CHURCHILL

CHURCHILL

Ashley Jackson

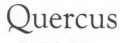

New York • London

Quercus

New York • London

ISBN 978-1-62365-622-5

Library of Congress Control Number: 2014931819

Distributed in the United States and Canada by
Hachette Book Group
1290 Avenue of the Americas
New York, NY 10104

Manufactured in the United States

10 9 8 7 6 5 4 3 2 1

www.quercus.com

This book is dedicated to my parents, Derek Paul Jackson
and Lesley Vivienne Jackson, with gratitude and love—
and happy memories of our lives together

CONTENTS

INTRODUCTION

"My life is its own message."

"I knew he always shaved himself with a safety razor before wallowing in a bath filled to the brim with water. From my bedroom I could hear the splashing as he sponged himself with the outsize sponge he always used. I listened for the signal which always told me Mr. Churchill's bathing was almost over. I did not have to wait long before I heard a noise like a whale 'blowing.'"[1]

Thus wrote Churchill's valet, Norman McGowan. The fact that we know so much about Churchill's bathing habits and often encounter him in a state of near or abject nakedness, looking like Humpty-Dumpty, as the Chief of the Imperial General Staff put it, speaks volumes about the man and his historical image. Not only do we read of him addressing generals and presidents while *déshabillé* or dictating to secretaries from the throne, we know a good deal about the colorful dressing gowns, jumpsuits, unusual hats, and Blenheim Bouquet cologne he wore. One can get carried away, in fact, with the idiosyncrasies and foibles of dress and manner that embellish his memory. The contrite Pug, the last lion, and the famous bulldog are familiar facets of the Churchill caricature, and along with hints of lovable Pooh Bear or irascible Mr. Toad, they can invest Churchill's image with cartoonlike elements that are unusual when considering the world's most important international leaders. While these aspects point to the sheer vitality and humanity of the man, and make him an incomparably more interesting biographical study than most politicians, it is necessary to remind ourselves that, above all else, Winston Churchill was a formidably powerful human being, a man whose achievements and greatness have become so interwoven with twentieth-century world history that it is easy to take them for granted. His achievements were awesome, and he was larger than life long before his death at the advanced age of ninety. "He was for me Pitt the Elder, Horatio Nelson and Benjamin Disraeli rolled into one; the cartoonists' John Bull too, no doubt, but a John Bull with culture, intelligence, style and what came over as the common touch."[2]

While history has rightly been kind to Winston Churchill's memory, he attracted far more criticism when he was alive than he has since his death. A surprising number of people nurtured a visceral loathing of the man, sometimes spiced by contempt for his relatives, who were often in the headlines for the wrong reasons. The Ulster leader Sir Edward Carson, who hated Churchill's liberal policies for Ireland, recorded his "savage satisfaction" at a Churchill special-election defeat: "I think W. Churchill really degrades public life more than anyone of any position in politics," he wrote.[3] In 1915, Prime Minister Asquith wrote that Churchill "was by far the most disliked man in my cabinet."[4] Evelyn Waugh, never a man to let prudence and politeness get in the way of his pronouncements, refused to take part in the "obsequies" when Churchill died. According to Waugh, Churchill was "always in the wrong, surrounded by crooks, a terrible father, a radio personality." Even during the war, Waugh had "despised his orations" broadcast on the radio.[5] So not everyone has been happy with Churchill, the man or the myth, and debunking him has become as central to some writers' careers as burnishing him has to others.

The problem with so many of these assessments and inchoate snapshots of "the greatest Briton ever," is that they apply to him, or demand of him, qualities of judgment and foresight that no human being has ever possessed, allow him to dominate in a way that in reality he never did, and divorce both his triumphs and his failures from their essential context. And yet still we try, to the tune of dozens of articles and volumes per year, to distill the Churchill essence. It is difficult for a man's spirit to remain free, when so many have tried to capture it. Yet despite the best efforts of an army of writers penning portraits of Winston Churchill, from old masters to cigarette package doodlers, he remains splendidly unreduced, perhaps because he is more enigmatic than one might expect: there is no diary, no recorded interview. He also remains enormous fun, because the iconoclasts have failed to tarnish him, while the idolaters have failed to reduce him to "great man" plasticity. Never omniscient or omnipotent, Churchill would make a poor demigod, because he would always be caught in the act, behaving badly, warming to the sound of his own rhetoric while colleagues cast their eyes heavenward, sticking his tongue out in the House of Commons, or nipping off for a pee.

But his evident humanity, which could so frustrate and anger his peers—even his wife—only adds to his appeal as a biographical subject. So, too, does the fact that his faults are visible to anyone who cares to examine his life. Even his family made candid reference to them. His daughter Mary acknowledged that he could be "maddening" and sometimes behaved like a "spoiled child." His son, Randolph, meanwhile, explained how Churchill hated whist for the simple reason that he wasn't any good at it: "Rarely," Randolph wrote, "even in later life, was Churchill apt to take an objective view of affairs. A game at which he did not prevail was naturally a bore. He was already developing that egocentricity which was to become such a predominant characteristic, and to which must be attributed alike his blunders and his triumphant successes."[6] Yet Churchill's egotism was tempered by humor, a marked lack of pomposity, mischievousness, and a capacity to back down, or be persuaded, even if it took a scrap to get there. His Harrow contemporary, Leopold Amery, might scold him in Cabinet; General

Sir Alan Brooke might compete with fist-banging resolution; his son, Randolph, might snap and snarl at the dinner or the card table ("Stop interrupting me while I'm interrupting you," Churchill might yell at him). "In the course of my life," he said, "I have often had to eat my own words, and I must confess I have always found it a wholesome diet."[7]

Of course, Churchill has only himself to blame for much of the skirmishing that has occurred around his reputation. The power of the image that he created of himself, and that his life left in the memory of ordinary people, still far outweighs the image created by the biographical pursuers who have variously followed in his footsteps and attempted to chase him. The magnitude of Churchill's achievements, the vibrancy of his character and lifestyle, and his sheer longevity have ensured his elevation above the realms of ordinary human life.

Winston Churchill was rooted in the heart of England at birth and in death and has been central to British national identity since the Second World War, a remarkable turnaround for a politician who, had it not been for Hitler, might have found his career consigned to the same scrap heap as that of his mercurial father. Winston was more than just the embodiment of the nation he led during its most dangerous years, for he lived in an age of empire and global ideological struggle. Because of the British Empire and his constant, if ultimately unrealistic, conception of it, his decisions and voice carried far beyond these shores. He was an international peacemaker but unflinchingly believed that peace could only come through strength, and sometimes through war. Indeed Churchill's lifelong preoccupation with the idea of an English-speaking civilization gave him the vision to see beyond even the vastness of empire to the rising power of America. In hitching Britain's fortunes to that power, first as an equal and later as a subordinate, Churchill helped define British foreign policy for decades, perhaps generations. He was also an advocate of closer European integration—hence the famous triumvirate of overlapping "circles," which in his view defined Britain's position in the world: empire-commonwealth,

Anglo-American alliance, and European harmony founded on the balance of power.

Because of his breadth of vision, his lengthy association with the affairs of the British Empire, and his pivotal position between 1939 and 1945, Churchill belongs not only to Britain, but to the world. He was the greatest international statesman of his age, to the extent that one can ever make such claims. He was an honorary citizen of the United States, champion of the freedom of small European nations, freeman of towns and cities around the world, warrior on imperial frontiers in Africa and Asia, summit visitor to ancient Middle Eastern capitals, holidaymaker and painter in Italy, and Atlantic and Mediterranean mariner. Scores of nations commemorated his death, or the anniversary of his birth, issuing postage stamps and a hodgepodge of souvenirs. Everybody wanted a piece of Winston Churchill, and the fact that he seemed effortlessly to cope with the demands of his impossible superman status (while robustly defending his privacy) has contributed to his enduring fame and fascination.

General Ismay, explaining to General Auchinleck that there was really no substitute for a personal meeting with Churchill, said that "you cannot judge the PM by ordinary standards, he is not in the least like anyone you and I have ever met."[8] This gives a sense of the utter uniqueness of the man. Churchill was a singularly intriguing and powerful human being: at once impetuous, generous, courageous, energetic, selfish, bombastic, and inspirational. Clement Attlee thought that his compassion was his most notable, though least acknowledged, character trait. His essential humanity and endearing qualities were blemished by irritating and downright unpleasant traits, the study of his life made all the more absorbing because the observer knows the heights he scaled during his life, and the depths to which his career sank. Beyond his talents and his longevity, he attracts attention because of the way he looked, the way he dressed, the manner in which he spoke, and his many idiosyncrasies. His evident ability to enjoy life to the full, while shouldering the burdens of state, has also held his admirers transfixed, as well as irritating the prudes and teetotalers. Some of the mud that has been slung at Churchill over the years has been as unfair as it has been predictable; the fact is, that if one were to pore minutely over the public and private correspondence and utterances of almost any man, especially when spread across several generations, one would be hard put not to encounter material that reflected poorly upon its author, especially when taken out of context.

But many criticisms of Churchill have also been unfair because he was not a biblical figure, and far from a saint. His flaws and mistakes were many and often egregious. To his critics, often outraged by his contemporary success as well as the veneration that history has afforded him, he was an unremarkable parliamentarian, a poor debater, a cause of British disarmament rather than the hero of Britain's most perilous hour. To some he was an untrustworthy political turncoat, a bully, a warmonger, an egotist; if not a downright liar, then a manufacturer of truth and distorter of the historical record; and an enemy of the common man. He was loathed by many in the Southern Hemisphere for allegedly abandoning Australia when Japan went on the rampage in the Far East and for squandering Anzac blood at Gallipoli; he has been accused of setting Iraq on course for an unsettled and bloody century; he advocated the use of poison gas against defenseless Africans (and also Germans and Russians) and killed Frenchmen in cold blood in order to prove a point about Britain's wartime resolve. Churchill's crime sheet, deserved or not, accurate or not, is a lengthy one. Quite apart from his historical reputation, Churchill was unpopular and notorious enough to require a bodyguard for most of his adult life.

But against most of these dramatic, often histrionic charges, Churchill can be defended in detail, or at least properly contextualized. They do little to dent his reputation—which always had two sides—or to diminish his achievements. Studying the life of Winston Churchill, cast against a backdrop of political, social, imperial, and personal foment and spread across ten decades, there are many qualities to admire, in addition to the undeniably beneficial work he conducted as a social reformer, war leader, writer, and international statesman of unique talent. These include his determination to succeed and his thirst for glory and notability; his belief in his own importance and his destiny as a shaper of national and international events; his bravery, loyalty, energy, and willingness to take the lead and provide ideas, even when the stakes were dauntingly high; his military and strategic acumen; his compassion and ability to apologize after he had erred; his devotion to his wife; his love of the countryside, of history, of tradition; his sentimentality; his inability to hold a grudge, even against those, like Lord Fisher, who very nearly ruined him; his time for hobbies; his capacity to write brilliant books and to paint skillfully; and his ability, apparently, to do all of this while serving in the highest offices of state and smoking a cigar. Geoffrey Best, one of the most perceptive writers ever to attempt a life of Churchill, wrote that he shared certain defining characteristics with his father, Lord Randolph Churchill: "Egotism, boldness, the need to be noticed, political ambition, bouts of depression, the ability to master complicated subjects, quickness of conception, energy, loquacity, cheek, humor, oratorical talent, impetuousness, irreverence, and sometimes disastrous tactlessness and failure of judgement."[9]

This book seeks to describe the contours of Winston Churchill's remarkable life and career while offering a sense of the man behind the piercing eyes and bulldog features. From thrusting junior officer to political pup in a hurry, from Cabinet outcast to the greatest war leader of modern times, from electoral loser to elder statesman on the international stage in the years of Cold War and imperial decline, this is the story of Winston Churchill's appointment with destiny.

1

Landscape for a Lifetime: Winston, Woodstock, and Oxfordshire

Winston Churchill's journey began at Blenheim Palace, the second-largest dwelling in Britain, covering seven acres with a 480-foot-long frontage, a magnificent building commanding thousands of acres of park and pastureland. "There is no house like it in the Western world," wrote J. H. Plumb.[1] This chapter examines the extent to which Churchill was rooted in English history and the history of his family because of the place of his birth and emphasizes his lifelong connections with Oxfordshire. The Blenheim fiefdom, located about nine miles north of Oxford, lies adjacent to the town of Woodstock. Despite its proximity, Woodstock remains distinct from the ancient university city, forming its own island in the heart of rural England, in many ways an annex of the great park it abuts. Like many small English towns, it possesses "an efficiency, culture, and charm which are the gradually matured expression of generations of settled life."[2] A handsome church and town hall stand amid long-established hotels, hostelries, and tearooms. Nestling in between are dignified town houses and wisteria-draped cottages, concealed courtyards, and English gardens glimpsed over honey-colored stone walls against which hollyhocks droop in summer months. Through gaps between buildings, views of the Oxfordshire countryside stretch into the distance as the town slides gently downhill to the water meadows of the River Glyme. The expansive 150-acre lake that this modest river feeds lies concealed behind Blenheim Park's eleven-mile-long encircling wall, monumental gates, and shelter belt of mature trees, adjacent to the town yet separated from it.

When George III visited Blenheim in 1786, he was prompted to remark: "We have nothing to equal this."[3] The scale of Sir John Vanbrugh's baroque extravagance is betrayed by another bold architectural statement visible from certain Woodstock streets, a monument that rivals Nelson's Column in height and declares an earlier hero of Britain's wars abroad: John Spencer Churchill, captain general of the English and allied forces in Europe in 1702–11, 1st Duke of Marlborough.* There he is captured in classical triumph atop Hawksmoor's hundred-foot Doric column, standing thirty-four feet in height, dressed as a Roman general and holding aloft a Winged Victory and eagles. And there the young Winston Churchill read about his triumphs in European warfare and was inspired.

On a beautiful spring day in early May 1874, his newlywed parents had arrived at the Woodstock railway station, where a public reception had been arranged. Attended by thunder and torrential rain, the couple were met by cheering tenants, who unharnessed their horses and dragged the carriage from the station to the palace. Though the Blenheim brass band was engaged elsewhere, the town was dressed with flags and bunting, and among the crowd was the Woodstock Lodge of Foresters. At the Bear Hotel, the mayor of Woodstock delivered an address of welcome as the carriage paused on its way from the station to the Triumphal Arch, from which vantage point Jennie Churchill caught her first glimpse of the palace. "The place could not have looked more glorious," she later wrote, "and as we passed through the entrance archway and the lovely scenery burst upon me Randolph said with pardonable pride, 'This is the finest view in England.'"[4]

---

* Spencer remained the family name of the dukes of Marlborough until 1817 when by Royal Licence the 5th Duke changed it to Spencer-Churchill

It was from a house on Park Street in Woodstock that Dr. Frederic Taylor was summoned to Blenheim to attend twenty-year-old Jennie Churchill on a winter's day in 1874. Hurriedly he made the short journey, entering the walled grounds through the Triumphal Arch, or Town Gate as it is known to locals, and proceeding along a drive that intersects the Mall. Here the breathtaking panorama of lake, palace, and Grand Bridge, with its thirty-three empty rooms, stretched out before him. His arrival was awaited by Jennie's anxious husband, Lord Randolph Churchill, second son of the 7th Duke of Marlborough and member of Parliament for Woodstock since February of that year. Because of her condition, Jennie had missed the Nobility Ball at the King's Arms in Woodstock, attended by Randolph, his mother, sister, and cousins. On November 24, she had had a slight fall, though on November 26, Randolph felt able to travel into Oxford to receive his master of arts degree in the Sheldonian Theatre. On November 28, Lady Churchill overexerted herself during a shooting party on the estate and then endured a bone-shaking ride back to the palace in a pony carriage. This brought on the pains. She remained in labor until Dr. Taylor delivered a boy at 1:30 a.m. on St. Andrew's Day, November 30, two months premature or, looking at the mathematics another way, seven and a half months after his parents' marriage. As Henry Pelling wisely leaves it, we must suspend judgment as to whether this was simply the first instance of Winston's impetuosity "or whether it also involved yet another example of Lord Randolph's."[5]

The London obstetrician who was supposed to have ushered Winston Churchill into this world was unable to attend. The telegram had got through, but the train timetables confounded his efforts to reach his distinguished patient. The Woodstock physician proved a capable substitute, and with the arrival of a baby boy, the church bells around Blenheim rang out, and Randolph and the Duchess of Marlborough wrote detailed letters to Jennie's mother in Paris announcing the birth. Winston's surprise arrival meant that a cradle had to be improvised, and clothes borrowed from the

Woodstock solicitor's wife. Dr. Taylor received the sum of twenty-five guineas and a letter from Lord Randolph thanking him for his "skilful management of and careful attention to her Ladyship during her confinement." With period condescension, the Duchess of Marlborough wrote to Mrs. Leonard Jerome, Jennie's American mother, saying that she had "only" had the Woodstock doctor, but that despite the absence of the London doctor or "an *accoucheur* from Oxford," "she could not have been more skillfully treated . . . than she was by our little local doctor."[6] The birth was registered in Woodstock on December 23, 1874, the baby's name appearing on the certificate as Winston Leonard, the latter being the Christian name of Jennie's father, Leonard Jerome, sometime American consul in Trieste, principal proprietor of the *New York Times* and founder of the American Jockey Club. Thus, in the words of Lord Randolph, a "wonderfully pretty" boy with "dark eyes and hair & very healthy" entered the world.[7]

Churchill's place of birth warrants our consideration, because he remained attached to this particular region of England throughout his life and chose to complete his life circle by being buried there. It shaped him profoundly. Blenheim Palace lies "at the heart of the Whig legend of that past which the English had manufactured in order to underpin their imperial ambitions and in which Winston Churchill had implicit belief."[8] His great ancestor's life was to provide a mental backdrop to Churchill's conception of himself and his actions, and on a more practical level his place of birth was to be the venue for countless holidays, house parties, and army camps as he grew up, as well as for family Christmas gatherings and research trips when he undertook to write biographies of both the 1st Duke, John Spencer Churchill, and his own father, Lord Randolph, and a place of refuge at moments of personal trouble. His birthplace is also of great importance because throughout his life, Winston Churchill was gripped by an almost primordial sense of place and the significance of time and history. This sense of history, and of his position within it, was developed at Blenheim and by what it represented. Churchill's birthplace is notable not only because it chimes well with his subsequent identification with England as both a historical and romantic landscape, but because he repeatedly returned to this part of the world and was eventually buried in the village of Bladon, nestling on the other side of the great lake near the point at which it flows into the River Evenlode. The church, visible from the windows of the palace's south face and the vast lawns before it, lies only a few hundred yards from the room in which he was born. Thus Churchill was both born and buried in a setting saturated with the history of England and of his own family, and the significance of it deeply influenced his conception of the world and the sense of personal destiny that was to be a lodestar throughout his life.

During his most formative childhood years, Churchill spent school holidays at Blenheim, shooting, scrumping fruit from the walled garden, playing "French and English," and riding his horse across the Grand Bridge to the Column of Victory or Rosamond's Well. With absentee parents heavily involved in the political and social life of the aristocracy, Winston was often cared for by his grandparents at Blenheim and spent many Easters and Christmases in the palace, sometimes with his beloved mother and father, more often without. The infant Winston spent his first Christmas at Blenheim with his parents, and on December 27, 1874, was baptized in the chapel of Blenheim by the duke's chaplain, the appropriately named Reverend Henry Yule.

At Blenheim he was "dazzled by the uniforms and armour, by the wonderful trophies, and by the battle scenes that decorated the walls."[9] Here he reflected upon the story of his famous ancestor, the 1st Duke of Marlborough, swashbuckling victor of Blenheim, Malplaquet, and Ramillies, savior of Europe. But Churchill's roots went beyond just Blenheim and the martial feats of the man for whom it was built: Churchill was infused with a sense of the ancient and medieval history with which Woodstock and the park adjoining it were associated, by the presence of oaks ancient enough to have been "gazed upon by Plantagenets" riding to the chase and the stories of the old kings of England who had once stayed there. As he wrote, "Roman, Saxon, Norman, Plantagenet, Tudor, [and] Stuart prefaced the 1st Duke's action at Blenheim. . . . The antiquity of Woodstock is not measured by a thousand years and Blenheim is heir to all the memories of Woodstock." "This great house," he said of Blenheim, "is one of the precious links which join us to our famous past, which is also the history of the English-speaking peoples, on whose unity the future of the free world depends. I am proud to have been born at Blenheim, and to be an Honorary Freeman of Woodstock."[10]

Sometimes political business brought the family to Woodstock, for the politics of the day was conducted across the candlelight and silverware of stately dining tables and to the clack of billiard balls, as well as in the Palace of Westminster itself. In 1874, the year of Winston's birth, Randolph had used his parents' ardent wish that he stand for election in Woodstock to win consent for his hasty marriage to Jennie. Having won his point, Randolph threw himself into canvassing. Since leaving Oxford he had been on call for this moment in order to prevent the seat falling to a radical. He was "popular with the farmers around Blenheim who had seen him since boyhood tearing over the countryside on horseback." "I took the chair at their dinner at the Bear Hotel and you have no idea how enthusiastic they were for me," he wrote to his brilliant, beguiling, and impulsive new wife.[11]

Churchill was often billeted at Blenheim when his parents were elsewhere. For Jennie, the London season held more appeal than the dullness of Woodstock and the formal life of Blenheim and its "dignified rhythm of existence,"[12] which included two-hour-long breakfasts in formal attire. In the summer of 1876, when he was nearly two, it was reported that "little Winston was now learning to creep in the top-floor nurseries, watched and cosseted by his nurse Mrs. Everest." In November 1880, Randolph persuaded Lord Salisbury to speak at Woodstock. This coincided with Winston's sixth birthday, "and the little boy had a first glimpse of the man who would be swept to the Premiership by his father's brilliance." In the winter of 1885, with Randolph having entered the Cabinet as secretary of state for India, canvassing in the Woodstock area for the forthcoming election was largely left to Jennie, driven hither and thither by Lady Georgina Curzon in her tandem as they scoured the countryside "with our smart turn-out, the horses gaily decorated with ribbons of pink and brown, Randolph's racing colors."[13]

At Blenheim, in the company of his brother, Jack, and cousin Sunny (later the 9th Duke), Winston played games in the endless corridors and rooms of the great palace, endured lessons, rode his pony Robroy across the open spaces of the Great Park and through its magnificent clumps of trees, and fished in the lake. His first letter to his mother, written at the age of eight in the neat but tentative hand of one new to the art, came from Blenheim: "My dear Mamma I hope you are quite well. I thank you very very much for the beautiful presents those Soldiers and Flags and Castle they are so nice."[14] Thus Blenheim helped to forge an interest in war and glory, as well as in history, and this was to color every aspect of Churchill's life. The very architecture proclaimed Marlborough's victory, stone cannonballs crushing French cockerels, the roofline embellished with martial trophies and, within, paintings and enormous tapestries detailing the battlefield. Later, when a schoolboy at Harrow, Winston drew detailed maps of the disposition of Marlborough's troops, his historical interests growing against the backdrop of the popular boyhood fiction he loved to read, including the works of G. A. Henty, Robert Louis Stevenson's *Treasure Island*, Rider Haggard's *King Solomon's Mines*, and tales told in person by a veteran of the Zulu War.

As a young man, Churchill remained a frequent visitor to Blenheim. He spent Christmas of 1893 there and visited the Dillon family at nearby Ditchley Park. He was at Blenheim again in the winter months of 1901, discussing intraparty intrigues with Lord Hugh Cecil. In August 1908, he was at nearby Nuneham House as a guest of Lewis, Viscount Harcourt, a member of the government. On

---

* Winston was later to race in these colors while serving with the army in India.

August 4, 1908, his brother, Jack, married Lady Gwendeline Bertie in a civil ceremony at Abingdon in South Oxfordshire, a religious service taking place in Oxford on the following day. Churchill described how the party swept down on Abingdon in cars from Blenheim, the proceedings feeling like an elopement. In the same month, he was also installed as a member of the Albion Lodge of the Ancient Order of Druids at Blenheim.

Churchill memorably said that "at Blenheim I took two important decisions: to be born and to marry."[15] In 1908, a young lady named Clementine Hozier was invited to Blenheim at Churchill's behest to join a small party that included the duke, Winston's mother, his great friend F. E. Smith (later Lord Birkenhead), and Mr. Clarke, a private secretary from the Board of Trade, the department of state to which Winston had been sent. Winston took the duke into his confidence, and the "Blenheim trip was arranged so he could propose to the beautiful girl with whom he was so deeply in love, in a setting which combined the romantic with the heroic, and where he felt so strongly the ties of family and friendship." Churchill wrote to persuade her to come: "I want so much to show you that beautiful place and its gardens. We shall find lots of places to talk in and lots of things to talk about."[16]

Yet despite this unsurpassed setting and all his planning, Winston nearly ruined the proceedings. Retiring for the night, he made a rendezvous with Clementine to walk in the Rose Garden after breakfast the following day, August 11, 1908. Never an early bird, in the morning he failed to appear. Clementine, furious, considered leaving. The duke stepped ably into the breach, however, dispatching a note to the still slumbering Churchill while persuading Clementine over breakfast to take a drive with him in his buggy. He whirled her round the estate for a while, returning to find Winston, finally out of bed, scanning the horizon.

During the course of the late afternoon, Winston and Clementine went for a walk in the grounds. The couple headed toward the Rose Garden and the Cascades, along a path flanked by cedars, beeches, and ancient oaks. Overtaken by a torrential rainstorm, they took refuge in a little Greek temple erected in 1789. This was the Temple of Diana, supported by four pillars with Ionic capitals and flanked by yews, enjoying a striking view of the lake cut through the trees. Here, by a bas-relief of Hippolytus offering a wreath to Diana, an unusually tongue-tied Churchill asked Clementine for her hand in marriage, and she consented. The following morning, Churchill picked a bouquet of roses for her and asked Clementine's mother for her blessing. Following a London wedding, the honeymoon began and ended at Blenheim, with a trip to Venice sandwiched in between. Arriving by train at Woodstock to begin their married life, Clementine and Winston were greeted by cheering crowds and the ringing bells of St. Mary Magdalene, the same scene that had greeted Winston's parents on their marriage thirty-four years earlier. Thus was forged a bond that was to remain unbroken until Churchill's death and was to anchor him throughout his turbulent life.

One of Churchill's most abiding links with Woodstock was provided by his military career. Shortly after he left the Regular Army in 1899 and following his escapades in South Africa as war correspondent and irregular soldier, he took a commission in a yeomanry regiment, the Queen's Own Oxfordshire Hussars, founded in 1798. So strong were the regiment's ties to Woodstock and Blenheim that it was known locally as "The Duke of Marlborough's Own." At first Winston joined the Woodstock Squadron (other squadrons being drawn from Banbury, Henley, and Oxford), in which he was posted as a captain and second in command. The duke commanded the squadron, and Winston's brother, Jack, was a lieutenant. His friend F. E. Smith was also an officer in the squadron, enhancing Winston's pleasure in soldiering with the Queen's Own even when he attained high political office in Asquith's Liberal government. Whether as undersecretary of state for the colonies, president of the Board of Trade, or home secretary, he took his part-time soldiering seriously. As he wrote to Clementine during the June 1911 camp:

> The weather is gorgeous and the whole Park in gala glories. I have been
> out drilling all the morning and my poor face is already a sufferer from

the sun. . . . We have three regiments here, two just outside the orna-
mental gardens, & a 3rd over by Bladon.[17]

The regiment's summer camp was the main feature of its training,
and the officers' ladies would descend to roost in Blenheim Palace and neighboring mansions, such as Nuneham. In April 1905,
Churchill attained his majority and assumed command of the
Henley Squadron, replacing Major the Honourable E. Twistleton-
Wykeham-Fiennes. Churchill had been keen to get away from the
Woodstock Squadron and its domination by the Marlboroughs,
seeking the opportunity to make his own mark on the men and,
no doubt, offer his cousin some competition. Henley also bene-
fited from its proximity to London and Whitehall, where Churchill
was now making his mark. Records show that Churchill was an
extremely attentive officer, concerning himself with the squadron's
training drill and its quartermastering arrangements and issuing
detailed squadron orders. His emphasis upon increased training
bore fruit when the Henley Squadron swept the board at the annual
regimental rifle meetings.

The handling of troops stimulated Churchill's desire to command large formations. As he wrote to Clementine on May 31, 1909,
after leaving summer exercises at Blenheim, "I would greatly love to
have some practice in the handling of large forces. I have much confidence in my judgment in things, when I see clearly, but on nothing do I seem to *feel* the truth more than in tactical combinations.
It is a vain and foolish thing to say—but *you* will not laugh at me."[18]
Winston's drive had a purpose, for, with a future war in mind, he
wanted his men to come up to the standard of the Regular Army's
cavalry. His efforts paid dividends, for when war came in August
1914, the Queen's Own were pitched into the fray on the Western
Front, gaining the distinction of being the first yeomanry unit to
engage the enemy.

The regiment's annual training exercises at Blenheim usually took place in the early summer, a forest of conical white tents
appearing at the foot of the Column of Victory. The gathering was

accompanied by the thunder of horses' hooves, dinners, dances, and sport. But this was by no means toy soldiering in an insignificant rural regiment, as the unit's deployment to France in 1914 was to show. The Queen's Own was a fighting unit that expected to be deployed in the event of a general war, as, indeed, had been the case during the Boer War, when the horsemanship of the imperial yeomanry had been much in demand. The regiment enjoyed impressive royal patronage: Queen Adelaide had granted the use of the "Queen's Own" title following a visit to Oxford in 1835 and had conferred her favorite color, mantua purple, as the regimental color. From 1896, the Prince of Wales, a close friend of the 9th Duke of Marlborough, was colonel in chief and remained so when he became King Edward VII. The regiment's appearance matched this impressive pedigree. The full-dress uniform was extremely ornate: navy-blue tunics with elaborate silver braid on the chest, sleeves, and collar and mantua-purple facings; mantua purple trousers with a silver stripe on each leg and silver braid above the knee; black fur busby hats with plumes of short purple vulture feathers and fifteen-inch-long ostrich feathers; and highly polished Hessian-style boots with silver edging at the top, a purple boss, and pink heels.

Visits to Blenheim were frequent at this stage of Churchill's life. He spent Christmas 1910 there and was there again in June the following year, writing to tell Clementine that "we are going to bathe in the Lake this evening." On this visit, he was again in uniform, and Churchill and his men watered their horses at the lake's edge, paraded in the stately courtyards of the palace, and charged across the broad acres of sculptured parkland. On one spectacular occasion, Churchill engineered a mass cavalry charge from one end of the park to the other. As he wrote to Clementine from Blenheim on June 6, 1911:

My dearest,
We all marched past this morning—walk, trot and gallop. Jack and I took our squadrons at real pace and excited the spontaneous plaudits of the crowd. . . . [A]fter the march past I made the general form the whole

Brigade into Brigade-Mass and galloped 1,200 strong the whole length of the park in one solid square of men and horses. It went awfully well. He was delighted.[19]

During the First World War, Churchill's visits to Blenheim were infrequent. He spent time there in 1916 after the Dardanelles campaign had caused him to leave the government, finding comfort by painting in the grounds. He happened to be at Blenheim when the war ended. It was Lord Blandford's twenty-first birthday, an occasion marked by a paper chase on horseback and an ox roast. The day concluded with fireworks and a gigantic bonfire topped by an effigy of the kaiser. Winston continued to visit Blenheim throughout the interwar years. Photographs show him enjoying the delights of the gardens, often in company with Clementine. When ejected from office at the beginning of his "wilderness years" away from government at the start of the 1930s, it was at Blenheim that Churchill researched and wrote much of his biography *Marlborough: His Life and Times*, the 9th Duke giving him special access to documents in the palace archives, as well as living quarters and stabling for his hunters. Much of this biographical masterpiece was "dictated in the Arcade Rooms beneath the Long Library," the research conducted during "many hours in the windowless strongroom" that is the palace's muniment room.[20] He was also able to indulge his passion for painting while at Blenheim. He would establish himself and his easel in one of the palace's magnificent rooms or at a vantage point in the grounds and break out his paints, brushes, and palette. Many of his paintings of Blenheim were completed in the early 1920s, and a number were subsequently given to his host, the duke, and his own children. A view of the lake was given to Field Marshal Viscount Montgomery, his champion at Alamein, and an enchanting study of *Wooded Water near Blenheim* was gifted to his private secretary, Sir Anthony Montague Browne.

Even when away from Blenheim, his place of birth and his ancestor's significance in European history were seldom far from

Churchill's mind. At Chartwell, the house in Kent that he made his home for over forty years, an enormous painting of Blenheim Palace hung before his desk, above the fireplace, and beneath the Union Jack hoisted in Rome by British soldiers in 1944. In his London home at 28 Hyde Gate Park, SW7, a canvas depicting the Battle of Blenheim loomed over the dining room table. When the queen made him a Knight of the Order of the Garter in 1953—the most distinguished commoner to join this, the highest class of knighthood—he was invested at Windsor Castle with the insignia worn by his forebear, the 1st Duke of Marlborough, in 1702.

World-changing battles of his own were to bring Churchill back to this corner of England when he acceded to the highest office of state in 1940, and the Battle of Britain and the Blitz dominated the skies above southern England. Even with the war focusing his tremendous energies on London and the world beyond Britain's shores, he spent a significant amount of time in the environs of Blenheim. He was instrumental in getting over four hundred schoolboys and their masters established at Blenheim to continue their studies when Malvern College was requisitioned by the Admiralty. In November 1941, Churchill took the future 11th Duke, then a schoolboy, on a visit to the city of Liverpool to inspect the damage wrought by Nazi bombs. As the duke recalls, his parents, aware that it would be cold, ensured that coupons were rounded up and a new overcoat procured, albeit two sizes too big for him.

War also forged a new link with Oxfordshire. Looking due northwest from Blenheim's Column of Victory, along the lengthy Grand Avenue of nearly seven hundred elms, lay the elegant Ditchley Gate. Beyond this began the land of Ditchley Park, and it was here that Churchill was able to establish a secluded home-from-home during the Second World War. It was owned by the millionaire Conservative MP Ronald Tree. With the onset of the Blitz, the prime minister's official country residence, Chequers in Buckinghamshire, was considered too dangerous for its intended purpose: a weekend escape from the pressures of official life in London. It was too visible and too well known, a tempting target. Ditchley, however, was not too distant from London, was unlikely to be known to the Luftwaffe, and was surrounded by a park of mature trees, making it inconspicuous from the air. The house, indeed, has an aura of rustic isolation and peacefulness unusual even in the tranquil setting of the English country house. As Tree was to write of his beloved home, "cut off from the main stream of life, the beauty of the place with its great avenues and woodlands of bluebells and primroses in the spring was to be an island of pure delight."[21] Having been advised not to visit Chequers "when the moon is high," Churchill asked Tree for the use of Ditchley. He readily consented, and Churchill subsequently found some of that tranquillity away from the maelstrom of war.

Churchill first visited Ditchley on the weekend of November 9, 1940, accompanied by Clementine and their daughter Mary. Special telephone lines were erected and a scrambler system installed, and accommodation was provided for Churchill's administrative staff and secretary, as well as billets for a full company of the Oxfordshire and Buckinghamshire Light Infantry detailed to guard the premises during Churchill's stay. During that first weekend at Ditchley, Churchill was aware of the Royal Air Forces's attack on Munich that was then taking place. On the following weekend, the city of Coventry, barely thirty miles from Ditchley, was visited by over five hundred German aircraft in a reprisal attack.

Churchill was to use Ditchley for twelve weekends in the following two years. The Trees were model hosts, going to considerable expense to entertain the Churchills and any guests Winston elected to bring, providing food, including vegetables and game from the estate, and wines from the excellent cellar. Guests included President Roosevelt's special envoy, Harry Hopkins; Averell Harriman; Anthony Eden; General Sir Alan Brooke, chief of the Imperial General Staff; General Vladislav Sikorski, prime minister of Poland; Edvard Beneš, prime minister of Czechoslovakia (for whom a Czech guard of honor was present); Lord Lothian, British ambassador to America; and people invited by the Trees, including the actor David Niven, whom Winston complimented for having given up his film career in order to join the army. ("Young man," he growled, "you did a very fine thing to give up a most promising career to fight for your country." After Niven had "stammered some inane reply," Churchill continued with a twinkle, "Mark you, had you not done so—it would have been despicable!'")[22] It was from Ditchley that Churchill wrote a long letter to Roosevelt, "one of the most important I ever wrote," that resulted in "the glorious conception of Lend-Lease." It was also at Ditchley that Churchill received a dramatic visit from the Duke of Hamilton to tell him of the arrival by parachute of Rudolf Hess in Scotland.

Churchill continued to visit Ditchley on a regular basis until 1942, by which time German bombing raids had become less severe. While there, he would sometimes take the opportunity to motor the four miles down the road to Blenheim in order to reacquaint himself with the park and the familiar haunts of his childhood. Ditchley became a welcome haven for the Churchill family away from the fatigued and battered capital. "Whenever the moon was high, we all repaired to Ditchley," wrote Churchill's daughter. "We were becoming so accustomed to the drabness and ugliness of war—khaki, mountains of sandbags, the blackout, and the dust and desolation of ruined buildings—that we gazed with keener appreciation on elegance and beauty, and glowing, lighted interiors."[23] And what interiors Ditchley possessed. The Trees had spent vast sums restoring the house to its original splendor, and Churchill must have wallowed in the peacefulness for which Ditchley is renowned as he wandered through the lofty Great Hall and the Velvet Room, its walls covered with Genoese silk since 1738, and enjoyed the view of the lake from his bedroom and of the Italian sunken garden and

---

* The following day after dinner Churchill "requisitioned" Niven for a walk around the walled garden, where "he talked at great length about vegetables and the joy of growing one's own. He made it clear that before long rationing would become so severe that 'every square inch of our island will be pressed into service.'" David Niven, *The Moon's a Balloon* (Harmondsworth: Penguin, 1994), p. 230.

Jellicoe pool from his study. It was clear that, despite the ceaseless nature of his work, he was able to relax here. As Clementine wrote to Mary in 1943, "I am at Ditchley for the weekend. Papa has got 'Prof' [Frederick Lindemann] & Uncle Jack who is also having a rest cure—& masses of films—War & Hollywood."[24] Churchill's main form of relaxation was watching films, and Tree remembers that he was particularly fond of *Lady Hamilton*, a film about the life and death of Nelson.

Following the war, Churchill had occasion to return to his birthplace when he was made a freeman of the Borough of Woodstock. Fatigued by the sheer number of invitations from communities eager to fête their war leader and share in his international celebrity, Churchill was at first reluctant to accept but was persuaded by Mary Marlborough, the mayor, and her promise of a political audience into the bargain. The day before the ceremony and his speech, Churchill spent the afternoon in the Grand Cabinet at Blenheim, relaxed with his shirt buttons undone. On the morning of Saturday, August 2, 1947, he received the Freedom of Woodstock from the borough council on a stage festooned with Union Jacks and bunting set up outside the main door of the eighteenth-century town hall. The party then processed along Park Street to enter Blenheim through the Triumphal Arch, cheered by ranks of townspeople lining both sides of the road. That afternoon Churchill addressed a Conservative Party rally held on the South Lawn of the palace, looking out from a high podium toward Bladon and its elegant little church tower, beneath which Churchill's parents lay in the family grave. His speech, attended by a throng of forty thousand people, was broadcast on the BBC World Service. In it he attacked Clement Attlee and declared that "the Socialist belief is that nothing matters so long as miseries are equally shared, and certainly they have acted in accordance with their faith."[25] In 1953, Churchill was again at Blenheim, this time on official business as a guest at the Blenheim Commonwealth garden party held to mark the coronation of Queen Elizabeth II. In the presence of Princess Margaret, he mingled with Commonwealth and Dominions visitors. His last visit to the place in which he had been born, and that had shaped his destiny, was in 1958.

In January 1965, Churchill came back to Oxfordshire for good when he was buried in the small churchyard at Bladon, within view of the palace where he had been born over ninety years before. They had been years of intense and extraordinary activity.

2

Cadet to Frontier Soldier: Warrior and Writer

Winston Churchill did not have an unusual childhood, as is some-times claimed: thousands of other Victorian boys played with soldiers, had difficult and distant relations with their parents, inhabited nurseries and gardens in fashionable London squares and great country houses, and then endured, rather than enjoyed, a pro-longed incarceration at boarding school (a background intended to produce independent-minded young men for the service of the empire). Overall Winston Churchill had a happy childhood, even when compulsory education and the manifold challenges of pub-lic school supervened. Before the legal violence of separation from family and home was visited upon him at the tender age of seven, Churchill's early years were characterized by the privilege attached to his social class. This meant playtime in the nurseries and grounds of whichever London residence or stately home he happened to be stationed at by his peripatetic family. It also meant regular sepa-ration from his parents and the companionship and devotion of a nanny, Elizabeth Everest. In all of this, his childhood differed little in its main contours from that of the majority of boys born into the English ruling elite. Nevertheless, Churchill was throughout his life an exotic individual—reflecting the nature of his personality, his appearance, and mannerisms. His place of birth and the celebrity status of his parents further marked him out among the scions of the aristocracy. It meant that he was always something of a social maroon, an oddity. There was no one remotely like him. This fact alone, regardless of the various eminences achieved in his life, makes him a brilliant biographical subject.

A "child of the Victorian era," as he described himself, Churchill grew up in an age that the First World War was to sweep away. He grew up in the "golden afternoon" of British world power, of Pax Britannica, of apparent stability in the world and security for Britain and its empire. In these halcyon late-Victorian days, he wrote, "the structure of our country seemed firmly set . . . its position in trade and on the seas was unrivaled, and . . . the realization of the greatness of our Empire and of our duty to preserve it was ever growing stronger."[1] From an early age, Churchill was alive to imperial and military matters, and the affairs of the British Empire and the British military formed a skein throughout his long life. Churchill came to view the British Empire, along with the "island story" of Britain's historical evolution as a nation state and force for international progress, as the prime buttresses of world stability and prosperity.

Churchill was always more interested in the empire as an extension of British power in the world than in the empire per se. To the imperial manner born, he viewed Britain's possession of a vast empire as part of the natural order of things. Both Churchill's father and grandfather had occupied positions of responsibility within the empire, as secretary of state for India and viceroy of Ireland respectively. When Winston was two years old, Lord Randolph removed his family to Ireland when he became secretary to his father, the 7th Duke of Marlborough, who had been appointed viceroy, or lord lieutenant, of Ireland, that closest and most awkward of Britain's imperial possessions. It was a move engineered to enable the family to evade the social ostracism resulting from a quarrel involving Randolph; his brother, Blandford; and the Prince of Wales—a quarrel that had almost led to a duel between Randolph and the prince. Disraeli offered the Duke of Marlborough the Ireland position as a way out of the impasse. The ostracism (marked by the prince's announcement that he would visit no house that welcomed the Randolphs) lasted from 1876 until 1884.

Though reluctantly accepted, the viceroyalty was the choicest proconsular position the empire had to offer. The Marlboroughs and the young Winston traveled to Dublin in January 1877, where they took up residence in the Little Lodge near to the Viceregal Lodge. Born into a palace replete with depictions of war, Churchill's earliest memory was also of a martial nature. When he was five, his grandfather unveiled a statue at which "I even remember a phrase he used: 'and with a withering volley he shattered the enemy's line.' I quite understood that he was speaking about war and fighting and that a 'volley' meant what the black-coated soldiers (Riflemen) used to do with loud bangs so often in the Phoenix Park where I was taken for my morning walk."[2]

Churchill later claimed that embarking on a military career "was entirely due to my collection of soldiers. I had ultimately nearly fifteen hundred." Churchill's collection had been inspired by the one at Blenheim. It was organized as an infantry division with a cavalry brigade, supported by field guns and fortress pieces. All other services were complete, short of transport, and his brother, Jack, commanded the hostile army. Even when he was fifteen, toy soldiers still turned his head, and he wrote to Jack from France in January 1892 that "I have seen here such beautiful soldiers," telling him to send money if he wanted some. Churchill's cousin remembered visiting his playroom, which "contained from one end to the other a plank table on trestles, upon which were thousands of lead soldiers arranged for battle. He organized wars. The lead battalions were manoeuvred into battle, peas and pebbles committed great casualties, forts were stormed, cavalry charged, bridges were destroyed." Toy soldiers, as Churchill put it, "turned the current of my life."[3]

He also played war with his relatives and friends. At one of Churchill's numerous childhood homes, Banstead Manor near

Newmarket (which his parents rented briefly until money troubles supervened), he and his brother constructed a log fort complete with a moat and drawbridge and a siege catapult that fired green apples. "The Den" was carpeted with straw and defended by intricate fortifications and a gun. The Churchill boys were delighted to have a country home of their own to play in. They accompanied the keeper on rabbit-hunting expeditions, and Winston drilled his brother and other children, progressing from toy soldiers to live boys on a course that would eventually lead to the command of British troops in action. (Banstead also saw Churchill's first experiments as a small farmer, involving chickens, ferrets, guinea pigs, and rabbits.)

True to form, in Ireland Churchill's parents were heavily engaged in the elegant duties and pastimes associated with high society and social position. Although he probably saw more of them here than if they'd been closer to the magnetic distractions of London, Winston lived at one remove from his parents, an observer peering over the banister rather than a participant in their daily lives. "My picture of her in Ireland," Churchill later wrote of his mother, "is in a riding habit, fitting like a skin and often beautifully spotted with mud." Nevertheless, and perhaps because of this distance, Churchill's reverence for his parents, indeed his lionization of them, developed from an early age. "My mother always seemed to me a fairy princess: a radiant being possessed of limitless riches and power." More regular and intimate companionship was provided by Winston's adored nurse, Mrs. Everest. She was "very proud of Kent her home county, where there grew strawberries, cherries, raspberries and plums. Lovely! I always wanted to live in Kent," and at a young age he went to stay with her and her sister on the Isle of Wight during the Zulu War (1879–80), and from the cliffs near Ventnor "saw a great splendid ship with all her sails set . . . a troopship . . . bringing the men back from the war"[4] All of this augmented the significance and glory of war that Churchill's wanderings around the tapestry-hung rooms of Blenheim Palace had inculcated. Clad in fancy-dress uniforms or a sailor suit, commanding armies in imaginary battles, it is easy to see why Churchill grew to believe that war and the conduct of war were natural to him.

SCHOOL DAYS

Much is made of Churchill's antipathy toward formal education, his dull-wittedness in certain academic directions, his misery and loneliness at school. Exaggerations, however, are made on all three counts. The simple fact is that, like thousands of others before and since, Churchill didn't much like school and, as a result, school didn't much like him. Winston's pugnacious and rebellious nature, according to his son, never adapted itself to discipline.

Churchill himself encouraged the picture of unhappy school days in his later writings. "In retrospect these years form not only the least agreeable, but the only barren and unhappy period of my life. I was happy as a child with my toys in my nursery. I have been happier every year since I became a man." But Churchill's school days were no worse than those of many children for whom severance from home and family came as a great trauma. His failures were balanced by successes on the sporting field and in the classroom—notably in history and English—and not all was gloom during his twelve-year school career. There is no doubt, however, that school did not best suit his precocious and independent-minded, gusto-fueled approach to life, and his natural penchant for buffeting against authority. But then, neither did the army, or political parties, or the established methods of cabinet government. Institutions and formal systems did not sit easily about him. He was never one to knuckle down, especially if he did not see the point, but was always one to question and seek ways to circumvent obstacles and free himself from structures that tried his poorly developed patience.

Even before school, the shadow of formal education had darkened Churchill's life. Like most boys of his class, he had to endure educators invading his home to begin life's instruction. What he termed the "dreaded apparition" of "The Governess" shook the security and irresponsibility of those early postnatal years, engaged in order to teach a young Winston the rudiments of reading. It was at about the age of five that Winston remembered being "first menaced by Education." His initial reaction was to do "what so many oppressed peoples have done in similar circumstances: I took to the woods."[5]

But soon "a much worse peril began to threaten: I was to go to school." The prospect was viewed with excitement as well as agitation as Winston approached a milestone on life's journey. He was a boy who, had he not been so combative, might have attracted bullies while at school: unable to pronounce the letter *s*, ginger haired (nicknamed, among other things, "Carrots"), and not particularly tall. It was at school that the intricacies and apparent irrelevancies of multiplication and grammar "cast a steadily growing shadow over my daily life." The separation from home galled him, and he missed the nursery where he had been so happy with all his toys. "I had such wonderful toys," he lamented, "a real steam engine, a magic lantern, and a collection of soldiers already nearly a thousand strong." Now it was to be all lessons, interspersed with trials of strength with schoolmasters who did their level best to offer correction to naughty boys.

His first experience of school, at an institution specializing in the preparation of boys for Eton (Randolph's school), justified his allergic reaction. It epitomized the worst elements of a system of boarding school education widely pilloried today. In Philip Guedalla's words, St. George's School, Ascot (which Churchill entered in November 1882), "divided its attentions between corporal punishment and the classics; and its latest pupil did not take to either." But then, he *was* a naughty boy, apt to be slovenly, and guilty of offenses such as putting his foot through the headmaster's straw hat after receiving a thrashing for stealing sugar. Anthony Storr suggests that the "intransigent disobedience" with which Churchill reacted to authority "was not only a way of discharging hostility, but a means of self-assertion . . . [for] a boy who, at that stage, felt himself to be weak physically, and who showed no disposition to excel."[6] Under the heading "general conduct," his school report stated that he was "very bad—is a constant trouble to everybody and is always in some scrape or other. He cannot be trusted to behave himself anywhere."[7] There was not the slightest chance of such behavioral defects going unpunished at St. George's. Here, flogging with the birch was a great feature. Boys were "flogged until they bled freely," punishment reinforced by frequent religious services in the school chapel. The headmaster was a generously bewhiskered sadist, the Reverend H. W. Sneyd-Kynnersley, who on one occasion continued beating a boy even though he had a spasm of diarrhea, "until the whole ceiling and walls of his study were spattered with filth."[8] Even by the standards of the day, this was a school marked by outrageous brutality. "How I hated this school, and what a life of anxiety I lived there for more than two years," Churchill wrote. But escape was eventually achieved; it appears that Mrs. Everest saw the welts left by the cane, showed Lady Randolph, and the boy was removed from the school.

Thus at the end of the summer term 1884, Churchill was transferred to a much gentler, less prestigious, school in Brighton. It was near the seaside and therefore considered good for his health, which at this stage of his life was frail. Here he remained for three years and did well enough at his studies to be positioned near the top of the class. He was allowed to study a range of subjects that interested him, such as "French, History, lots of poetry by heart, and above all Riding and Swimming."[9] "He lapped up the patriotic and imperial history that was usual in those years, mostly kings and queens, wars and battles and heroes."[10] But examinations, he ruefully recorded, remained "a great trial to me."

He threw himself into a range of extracurricular activities, including amateur dramatics and the preparations for the celebration of Queen Victoria's Golden Jubilee (June 21, 1887). He also got stuck into sports other than those with which he became associated in adult life; he made it into the first XI football team and took up cricket (even witnessing a W. G. Grace half-century for Gloucestershire against Sussex in May 1887). He read classic boys' literature of the period such as Henry Rider Haggard's *She* and *Jess*, both

titles hot off the press in 1887. He took up stamp collecting while
at this school and often wrote to ask his father for autographs, as
his schoolmates wanted them as a result of Randolph's growing
political celebrity ("I only want a scribble as I know that you are
very busy").

His time in Brighton was marred by a life-threatening case of
pneumonia in March 1886 ("my boy at school at Brighton nearly
died of inflammation of the lungs last week," wrote Randolph to
the Conservative leader, Lord Salisbury). Despite the serious-
nesses, his parents weren't around, and the trusted family doctor,
Robson Roose, kept Randolph informed through regular bulletins
(March 15: "we are still fighting the battle for your boy"). Winston
maintained affectionate correspondence with Mrs. Everest and
his aunt the Countess of Wilton, a kind benefactress, while his
parents remained detached, continuing his semirelationship with
his mother and his nonrelationship with his father. According to
Churchill's son, "the neglect and lack of interest in him shown by
his parents were remarkable, even judged by the standards of late
Victorian and Edwardian days."[11] His father was a clever, insolent,
sometimes charming, often offensive individual who coveted attention, a shooting star popular with the newspapers he sedulously
courted, though his physical deterioration and suicidal political tendencies ensured that he never became a fixture in the political firma-
ment. Jennie Churchill was a fleeting mother when Churchill was a
schoolboy. Both parents were too self-obsessed to really cater for
another being clamoring for their attention. While they did not lack
affection for their son, they seldom saw him, and as a consequence
he felt profoundly neglected. Churchill's letters to his parents, until
well into his teens, told of this. "Please do do do do do do come
down to see me. . . . Please do come I have been so disappointed so
many times about your coming."[12]

It is no surprise that his attachment to his nanny lasted for so
long, and that as a schoolboy, Churchill was willing to court the jeers
of his fellows when showing Mrs. Everest around Harrow, walking
with her arm in arm. As a result of their neglect, both parents were

viewed through roseate lenses by the young Winston: his father adored and revered, compensating for the absence of sustained contact and love; his mother idolized as the epitome of womanhood. Nevertheless, perhaps another way of looking at Churchill's relations with his parents is to emphasize the point that he was an extremely *demanding* child, emotionally undernourished yet emotionally insatiable. The arrival of a brother in 1880 cannot have suited Churchill, and he would tease and torment him. Throughout his life he remained demanding and prone to selfishness, and those who found themselves in his way, and often mishandled as a consequence, were only ever partially mollified by his humor, self-effacement, and kindness. There is little doubt that, in later life, an embellished story of adversity in childhood was a useful sympathy winner.

Though Churchill's relationship with his father was always distant and strained, he inherited his desire to cut a dash in society, an urge that was supercharged from 1895 by the conviction that he might, like his father, die young. During his son's school days, Lord Randolph became convinced that Winston had little academic ability, though it was clear that where he enjoyed a subject, he attained excellent marks. But Randolph was usually willing to see the worst in his son and to pointedly rake over his misdemeanors, possibly projecting onto Winston a chastisement of himself. Those with more patience and less self-absorption than Randolph Churchill looked beyond the cheekiness and naughtiness. The Duchess of Marlborough wrote to her son Randolph on January 8, 1888, remarking that Winston was "a clever Boy & really not naughty but he wants a firm hand." But even indulgent souls were tired by Winston's incessancy; two weeks later the duchess wrote: "Winston is going back to school today. *Entre nous* I do not feel very sorry for he is certainly a handful."[13]

Coming to the end of his primary education, Churchill sat the entrance examination for Harrow, an inauspicious experience involving a Latin paper on which he was able to answer not a single question but only, he later claimed, to write his name. He was admitted anyway by a headmaster who saw, Churchill speculated, his innate talent shining through. A more likely explanation is that he was a headmaster unprepared to turn down the son of a famous politician. At first, Churchill was put into a small house, but with the promise that he would transfer to the headmaster's, the Reverend J. E. C. Welldon's, in due course. Churchill was placed in the fourth form, the school's lowest.

At Harrow, which he entered on April 17, 1888, Churchill did not excel, though he swam for his house and won the boarding school fencing championship in 1892, as well as achieving proud distinction by winning a prize for reciting 1,200 lines of Macaulay's *Lays of Ancient Rome* to the headmaster without making a single mistake, a phenomenal achievement. But Churchill continued to perform indifferently at his books, finding it almost impossible to enthuse or excel at subjects in which he saw little purpose, such as quadratic equations and differential calculus. "I have never met any of these creatures since," he later wrote, as if confirming their intrinsic irrelevance. In short, this stubborn and questioning youngster was a typical schoolboy of the individualist mold, tending toward the slovenly, flouting rules, getting into trouble for throwing stones and misbehaving, and rarely ready to submit humbly to his just deserts without indignantly defending his actions. He was "Just Winston," and these traits remained with him for life. Be it at school, in the army, or in Parliament, Churchill had a peculiar capacity for behaving in a manner most likely to offend against rules of propriety, showing scant regard for rank or seniority. As his first housemaster, H. O. D. Davidson, put it, he was not "*wilfully troublesome*: but his forgetfulness, carelessness, unpunctuality, and irregularity in every way, have really been so serious, that I write to ask you, when he is home to speak very gravely to him."[14] Nevertheless, such written evidence did little to diminish Churchill's irrepressible, and defiant, optimism—one of his most important character traits. Upon being scolded by his mother for a "*very* bad" report one week, in the following week he told her that next time round he was "*bound* to get a good report."[15] It also failed to dampen his zeal for impromptu adventure, leading into trouble when, for example, he and a group of friends decided to smash the windows in a disused factory in Harrow.

At Harrow, the martial and imperial themes already noted in Winston's life were nurtured. He enjoyed school songs, with their "tales of great deeds and of great men," which caused him to wonder "with intensity how I could ever do something glorious for my country" (as he told his son Randolph in 1940), and remembered particularly in later life a celebratory account of Waterloo. A lecture on Imperial Federation made a deep impression upon him, G. R. Parkin telling the school how "at Trafalgar, Nelson's signal—'England expects that every man will do his duty'—ran down the line of battle, and how if we and our Colonies all held together, a day would come when such a signal would run not merely along a line of ships, but along a line of nations."[16] He won a prize for composing a poem that features the verse "God shield our Empire from the might / Of war or famine, plague or blight / And all the powers of hell, / And keep it ever in the hands / of those who fought 'gainst other lands / who fought and conquered well."[17] There were other extracurricular activities. In May 1889, he bought a bike ("a beautiful little machine," as he told his mother when thanking her for the funds that had procured it), though a month later he was consigned to the sickroom for a week after falling off it. He enjoyed drill and shooting as a member of the school's rifle corps and competed in mock battles against other boarding schools.

His parents maintained their detachment. Lady Randolph was "increasingly caught up in the world of fashion and society and was more and more surrounded by a competitive band of handsome young admirers" while his father was absent abroad or busy.[18] Jennie would even put Winston off from visiting for no reason other than her social engagements; in July 1891, for example, "just" managing to put him up for a night, but at some inconvenience. In that same month, her then beau, Colonel Kinsky, took Winston to the Crystal Palace to see a show put on for the visiting German emperor. At the time, Lord Randolph was touring southern Africa (making some useful investments and writing *Men, Mines and Animals in South Africa*), while also writing columns for the *Daily Graphic*, a ploy his son was soon to excel at. While Randolph regretted that he probably wouldn't be able to bring home a "tame antelope" for his son, he did concede in a letter in June 1891 that he could obtain the Bechuanaland stamps that Winston had requested.

Soon his parents were battling to send him to France for his holidays, in support of Reverend Welldon's wishes, in order to learn the language. Churchill fought a vigorous, though ultimately futile, rearguard action, deploring their conspiracy to send him to "some horrid French Family." He was, his parents concluded, at the "ugly" stage, "slouchy and tiresome."[19] They resented Winston's tone, though seeing his parents so rarely meant that it was not possible for him to always write with an angelic voice when he dissented from their opinions. The "tone of your letter is not calculated to make me over lenient," his mother wrote in December 1891 after threats and ultimatums regarding his visit to France. She told him that she would determine what was best for him: "I tell you frankly that *I* am going to determine and not *you*." One of his letters she sent back to him, to which he replied despairingly, "Darling Mummy I am so unhappy but if you don't read this letter it will be the last you'll have the trouble to send back."[20] Clearly there were faults on both sides, as there often are when family trials of strength are played out, and Churchill fought through his teenage years.

Churchill spent three years in the army form at Harrow, as it had been decided that he was to be a soldier, though he had to make three attempts to get into the Royal Military Academy at Sandhurst. After his second failure to pass the exam, he was sent to a crammer run by Captain W. H. James. His poor math had prevented him from getting into Woolwich, the academy for the artillery and the engineers. Captain James believed that Winston thought too highly of his own abilities, and in March 1893 reported that "all of the tutors complain that while he has good abilities he does not apply himself with sufficient earnestness."

Churchill finally succeeded in passing the dreaded exam in the summer of 1893 (largely because by chance he had mugged up on New Zealand, on which a question appeared), but he did not do enough to qualify for the infantry, a further source of irritation for Lord Randolph, who roundly chastised his son in a withering letter. But he had passed in all subjects (he was placed 95th out of 389), and only 12 out of 29 Harrovian army candidates succeeded. Nevertheless, his father blasted him for his "folly & failure" and the risk he ran of degenerating "into a shabby unhappy and futile existence" as a "social wastrel."[21]

Churchill's transition from schoolboy to soldier cadet was delayed when in January 1893 he fell off a bridge and lay unconscious for three days. His aunt, Lady Wimborne, had lent the Churchills her comfortable estate at Bournemouth for the winter, and in the grounds there were forty or fifty acres of pine forest descending to a beach. Here, while trying to evade being caught in a game of chase, he plunged off a bridge and plummeted over thirty feet, breaking his fall in the branches of a tree. As a result, he was confined to bed for over three months with, among other injuries, a ruptured kidney. In order to recover fully from his fall, Winston was transferred to his father's house in London. Here, while convalescing, he watched from the gallery as "many of the leading figures of the Parliamentary conflicts" visited, including luminaries such as Balfour, Chamberlain, Rosebery, Asquith, Morley, and Carson. "It seemed a very great world in which these men lived."[22] Though Sandhurst and the army beckoned, it was little surprise that Winston Churchill's head had already been turned by the lure of politics and power.

SANDHURST AND THE ARMY

In the period between Harrow, which he left in December 1892, and Sandhurst, which he entered in September 1893, Churchill spent time in Versailles in an attempt to improve his French and was sent by his father, in the company of an Eton master and his brother, Jack,, on a walking tour in Switzerland. Churchill qualified for a cavalry cadetship at Sandhurst and ranked horses as his greatest pleasure while there. He had been lucky to get in, on health as well as intellectual grounds. His recurring chest ailments meant that he almost failed the medical. The competition to enter Sandhurst as part of the infantry class was keener, as the cavalry was so much more expensive. This was a prime consideration for the Churchill family, which had just started house sharing with Duchess Fanny at 50 Grosvenor Square in order to economize. They had also given up their country home, Banstead, as a result of their financial difficulties. While this didn't deter Churchill, it governed his father's attitude to the matter. "What fun it would be having a horse! Also the uniforms of the cavalry were far more magnificent than those of the Foot. It was therefore in an expansive mood that I wrote to my father. I found to my surprise that he took a contrary view. He thought it very discreditable that I had not qualified for the infantry."[23] Lord Randolph was particularly put out by the expense he would have to meet, including two official chargers, one or two hunters, and the indispensable string of polo ponies. His father was exercised enough by the triumphant manner in which Churchill announced his results to roundly chastise him in a letter that cut Churchill to the quick.

Despite his father's warnings, Churchill was a great success at Sandhurst, graduating near the top of his class, though his father died before this incontestable triumph was announced. Joining the army altered Churchill's relationship with his father in some ways, but not in others. "When I became a gentleman cadet I acquired a new status in my father's eyes. . . . But if ever I began to show the slightest idea of comradeship, he was immediately offended." On Churchill's own count he had only "three or four intimate conversations" with his father.[24] When Winston joined the army, Lord Randolph "proceeded to talk to me in the most wonderful manner about school and going into the army and the grown-up life which lay beyond. I listened spellbound to this sudden complete departure from his usual reserve, amazed at his intimate comprehension of my affairs."

Churchill's arrival at Sandhurst brought to a close twelve years of school, and he thrived at this elite military academy. He stood five feet six and a half inches in height and, with an unexpanded chest measuring thirty-one inches, was considered undersized and in need of development if he were to survive the physical demands of army life. He flowered as a self-confident though still self-centered youth and was soon able to indulge his love of danger. Here, he wrote, "I had a new start. I was no longer handicapped by past neglect of Latin, French or Mathematics." The task was now to learn the ropes as a young cavalryman, including all the requisite horsemanship, cavalry maneuvering in column, and fighting in line. Tactics and fortifications, to Churchill's delight, replaced math and Latin as subjects of study. He was impressed by cavalry units as they were handled in the field and later recalled an occasion when General Luck, the inspector general, maneuvered a cavalry division of thirty or forty squadrons as if it were a single unit.

At Sandhurst, Churchill developed a habit of private study that was to be the wellspring of his future success as a writer, orator, and politician. Focused upon achieving something notable in his life, he developed powers of intense concentration. Beyond the basics of military tactics and soldiering, Churchill had occasion to consider the higher levels of the strategic direction of war, the study and practice of which were to be a central feature of his life, and to dabble in the exhilarating world of public oration. On the former count, he was sometimes invited to dine at the nearby Staff College at Camberley, an educational establishment for higher-ranking officers. Here "the talk was of divisions, army corps and even whole armies; of bases, of supplies, of lines of communication and railway strategy. This was thrilling."[25] It was very much Churchill's line of territory, as even at this early stage, he was convinced that the gifts of military and political leadership were in his blood and that the direction of great campaigns would represent the best use of his talents. While at Sandhurst, he received his first taste of preparing and delivering public speeches in an attempt to woo opinion when he gave a speech for the Entertainments Protection League, formed to oppose moralists seeking to screen off the bar of the Empire Theatre, Leicester Square, where "undesirable" ladies occasionally congregated. He had a letter published in the *Westminster Gazette* and carefully prepared and rehearsed a speech that he committed to memory ("Ladies of the Empire, I stand for Liberty!").

Sandhurst brought its usual share of frolics to the young Churchill (he made a convincing Pierrot at the May 1894 Half-Mile Donkey Derby), yet his poor relations with his father continued. Lord Randolph's persistent low opinion of his son was graphically demonstrated when in March 1894, Churchill lost a pocket watch his father had given him. Though showing great ingenuity in searching for it, hiring twenty-three men and diverting the course of a river in the hunt, his father boiled with a rage that was communicated, as usual, not in person but on paper. It was not until October 1894, three months before his death, that Churchill became aware of the seriousness of his father's illness (long believed to have been advanced syphilis, more likely to have been the result of a brain tumor, but still unknown).

Churchill completed his Sandhurst cadetship in 1895, a year in which the Churchill family suffered a spate of deaths. Lord Randolph "died by inches in public," continuing to make speeches though visibly in decline. He died on January 24, his wife and two sons at his bedside. A memorial service was held in Westminster Abbey, attended by Lord Rosebery, and a simultaneous funeral took place in Woodstock, followed by a burial in the family plot in the churchyard at Bladon. "The snow lay thick in the long avenue stretching through Blenheim Park from the Woodstock arch to Bladon. . . . Lady Randolph Churchill, supported by her sons, stood at the grave [and] . . . scattered lilies of the valley in the coffin."[26] Three months later, Jennie's mother passed away. Then, in July, the cherished Mrs. Everest died as well. Upon hearing that she was seriously ill, Churchill had gone to London to see her, reaching Sandhurst for early morning parade by the last train before returning again to her bedside. He organized her funeral and later paid for the erection of a headstone and for the upkeep of the grave.

Randolph's death had a profound influence upon his son. The only silver lining was that it meant he was able to have his way and join the cavalry. Despite his father's clear wish that he join the infantry, Churchill had, irrespective of his exam results, developed a fancy for the 4th Hussars, whose commanding officer, Colonel Brabazon, he admired. Churchill had set about pulling the necessary strings, his head turned, as he put it, by "the stir of the horses, the clank of their equipment, the thrill of motion, the tossing plumes, the sense of incorporation in a living machine, the suave dignity of the uniform."[27] A week after his father's death he asked his mother to write to no less a personage than the Duke of Cambridge, commander in chief of the British Army. He was all in favor of the young Churchill going into the 4th Hussars, and so it was neatly arranged.

Even while at Sandhurst, gearing up for a career in the army, Churchill had decided that he wanted to become a politician, possibly spurred on by his father's death. He wrote prescient commentaries on political events in letters to his mother, as if rehearsing for what would come. On August 3, 1895, he described politics as "a fine game to play," for which it was "well worth waiting for a good hand before really plunging."[28] In the same month, he conceived the idea of spending a couple of hours a week with one of Captain James's "cramming" tutors when in London—"if you know what I mean, I need some one to point out some specific subjects to stimulate & to direct my reading." He was conscious of the fact that his mind hadn't received the "polish" that Oxbridge might have given it and wanted to rectify this perceived omission.

WAR TOURIST

Churchill entered the British Army burning with ambition and with a lot to prove. Achievement early was the order of the day, now in pursuit of his father's memory, a more liberating hunt than seeking his approval during his lifetime had ever been. He was the ultimate "young man in a hurry," prepared brazenly to use his connections in order to get on and never afraid to put himself forward, an unashamed thruster motivated by ambition and burgeoning talent. Of course, Churchill would have defended himself vigorously against all charges along these lines. What else was he supposed to do? Sit idle and treat the world as if it owed him a living? Languish with his contemporaries, playing cards and waiting for the slow, slow progress through the army's rank structure? Churchill eschewed these tempting options and decided to act upon the world. Though he exploited his family's connections where possible, they alone were not a decisive factor. Family connections would have been "to no avail without his own primordial thrust. . . . Though he took the fullest opportunity of connections which he had inherited from his father, it was his own daemon which led him on to fame, prosperity and honour."[29] What now followed were four years of phenomenal military and literary activity, which sculpted Churchill's adult character and prefaced his career as a politician.

Of course, the British Army of this period was a much smaller force than that which was to languish in the trenches and endure lengthy campaigns in Flanders, Turkey, Mesopotamia, and East Africa in the First World War. Churchill remembered that a young cavalry captain with whom he had exercised while at Sandhurst, Douglas Haig, was later to bemoan the fact that he "only" had forty British divisions and four hundred brigades of artillery, a scale of military resource that would have been unthinkable even to the military visionary a few years before. "I wonder," Churchill mused, "whether any other generation has seen such astounding revolutions of data and values as those through which we have lived. Scarcely anything material or established which I was brought up to believe was permanent and vital, has lasted. Everything that I was sure or taught to be sure was impossible, has happened."[30] But in the mid-1890s, the world was still unchanged; God, it appeared, was in his heaven, and despite some discernible challenges, the British Empire was secure, and Britannia ruled the waves. This state of affairs, however, was not entirely to the liking of a young man looking forward, especially a young soldier—for it meant precious few opportunities to win the glory he craved.

Soon a problem that would remain a factor throughout most of Churchill's adult life began to plague him: money. His salary as a second lieutenant in the hussars was £120, yet it was reckoned that in such a smart unit an additional £500 was needed just in order to get by. Not having enough money was not just a personal worry and constraint but could lead to public embarrassment, and Churchill was implicated in an unsavory episode of bullying in which a fellow junior officer, Allan Bruce, was driven out of the regiment for (among other things) having an allowance of "only" £500 a year.* Such an amount could not easily be borne by the Churchills, though Winston did manage to lever more money out of his mother.

Having joined the right kind of regiment, Churchill now needed to find the right kind of campaigns. Like most army officers, Churchill hankered after action, because that was the way to win medals and get noticed, invaluable springboards to personal advancement in both the army and wider society. For Churchill, this was doubly important, because he had vaulting ambitions far beyond the slow rise toward his majority, battalion command, and the vague hope of possible promotion into the red-tabbed world of senior officers. Churchill was possessed of the conviction that life had much more in store for him than this. As he put it rather endearingly to Asquith's daughter, Violet, "we are all worms. But I do believe that I am a glow-worm."[31] He was irresistibly drawn toward the idea of emulating his father in politics. This sense of promise to be fulfilled, and of glories to live up to, was intensified by the reaction of other people to *him* as the son of an exceptional man born of a famous line. Because of his father's meteoric rise and subsequent fame—seen by some as Disraeli's true successor, widely mentioned as the next Conservative prime minister after Salisbury—everyone had an interest in seeing what the young offshoot was like, including the army's senior officers. The Duke of Cambridge set the tone when on an official visit to Aldershot, he asked for Churchill as

---

* There were also allegations of race fixing at the Subalterns' Challenge Cup, for which Winston sued and received a full apology and £500.

an escort, and everywhere Churchill went,, he gained access to the upper echelons at least in part because his elders and betters couldn't resist having a peek at him. An air of celebrity surrounded Churchill from birth, and this was a factor in shaping his character and how he viewed the world and his place in it.

As a young blade searching for distinction, Churchill was entirely representative of his caste in regretting that the world, when viewed from the vantage point of the early 1890s, was growing so "sensible and pacific," as he put it; there was no chance of the twenty years of war that one "would have got if it was 1793 as opposed to 1893." British troops hadn't fired at white troops since the Crimea. "Luckily, however, there were still savages and barbarous peoples," he wrote. "There were Zulus and Afghans, also the Dervishes in the Soudan. Some of these might, if they were well-disposed, 'put up a show' some day."[32]

It was completely in character for Churchill to seek to circumvent the difficulty that this irritating dearth of conflict presented. In doing so, he illustrated the determination, initiative, and self-confidence in his own ability and destiny that marked him apart from most men. Churchill knew full well that the swift road to advancement lay in active service, "the glittering gateway to distinction," as he put it. Sporting prowess was all very well, but having been "under fire" had a special aura. Besides, all his money had been spent on polo ponies, so he couldn't afford to hunt during the leave period of 1895, as was the norm. Yet, though a man of colossal determination, even Winston Churchill could not cause a war to erupt in order to expedite his search for personal glory and renown. He could, however, do the next best thing: get involved in someone else's.

In getting himself into a war zone, Churchill displayed the hallmarks of his pell-mell, thrusting early career—audacity, innovation, and the pulling of strings, most of them in the hands of his mother and other relatives. He scoured the world for war and found the peace of the 1890s broken only in one quarter of the globe: in Cuba, where the beleaguered Spanish Empire was fighting a tricky counterinsurgency campaign. His proposed venture met with the approval of the 4th Hussars' commanding officer, indeed was considered to be almost as good an idea as a season's hunting, "without which," Churchill wrote, "no subaltern [junior officer] or captain was considered to be living a respectable life."[33] This hurdle cleared, a letter was dispatched to the British ambassador in Madrid, Sir Henry Drummond Wolff, who happened to be an old friend of Winston's father. The Spanish minister of war duly wrote to Marshal Campos, commanding operations in Cuba. These contacts ensured excellent introductions, and Churchill was told that he had only to reach Havana to be warmly welcomed by no less a person than the captain general himself. Not content with this, Churchill reached even higher, obtaining a personal interview with the new commander in chief of the British Army, Field Marshal Lord Wolseley, in order to seek formal permission for his trip. Wolseley, who had also been a friend of his father, was happy to oblige. As an added bonus and official imprimatur, the director of military intelligence asked if Churchill could collect military information. One can only admire how Churchill played his hand.

It was thus that Churchill headed for Cuba via New York in November 1895. "Often I had imagined in dreams and day-dreams the sensations attendant upon being for the first time under fire," and his dreams were about to be fulfilled.[34] The trip to Cuba, in the company of a fellow junior officer, Reginald Barnes, was intended to accomplish this essential first step: "I thought it might be as well to have a private rehearsal given my choice of profession." And so, for the first time, Churchill left Europe behind. The ship called at New York before onward passage to Cuba, where a meeting took place that presented another example of his mother's influence. Churchill and Barnes were met on the quayside by Bourke Cochran, an influential American politician and friend of Lady Randolph's who was to have an important impact upon Churchill as a politician and orator. Cochran put them up in his Fifth Avenue apartment and impressed Churchill markedly, particularly with his exhilarating conversation. Later in life, Churchill claimed that he had never met

Cochran's equal in conversation and comprehension. A correspondence between the two men developed, Bourke sending Churchill copies of his speeches. In New York, Churchill developed impressions of America, remarking upon paper money, the transport system, the strictness of the regime at West Point Military Academy, and the smartness of the cruiser USS *New York*.

Following this New York sojourn, Churchill and Barnes sailed for Cuba. "When first in the dim light of early morning I first saw the shores of Cuba rise and define themselves from the dark-blue horizon, I felt as if I sailed with Long John Silver and first gazed on Treasure Island."[35] Churchill had devoured "with delight" Robert Louis Stevenson's classic novel about pirates, shipwrecks, and treasure at the age of nine. Upon their being received and welcomed by the Spanish authorities, it was suggested that the two junior officers join a mobile force if they wanted to see some fighting. A three-thousand-strong column had started from Santa Clara heading for Sancti Spíritus, a town beset by rebels. They caught up with the column and were cordially received by General Valdez, who saw in their visit a token of moral support from Britain.

As well as acquiring a taste for Havana cigars and siestas, Churchill made useful observations during his visit to the troubled island. He discovered that foreigners had "the same feelings about colonies as we do," and that the Spaniards talked of Cuba "as we talk of Ireland." Despite this, he couldn't see how the Spanish could win, given the immense cost of maintaining large forces so far from home, fighting a war in which the enemy only needed to avoid defeat in order to win. Cuba for Spain was "like a dumb-bell held at arm's length." Across the island the Spanish forces "moved like Napoleon's convoys in the Peninsula," Churchill wrote, "league after league, day after day, through a world of impalpable hostility, slashed here and there by fierce onslaught."[36]

Churchill was straining at the bit for something to happen, and on November 30, 1895, his twenty-first birthday, it did. "For the first time I heard shots fired in anger, heard bullets strike flesh or whistle through the air," a bullet even passing through the hut in which he was sheltering. Immediately he began to take a more circumspect view of being "under fire."[37] "Nothing in life is so exhilarating as to be shot at without result." He witnessed several contacts between the Spanish column and the Cuban insurgents. He was even awarded a Spanish medal for gallantry, causing a rumpus at home, where the Spanish action was unpopular, and inviting questions as to what on earth young Churchill was doing in Cuba at all. Nevertheless, the receipt of silverware ticked another item off the list of things required if he were to get on. The trip also introduced him to what was to become one of the major vehicles for establishing his name, and a crucial strand of personal income for the rest of his life—writing for the newspapers. Taking a leaf out of his father's book, he had contracted with the *Daily Graphic* to provide letters at £5 a piece from this distant war zone. From this point on, writing was central to Churchill's life, inseparable from his political and public life. He found in it not only power and profit, but solace. As he described it in 1908, "I often fortify myself amid the uncertainties and vexations of political life by believing that I possess a line of retreat into a peaceful and fertile country where no rascal can pursue me and where one need never be dull or idle or even wholly without power. It is then, indeed, that I feel devoutly thankful to have been born fond of writing."[38]

SOLDIER AND WAR CORRESPONDENT: INDIA AND AFRICA

Returning to England, Churchill sought every opportunity to meet the "right sort" of people and discuss the affairs of the day. In January 1896, he stayed at Tring with the Rothschilds, where the talk was of Cecil Rhodes and the Jameson Raid into the Transvaal. In spring 1896, his regiment marched to Hounslow and Hampton Court, preparatory to departure for India. While waiting to sail, Churchill passed an agreeable six months that he described as the "only idle spell I've ever had." He was able to live at home with his mother, play polo at Hurlingham and Ranelagh (he had five polo ponies), and enjoy the trappings of the London Season. In describing this world of the 1890s from the vantage point of the 1920s, Churchill wrote of how "in a very large degree, everyone knew everyone else. The few hundred great families who had governed England for so many generations and had seen her rise to the pinnacle of her glory, were interrelated to an enormous extent by marriage."[39] In the intervening thirty years, this was all to change immensely, the great London houses turned into hotels or flats and the aristocracy immeasurably weakened. Naturally, Churchill deplored such changes, just as he deplored what he termed the "democratization of the battlefield" brought about by the industrialization of conflict, a far cry from the warfare depicted on the grand tapestries at Blenheim Palace that had so influenced his childhood thoughts. Yet regretting what he perceived to be changes for the worse never prevented him from keeping abreast of modern developments and dealing effectively with them, whether in his private or professional life.

The London that Churchill launched himself upon in the summer of 1896 was one where all minds were turned to Queen Victoria's Diamond Jubilee the following year: the First World War, and the immense changes it was to effect, were part of a future as yet unknown. Churchill was determined not to waste the final summer before the start of his regiment's lengthy stint in India. At social functions he met, among others, a former home secretary, two future prime ministers, the Leader of the House of Commons, the First Lord of the Treasury, the colonial secretary, the commander in chief of the British Army, the president of the Local Government Board, and the chancellor of the Duchy of Lancaster. At a house party at Deepdene, home of Lord William Beresford and Lilian, widow of Churchill's uncle the 8th Duke of Marlborough, he also met General Sir Bindon Blood. "On the sunny lawns of Deepdene I extracted a promise that if ever he commanded another expedition on the Indian frontier, he would let me come with him."

The rambunctious Churchill realized, sometimes, that he needed to curb his natural tendencies in order to operate successfully in such exalted company. Nevertheless, it must have been very difficult to do so while mixing in the lofty circles to which his family background (and his father's fame) entitled him and never having been one to defer to others just because they were older or more important. He attended a weekend party given by the Prince of Wales (a family friend and sometime enemy, now firmly returned to friendship and even intimacy with Lady Randolph) to which the colonel commanding his regiment was invited. He had, therefore, to be on his best behavior—"punctual, subdued, reserved, in short display[ing] all the qualities with which I am least endowed."[40]

Over the course of this summer, he energetically maneuvered for future advantage. He heard that Kitchener was organizing an expedition to reclaim the Sudan and attempted to join Sir Frederick Carrington's expedition to Matabeleland. Churchill's appetite for politics remained undiminished, as did his desire to hone his communicative skills and augment his knowledge. In April 1896, Bourke Cochran commended the study of sociology and political economy, because "with your remarkable talent for lucid and attractive expression you would be able to make great use of the information" acquired.[41] He hungered for immediate glory and for political renown and was reluctant to pay his dues in order to get there, unprepared to wait his turn. The prospect of eight years of garrison duty in India appalled him. As he wrote to his mother on August 4, 1896, "The future is to me utterly unattractive. I look upon going to India with this unfortunate regiment . . . as useless and unprofitable exile."[42] He was already determined to become a politician and impatient for the opportunity to change career.

But not even Churchill could turn the wheel of fate at a moment's notice. In September 1896, he was off to India, unfortunate or not, aboard the SS *Britannia*. Colonel Brabazon's farewell address referred memorably, Churchill recalled, to "India, that famous appanage of the Bwitish Cwown." Along with the 1,200 men of his regiment, he sailed from Southampton, landing in Bombay twenty-three days later. The journey was spent playing chess and piquet (a two-handed card game) and conducting debates. Alighting from the ship, he fell and badly injured his shoulder, a wound that crippled him at polo and prevented him from using his sword at the Battle of Omdurman two years later. From Bombay the regiment moved via Poona to Bangalore, the main military cantonment of the Madras Presidency. Settling in, among an officer's first tasks was to collect about him his "cabinet" of servants, finding (or inheriting from a departing regiment) a dressing boy, an attendant, and a butler. Again favored by his stellar background, Churchill was invited to dine at Government House. Thus after a day spent chiding troops for failing to wear their pith helmets, he was able to enjoy a "banquet of glitter, pomp and iced champagne" and began to develop an imperialist's sense of the "great work that England was doing in India and of her high mission to rule these primitive but agreeable races for their welfare and our own."[43]

In Bangalore, Churchill, along with Reginald Barnes and Hugo Baring, "took a palatial bungalow, all pink and white, with heavily tiled roof and deep verandahs sustained by white plaster columns, wreathed in purple bougainvillea, in two acres of land and surrounded by rose trees."[44] Here Churchill took up a hobby he had toyed with during childhood and built a collection of the exotic butterflies that fluttered in the garden, though it was soon destroyed by a rat. The abundant roses in the garden meant that "every morning I can cut about three great basins full of the most beautiful flowers. Flowers, flowering shrubs and creepers blossom in glorious profusion," he wrote, "snipe (and snakes) abound in the marshes; brilliant butterflies dance in the sunshine."[45] A large barn was built to cater for thirty horses and ponies, and soon the regiment acquired twenty-five polo ponies from the Poona Light Horse, a stable that was to form the nucleus for the 4th Hussars' assault on the Inter-Regimental Polo Tournament. As Churchill explained, this devotion to horsemanship and winning polo tournaments sustained the regiment's intensity of purpose.

But horses and pith helmets alone were unlikely to be enough for the questing mind of Winston Churchill and the ticking clock of his ambition. He found Anglo-Indian society "vulgar," reporting to his mother that they had commented on "my not 'calling' as is the absurd custom of the country."[46] In this social desert, he again enlisted his mother and her contacts, desperate to meet the "right type" of people. In fact, he found the routine of army life dull and boring. He kept revolving the proposed Egyptian campaign in his mind—"action this day" being a personal leitmotif that he was later to inflict upon other people—and frequently thought about parliamentary elections back at home. He sharpened his political talons in letters, writing, for example, a voluminous response to Lord Lansdowne's proposal to increase the size of the army. In a lengthy disquisition to his mother he referred to his "stupid speech" and the fact that the strength of the Royal Navy negated a large army (material later to be used when, as a young MP, Churchill took a leading role in opposing Brodrick's army reforms). Letters to his mother begged her to obtain him a transfer. Jennie, to her credit, sought to soothe his tormented ambition, recognizing (and therefore tolerating) a greedy appetite for life that resembled her own. Her efforts met with some success; in December 1896, Lord Kitchener agreed to put Churchill's name down for special service with the Egyptian Army in the event of a campaign.

Thinking constantly about his future and his destiny, Churchill decided that he needed to study more widely and intensely than he had ever done before. This was to overcome his lack of a university education, about which he was self-conscious, and to acquire the breadth of knowledge he considered essential for a man of his boundless ambition. Of his university-educated peers he wrote that he "sometimes resented the apt and copious information which some of them seemed to possess. . . . So I resolved to read history, philosophy, economics and things like that." He asked his mother to send books, including Gibbon's *Decline and Fall of the Roman Empire*, Macaulay's collection of ballad poems *Lays of Ancient Rome*, Smith's *Wealth of Nations*, and also the parliamentary debates of the previous six years. "From November to May I read for four or five hours every day. . . . I approached it with an empty, hungry mind, and with fairly strong jaws."[47] This store of knowledge was to stand Churchill in good stead for the rest of his life, though he continued to regret the fact that he learned without the benefit of tutorial enquiry and critical dialogue. Churchill was a self-educated man, and as A. J. P. Taylor noted, "The theme of his education was statesmanship."[48]

In these formative years, Churchill conceived a view of the world influenced by Darwinism and history more than God. Civilized races progressed; backward races were there to be aided, though they were not to be allowed to stand in the way of progress. Non-Europeans might *currently* be inferior to Europeans, but they could be "uplifted," and this was clearly Britain's imperial mission. Churchill, writing to Wilfrid Scawen Blunt, said that the empire was a lot of bother to Britain; "The only thing one can say for it is that it is justified if it is undertaken in an altruistic spirit for the good of the subject races."[49] England—soon extended in Churchill's conception of the world to become the "English-speaking peoples"—was a force for good in the world, and this was the key to his belief in the British Empire. It was a driver of progress and enlightenment, and for this reason Churchill was quick to condemn actions that besmirched Britain's reputation as a fair, wise, and judicious imperial power. He eschewed jingoism and crass yellow-press nationalism, though he was in no way anti-imperialist. Having seen men die horrible, prosaic deaths and having witnessed the slaughter of wounded foes on the battlefield, jingoism was not for him. But he did reflect the "Jolly Old Empire" attitude common among his class and didn't question Britain's right to hold dominion over palm and pine. A. J. P. Taylor wrote:

> His deepest devotion was to England, as she had matured through the ages, and, though it would be unfair to call him a Little Englander, he was never an Imperialist in the ordinary sense. Perhaps Great Englander would be the right term. In his view the British Empire was another form of the benevolence which he sought to practice at home in social affairs. Far from being a source of profit to be exploited, Churchill's Empire was simply the white man's burden—a responsibility imposed by conscience on a great power. Similarly, he did not

regard the Dominions as equals and he saw the Commonwealth (a word he detested) as a family of children, loyally sustaining the venerable mother to whom they owed so much.[50]

Churchill continued to yearn for the British political scene, his appetite whetted by the three thousand miles separating Westminster from the suffocating plains of southern India. As he wrote to his mother, "the more I see of soldiering—the more I like it—but the more I feel convinced that it is not my *métier*." He seems to have been more content when given more responsibility, as when, in February 1897, he was acting as brigade major and getting stuck into the interminable administration that accompanies military affairs, becoming "a very 'correct' soldier" full of zeal. Even at this early stage in his army career, Churchill (like many junior officers before and since) was putting a mental time limit on the length of his service—perhaps two years—and writing candidly to his mother about how he should best use his time as a springboard for a public career thereafter, constantly seeking to put himself "before the public." "A few months in South Africa would win me the S. A. medal and in all probability the [British South Africa] Company's Star. Then hotfoot to Egypt—to return with two more decorations in a year or two—and beat my sword into an iron dispatch box."[51] Churchill considered military service an essential prerequisite for political life and was increasingly convinced that fate, destiny—call it what you will—had something more in store for him than was the lot of ordinary man, even the "ordinary" man of high birth and exceptional talent. His early exposure to the life and works of his great ancestor John Spencer Churchill, so powerfully enshrined in stone and tapestry at Blenheim, his belief in the importance of hereditary blood, his adoration of his father's achievements and foiled ambitions—all of these things left him yearning for dramatic distinction on the grandest stage. As Clement Attlee was to write, "If there was one thing that marked him off from the comparable figures of history, it was his characteristic way of standing back and looking at himself—and his country—as he believed history would."[52]

Despite these lofty ambitions, however, the tedious gap that often exists between income and expenditure was a significant inconvenience to Churchill. Much of his correspondence with his mother revolved around money, or rather the lack of it—Churchill cast in the role of the schoolboy writing home for seedcake and yet another postal order. Jennie scolded him, not without affection, for extravagance, thoughtlessness, and pomposity. The admonishments increasingly went the other way, too, Churchill chastising his mother (sometimes in bullying tones) for her renowned extravagances and financial mismanagement while reminding her of her duty to both him and Jack. While Jennie might bemoan a bounced check, Churchill pointed out her responsibility for squandering the family's limited fortune. He could be both ungenerous and ungrateful but sometimes had good cause. A consolidation loan of £17,000, which he was roped in to help secure, gave him a legitimate voice as the Churchills' battered finances soldiered on. As Winston wrote to his mother, "The pinch of the matter is that we are damned poor,"[53] not poor like farm laborers, but poor in a world where ball gowns and cavalry chargers at £200 a go were considered necessities. Though Churchill's renowned insensitivity shaded his financial dealings with his mother, to his considerable credit he worked hard throughout his life to earn the money to support his family, all the more creditable because his parents had set such a bad example. As he ruefully remarked, "Saving is a very fine thing. Especially when your parents have done it for you."[54] But Lord and Lady Randolph hadn't. Upon their marriage, the Duke of Marlborough and Mr. Leonard Jerome had between them settled £3,000 a year on the couple, a princely sum, yet one they had consistently managed to live beyond, partying, horseracing, and keeping up with the Prince of Wales's social set.

For the time being, Churchill remained discontent with the routine of army life, though there was triumph on the polo field when the 4th Hussars team won a first-class tournament at Hyderabad. After this, he was allowed three months' leave, sailing from Bombay in May 1897. Always espying windows of opportunity, Churchill conceived the idea of stopping off en route in order to cover the Greek-Turkish War for a newspaper. As he wrote to his mother on April 21, he would view the imminent conflict from whichever side he could gain the best vantage point, and he asked her to use her contacts, including the king of Greece. Unfortunately for Churchill, however, the Greeks had already been defeated by the time his ship reached Port Said. Ever ready to leap from one opportunity to another, he decided instead to spend two weeks in Italy, visiting the monuments of ancient Rome, about which he had been reading, before returning to England for another crack at the London Season (including an appearance at the famous fancy-dress ball thrown each year by the Duchess of Devonshire, an invitation obtained by his mother).

It was from the manicured lawns of Goodwood during another fine English summer that Churchill heard that the Pathan tribesmen of India's North West Frontier were revolting. He read that a field force of three brigades was being gathered under the command of Sir Bindon Blood. Opportunity knocked. Churchill telegraphed the general, reminding him of the promise he had made at Deepdene the summer before, enlisted other worthies to lobby in his cause, and headed off for India. He left England with unseemly haste, forgetting items of equipment, including his polo sticks and his dog Peas, which he cabled for from Aden. Thus, on an outside chance of being near the action, Churchill forewent three weeks of leave, playing for medals and experience that could then be converted into a political career. Blood's response was discouraging, but not an outright rejection. "Very difficult; no vacancies; come up as a correspondent will try to fit you in. B. B."[55] And so Winston Churchill entered the first of three wars in which he was to occupy a remarkable position as free-ranging soldier cum newspaper reporter. In each of these skirmishes on the frontiers of Britain's expanding empire, Churchill was driven by his desire to make a name for himself in the papers back at home while earning extra cash on the side.

He was commissioned as a correspondent by the *Calcutta Pioneer*, a result of Blood's good offices, and his mother secured

£5 a column from the *Daily Telegraph*. Churchill was subsequently annoyed that, when published, these letters bore only his initials: "I had written them with the design, a design which took form as the correspondence advanced, of bringing my personality before the electorate." A peeved Churchill carried on, revealing the essence of his approach to life at this time: "If I am to avoid doing 'unusual' things it is difficult to see what chance I have of being more than an average person. I was proud of the letters and anxious to stake my reputation on them."[56] Jennie Churchill helped oil the works for this latest assault, writing, for instance, to the Prince of Wales, telling him to keep an eye open for her son's newspaper reports. Thus continued what had begun in Cuba: the turbocharged progress of the warrior-writer. Churchill was off to the wars, and he was in a hurry to reach them. With his dressing boy and campaigning gear in tow, Churchill "sped to the Bangalore railway station and bought a ticket for Nowshera," 2,028 miles away. From there he traveled forty miles across the plains in great heat before beginning the climb upward to the Malakand Pass. Here he had to buy two horses, engage an attendant, and assemble military effects from dead brother officers, sold at auction, as was the grim but eminently practical army custom.

It was on one of his newly purchased mounts that Churchill set about getting himself noticed, riding up and down the skirmish line on a striking gray. He wished to create the impression that he was impervious to enemy fire, desperate for a reputation for bravery (juxtaposed, in a letter to his brother, with his self-confessed cowardice while at school). As he put it squarely, when there was an audience, there was "no act too daring or noble." Personal distinction was Churchill's goal, and danger wasn't going to be allowed to stand in the way. "I am so conceited I do not think the gods would create so potent a being for so prosaic an ending."[57] By his dashing about, Churchill certainly did manage to get himself noticed while also performing valuable battlefield tasks; General Blood told Churchill's commanding officer that he was worth two junior officers and even mentioned him in dispatches. This delighted Churchill no end.

The campaign was a pretty standard North West Frontier affair. Tribesmen had attacked the garrisons holding the Malakand Pass and the fort at Chakdara. Therefore, across a swinging rope bridge, a punitive force of about twelve thousand men and four thousand animals marched into the mountains. Churchill joined a brigade sent to retaliate after an attack by tribesmen. "At earliest dawn on September 16 our whole Brigade, preceded by a squadron of Bengal Lancers, marched in warlike formation into the Mamund Valley."[58] Churchill left his horse and joined some Sikh infantrymen and their British officers climbing a hill at the head of the valley to "punish its farthest village." The village was deserted, and the captain ordered a withdrawal. But he had been mistaken. As Churchill recorded, "Suddenly the mountain-side sprang to life. Swords flashed from behind rocks, bright flags waved here and there." Churchill tried to rescue wounded soldiers, taking a Martini Henry rifle from a stricken comrade and brandishing a revolver amid the yells, powder smoke, and calls to withdraw. It was a very close-run thing, the Buffs (East Kent Regiment) arriving in the nick of time and putting in a charge to drive the enemy off. Churchill marched back to camp with the Buffs and the much-mauled 35th Sikhs. The brigade commander exchanged messages by heliograph with his superior, General Blood, and was ordered to stay in the Mamund Valley and lay it waste in vengeance. This the brigade set about "in punitive devastation," destroying crops, felling shady trees, breaking reservoirs, and burning homesteads.

Given its significant losses, General Blood emergency-posted Churchill to the 31st Punjab Infantry. All of this made good copy for Churchill's two newspapers, and he managed to successfully file his reports even though under field conditions. While naturally not revealing the full horrors of the battlefield, Churchill's experiences here contributed to his growing and vocal disapproval of the British government's "forward policy" (the belief that the passes leading from India into Afghanistan needed to be held by the British and their allies, particularly in order to forestall Russian penetration southward) in imperial affairs, and he offered brave criticism of this policy in the books that described the first two campaigns in which he was engaged, *The Story of the Malakand Field Force* and *The River War*. As Richard Toye makes clear, however, Churchill objected more to the forward police on grounds of cost and because he believed the government should be honest with the public on this score.

Churchill's subsequent writings on the action in which he had taken part reveal a great deal about his views on empire and war. He was not a jingo. Having seen action, he did not seek to glorify it, finding the realities of the battlefield repulsive, and wrestled with the ethical issues associated with war. In particular, he demanded the best treatment for a defeated foe. Though he was proud of Britain's imperial achievements, he was very critical when the empire fell short of the "ideal." He told his mother that the Malakand Field Force was "financially ruinous . . . morally . . . wicked, and politically it is a blunder," made necessary only by the Government of India's misguided "forward policy."[59]

Churchill returned to his regiment at Bangalore in October 1897 after six weeks on the frontier. The more powerful Afridi tribes of the Tirah region east of the Khyber Pass had now joined the revolt. The Government of India decided to send an expedition comprising two whole divisions—about thirty-five thousand men—under Sir William Lockhart, to do what Blood had been doing in the Malakand region. Churchill made strenuous efforts to join the Tirah Expeditionary Force in order to be part of what promised to be the next high-profile frontier adventure. He knew none of the "high-ups" involved, however, and besides, the colonel of his regiment was pressing for his return to Bangalore, where the general sense was that he'd had quite enough leave and adventure and should now settle down to the routine of army life, for which he was in fact being paid. Thus, after seeing real war, "I found myself popping off blank cartridges in sham fights two thousand miles away."

Meanwhile the Tirah campaign rumbled on, as did Churchill's interest in it. Having largely failed to achieve its objective of cowing the Afridis, the Tirah Expeditionary Force planned a second round of hostilities, and Churchill made strenuous efforts to be involved this time around, dragooning his mother into helping with the lobbying. "Under my direction she had laid vigorous siege both to Lord Wolseley and Lord Roberts. These fortresses resisted obdurately." Churchill therefore decided to go to Calcutta, the seat of Indian military command, where he engineered an introduction to the viceroy himself, Lord Elgin, and dined with the commander in chief, General Sir George White, as well as winning the fortnightly Calcutta point-to-point. But despite his social and sporting triumphs, his trip did not meet with success. All appointments were made by the adjutant general's department, he was informed, and the adjutant-general refused point blank to see this pushy young junior officer. Churchill returned reluctantly to his regiment at Bangalore.

This setback did not prevent Churchill, ever active on a number of different fronts, from conceiving and successfully executing an excellent plan calculated to earn cash and win public attention. This was to convert his notes and dispatches from the Malakand Field Force into a book. Striking while the iron was hot, he wrote during the hours in the middle of the day that his peers devoted to slumber and cards, discovering "a great power of application which I did not think I possessed."[60] The manuscript was finished shortly after Christmas, and his mother, playing a stalwart role as business partner and career adviser in these crucial formative years, ensured the book's rapid publication by Longman.

Churchill's book about the frontier war, *The Story of the Malakand Field Force*, was published to great acclaim in the spring of 1898, achieving all that he could reasonably have desired from his first venture in this direction. The many glowing reviews gave great pleasure to someone who had, until now, received scant praise for his academic efforts. From the Prince of Wales down, he was widely congratulated, and this thrilled him. "I felt a new way of making a living and of asserting myself, opening splendidly out before me." "Writing a book was an adventure. To begin with, it was a toy, an amusement; then it became a mistress, and then a master, and then a tyrant."[61] In a few months, the book had earned him the equivalent of two years' pay. What is more, and typical of Churchill's ability to short-circuit conventional customs of rank and propriety, the book meant that though only a lowly life form in army terms, he was able to communicate above the heads of his seniors. The book enabled him to address a wider audience and to censure the strategies and tactics of those at the military summit. He received invitations to write on military themes—the editor of the influential *United Services Magazine*, for instance, asking for articles on the ethics of Britain's frontier policy. The book was written with astonishing speed, largely motivated by the desire to beat a competitor's effort into the public domain. One of the prices for such a rapid publication, however, was that Churchill entrusted the proofreading to someone else (Morton Frewin, known by the sobriquet "Mortal Ruin"), who, alas, allowed errors to creep in, or to remain undetected. Churchill felt a sense of "disgrace" at the errors and the slovenly impression they might convey; "literary excellence is what I aim at."[62] But the errors did little to impede the book's enthusiastic reception.

"Having contracted the habit of writing," Churchill thought that, for his next trick, he'd try his hand at a novel, finished in two months and published under the title *Savrola: A Tale of Revolution in Laurania* in 1899. "I have consistently urged my friends to abstain from reading it" was his later judgment upon his first and last venture into fiction. But to have written a novel at all, at such a young age and with so many other calls upon his time, was amazing, and the novel itself was of sufficient quality to earn favorable reviews in a number of respected journals. It still reads well enough today, a tale of high politics and intrigue typical of its age, though rarely read by anyone "who does not have a greater interest in the author than in the book."[63] Meticulously well written by a man of twenty-three, perhaps somewhat wooden for modern tastes, it is an enduring testament to the remarkable energy, talent, and ambition of its author and provides a unique self-portrait and window into the mind of the young Winston.

Even though there was the serious matter of books and an interregimental polo tournament to keep him occupied, Churchill was still desperate to get to the Tirah. He contacted his friend Colonel Ian Hamilton, one of the expedition's brigade commanders. It transpired that the only exception to the general rule that had prevented Churchill from being sent was in the case of people appointed to Sir William Lockhart's personal staff. Churchill therefore decided to risk bunking off from his regiment in order to go to Peshawar and see what he could do to persuade Lockhart's ADC (aide-de-camp), Captain Haldane, in his direction. This ploy worked, and he was appointed as an extra orderly officer on the general's staff. Haldane's opinion on first meeting him was that he was cut out on a vastly different pattern from any officer of his years he had so far met. Having stuck his neck out, Churchill behaved as demurely as possible among the more senior officers who comprised the general's staff. His chance to get noticed came, however, when Captain Haldane revealed that a newspaper correspondent had written a critical account for the *Fortnightly Review*. Churchill advised on how best to respond in order to prevent its publication without the need to engage General Lockhart in an undignified correspondence on the matter.

The episode was a harbinger of much that was to come in Churchill's career; while he earned the plaudits and gratitude of some, others were not amused. Important people in the War Office and the Indian Army thought the precocious junior officer had no business in the affair, and *The Broad Sword* (the organ of Britain's military establishment) was hostile. As regards the campaign, to Churchill's disappointment, negotiations soon won out over a return to war, and the expeditionary force dispersed. Bangalore and regimental duties beckoned once again. He fared little better at polo. At the regimental tournament in Meerut in February 1898, the 4th Hussars team was knocked out by the Durham Light Infantry. As Churchill pondered intensely over the career choices open to him, Colonel Ian Hamilton offered some sagacious advice: "Art is long, life is short—so get on the right track as soon as possible and stay on it." His point was that no one could do all things at once, and that Churchill needed to decide, now, whether he was to be a politician or a soldier.[64]

Fresh news was filtering through of war clouds in the Sudan, thousands of miles to the west. As we have seen, Churchill's keen ear had been tuned to the heralds of this new conflict for some time, and a Churchillian campaign to secure his involvement commenced for the third time. On May 22, 1898 he wrote to his mother: "Redouble your efforts in this direction. My plans for the future will be much influenced by this." Churchill's apparently footloose ways, and his ability to persuade reluctant senior commanders and to follow the action while his regiment carried out its humdrum duty, were generating suspicion and animosity toward him. "A great sense of destiny, of power and of greatness was deeply impregnated in Churchill. He was, by this time, markedly egocentric and self-expressive."[65] He was a "self-advertiser" and a "medal-hunter." Furthermore, many of his brother officers thought that the role of war correspondent sat ill alongside that of professional soldier and broke the unwritten code of officers not commenting on military affairs or publicly criticizing the actions of their superiors. Churchill lived, as his son put it, in "the twilight of a Victorian era in which many of his activities were regarded as 'ungentlemanly.'"[66] But Churchill was undeterred: enjoining his mother to pull strings as never before, he wrote: "It is a pushing age, we must push with the best."[67]

Among those who had taken agin the young Churchill was the sirdar of the Egyptian Army himself, General Sir Horatio Herbert Kitchener. This was unfortunate, because it was his army Churchill now wanted to join as it prepared to reconquer the Sudan and sort out the followers of the mahdi's successor, the caliph, while avenging General Gordon once and for all. Though the War Office approved Churchill's application and his own regiment was prepared to grant leave (and the 21st Lancers to accept him), Kitchener was having none of it. Given that he had leave owing following his Tirah service, Churchill decided to go to London to take up the cudgels, another example of the lengths to which this indefatigable young man was prepared to go to get his way.

But Kitchener was too powerful an enemy and too implacable an obstacle for Churchill and his string pulling to shift on his own.

It was a slice of luck, therefore, that Prime Minister Lord Salisbury happened at that moment to be reading *The Story of the Malakand Field Force*. Having enjoyed it, he asked to see Churchill, and as a parting pleasantry asked Churchill to contact him if there was ever anything he could do for him. Churchill didn't need to be asked twice, and he acted on it promptly, as time in which to effect his attachment to the Egyptian Army was fast running out (this was July, and the march toward Khartoum was to begin in August). A telegram was duly sent from the prime minister, though Kitchener's reply was that he had all the staff officers he needed and that, in the event of vacancies cropping up, there was a queue well ahead of young Churchill.

In the meantime, another stone had been unturned in the form of Sir Francis Jeune, a friend of the family whose wife, Lady St. Helier, was intimate with Sir Evelyn Wood, the adjutant general of the British Army. Wood was of the opinion that Kitchener should not be allowed to pick and choose officers in disregard of War Office wishes, and that besides, while Kitchener was sirdar of the Egyptian Army, the composition of *British* Army units attached to it was War Office business. Two days later, a telegram arrived from the War Office appointing Churchill a supernumerary lieutenant with the 21st Lancers (meaning that he went at his own expense and that the army would do nothing to repatriate him or his remains if he were killed or wounded). A friend's father was the proprietor of the *Morning Post*, the most influential Conservative newspaper of the day, and so Churchill was also able to secure employment as a correspondent at £15 a column. So, in July 1898, Churchill was off to the wars again, though not before he had made a speech at Bradford, testing political waters that he hoped soon to plunge into. Six days after catching the train to Marseilles, he was reporting to Regimental Headquarters in Cairo. Though this was traveling at speed, it was lucky that he did not arrive sooner, for the officer who took the troop of lancers from Cairo to join Kitchener's army—the troop that had been intended for Churchill—soon fell, along with ten of his men.

So began Churchill's involvement in what he named (in the book that soon followed) the River War, and its famous set-piece battle at Omdurman, a cipher for Victorian military triumph over "savage" enemies on the imperial frontier. From Cairo the 21st Lancers moved fourteen hundred miles into the depths of equatorial Africa, by train and river steamer to Aswan, then on foot and on horseback, a significant feat in a war noted for its logistical achievements, especially the use of machine guns, trains, and gunboats. During the journey, Churchill speculated about the role that might be performed by the only cavalry regiment attached to Kitchener's army and fretted about how the sirdar would receive him, given the fact that his rejection of Churchill had been overcome through string pulling and bloody-minded persistence.

On August 28, the army began its final advance toward Khartoum and the nearby city of Omdurman, moving in full battle order. It marched alongside the Nile, from where water could be drawn for thirsty men and horses, and stores taken from the steamers and the river gunboats that, as Churchill wrote, "scrutinized the banks with their guns." "We filed down in gold and purple twilight to drink and drink and drink again from the swift abundant Nile."[68]

On September 1, and only eighteen miles or so from Omdurman, Churchill was riding with the advanced screen reconnoitering ahead of the main body of the army. From the vantage point of a broad swell of sand, he saw, scarcely a mile away, "all our advanced patrols and parties halted in a long line, observing something which lay apparently immediately across their path." A "long brown smear" visible in the distance was in fact the enemy. Churchill was sent galloping to consult with the colonel in the advanced line. Colonel Martin reported that the enemy was advancing fast and that Churchill should report this to Kitchener, marching about six miles behind with the infantry. Pausing to observe the scene, Churchill saw a "truly magnificent" sight:

> The British and Egyptian army was advancing in battle array. Five solid brigades of three or four infantry battalions each, marching in open

columns, echeloned back from the Nile. Behind these great blocks of men followed long rows of artillery, and beyond these there trailed out interminable strings of camels carrying supplies. On the river abreast of the leading brigade moved masses of heavily laden sailing-boats towed by a score of stern-wheel steamers, and from this mass there emerged gleaming grimly seven or eight large white gunboats ready for action. On the desert flank and towards the enemy a dozen squadrons of Egyptian cavalry at wide intervals could be seen supporting the outpost line, and still further inland the grey and chocolate columns of the Camel Corps completed the spacious panorama.[69]

Churchill found Kitchener marching beneath a red banner and made his report, informing the sirdar that he probably had an hour or an hour and a half. Churchill was then invited to lunch by a staff officer and beheld a low wall of biscuit boxes, a white cloth spread across them, and dishes of bully beef, mixed pickles, and "many bottles of inviting appearance." Everyone was in high spirits. The event was "like a race luncheon before the Derby. . . . It really was a good moment to live. . . . This kind of war was full of fascinating thrills. It was not like the Great War. Nobody expected to be killed."[70]

The following day, Churchill and the lancers stayed as close as possible to the great mass of the Dervish army in order to report their movements to headquarters. Thus the battle drew near. Churchill and his troop occupied a ridge four hundred yards from the enemy, a distance soon closed to two hundred yards as they came on. From their vantage point, Churchill and his men were able to see both sides, the twenty thousand British and Egyptians with their backs to the Nile, the Dervishes climbing toward them. Churchill witnessed the first shots as the armies engaged, and saw the "full blast of Death" as the British gun batteries and river gunboats poured fire into the white-flagged mass of about sixty thousand men. Churchill was then called back by his commanding officer into the shelter of a zareba (a protective enclosure, usually thornbushes) as the infantry were about to open fire. Now the two forces fully engaged, and "the weapons, methods and the fanaticism of the Middle Ages were brought by an extraordinary anachronism into dire collision with the organization and inventions of the nineteenth century."

After great slaughter, Kitchener wheeled his five brigades south and marched toward the city of Khartoum with the Nile on his left flank, intending to cut off the remnants of the Dervish army from their capital and chief supply base. But the Dervish army still had a left flank as yet unblooded, and a reserve of perhaps fifteen thousand men. This force now advanced upon Kitchener's army, which was no longer dug in, but in line of march. All along the line, the enemy succeeded in getting to within two hundred yards, only to be stopped by the hitting power of the modern guns, as "discipline and machinery," in Churchill's words, "triumphed over the most desperate valour."

The 21st Lancers "were the only horsemen on the left flank nearest Omdurman." They had been ordered to scout and discover what forces lay between Kitchener's army and the city and, if possible, to drive them back and clear a line of passage for the advancing army. Thus began Churchill's participation in what was to be the British Army's most famous cavalry charge since the Crimean War. Ascending the slopes of Jebel Surgham, the lancers soon saw "the whole plain of Omdurman with the vast mud city, its minarets and domes, spread before us six or seven miles away." Churchill commanded a troop of about twenty-five lancers, strung out in line ahead along with the fifteen other troops that comprised the regiment. As they moved forward, the lancers expected at some point to be ordered to charge, the time-honored role of the cavalry. Three hundred yards away, the enemy were spotted on the column's flank, and the trumpet sounded "Trot." The line of enemy soldiers, thought at first to be spearmen, began firing at the mounted figures with rifles. Unable to approach the enemy, the colonel ordered "right wheel into line" and "almost immediately," Churchill wrote, "the regiment broke into a gallop, and the 21st Lancers were committed to their first charge in war!"[71]

Essentially, the lancers had been taken by surprise at a moment when it was too late to do anything about it other than gather speed and hope for the best. As Churchill put it, "it is very rarely that stubborn and unshaken infantry meet equally stubborn and unshaken cavalry." But this is what happened. Churchill chose his Mauser pistol rather than his sword as the charge began, a result of the injury sustained in India two years before. As they galloped toward the blue-black line of the enemy and made first contact, Churchill beheld a depression (a dried watercourse) behind the enemy line, "crowded and crammed with men rising up from the ground where they had hidden. Bright flags appeared as if by magic, and I saw arriving from nowhere Emirs on horseback among and around the mass of the enemy." The lancers had been taken by surprise, committing themselves to a charge against an enemy that outnumbered them by at least ten to one. The lancers rode into the watercourse, Churchill's horse dropping "like a cat four or five feet down . . . and in this sandy bed I found myself surrounded by what seemed to be dozens of men," though in a flash Churchill found himself scrambling up the other side of the depression, regaining "the hard, crisp desert, my horse at a trot." Immediately a Dervish drew back his sword to slash at the horse's hamstring, which Churchill avoided and shot him down. Another appeared and Churchill fired, so close that the pistol struck his foe; then he shot an Arab horseman to his left at ten yards.

Those unlucky enough to be stopped by the Dervish mass were pulled from their horses and stabbed and hacked to death, though at this point Churchill considered the lancers to be masters of the field. Soon, however, he began to feel that he was totally alone on the battlefield, and experienced "a sudden sensation of fear" as he discerned three riflemen taking aim at him. He spurred his horse and galloped away and found his troop faced about and forming up, the other three troops of the squadron forming up close by. Churchill shot a man who sprung up amid the troop, then reloaded his Mauser. From the jumble of fighting men, "a succession of grisly apparitions" emerged as horses and men in various states of bloody distress appeared, "gasping, crying, collapsing, expiring." Instead of charging again, two squadrons were ordered to dismount and use their carbines to enfilade the watercourse, forcing the Dervishes to retreat.[72]

"We therefore remained in possession of the field. Within twenty minutes of the time when we had first wheeled into line and begun our charge, we were halted and breakfasting in the very watercourse that had so very nearly proved our undoing." Among the Dervish corpses that had not been carried from the field lay the bodies of over twenty lancers, "so hacked and mutilated as to be mostly unrecognizable."[73] In the space of about two or three minutes, the regiment had lost five officers and sixty-five men killed and wounded, along with 119 horses. Despite this extremely high casualty rate, the action was successful. As for the wider action, the British and Egyptian forces had scored a crushing victory, killing over ten thousand Dervishes. In a letter to his mother, Churchill described the stench of bodies littering the field of battle. Given the finality of this victory and the expense of maintaining cavalry, Churchill's regiment was released three days after the battle and marched northward on the journey home. Churchill hitched a lift on a Nile sailing boat carrying the Grenadier Guards. In Cairo, he was obliged to render up a piece of flesh from his forearm so that a colleague from the 21st Lancers, wounded in the charge at Omdurman, might have a much-needed skin graft. As the Irish doctor explained: "Ye've heeard of a man being flayed aloive? Well, this is what it feels loike."[74]

HOME AND BACK AGAIN: ENGLAND AND INDIA

After this latest adventure, and now having been blooded in both Africa and Asia, Churchill thought long and hard about his next move. Time pressed, and he'd already been a soldier for three years. He had considered leaving the army for some time, and the lure of politics grew stronger by the year. His father, in Churchill's words, had died at a moment when "his fortune almost exactly equalled his debts," about £70,000, which shares in South African mines took care of. Jennie Churchill, however, still had the property, and this was enough "for comfort, ease and pleasure," but not enough for two adult sons.[75] Churchill was determined not to add to his mother's financial burden. He concluded that the army could never allow him to be independent, at least not if he were to maintain polo-type expenses and a lifestyle in which old brandy and Havana cigars were considered essential groceries. It was on the basis of this calculation that Churchill planned his assault on the year 1899. He would return to his regiment in India and play in a polo tournament; write a book on the war in the Sudan in which he had so recently fought; accept any journalistic commissions that came his way; and look for an opportunity to enter Parliament.

As a result of his writing, Churchill's stock was rising. His *Morning Post* reports from the Sudan had been generally well received, and he found that he was something of a celebrity. Not all felt comfortable with this, however, and the Prince of Wales wrote in October 1898 to suggest that he stick to being a soldier and leave off the writing. If not, then he should go for the parliamentary and literary life he clearly craved. "Life in an Indian station can have no attraction for you—though fortunately some officers do put up with it or else we should have no at all!"[76] Falling in with a group of young Conservative MPs, including Lord Hugh Cecil, Churchill's political appetite was sharpened. Among this smart set, however, Churchill felt himself "the earthen pot among the brass." They were all silver tongued, former scholars of Oxford or Cambridge, and now, though only a few years older than Churchill, "ensconced in safe Tory constituencies." Despite his high birth, privileged upbringing, and family fame, Churchill was still self-conscious about perceived educational and social deficits and the chasm between where he was and where he wanted to be. He thought that in order to join in the quick-witted and educated banter to which he was exposed, self-learning was not enough and that he should go to Oxford when he returned from India. But there was the entrance exam, and "I could not contemplate toiling at Greek irregular verbs after having commanded British regular troops."[77] So it was upon sedulous self-education and a professional attitude toward the pursuit of political recognition that he came to depend. In an age when politicians were generally to the manner born, and the cult of the amateur at its height, this was to doubly mark him out as one to watch, a zealot as well as a naturally talented, impetuous, elemental force, questing for renown.

Between his adventures in the Sudan and returning to his regiment in India, Churchill lined up his political contacts, addressed Conservative meetings, cultivated political agents and made friends with the newspaper baron Alfred Harmsworth. Churchill had made his maiden political speech at a Bath meeting of the Primrose League, founded by his father at Blenheim and named in memory of Disraeli (whose favorite flower was the primrose). His contacts ensured that reporters were dispatched to cover the event. He spoke in support of a bill to protect people injured while at work, removing "the question from the shifting sands of charity" and placing it "on the firm bedrock of law." He then went on to strike an ebullient note concerning Britain's place in the world, symptomatic of late-Victorian confidence in the face of emerging challenges. "There are not wanting those who say that in this Jubilee year [1897] our Empire has reached the height of its glory and power, and that now we shall begin to decline, as Babylon, Carthage, Rome declined. Do not believe these croakers but give the lie to their dismal croaking by showing by our actions that the vigour and vitality of our race is unimpaired."[78] The speech went well; the *Morning Post* devoted a whole column to it the following day, though the *Eastern Morning News* was less taken in, writing that he was "in danger of being spoilt by flattery and public notice" and warning that "political talent is the least hereditary of our tendencies." But Churchill had been launched upon the turbid waters of British politics. In a speech to the Southsea Conservative Association in October 1898, he reflected on Britain's need for "the Imperial spark" in order to retain its position in the world. This required "a free people, an educated and well fed people."[79] Given this, he claimed, he was in favor of social reform, such as the introduction of old-age pensions. "Imperium et Libertas" was his motto, and that of the Primrose League. While in

Britain after the Sudan campaign, he engaged in the press debate surrounding the ethics of killing wounded on the battlefield and made speedy progress with the manuscript of *The River War*.

Churchill had decided to leave the army in order to pursue a place in Parliament, though a final, polo-dominated fling with his regiment began when he sailed for India in January 1899. Having swept across the continents of a British-dominated world, he now knuckled down to the serious business of regimental polo at Meerut, to where the team journeyed with its thirty horses and five hundred tons of gear. While in Jodhpore en route, Churchill had a fall and dislocated his shoulder. "I trust the misfortune will propitiate the gods—offended perhaps at my success & luck elsewhere," as he told his mother.[80] Despite this accident, the captain of the polo team decided to play Churchill anyway rather than bring in the reserve, a measure of how good Churchill's polo was. As the 4th Hussars' team progressed, Churchill played with his bad arm strapped to his torso and in the final scored some of the goals that won the match. After this triumph, and providing another instance of the good fortune of having well-connected parents, he stayed for a week in Calcutta with the recently appointed viceroy, Lord Curzon, and was charmed by a man whom he had previously viewed with hostility. With leave owing, Churchill returned to Britain.

In his spare time, Churchill had been preparing his book *The River War*, reading scores of accounts and histories of the Sudan, and attempting in his writing "a combination of the styles of Macaulay and Gibbon, the staccato antithesis of the former and the rolling sentences and genitival endings of the latter; and I stuck in a bit of my own from time to time." On his way home, he made friends with G. W. Steevens, a brilliant young journalist writing for the recently launched *Daily Mail*, a contact with the Harmsworth press that was to be of use. Steevens had just published the iconic *With Kitchener to Khartoum* and happily read Churchill's proofs and offered advice. Steevens wrote him up in the *Daily Mail* as "The Youngest Man in Europe," crediting him with almost superhuman powers that would sweep him into Parliament and high office. Stopping off in Cairo,

Churchill was able to meet some of the leading actors in the recent Sudan war, and even had his manuscript commented upon by Lord Cromer, Britain's consul general in Egypt.

Taking a leap in the dark, Churchill resigned from the army in spring 1899. He was playing for high stakes, and risk was therefore inevitable. Jennie Churchill, as usual, helped all she could, and "during this vivid summer my mother gathered constantly around her table politicians of both parties, and leading figures in literature and art, together with the most lovely beings on whom the eye could beam." Churchill was selected to contest a parliamentary seat in a special election in Oldham in July 1899 and threw himself into traveling and speech making on the campaign trail. He realized that the old methods of electioneering would no longer do and that politicians needed to reach out to an audience and seek to make a distinctive impression on the public mind: Churchill remained into old age intensely interested in what people thought of him, his speeches and actions. He espoused the cause of "Tory Democracy," claiming that the main aim of government should be to improve the lot of the British people. He also believed that MPs should be paid, that there should be a system of progressive income tax, and that the size of the army should be limited—the army, as it stood, was sufficient to protect the interests of a maritime power whose security rested on salt water and the world's most powerful navy.

Despite a good campaign, he was in his own words "well beaten" at the polls, failing to hold what had been a Conservative seat. "Then came the recriminations which follow every kind of defeat. Everyone threw the blame on me. I have noticed that they nearly always do. I suppose it is because they think I shall be able to bear it best."[81] Thus wrote Churchill much later on, evincing a tendency to magnify the scale of the obstacles he had to overcome, and casting himself in the role of an outsider struggling to get on. The result was not a great surprise, because the government was then in the kind of midterm doldrums that make special elections ideal for those seeking to vent their displeasure toward an incumbent administration. While receiving congratulations from party grandees such as Balfour and Chamberlain, there was a flicker of his future defiance of the party whip as Churchill inveighed against the government's Clerical Tithes Bill. But despite this sign of things to come, Churchill had impressed by his performance and his graciousness in defeat.

The experience was a political beginning, and meanwhile Churchill completed the manuscript of *The River War*. It was a much more ambitious book than *The Story of the Malakand Field Force* in its sweep of historical context, its reportage, and its pronouncements on the conduct of the war. It was published in the spring of 1899, only a year after his Malakand book had appeared, representing a truly prodigious literary turnover. It immediately became the standard work on the subject, running to 950 pages over two volumes. In it, Churchill showed a characteristic, though at the time uncommon, capacity for empathizing with the enemy. "Why should we regard as madness what we would find sublime in civilized men?" he wrote of the determination and spirit of the Dervishes. He openly censured the army commander, the famous Kitchener, despite his status as a national hero. Not everyone liked it, though the wind blew strongly in his favor. On the negative side, the *Saturday Review* considered both of Churchill's military narratives "ponderous and pretentious" and wrote that "the annoying feature in the book is the irrepressible egoism of its author. . . . The airs of infallibility he assumes are irritating." Read today, the book's mature and assured style retains freshness and relevance. The Prince of Wales praised the book, and the prime minister, to whom it was dedicated, summoned the author to Downing Street. It was a notable triumph for a young man and greatly aided Churchill's relentless campaign to get his name "before the public," a public that, as he fully appreciated, carried votes in their pockets following the electoral reforms of the 1880s. As luck would have it, a situation now arose that not only returned Churchill to the colors and to Fleet Street, but made him famous throughout the world.

THE SOUTH AFRICAN WAR

"25 years old, about 5 ft 8 in tall, average build, walks with a slight stoop, pale appearance, red brown hair, almost invisible small moustache, speaks through the nose, cannot pronounce the letters, cannot speak Dutch." This, according to Boer forces trying to capture him, was the *fin de siècle* Winston Churchill. The collision between the British government and the Boer Republics of the Orange Free State and the Transvaal had been coming on for years, foreshadowed most dramatically by the First Anglo-Boer War of 1880–81 and the infamous Jameson Raid of 1895. The British claimed suzerainty across the whole of southern Africa; heedless of this, the Boer Republics proclaimed their independence and nursed a deep hostility to British encroachments. With inflexible attitudes and stony personalities presiding on all sides, "the atmosphere," as Churchill put it, "gradually but steadily became tense, charged with electricity, laden with the presage of a storm."[82]

As soon as the Boer ultimatum to the British to withdraw their forces from the frontiers of the republics had expired, Churchill was appointed principal war correspondent by the *Morning Post*. "£250 a month, all expenses paid, entire discretion as to movements and opinions, four months' minimum guaranteed employment—such were the terms; higher, I think than any previously paid in British journalism to war correspondents, and certainly attractive to a young man of twenty-four with no responsibilities but to earn his own living." Churchill, using his connections, sought and received an audience with the colonial secretary, Joseph Chamberlain, himself before heading off. The ship on which he sailed with his extensive gear and five dozen bottles of champagne and brandy, the *Dunottar Castle*, also carried the new commander in chief, General Sir Redvers Buller, and his headquarters staff. On board, the consensus was that it would all be over before they arrived, another colonial jolly against amateurs (albeit white ones this time) that couldn't even wait until Christmas to be over. Though no longer in the army (but still a territorial soldier), Churchill became deeply involved in the

conflict after his arrival on October 31, 1899. He obtained a commission in the Lancashire Hussars and sailed for Durban and the
war's most active front. Against an underestimated enemy that was
motivated, well led, well organized, well armed, and that knew the
country, the war went from bad to worse for the British in its opening stages. Churchill found it strange to be fighting against European settlers and, importantly, came to sympathize with the Boer
desire for independence.

Churchill's intention was to get to Ladysmith, where his old
friend Sir Ian Hamilton was stationed. But the Boers had cut off
the rail link on the Tugela River and laid siege to most of Natal's
defenders within the town. He therefore waited at Estcourt, from
where cavalry patrols issued forth scouting for the enemy, sometimes riding almost within sight of besieged Ladysmith. The commanding officer decided to add the weight of an armored train to
their operations along the sixteen miles of intact railway. Thus an
armored train containing a company of the Dublin Fusiliers and a
company of the Durban Light Infantry, together with a naval gun,
set out on November 15, 1899, under Captain Aylmer Haldane,
whom Churchill knew from the Tirah episode. Looking for news-
worthy action, Churchill offered to join the column, and Haldane
gladly accepted.

The lumbering train presented a tempting target to the Boers.
By the simple expedient of placing an obstacle on the track, it was
ambushed. Churchill, though strictly a noncombatant, showed
great endeavor, initiative, and bravery in trying to rescue the situation. The halted and partially derailed train acted as cover for the
troops as they vainly returned the heavy fire of a large Boer force
overlooking the railway cutting. Churchill took the leading role in
attempting to remove the blockage on the line so as to enable the
train to get moving. Altogether, an hour and ten minutes were spent
under fire. Churchill was instrumental in seeing the damage
partly righted, allowing the engine and some of the force, including forty wounded, to escape. But he was not so lucky. Encountering
two Boers on the line who fired several shots at him, Churchill

scrambled up out of the cutting, determined to make for the cover of a nearby river. But his luck ran out, and he was captured by a mounted Boer after losing his pistol. This was in some ways fortunate, and as he was marched off into captivity, Churchill managed to rid himself of two clips of ammunition, a vital precaution if he were to be taken seriously as a noncombatant, a status that, Churchill earnestly hoped, would secure his early release.

Thus began a celebrated interlude as a prisoner of war, spent at the State Model School in Pretoria. The news of his capture spread around the world, for he bore a famous name and was already well known for his military and literary exploits. The Boers were aware of the part played by Churchill in the action, and were disinclined to grant him noncombatant status. Besides, such a well-known figure might act as a useful bargaining counter. Boer intransigence might have been a considerable hindrance to the onward march of Winston Churchill. Indeed, it might have represented a history-changing full stop, for some of his captors wanted Churchill shot for bearing arms. As it was, the episode created another ladder up which his reputation could scramble, providing prominence far beyond his years and a taste of international celebrity.

An escape scheme was hatched by Churchill, Haldane, and another inmate. All did not go according to plan, however, and Churchill broke out on his own, garnering retrospective admiration on the one hand and a measure of lingering disapproval on the other. (Should he not have waited to escape with his brother officers? Did not his solitary escape make their subsequent attempts more difficult?) The reaction to Churchill's solo flight illustrated the price he had to pay for his thrusting ways. It ruffled feathers, particularly of his elders and betters as he overtook them. Anything that could be used to label him "unreliable," such as his father's reputation or his failure to escape with his brother officers, was taken up by his detractors. (A cumulative mass of disapproval accompanied Churchill throughout his life, until his role in the Second World War cleaned the slate for all but his most ardent opponents.) The issue of his escape dogged him for decades to come, though it is difficult to sustain the view that Churchill did anything particularly wrong. When he went over the wire, he waited for a long time on the other side, at risk of discovery, for the others to follow him, even conversing through the wall with one of the inmates. In the end, he had little choice but to go on; he could hardly break back in. If anything, Churchill was "guilty" of getting on with it while others dithered, and of looking after number one, necessary qualities in war as in politics.

Anyway, escape he did, and Churchill was soon at large in the midst of the enemy's capital city. He knew that the alarm would be raised by daybreak at the latest. His plan, therefore, was to stow away aboard a train to Delagoa Bay in neutral Portuguese East Africa and from there rejoin British forces. He climbed aboard a goods train, where he slept among empty coal sacks and trusted to his luck. Waking before daybreak, he jumped from the still-moving train and set out on foot for nearby hills. Sheltering among some trees to wait for night to fall, he was kept company by a gigantic vulture, "who manifested an extravagant interest in my condition, and made hideous and ominous gurglings from time to time."[83] By this time, the initial elation of escape had evaporated, and he was hungry and unsure of what to do. Resolving to approach an African village that was visible by firelight, it became apparent as he approached that it was in fact a group of stone houses. He was greeted, at first suspiciously, by an English mine manager, John Howard, who readily agreed to help him hide from the inevitable pursuit (a £25 dead-or-alive reward had been placed on his head, so anxious were the Boers to retrieve their famous captive) and then to make good his escape. This involved lying low in a mine shaft for a number of days in rat-infested darkness, fed and supported by English miners, including one from Oldham who assured him they'd all vote for him next time around (referring to his recent special-election defeat). Churchill whiled away the tedious and nerve-racking days reading Robert Louis Stevenson's *Kidnapped.*

Churchill's protectors soon smuggled him aboard a train loaded with wool and bound for Delagoa Bay. Meanwhile, as he awaited

events that December 1899, newspapers around the world speculated about his whereabouts. When the train entered Portuguese
territory, Churchill's elation overflowed. He whooped aloud and
fired shots into the air. By late afternoon, the train had reached Lou-
renço Marques. There one of the miners was waiting for him and
led him surreptitiously to the British consulate, where Churchill
noisily announced himself.

Soon word was out: the captive Churchill had made it through
to friendly lines. His dramatic escape occurred at a time when the
British public, reared on a rich diet of imperial heroes and easily
defeated native foes, was being starved. The Boer War was producing little but defeats and casualties, so there was a vacancy for a
hero. "The news of my arrival had spread like wildfire through the
town," and armed Englishmen arrived at the consulate to resist any
recapture attempted by local Boers. He was marched through the
streets and promptly put on the weekly steamer to Durban, where
he arrived "to find myself a popular hero."[84] Bands, flags, and crowds
lined the wharf. The mayor, an admiral, and a general waited to
greet him, and he was carried shoulder-high to the town hall, where
a speech was demanded and duly delivered. Yet even at this moment
of euphoria, distaste and dislike continued to afflict him. As he later
recalled, he received a cable from England that simply stated, "Best
friends here hope you won't go making further ass of yourself."[85]

Churchill was never one to let the grass grow under his feet, and,
deciding to remain in South Africa, he soon rejoined the army. As he
put it, "Youth seeks Adventure, Journalism requires Advertisement.
Certainly I had found both. I became for the time quite famous."[86]
Interviewed by General Sir Redvers Buller himself, Churchill asked
for a commission in one of the irregular corps. Buller was concerned about his status as a war correspondent, as his past elision
of these roles in India and the Sudan had led to considerable criticism. Buller mulled over this thorny problem, pacing around the
room. "Then at last he said: 'All right. You can have a commission in
Bungo's regiment. You will have to do as much as you can for both
jobs. But,' he said, 'you will get no pay for ours.'"[87]

Thus Churchill became a lieutenant in the South African Light Horse, a regiment of over seven hundred mounted men with a battery of galloping Colt machine guns, raised by Colonel "Bungo" Byng. "I stitched my badges of rank to my khaki coat and stuck the long plume feathers from the tail of the *sakabula* bird in my hat, and lived from day to day in perfect happiness."[88] With this unit, Churchill was present at the tragic defeat at Spion Kop, passing messages between the headquarters of Sir Charles Warren and Colonel Thorneycroft at the top of the hill. He also had the feathers in his hat trimmed by an enemy bullet. His regiment had frequent skirmishes with the Boers, and Churchill dispatched a continuous stream of letters and cables to the *Morning Post* "and learned from them that all I wrote commanded a wide and influential public." His reports reflected not only the conduct of the war, but also the broader political and strategic aspects, such as how best to treat with vanquished foes in order to secure harmonious relations once victory had been won. His forthright views on the war were, on the whole, well founded (as time would tell), though they attracted criticism from those who thought them "disloyal" or badly timed. But Churchill had the conviction to stick to his guns. As he was later to advocate in Ireland, and again during the General Strike, while enemies had to be conquered, their grievances had then to be met. This opinion became one of his several differences with the Conservative Party for whom he was soon to become a member of Parliament, presaging the manner in which his liberal, indeed Liberal, tendencies would eventually lead to a clash with the party of his father and his kin.

Churchill enjoyed this phase of the war, roaming where he chose, filing reports and joining in various actions. "One lived entirely in the present with something happening all the time. Care-free, no regrets for the past, no fears for the future; no expenses, no duns, no complications, and all the time my salary was safely piling up at home!"[89] Adding to Churchill's pleasure in these months was the presence of his brother, Jack,, and soon his mother serving aboard a hospital ship.

Churchill was present at the relief of Ladysmith, riding into the town as the siege was lifted. After this, and impatient to get to what was becoming the main crucible of war as Lord Roberts advanced from Cape Colony toward the Orange Free State, Churchill obtained leave from the South African Light Horse and attempted to join Roberts's army. He spent a pleasant few days in Cape Town while he awaited the completion of the formalities, meeting the high commissioner, Sir Alfred Milner, and, with his aide-de-camp the Duke of Westminster, hunting jackal with foxhounds beneath Table Mountain. An obstacle had arisen, and it transpired that the block was the commander in chief himself; Roberts's chief of staff, Lord Kitchener, had taken exception to a passage in *The River War* in which Churchill had openly criticized Britain's most exalted military hero, and Roberts did not want to upset him by favoring its author (Churchill had roundly criticized Kitchener for callousness toward enemy wounded on the battlefield and had deplored the desecration of the mahdi's tomb). Roberts had his own grievance to boot, following a *Morning Post* column in which Churchill criticized an eve-of-battle sermon preached by an army chaplain, touching a raw religious nerve. So, too, it later transpired, did General French, naturally disapproving of "the hybrid combination of a junior officer and widely followed war correspondent." Nevertheless, Churchill's friends carried the day, though he had to accept a ticking off from the commander in chief's military secretary. In the end, Churchill was told, Roberts decided to take him "*for your father's sake.*"[90]

Freed to move north, Churchill began roving around the front "wherever there was a chance of fighting" and had his horse shot from under him during an action involving mounted scouts. Churchill advanced as Roberts's force marched on Johannesburg and Pretoria in the summer of 1900, even managing to cycle in civilian clothes through Johannesburg before it had surrendered, thereby getting an important message through to Lord Roberts. He had the pleasure of running up the flag on the State Model School, where he had so recently been incarcerated, and took part in the

Battle of Diamond Hill, where he displayed "conspicuous gallantry." Churchill continued to write for the *Morning Post* and rushed out more books: *Ian Hamilton's March* was published in October 1900, selling eight thousand copies. Its predecessor, *London to Ladysmith via Pretoria*, was published five days before the relief of Mafeking and sold fourteen thousand copies. This military activity and copious literary output in this period was remarkable, and quite unique.

It was when the Union Flag was raised in the enemy capital of Pretoria on June 5, 1900, that Churchill decided to return home. The conventional war had been won and the enemy's capital cities conquered. There remained a lengthy guerrilla phase that "promised to be shapeless and indefinite," and this was not for Churchill. He had formed the lasting—and through two world wars, important—impression that war was far too serious a business to be left to generals and that the Victorian army was poorly placed to fight a modern war. Also in his mind was the prospect of a general election, as well as a store of cash and public capital at home that needed to be exploited. The nineteenth century, and a half decade of intense Churchillian activity and development, were over. The twentieth century, which was to witness Churchill's colossal contribution to world history, had dawned.

3

Pundit and Politician: A Rising Star

In the decade following his election to Parliament, Winston Churchill moved swiftly through the political gears, gathering speed at an unheard-of rate as he advanced from parliamentary debutant to senior Cabinet minister. It was a rise made all the more remarkable by the fact that he left one political party for another, crossing the floor of the House of Commons in a daring move that could make or break his fledgling political career. Those who encountered Churchill rarely forgot him, most recognizing his extraordinary nature, whether they approved of him or not. At the turn of the century, Captain Percy Scott of HMS *Terrible* predicted that one day he would be prime minister, for he possessed the two necessary qualifications, "genius and plod."[1]

Having left the Boer War behind, Churchill had returned to Britain determined upon politics. He had had a "good" war and was accorded a hero's welcome in Oldham, entering the town through crowded streets in a procession of ten landaus, to regale a packed Theatre Royal with the tale of his escape from captivity. Jubilant cheers rang out when he mentioned the name of one of his

Oldham-born saviors and it was discovered that his wife was in the gallery. The Conservative government was determined to cash in on the general optimism following the fall of Pretoria and Johannesburg, the debilitating guerrilla war not yet having set in. Churchill campaigned as a pro-war candidate and criticized the Liberals for opposing it. He took one of the town's two seats by a narrow margin in the "khaki" election of 1900. Congratulations and demands to speak in support of other candidates flowed in, from Prime Minister Lord Salisbury and Arthur Balfour (Salisbury's successor in July 1902) down. Churchill's success in Oldham, and his celebrity, meant that he was much in demand. "For three weeks I had what seemed to me a triumphal progress through the country": twenty-six years old and fêted throughout the land.[2]

How did this young dynamo appear to his fellow men as he swapped khaki and press dispatches for the frock coat and parliamentary flourish? He was "five foot six and a half inches, slender built, with a 31-inch chest, rounded shoulders, delicate skin, ginger hair and a pugnacious baby face with twinkling blue eyes . . . striking but not handsome." His personality struck people forcibly, even if his looks did not. Some he repelled; others he fascinated. Wilfrid Scawen Blunt described him as "a little, square-headed fellow of no very striking appearance, but of wit, intelligence, and originality. In mind and manner he is a strange replica of his father, with all his father's suddenness and assurance, and I should say more than his father's ability. There is just the same gaminerie and contempt of the conventional."[3]

He had swapped paid employment for unpaid, and so his search for money continued. Back salary from the *Morning Post*, plus the sale of his books on the Sudan and South Africa campaigns, netted him over £4,000, but he spotted an opportunity to add significantly to this sum: sensing that his earning potential as a celebrity lecturer was at its zenith, he began planning a lecture tour of America, Britain, and Canada, recounting his Boer War escapades and explaining his political opinions. Churchill stayed with the governor general in Canada, where, aided by magic lantern displays, he addressed packed gatherings about the war and his part in it, rarely earning less than £100 a night. In one month—November 1900—he banked over £4,500. Despite these earnings, he remained relatively hard up. But he was at least able to relieve his mother of the annual £500 allowance and from this moment began his financial independence.

When Churchill took up his parliamentary career in earnest after returning from this tour, he soon marked himself out as a man of potential and controversy. He took up his seat on February 14, 1901, in "the historic arena where he was to live his life and fulfill his destiny" and which he had envisioned in countless daydreams since childhood.[4] His maiden speech was delivered to a packed house four days later and was widely reported in the press; through the advance release of the text, Churchill had ensured that it would be. The *Daily Express* considered it "spellbinding." In the speech, he graphically portrayed himself as his father's son and courted the displeasure of his party by making a reference to the justness of the Boer cause when viewed through Boer eyes, remarking that if he were a Boer, he would be fighting against the British. He struck a fair-minded, as opposed to jingoistic, tone, saying that the government's policy "ought to be to make it easy and honourable for the Boers to surrender, and painful and perilous for them to continue in the field."[5]

As was to be the case throughout his life, Churchill's preparation for the speech had been meticulous, for he was not a gifted off-the-cuff speaker. "Just preparing my impromptu remarks" was to become a feature of his approach to public speaking. There was very good reason for this use of the "concocted impromptu," for shortly after entering Parliament, he had the horrifying experience of forgetting what he was saying. He rose to speak in the House on the Trades Unions and Trade Disputes Bill, in which he intended to attack his own government for not being radical enough in protecting workers. He began "with all the vigour, brightness and freshness of expression and courage" for which he was known, a reporter wrote. But after forty-five minutes, he dried up. He tried several times to remember what he had to say. He cast around for pieces

of paper, searching his pockets and the floor. Finally he sat down
after thanking the House for its kindness in having listened to him.
"He searched the roof with upturned eyes." Next day the headlines
declared "Mr. Churchill Breaks Down" and "Moving Incident in
the House." Many people thought he had suffered a stroke, though
"these anticipations were happily premature," as he wrote later. "But
the experience was disconcerting to the last degree, and it leads me
to utter this solemn warning to public speakers: 'Never trust your
memory without your manuscript.'"[6]

The usual custom for new members of the House was to maintain a decorous parliamentary silence for some time following their
maiden speech. But there was little chance of Winston Churchill
observing this custom. In the following week, he intervened twice
on South Africa, and on March 12, he defended the government in
a significant speech, eliciting the gratitude of the secretary of state
for war, St. John Brodrick. In his first eleven months in Parliament,
he made nine speeches in the House, thirty speeches in the country, and twenty in towns.[7] He spent twelve afternoons playing polo
during this period, fourteen days hunting, two days shooting, and
eighteen days holidaying abroad.

His maiden speech marked the start of what would become a
seminal relationship in Churchill's political life—his association
and friendship with David Lloyd George, leader of the radical wing
of the Liberal Party. After the rising Liberal star had met "the new
Tory bully" (as he described Churchill) on the floor of the chamber, he sought him out to congratulate him. Churchill soon came
to look up to this remarkable Welsh politician and was to seek his
counsel and advice through many political vicissitudes.

Churchill's debut as a parliamentary speaker bore within it the
seeds of discord. He was a Conservative MP—but as he had written
to his mother in 1897, "I am a Liberal in all but name." Only on the
issue of Irish Home Rule did Churchill's views vary from those of
the Liberal Party. Almost as soon as he had set out on his parliamentary career, Churchill began to challenge his own government's
policies, ferociously criticizing proposals for an increase in the size

of the British Army tabled by the secretary of state for war (while upholding the Royal Navy as the guardian of British and imperial security, a view that was shared by many within his own party, as well as on the Opposition benches). For a three-year period from April 1901, Churchill attacked Brodrick's proposed army reforms. As he said in the Commons on May 13, 1901, "I wish to complain very respectfully, but most urgently, that the Army Estimates . . . are much too high. . . . I think it about time that a voice was heard from this side of the House pleading that unpopular cause."[8] His position was that the army was bad value for money. It was not big enough to rival the armies of the continental powers and should confine itself to the job of garrisoning the empire—the wider security of Britain was the job of the navy: "The Empire which has grown up around these islands is essentially commercial and marine."[9] He claimed that "the first and main principle which should animate British statecraft in the realm of imperial defense was the promotion of a steady transfer of expenditure from military to marine."[10] He chided the government and Brodrick in particular for imitating the Germans and advocating a big army. As he told laughing constituents in Oldham in January 1903, "Sometimes I think the whole Cabinet has got a touch of German measles, but Mr. Brodrick's case is much the worst. He is spotted from head to foot, and he has communicated the contagion to the Army."[11] That same year, he was to begin making fun of Joseph Chamberlain in his speeches as the issue of tariff reform came to dominate party politics. For a twenty-something parliamentary debutant, and one with vaulting political ambitions, to start his career by laying into his party's senior ministers was brave to the point of recklessness. But as Churchill's extraordinary political rise bore witness, he seemed to know what he was doing.

Clearly, party loyalty was not of great consequence to Churchill, and it never would be. Many would come to despise him for this reason. But as he told an audience in Liverpool in November 1901, "Nothing would be worse than that independent men should be snuffed out and that there should be only two opinions in England—the Government opinion and the Opposition opinion.

The perpetually unanimous Cabinet disquiets me. I believe in personality."[12] Churchill's convictions differed from those of the majority of his party. He had contacts, such as the radical politician and free-thinker John Morley, and social ideas that were anathema to most Tories (such as progressive taxation and disapproval of the Church of England's protected position). His contact with Lloyd George nurtured the seeds of liberalism implanted in Churchill's breast. He did not, however, set out to be a rebel, and it was not unusual for a young man to "be in a hurry." Churchill was sensible enough to couch his opposition to the government's policies in terms of loyalty, saying, for example, that if Chamberlain's tariff reform proposals were adopted, the old Conservative Party would disappear (a view many Conservatives would have endorsed). When he disagreed with his party, he was apt to say that the party had moved away from *him*, not vice versa, and he reserved much of his fire for "socialism" as espoused by the emerging Labour Party, castigating its "all yours is mine" philosophy.

While Churchill had little time for party political warfare, he was also uninterested in personal rivalries. His lack of party loyalty led many politicians to distrust him, and his brusque, often rude style put backs up from the start of his career. As a young politician, he was very aggressive in his parliamentary speeches and prone to making personal attacks. After leaving the Conservatives to join the Liberals in 1904, he was asked to moderate his abuse of the Conservative leadership by his Liberal Party superiors. Balfour's elegant censure was that "if there is preparation there should be more finish, and if there is so much violence there should certainly be more obvious veracity of feeling."[13] Despite the rancor he attracted, it was remarkable how little enmity he felt toward those who attacked him. He had the skin of a rhinoceros, which was just as well, for not only had he made himself unpopular in certain military circles, once he entered Parliament, he succeeded in making himself an unloved, even a hated, figure in some quarters, more especially after he had abandoned the Conservative Party. But his guileless disregard for, and indeed ignorance of, what other people on an individual basis thought about his actions was one of his greatest political strengths.

Churchill's loyalty to the Tories was undermined by the process of writing his father's biography (commenced in 1902, completed in 1905, published in two volumes in 1906). He came to believe that Lord Randolph had been ill used by the party's hierarchy, and this affected his political expressions. Earl Winterton was "convinced that this behavior, which caused him to be the most unpopular man in politics and society at the time, was due to what amounted to an *idée fixe* about his father. . . . He believed that the latter had been abominably treated by the social and political world who had together plotted his downfall."[14] His father had been the natural successor to Disraeli, the man who had revived Tory fortunes after the 1880 election defeat and the great leader's retirement. And yet he had been abandoned by his party and his so-called friends. Churchill had an ardent desire, therefore, to be seen to be carrying on his father's disputes. He was an egocentric individual and, unlike most politicians, took no steps to conceal it.

During these early parliamentary years, Churchill surveyed the metropole and contemplated his new career from rooms at 105 Mount Street, seeing out a lease on the property taken by his cousin the Duke of Marlborough (as well as the gift of this two-year lease, his generous cousin gave him £500 toward election expenses). Having joined the set of youthful MPs who had so impressed him a few years before, Churchill soon became a key member of a group known as the Hooligans or "Hughligans," after Lord Hugh Cecil. It was an informal House of Commons dining club through which a select band of mischievous youngbloods sought to get themselves noticed by the prominent people they invited to attend. They dined more often with members of the Liberal Party's right wing than with fellow Conservatives, very much to the liking of the transparty Winston Churchill. Though still very early in his parliamentary career, he was already seeking to forge a new political grouping that would concentrate like-minded men from both main parties. As he wrote to the aged Lord Rosebery in October 1902, he longed to "create a wing of the Tory party which could either infuse vigour into the parent body or join a central coalition. . . . The only real difficulty I have to encounter is the suspicion that I am moved by mere restless ambition: & if some issue—such as [tariff reform]—were to arise—that difficulty would disappear."[15] Churchill's scant regard for the proprieties of party membership stoked the fires of those who disapproved of him and was an important facet of his image in the long years before he became a national hero.

Churchill's attachment to the Conservative Party was further weakened when one of its leading lights, Joseph Chamberlain, began to espouse the cause of protectionism, or tariff reform, that if adopted would lead to the levying of duty on imports from nonempire countries, signaling a move away from the free-trade precepts ushered in by the Corn Laws. It began an internecine struggle for the heart of the Tory party that was to do it great damage. Having drifted so far from the rather loose Tory moorings that had tethered him, it was inevitable Churchill would leave the party. Warned by Joseph Chamberlain, the party's leading proponent of tariff reform, to look out for it as the "coming" big issue in British politics, Churchill sedulously prepared himself for the fight. He opposed protectionism because although the vast British Empire contained many of the raw materials and markets that Britain's global trading economy depended upon, it could not act in isolation from the rest of the world; ultimately, a turn to protectionism would spell disaster. Churchill was adamant that he did "not want a self-contained Empire. It is very much better that the great nations of the world should be interdependent." In the event of a European war, "do you not think it very much better that the United States should be vitally interested in keeping the English market open?"[16] As he wrote to Ernest Fletcher:

> It would seem to me a fantastic policy to endeavor to shut the British Empire up in a ringed fence. It is very large, and there are a good many things which can be produced in it, but the world is larger & produces some better things than can be found in the British Empire. Why

should we deny ourselves the good and varied merchandise which the traffic of the world offers, more especially since the more we trade with others, the more they must trade with us. . . . Our planet is not a very big one compared with the other celestial bodies, and I see no particular reason why we should endeavor to make inside our planet a smaller planet called the British Empire, cut off by impassable space from everything else.[17]

The free-trade versus protection battle gave Churchill his first experience of taking campaigns to the country through the mechanism of a "league," a common means of garnering support and publicity for a cause. He became a prime mover in the Free Food League, an organization created to rival the Tariff Reform League. The issue of tariff reform caused the final breach between Churchill and the Conservative Party, and he announced his resignation in a speech on March 29, 1904. Knowing what was coming, when Churchill rose to speak, the prime minister left the chamber, soon followed by his ministers. Tory backbenchers then began to leave, some remaining at the door to jeer Churchill ("the most marked discourtesy which I think I have ever seen," in the words of the Tory MP Sir John Gorst). But Churchill joined a party in the ascendant. He cast aside all criticism and defended his actions. As he was to say in 1906, the year of the Liberals' landslide victory at the polls, "I said a lot of stupid things when I was in the Conservative Party, and I left because I did not want to go on saying stupid things."[18] Churchill spoke on behalf of the Liberals at a special election and spoke out against the government's position on tariff reform, actions that forced his Oldham constituency to disown him. He became the Opposition's most knowledgeable and effective antiprotectionist speaker in the last days of the Tory administration.

Churchill crossed the floor of the House and took his seat on the Liberal benches in such a way as to emphasize his newfound relationship with Lloyd George. His desertion of the Tories was a defining moment in Churchill's career, and while beneficial in many ways, it was personally damaging. Conservatives felt bitterly betrayed, and his reputation for opportunism, forged while a maverick soldier-cum–war correspondent, became an article of faith in some quarters. The Liberals, meanwhile, were naturally suspicious of a man who had ditched his party; he might (and he did) do it again. He acknowledged the reasons for hostility toward him in Conservative circles. As he wrote to Lord Salisbury in November 1904, "I readily admit that my conduct is open to criticism—not—thank heaven—on the score of sincerity, but from the point of view of taste. I had to choose between fighting & standing aside."[19] He had to quit the Carlton Club when he left the Tory party and was even blackballed from the Hurlingham Club, the home of British polo.

Churchill was a classic inside-outsider. Despite his noble birth, he looked different, sounded different, and acted differently from the lathe-turned aristocrat of his day. He eschewed idleness and leisure; he was publicity seeking among a class that pretended to shun publicity; he defied convention; he was seized with ambition and a desire for professional standards in an age when English gentlemen were supposed to cultivate an air of amateurism, languor, and laissez-faire. But Churchill found it impossible to "laissez-faire" anything.

Socially he remained privileged despite cutting a strikingly different figure from those around him. Even the Prince of Wales, so close in many ways to both Churchill's parents, took an interest in his activities, and this continued when he became King Edward VII in 1901. In the autumn of 1902, he invited Churchill to stay at Balmoral, the kind of invitation few young backbenchers could display on their mantelpiece. Determined to wring every possible advantage from his contacts, he exhorted his mother, who would be seeing the king soon after: "Mind you gush to him about my having written to you saying how much etc. etc. I had enjoyed myself here."[20] Even when his politics turned against the Tories, his cousin Sunny, Duke of Marlborough, remained friendly, and Blenheim was always at his disposal as a haven. The duke even allowed him to have Lloyd George, author of the "People's Budget," to stay there (though relations between the Churchills and the duke soured for a couple of years when His Grace discovered Clementine writing to the Welshman on Blenheim stationery).

Churchill kept up his prodigious literary activity during this period. With five books already to his name, between 1903 and 1905 he embarked on a major biography of his father. He secured a lucrative deal with Macmillan, and the book was published to critical acclaim in 1906. In preparing it, he made extensive use of the Blenheim archives. Sunny gave him rooms, loaned him hunters when he was working there, and later gave him all Lord Randolph's political papers bound in thirty-two blue morocco volumes.

Having switched parties, Churchill needed a new seat and agreed to run as Liberal candidate for Manchester North West, where free trade was strongly supported. Many of his supporters in this campaign came from the Jewish community, as he was a significant critic of the Aliens Bill, establishing his reputation as a leading opponent of discrimination against minorities and a Zionist sympathizer. Churchill's mother campaigned with her son in Manchester, as she had done with Lord Randolph many years before. As Ann Leslie wrote, "Jennie never ceased to work for her elder son. Jack, whom she loved equally, worked away in the City under Cassell's guidance, but it was the demanding, the tyrannical, fascinating Winston who kept her on the go."[21] Churchill won his poll on January 13, after leading the Liberals' fight in the whole area.

JUNIOR MINISTER

The Liberal Party won a landslide victory in the general election of January–February 1906. Churchill attained office in the new government. Offered the most senior of the junior ministerial posts—financial secretary to the Treasury, where he would have worked under Herbert Asquith, the party's coming leader—Churchill asked for the lowlier office of undersecretary of state for the colonies. This was a shrewd move because it meant working for a secretary of state who was twenty-five years his senior and not known for his dynamism and who, as a member of the House of Lords, could not represent the department in the House of Commons. Enter Churchill, who would lead on all matters related to the colonies in that chamber and, because of this, be to the fore in a way that was uncommon for a junior minister. In doing so, he was to exhibit a real talent for conducting government business effectively in Parliament.

His boss, Lord Elgin, relished the quiet life on his Scottish estate. While certainly no pushover, and indeed rather adept at curbing Churchill's excesses, this was just the kind of boss for a young thruster, though throughout their relationship Churchill behaved with a becoming sense of loyalty and propriety. Elgin was not subdued by Churchill's obvious talent or bamboozled by his exuberance and energy. As he put it, "When I accepted Churchill as my Under-Secy I knew I had no easy task. I resolved to give him access to all business—but to keep control (& my temper)."[22] But Elgin did require a measure of protection; his staff devised an early-warning system that gave them notice when Churchill left his office to make for Elgin's upstairs, allowing them to head Churchill off and oblige him to approach Elgin via his secretary.

What followed was a period in which Churchill's dash and energy, and his habitual pronouncement upon all issues under the sun regardless of whether they were within his purview or not, contrasted and complemented the more leisurely pace at which Elgin conducted his department's affairs. Randolph Churchill neatly summarized his father's approach: "While he was a backbencher, Churchill had spoken as if he were an Under-Secretary, now, as an Under-Secretary, as if a member of the Cabinet; and when he reached the Cabinet he was apt to speak as if he were Prime Minister."[23] His tenure at the Colonial Office was to see Churchill concoct a stream of minutes and reports of extreme audacity. They often irritated his superiors but demonstrated Churchill's insistence on fundamental principles of British life, such as the rule of law, being applied in the colonies. He argued for the need to understand the perspective of indigenous peoples subjected to alien rule.

Churchill chose as his private secretary Edward ("Eddie") Marsh, two years his senior, who was to follow him through eight departments of state. He joined a band of "behind the scenes" people, such as nannies, secretaries, researchers, and valets, who kept Winston Churchill on track during his lengthy career. Without these important people, Churchill would have found it difficult to acquire crucial political and literary information, to manage masses of data and juggle large projects and offices of state, or even to feed himself and get dressed.

Like all incoming governments, which until recently have subjected the incumbent administration to withering criticism from the relative safety of the Opposition benches, the Liberal government that took office in 1906 was expected to deliver on a raft of pledges. For the Colonial Office, nowhere was this more important than with regard to Britain's relations with South Africa, so recently the scene of bitter fighting and with a peace still to be lost or won. The new government had to show that, unlike the Tories, it could reconcile the defeated Boers and offer them status equal to that of South Africans of British descent. Churchill was heavily engaged in determining the future of the newly united South Africa, a country in which he had so recently fought and that now required political reconstruction. This was one of the most important imperial issues of the time, ranking alongside political reform in India and Ireland. The puzzle was how to transform the two recently conquered states from Crown colonies under the authoritarian rule of Sir Alfred Milner and his successor, to a political status that at least reconciled the vanquished Boers to British overlordship by providing them with a large measure of autonomy. Attempting to square the circle of nationalism and imperialism was to become a familiar theme of twentieth-century imperial politics. As we have seen, Churchill sympathized with Boer demands for independence; the question was, could he devise an acceptable form of "independence" that kept them and South Africa within the British Empire?

Churchill argued strongly that a complete break with the previous government's constitutional plans was required, and that they should stop at nothing short of "one man one vote." He therefore pressed hard for full responsible government, even though the then high commissioner, Lord Selborne, thought the end result would be Boer majority governments (which it was). But it was a progressive and liberal solution, despite the fact that it meant selling the nonwhites down the river in pursuit of the politically attainable and contributed to the Union of South Africa remaining a part of the British Empire. Churchill managed to convince his colleagues of the rightness of his plan for early responsible government, elevating South Africa to the same status of autonomy within the empire as was enjoyed by Australia, Canada, and New Zealand. Jan Smuts, the former Boer general who was for many decades to be Britain's main ally in negotiating the tightrope between Boer and Briton, instantly saw this as a significant olive branch proffered to his people. Thus in February 1906, the Cabinet agreed self-government would be granted sooner rather than later. Churchill told the king in mid-August 1906 that he had conducted all the South African business in Parliament, answering around five hundred questions.

Also relating to South Africa, Churchill had to wrestle with the thorny problem of Chinese indentured laborers, who had been imported to work in the mines on the Rand. This was an issue ruthlessly exploited by the Liberal Party when in opposition, so when they inherited the problem, they risked accusations of hypocrisy if they failed to swiftly resolve it. It was at this time that Churchill blundered badly in the Commons by launching a vehement attack on Sir Alfred Milner, showing a customary lack of awareness of the feelings of others or the likely results of his actions. Some Liberals had tabled a motion of censure against Milner when it was learned that he had sanctioned the flogging of some Chinese laborers. The subsequent spectacle of the bombastic and belligerent young Churchill tearing strips off a senior imperial proconsul, even taunting him, confirmed the worse suspicions about Lord Randolph's impetuous offspring. The king told a distant kinsman of Churchill that his behavior was "simply scandalous." The episode earned him the lasting enmity of many Tories, and Churchill had, not for the first or the last time, provided grist for the mill of those who wished to hate him. Sir William Anson, warden of All Souls and MP for Oxford, wrote that Churchill "seems to have been both pompous and impertinent. . . . It is terrible to think what harm that young jackanapes may do with a big majority behind him and an incompetent prime minister to look after him."[24] But in belittling Milner, Churchill had been attempting to shield him from parliamentary censure. Another scrape for what the *Pall Mall Gazette* called "The Blenheim Pup" occurred when Churchill claimed that Westminster could overrule the new self-governing South African colonies on matters relating to the treatment of the African population. Churchill was, of course, correct, but saying so affronted settler sensibilities regarding their precious autonomy.

The affair blew over, however, and the headline fact was that Churchill, in a year, had dealt with two of the most pressing problems facing the British government in colonial affairs—the Transvaal and Chinese labor—showing commendable skill and audacious confidence. He also continued to evince a liberal outlook regarding the treatment of indigenous people. He condemned punitive raids and suppressions that took place in Natal and East and West Africa and questioned the actions of settlers and administrators. Lady Lugard (the wife of a famous colonial official), staying at Blenheim in 1906, was appalled by his "rank Little Englandism," in this instance an unintended compliment to Churchill's liberal proclivities.[25] After proposing reprisals when the Munshi people had burned a Niger company station, Lugard was met by this Churchillian riposte: "The chronic bloodshed which stains the West African season is odious and disquieting. Moreover, the whole enterprise is liable to be misrepresented by persons unacquainted with Imperial terminology as the murdering of natives and stealing of their lands."[26]

In 1908, Churchill decided to make a tour of British colonial possessions in Africa. Elgin thought this might provide relief from his eager subordinate's constant initiatives, but he was wrong: Churchill sustained his bombardment by sending missives on all manner of subjects back to London. Potentially more worrying, rather than just being the private "sporting" (i.e., big-game shooting) holiday that had been planned, Churchill's character, his important political position, and his fame transformed it into a semiofficial state progress from Britain to East Africa by way of the empire's stepping stones in the Mediterranean and Red Sea. His tour took on the characteristics of an official enquiry into colonial affairs, from native administration to sleeping sickness and railway construction. Churchill visited Malta, where he met the cruiser HMS *Venus*, put at his disposal by the Admiralty. The journey eastward continued, punctuated by various stops—Cyprus, and then Port Said, where "I bought a Japanese *kimono* for a dressing gown in passing through,"[27] possibly the first appearance of the brightly colored evening wear he was to sport throughout his life.

Churchill recorded his tour for the *Strand Magazine*, which had commissioned him to write a series of articles at £150 apiece, a now familiar Churchill ploy when traveling overseas, as was his keenness to turn the articles into a book posthaste upon returning home (he did so even though this conflicted with his honeymoon in August 1908; the book appeared as *My African Journey*). His letters were "written in the long hot Uganda afternoons," as he put it, "after the day's march was done." His customary panache was evident from the book's first sentence: "The aspect of Mombasa as she rises from the sea and clothes herself with form and color at the swift approach of the ship is alluring and even delicious."[28] He was welcomed with a fanfare when he arrived at Mombasa after stops at Berbera and Aden.

As well as flooding the Colonial Office with memoranda, he became deeply involved in the business of the places he visited ("I shall spend I think two days looking into the affairs of the Somaliland Protectorate—upon which we spend £76,000 a year with uncommonly little return," he wrote to his mother).[29] Churchill traveled from Nairobi to Lake Victoria along the railway line whose development he had championed. At Kisumu, he boarded a steamer to Entebbe. In between official dinners and receptions, the energetic undersecretary did manage to get in some trophy shooting as he moved from Kenya to Uganda, though even this was not without a businesslike purpose; moving with four hundred porters, the Churchill safari had as its practical aim the reconnoitering of a possible railway extension linking Lakes Albert and Victoria. Running up and down the railway line on a trolley, Churchill took potshots at the wildlife. "*The plains are crowded with wild animals*," he wrote. "From the window the whole zoological garden can be seen disporting itself."[30] He sympathized with the "noble" beasts slaughtered in the name of sport though still found himself able to shoot them.

Churchill evinced ideas about subject races as well as wildlife that were common and uncontroversial at the time, but would now be considered deeply flawed on both racial and conservational grounds. Africans were viewed as "childlike" and "dignified" when they conformed to British stereotypes of "traditional" African society, while colonial officers were viewed as guardians protecting the Africans from those who would exploit them—by which Churchill meant the white settlers. The Kikuyu, he wrote, were "light-hearted, tractable, if brutish children" for whom it would be "an ill day" if "their fortunes are removed from the impartial and august administration of the Crown and abandoned to the fierce self-interest of a small white population." In Churchill's view, colonial rule was bringing to Africa the manifold benefits of civilization and protecting docile Africans from the predations of slave raiders and unscrupulous traders and from their own violence, a classic justification for the Pax Britannica. This did not prevent him from striking a cautionary note about the dangers of unchecked white settlement, for both the native African and the Indian population. He also saw in these recently acquired British domains rich fields of opportunity, not least because of the potential of their untapped natural resources. In Churchill's mind, resources such as water were placed on God's clean earth to be developed in the name of "progress," just as game was there to be shot with gay abandon in the name of sport. He viewed the presence of the white man as an unsolicited boon for the indigenous people, uplifting them from a state of backwardness by his very presence. Nevertheless, Churchill did display some more enlightened thinking about these matters, akin to his liberal and reformist attitudes toward social issues in Britain. Though a staunch paternalist, he was considerate and empathetic toward subject peoples, questioning the belief that colonial officials were always right when Africans complained about their rulers. He deplored, here as in India, the employment of punitive expeditions to discipline alleged recalcitrants.

The Governor of Uganda, Sir Hesketh Bell, wrote that Churchill "is a difficult fellow to handle, but I can't help liking him. . . . He sees things *en grand* and appreciates adequately the great possibilities of industrial development that are latent in this remarkable country."[31] Churchill was blithely confident in the ability of industrial society to tame these "wild" places and harness them, for Britain's benefit and also that of the native inhabitants. He was much impressed by the railway, with "its trim little stations, with their water tanks, signals, ticket-offices, and flower-beds complete and all of a pattern, backed by impenetrable bush. In brief one slender thread of scientific civilization, of order, authority, and arrangement, drawn across the primeval chaos of the world." While Churchill was clever enough to see some of the real problems inherent in the racial composition of the nascent protectorate, the reports he wrote smack of the chancing journalist, long on opinion but short on detailed knowledge. He was an "expert" on the affairs of the Baganda after only a couple of days in their midst. Here, for example, he expatiates on Britain's task among the people of Uganda:

> What an obligation, what a sacred duty is imposed upon Great Britain to enter the lists in person and to shield this trustful, docile, intelligent Baganda race from dangers which, whatever their cause, have synchronized with our arrival in their midst! And, meanwhile, let us be sure that order and science will conquer, and that in the end John Bull will really be master in his curious garden of sunshine and deadly nightshade.[32]

In 1908, such sentiments were common. Churchill's visit was not without purpose, and he was only trying to act on the world as it was presented to him and exercising his innate capacity for trying to put the world to rights. In Uganda, he deduced "the need for machinery and cheap power to replace cheap labor and transform Africa—on this we talked—or at least I talked—while we scrambled across the stumps of fallen trees or waded in an emerald twilight from one sunbeam to another across the creeper flood."

MARRIAGE AND A SEAT IN CABINET

Returning to England, Churchill was going to stay at the Ritz, but Lord and Lady Ridley placed at his disposal a flat in Carlton House Terrace. Churchill had thrown himself wholeheartedly into the affairs of the Colonial Office, though he was not one to settle for long while the metronome of his ambition marked time, and he displayed what was becoming a trademark propensity to concern himself with the affairs of departments of state other than his own. During his time at the Colonial Office, he maintained his interest in social reform, reading books, holding discussions, and writing memoranda to his colleagues as he looked to the future prospects of both himself and the government in which he served. In this first decade of the twentieth century, new class antagonisms, new political parties, and new socialist doctrines were entering the mainstream of British politics as never before. Political leaders, therefore, had to consider and deal with issues alien to their predecessors.

It is a measure of Churchill's political convictions and his ambition that in this period he became nationally acknowledged as one of the two most significant social reformers in high office. He espoused the need for a minimum standard of living and work for all, regardless of class and wealth. By 1907, his mind ranged busily on the subject of his next promotion, for which he pressed regularly. The moment came in 1908, following a stroke that rendered the prime minister, Henry Campbell-Bannerman, incapable, forcing him to resign in favor of Herbert Asquith. After having turned down tentative offers of the Local Government Board or the Admiralty, in April 1908 Churchill was offered the presidency of the Board of Trade, a promotion to full ministerial status at the young age of thirty-four. April turned into a busy month: not only did he have to fight a special election because convention required new Cabinet ministers to seek reelection to Parliament, he also became engaged to Clementine Hozier. The wedding proposal went better than the election, which he lost. Defeated in Manchester, he had quickly to find another constituency, which turned out to be in Dundee.

Churchill's private life in this period was of secondary importance to his political life, but he clearly wanted to marry. He had had something approaching an "understanding" with a young lady called Pamela Plowden, though apparently she also had "understandings" elsewhere and plumped for the hand of the Earl of Lytton. In a backhanded compliment that probably says a lot about why they didn't marry, Plowden commented that "the first time you meet Winston you see all his faults, and the rest of your life you spend discovering his virtues."[33] Churchill's public image was dominated by his energy, devotion to politics, self-publicity, and conceit. He was variously considered charming, forgivable, or infuriating, depending on where you stood. But as a romantic, he was unusually tongue-tied, as well as being tender and gentle. He had plenty of affection to give, even if it was often delivered by telegram rather than in person, as his politics took him away from house parties and dinner parties and even, later, from the marital home.

In 1904. Churchill had insisted his mother introduce him to Clementine Hozier at a ball at Crewe House, so impressed was he by her beauty. Their respective mothers knew each other and were able to effect the introduction. Once it had been done, Churchill stood speechless and stared, until Clementine was rescued by a more forward admirer. According to his son, "All his life Churchill was always apt to be gauche when he met women for the first time. He had no small talk. He greatly preferred talking about himself."[34] Throughout his life, Churchill admired and was impressed by female beauty, hardly an unusual male trait. Churchill soon met Clementine again at the home of Clementine's aunt, Lady St. Helier, where they sat next to each other at dinner, and then in April 1908, on the weekend when Asquith was announcing his new Cabinet, Lady Randolph invited her and her mother, Lady Blanche, to Salisbury Hall at her son's request. It was on the weekend of this house party that Churchill became president of the Board of Trade. Soon after, he was off to fight for his seat in Manchester, and a couple of days later, Clementine left for Germany. Thus began an exchange of letters that was to last for over half a century. On April 27, Churchill ended a scrawl with the words "Write to me again—I am a solitary creature in the midst of crowds," a hint of melodrama and self-regard creeping into the words of an important young man, ardent and in love.

Naturally, society tongues wagged about the marriage prospects and the position of eligible youngsters. Churchill, in his mid-thirties, fell squarely into this category. Winston's mother wanted him to find a mate, realizing that her son was brilliant, but very hard to suit. One of the period's great gossips, Violet Asquith, commented that Churchill "did not *wish* for—though he needs it badly—a critical reformatory wife who would stop up the lacunas in his taste etc. & hold him back from blunders."[35] Clementine Hozier, although she did not bring a fortune, certainly brought those things. Though, from the very outset, politics was to be an indefatigable competitor for Churchill's devotion, she offered him a highly successful life partnership. Jennie was delighted. "She will be the perfect wife for him. You see my Winston is not *easy*; he is very difficult indeed and she is just right." Lady Blanche also approved and had a shrewd opinion of the young suitor, writing to Wilfrid Scawen Blunt that he had some of Lord Randolph's faults and all of his qualities: "He is gentle and tender, and affectionate to those he loves, much hated by those who have not come under his personal charm."[36]

Fittingly, the summit meeting took place at Blenheim Palace, as has been seen. Churchill caused Clementine to be invited to join a house party there, and wrote on August 8 to say that he would collect her from Oxford station. She hesitated, but, although down to her last cotton frock and without a maid, she made the journey, and as Ann Leslie remarked, "Her dryad beauty, her glowing red hair and huge blue eyes were off-set by not being over-ironed."[37] In persuading her to come, Winston had emphasized the charms of the estate: "It has many glories in the fullness of summer. Pools of water, gardens of roses, a noble lake shrouded by giant trees; tapestries, pictures, and monuments within."[38] The party gathered at the palace on August 10, and Churchill's hesitant proposal in the Temple of Diana soon followed.

Fruit and vegetable mongers in pearly suits danced outside of St. Margaret's, Westminster, where they were wed. Though their wedding in September 1908 was out of season, Churchill and Clementine still mustered over thirteen hundred guests at their reception at the Portland Place home of Lady St. Helier. Here an array of wedding presents was displayed, including a gold-capped Malacca cane bearing the Marlborough insignia from the king and a silver tray engraved with the autographs of all Churchill's Cabinet colleagues. A brief honeymoon was spent at Blenheim, Lake Maggiore in Lombardy, and Venice. It was a hurried trip because Churchill needed to be back in London to attend to his new ministry. Politics came at a price for marriage and personal life, and even at this early stage, Clementine found herself unwelcome in the houses of certain Tory "friends" because of the man she had married.

The newlyweds' early life was spent "squatting" around London—a little house in Bolton Street near Green Park, which had been Churchill's bachelor pad, then the lease of a house in Eccleston Square in Pimlico from March 1909. Winston was a caring husband and most attentive during Clementine's first pregnancy. Churchill described the newborn to Charles Masterman, Lloyd George's secretary, as "the prettiest child ever seen." "Like her mother, I suppose," Masterman replied. "No," was his reply. "She is exactly like me." Winston's endearing, childlike qualities suited him for family life. He was observed at his birthday on November 30, 1909, with "a birthday cake with 35 candles. And *crackers*. He sat all evening with a paper cap, from a cracker, on his head. A queer sight . . . He and she sat on the same sofa, and he holds her hand. I never saw two people more in love."[39] The Churchills were to become known for their open expressions of tenderness and affection. Churchill was also gaining a middle-aged spread, not helped by his appetite and a general lack of exercise at this time—the occasional day's shooting, or a round of golf (a game he was not very good at because he talked too much) being about the limit.

Churchill's marriage was of fundamental importance to his subsequent career. It was, to modern eyes, a marriage not without its oddities, though perhaps more "normal" when viewed in its proper aristocratic setting. Devotedly in love they may have been, but their dissimilarities were pronounced, and as the grand total of at least seventeen hundred letters, notes, and telegrams exchanged between them during fifty-seven years of wedlock indicates, they were often apart. Their tastes in people differed markedly—Clementine disapproved of many of Churchill's intimates, describing them memorably as being like "dogs around a lamppost." Their daily routines also differed, as did their preferences for leisure and holiday venues.[40] In fact, they often lived quite separate lives, though overlapping sufficiently to form a rock-solid marriage. It was not without its trials: Clementine was highly strung and often suffered from bouts of depression and overanxiety, though little is known about Churchill's private reactions to this. Clementine's "impression of serenity," according to her daughter, was an artifact "of a long lifetime of self-control."[41] Churchill, for his part, was a loving husband, "and he always wanted Clementine to 'be there'; but his self-centeredness, combined with his total commitment to politics, did not make him a very companionable one."[42] Reading their correspondence, one is struck by how very often he was absent, even at significant moments, and how often his undoubtedly heartfelt words of love and adoration were expressed by the written, rather than the spoken, word.

Now a fully fledged member of the Cabinet, Churchill entered the Board of Trade with a radical manifesto in mind. He did so at a time when the working class was becoming more militant and politically powerful, and when the issue of Irish Home Rule (and a simmering feud between the Liberal government and the Tory establishment) was coming to a head. The depression of 1907–8 made the new government more prepared to be adventurous in tackling social and economic problems, and Churchill took a radical position on all issues: he advocated the nationalization of railways and canals and discovered that the Board of Trade could be an instrument for unprecedented experiment in social welfare. Since the start of 1908, he had been studying employment exchanges and unemployment insurance, especially in Germany (in 1909 he was invited by the kaiser to attend the German army's maneuvers and found time to visit labor exchanges in Strasbourg and Frankfurt am Main). As he wrote to Asquith, "Dimly across gulfs of ignorance I see the outline of a policy which I call the Minimum Standard."[43] The Board of Trade, in Churchill's own words, was "a great apparatus of beneficent government organization, a great accumulation of knowledge." Working with both employers and unions, its "three great principles were 'Confer, Conciliate and Compromise.'"[44] The board's responsibilities included import and excise duties, conciliation in industrial disputes, and labor conditions, and it had an important role in disbursing central government revenue.

Despite his department's extensive responsibilities, no sooner was Churchill in the Cabinet than he was attacking the army estimates prepared by his colleague and circulating detailed proposals for the reform of other departments. Churchill and Lloyd George began a period of constructive cooperation as they sought to push through a legislative program characterized by social radicalism. Clement Attlee was of the opinion that "Winston felt himself superior to anyone he had ever met, with one exception: Lloyd George."

Churchill had been attracted to the Board of Trade because of the potential it offered to make a mark as a social reformer. He was deeply interested in social reform, though his significant achievements in this field are usually drowned out amid the clamor surrounding his war record. Churchill recruited William Beveridge to devise a nationwide scheme of labor exchanges and kept in close and friendly touch with Beatrice and Sidney Webb, the noted social thinkers. He was attempting to deal with increasing unemployment in 1907–8 and, inspired in part by the Webbs and the example of German and Australian legislation, pioneered labor exchanges. Beatrice Webb offered the following assessment of Churchill at this stage of his career: "Bound to be unpopular, [he is] too unpleasant a flavour with his restless self-regarding personality and lack of moral or intellectual refinement. . . . But his pluck, courage, resourcefulness and great tradition may carry him far, unless he knocks himself to pieces like his father."[45]

Work frequently kept Churchill away from the family home, and the affectionate correspondence between husband and wife blossomed. His letters demonstrated the manner in which Clementine became the lodestar, the rock upon which his ambition and talent could build: "I have missed you a great deal," he wrote a year after their marriage. "Your room is very empty. The poor pug pules disconsolate." In their letters and notes, Churchill was Clementine's Pug, Pig, or Amber Dog; she his Cat, Kat, or Pussy Bird. Their pet names were often illustrated with little sketches of cats or pugs. "Your sweetness & beauty have cast a glory upon my life," Churchill wrote in November 1909.[46] Over the course of the next six decades, Clementine was never left in any doubt as to how much she meant to him. She kept the show on the road, and since she "was primarily interested in Winston and so was Winston, their relationship to each other was always closer than that with their five children."[47]

The alliance between Churchill and Lloyd George attained its fullest bloom in the years 1908 to 1910. Known as the "terrible twins," together they were responsible for a barrage of radical legislation that changed the relationship between the people and the state for good, signaling the end of the laissez-faire politics of the nineteenth century and heralding the dawn of the managerial and interventionist state, of social security and greater government centralization. They fought side by side in these years against a phalanx of the British elite over the issue of the "People's Budget" and the reform of the Tory-dominated House of Lords that refused to pass it into law.

The issue arose when Lloyd George sought to raise money to fight poverty and to fund the old-age pensions scheme, as well as new naval construction. To do so, he proposed to tax the better-off, particularly property owners, introducing wealth redistribution into the tax systems. A minority in the Commons, the Conservatives sought to thwart the budget in the Lords. Churchill's involvement in this gigantic prewar political battle came as a result of his keenness for social reform. His Cabinet colleagues did not generally share his aggressive stance toward the Lords. But Churchill was angry with the upper chamber because it had rejected the Licensing Bill, aimed at reducing the number of pubs in order to curb working-class drunkenness. Lucy Masterman recalls an infuriated Churchill saying that "we shall send them up a budget in June as shall terrify them. They have started the class war, they had better be careful."[48]

He was bellicose on the issue of the reform of the Lords should they fail to pass the 1909 budget, with the result that he was seen by many as a traitor to his class. But his fire strengthened the prime minister's resolve to stand firm on the issue, leading to the 1911 Parliament Act that limited the power of the Lords. "The issue," Churchill told an audience in Leicester in September 1909, "will be whether the British people in the year of grace 1909 are going to be ruled through a representative Assembly elected by six or seven millions of voters about which everyone in the country has a chance of being consulted, or whether they are going to allow themselves to be dictated to and domineered by a miserable minority of titled persons, who represent nobody, who are responsible to nobody, and who only scurry up to London to vote in their party interests, in their class interests, and in their own interests."[49] In Burnley in December, he brought the house down with his ribbing of Lord Curzon, who had defended the hereditary principle in the House of Lords, saying that "all civilization has been the work of aristocracies." "They liked that in Oldham," Churchill said. "There was not a duke, not an earl, not a marquis, not a viscount in Oldham who did not feel that a compliment had been paid to him. . . . 'All civilization has been the work of aristocracies,'" Churchill repeated. "Why, it would be much more true to say the upkeep of the aristocracy has been the hard work of all civilizations." Churchill's speech ended with loud cheers and shouts of "say it again."[50] In July, he had questioned the "self reliance" of the rich in a speech in Norwich: "It is very easy for rich people to preach the virtues of self reliance to the poor. It is also very foolish because, as a matter of fact, the wealthy, so far from being self reliant, are dependent on the constant attention of scores, sometimes hundreds, of persons who are employed in waiting upon them and ministering to their wants."[51] Churchill returned to this theme again and again, ridiculing the hereditary principle. In Liverpool on December 8, 1909: "There are four or five hundred backwoods peers meditating upon their estates on the great questions of government or studying *Ruff's Guide* [*to the Turf*] and other Blue books or evolving problems of Empire at Epsom. Every one of them, a heaven-born or God-granted legislator, knows what the people want by instinct and every one of them with a stake in the heart of the country."

In the final years of Edward VII's reign, which coincided with the great period of Liberal reform, Churchill successfully linked imperialism to social progress at home. As he wrote in the *Morning Post* as early as 1898, "To keep our Empire we must have a free people, an educated and well fed people. That is why we are in favor of social reform. That is why we yearn for Old Age Pensions and the like." In 1909, Churchill said that the greatest threat to the empire and the British people was not to be found in enemy military power overseas or problems on the fringes of empire. "No, it is here in our midst, close at home, close at hand" in cities and underpopulated villages. The "seeds of imperial ruin and national decay" lay in the unnatural gap between rich and poor, physical degeneration, and child labor.[52]

Some, naturally, were amused by Churchill's championing of social reform, though it only demonstrated his keenness, industry, and political instinct, not to say his social conscience, which is better to have than to not. Charles Masterman wrote that "Winston is full of the poor, whom he has just discovered. He thinks he is called by providence—to do something for them."[53] But though it was easy to scoff, having a senior British politician vigorously trying to "do something" for the poor was a good thing. Besides, Churchill's interest in poverty was not a hastily adopted, vote-winning sally. As a young parliamentarian, Churchill had begun to develop an interest in social policy and the plight of the disadvantaged, a side of his political character that is often overlooked because of his towering reputation as a war leader. His contact with John Morley led him to read Seebohm Rowntree's book *Poverty: A Study of Town Life*, which "fairly made my hair stand on end."

With Lloyd George at the Treasury and Churchill at the Board of Trade, the prime minister had the two brightest ministers in the land at the vanguard of delivering a new approach to problems of social welfare, acting as conduits through which the ideas of social reformers could be translated into effective policy. Together Churchill and Lloyd George stole the limelight from the Labour Party and, according to Beatrice Webb, stood "out as the most advanced politicians" in the land.[54] During these years, the government enacted a mass of radical legislation that changed the face of Britain. In piloting these reforms, Churchill and Lloyd George were the fulcrum of a defining moment in British political history. Though some chose to see Churchill as a traitor to his class, it was surely more palatable to have a scion of the aristocracy imploring the rich to help the poor than to have the message forced down their throats by firebrand radicals. On February 5, 1909, Churchill spoke at Newcastle on "the great mission of Liberalism," which was to elevate the poor, and "to open all careers freely to the talent of every class."[55] He had to convince the Cabinet, as well as Parliament and the country, that this was the thing to do.

As president of the Board of Trade, Churchill brought the Port of London Act onto the statute book and was instrumental in establishing a network of labor exchanges. The first one opened in February 1910, and there were 214 within two months. Churchill also did a great deal of work toward a scheme of compulsory unemployment insurance, which came into law in December 1911. He recommended delaying the unemployment insurance scheme in December 1908 so that it could be presented as a whole—which robbed him of public acknowledgment of his role in delivering it. When it eventually came before the House, Churchill said that "there is no proposal in the field of politics which I care more about than this great insurance scheme."[56] His 1909 Trade Boards Act introduced minimum wages in a number of "sweated" trades.

Churchill's passion as a social reformer saw him engage in a ferocious campaign against the battleship building program proposed by the First Lord of the Admiralty, Reginald McKenna. Though historical memory casts Churchill primarily as a war minister, he was in this period more concerned with remedying domestic ills than with the defense of the realm. Churchill put his own office of state and its responsibilities first, and this naturally brought him into conflict with fellow ministers vying for Treasury funds, particularly the service ministries. At this point, Churchill did not believe that war with Germany was imminent, and he eschewed the scaremongering that had for some time been stirring. Later, Churchill was to acknowledge that he and Lloyd George had been wrong in this period "in relation to the deep tides of destiny" and should not have so opposed McKenna.[57] But at the time, he was looking forward rather than back.

Churchill's formidable oratory made him a powerful voice in support of any cause, and Asquith saluted the signal contribution of his speeches during these years, claiming that they would be remembered by history. Churchill could, however, overstep the mark, and in supporting the budget earned rebukes not only from his easygoing superior the prime minister, but even from the king. But Churchill remained extraordinarily resilient, a vital strength for those aiming for the political summit. He was rarely abashed; though still much younger than all his Cabinet colleagues and so recently promoted to Cabinet rank, he was perfectly happy to send the most uninhibited letters, offering opinion and policy advice on any subject, whether or not it came within his own department's purview. In participating in the "peers versus people" debates, it was not lost on some that if his cousin were to die, Churchill would find himself Duke of Marlborough. Despite his interest in social reform, Churchill was not a revolutionary, and the existing social order was perfectly acceptable to him. His concern for the working class was paternalistic—he was a squire dispensing alms to the poor. The social-engineering elements of the budget's land taxes were abandoned in a final compromise, though the myth of the "people" beating the super-rich remained thereafter.

As a result of the struggle surrounding the budget, Parliament was dissolved, and in the ensuing election of January 1910, Churchill registered a big win in Dundee. The campaign was fought under a "who rules?" banner, and Churchill gave impressive speeches, noted by the prime minister and knitted together for publication as an election handbook entitled *The People's Right*. The first election of 1910 saw a Tory recovery and left the Liberal government dependent on the support of the Labour Party and the Irish MPs. Churchill's excellent record at the Board of Trade, and his vocal support of his government's policies, convinced the prime minister that he merited promotion. Asquith offered him the Irish Office; Churchill, with typical boldness, said thanks, but no thanks, and asked instead for much higher ministerial positions: "The office does not attract me now. There are many circumstances connected with it which repel me . . . for myself I would like to go either to the Admiralty . . . or to the Home Office."[58] Asquith gave him the Home Office, Churchill becoming the youngest incumbent since 1822, just the kind of statistic that caught his imagination and caressed his ambition and pride (as it would almost anyone in a similar position).

The Home Office was the chief ministry of state for domestic affairs, and one of the four most senior Cabinet positions. As home secretary, Churchill's powers and responsibilities were manifold, including prison reform, the fire service, immigration, censorship of theater, protection of game birds, betting and gambling legislation, issues relating to drugs, and the casting vote in cases involving the death sentence. It was also the customary duty of the home secretary to write a daily letter to the monarch reporting on business conducted in the Commons. This was an onerous task, though Churchill entered into it with gusto, composing eighty-four handwritten missives during his fourteen months in office. The tone of his reports led him into a dispute with the king, conducted through his private secretary. Churchill was unabashed, and the episode provided an interesting insight into his attitude to the monarchy. Although a staunch monarchist throughout his life, prizing the institution's stabilizing influence in British and international affairs, he upheld the supremacy of Parliament. While Kings Edward VII and George V might not have considered Churchill respectful enough of their person or prerogatives, he in turn opposed royal interference in parliamentary matters and played a role in ensuring that the monarchy had less power in political affairs at the end of his parliamentary life than it had at its beginning.

At the Home Office, Churchill drove through a Mines Act, intended to relieve the lot of the many men who worked in appalling conditions in Britain's extensive coalfields, and took steps to help those trapped in "sweated" labor employment. He also did a great deal to reform the treatment of prisoners in Britain's prisons, speaking forcefully as someone who had endured incarceration himself. He legislated against solitary confinement and for the provision of entertainments for prisoners, a novel concept for a penal system fixated with punishment. As Churchill convincingly argued, the way that a society treated its prisoners was "one of the most unfailing tests of the civilization of any country." As home secretary, Churchill was an obvious target for the attention of the suffragettes, struggling to win the vote for women. His public meetings were targeted by female hecklers; he was attacked by a woman wielding a dog whip at Bristol railway station and had a scuffle on the steps of 10 Downing Street. This treatment had the reverse effect from that intended, for it roused Churchill's ire and sense of constitutional propriety.

Meanwhile, skirmishing around the "People's Budget" continued, and both sides prepared for the next set-piece battle. There had been a compromise budget in April 1910, but Asquith was set on curbing the power of the Lords and planned to swamp it with newly created Liberal peers unless they passed the budget. In this cause he was ably assisted by Churchill and Lloyd George. It was the political fight of the Edwardian era, though a temporary truce prevailed after the death of King Edward VII in May 1910. During the summer, Churchill and Lloyd George discussed with sympathetic Conservatives the prospect of a coalition government as a way of bridging the party divide.

Churchill adopted a lifelong habit in these early political years, taking regular and extensive holidays overseas, usually on the Continent. He was, however, unable to holiday without continuing to work, and on these trips he composed lengthy policy documents with which to best his colleagues, as well as making progress on his private writing projects. Since he was a confirmed workaholic, these holidays enabled him to marshal his forces and maintain his intense work rate. In 1910, the holiday involved a six-week Mediterranean cruise. There was yet another general election in December 1910, at which Churchill did less well at the polls than in the first, mirroring his party's failure to improve its position.

Churchill's reputation for being a very "hands on" politician was set during this period, particularly by his involvement in dealing with a wave of strikes that broke out across the country. This did not do him a great deal of good, as it augmented his reputation for overkeenness. The characteristics of drive, egocentrism, energy, and innovation that enabled him to push himself further and further forward were exactly what many people disliked in him. The shadow of his father counted against him—he was considered by some to be "unsound." Some disapproved of his style, sniggering at the figure he cut, standing in his frock coat with a pronounced forward stoop, hands on hips, striking a dramatic parliamentary pose part his own, part his father's. Drama was central to Churchill; he could invest a measure to improve pit latrines with a sense of national purpose. He saw events through dramatic lenses and cast himself in a heroic role, and his ability to tell dramatic tales was the secret of his success with the spoken and written word, though some people always found his rhetoric too florid for their tastes.

The strikes and riots of 1910–11 led to the dispatch of troops to many parts of the country. The unions were growing in power and chose to flex their muscles during a period of almost full employment. In November 1910, miners rioted at Tonypandy in the Rhondda Valley. Troops were ordered to the area without Home Office authority, and when Churchill became involved, he ordered that the troops be kept in reserve and the local police reinforced from London. He decreed that police, not troops, were to deal with the situation. He appointed General Neville Macready to command both troops and police, though he stressed that the police must form a buffer between the strikers and the troops. By this mechanism, authority was removed from the local body—who might have been tempted to employ both the troops and the police as strikebreakers. This was regarded as a wise decision: there was no loss of life, and Churchill had acted with restraint. Yet still he was branded a heavy-handed enemy of the working man, even though "careful scrutiny shows that Churchill sought to avoid sending soldiers at all and then, when he judged that some show of military force was unavoidable, instructed General Macready not to act, or to seem to be acting, other than in support of the civil power."[59] On this occasion, he was criticized in Parliament for not employing the military more rigorously, though later in the year, when troops were used to break a nationwide rail strike, he was criticized for deploying them.

In 1911, Churchill was involved in the unimportant but extensively reported "Battle of Sidney Street," an incident that augmented his reputation for rashness. He was photographed, in frock coat and top hat, observing and conducting a police and army siege of an East End house in which a dangerous gang had taken shelter. Whether guilty or not of rashness and poor judgment, it was a cap that his critics always managed to make fit. The Tory press said he had brought his office into disrepute by being so close to the action, just as it had accused him of being "aloof" over the strikes in the Rhondda Valley. Despite his indisputable record as a social reformer—second only to Lloyd George in promulgating effective legislation against society's ills—these episodes ensured Churchill was cast in many people's minds as an enemy of the working class, "a triumph of propaganda over reality." Winston's love of action, often too closely involved when distance and patience would better have served him, is wonderfully summed up by Clement Attlee, who had first seen him during the Sidney Street siege:

> When Asquith managed to call off the railway strike, his face fell. "Somebody has got to break the news to Winston that it's off." A reluctant Lloyd George was sent around to the Home Office. He found Winston in his room, on all-fours, with large scale plans of various railway stations and goods yards spread in front of him, and small blocks of wood, representing troops, being moved in and put into position. "It's off, Winston," said Lloyd George. "Bloody hell!", said Winston, or words to that effect: then he got up and kicked the troops and the maps across the room. Winston had become so enthused about his job that he wanted to go ahead and finish it. Animosity against the strikers had nothing to do with it.[60]

In the same month as the "Battle of Sidney Street," Churchill was also present at the "Battle of Downing Street." Arriving there to see a scuffle involving the prime minister, Churchill roused a group of policemen who were dealing with Anne Cobden-Sanderson and told them to take her to prison. This remark was overheard, and four days later, after addressing a meeting in Bradford, he was attacked with a whip in the dining car of the train, to the words "take that, you dirty cur."[61]

Given Churchill's growing, if undeserved, association with over-activity and a mailed-fist approach to public disorder, it was little surprise that Asquith formed the opinion that he was too much of a firebrand for the Home Office. The soldier in him, Asquith feared, might win out, and he was considered unsuited to the role of conciliator, partly because he talked too much. Besides, Winston was getting restless, mainly because during the course of 1911, his thoughts had turned to the world situation and the defense of the empire during a future war, in particular its naval defenses. It was the Agadir crisis, in which Germany used the gunboat *Panther* to send a pointed message to the French and the British, that fully alerted Churchill to the true nature of the German menace. From this point on, the security of the British Empire became a dominant theme in his mind, and he even managed to find a Home Office reason—its responsibility for guarding cordite magazines near London—to take emergency precautions. He wrote an extraordinarily percipient and accurate assessment of what the first forty days of a large-scale European war would look like—a military timetable of the German invasion of France and Belgium in 1914 and when it would be halted—which he circulated to the Committee of Imperial Defence.

Given all this, Asquith decided to decouple Churchill from home affairs and let him loose on defense and strategy. The Admiralty, in Asquith's mind, was lagging behind the organizational developments that had been taking place at the War Office. The Royal Navy did not have a war staff as the army did, and its grand strategic plans were supposedly locked away in the recesses of the most senior admiral's mind. Incredibly, the Admiralty had no fixed plans to transport and secure a British expeditionary force across the Channel to France in the event of war. This would not do, given the looming threat of war. Things needed to change, and the navy needed to prepare properly to cooperate with the army. Churchill could provide the impetus for these things to happen and, what is more, if he replaced the First Lord, Reginald McKenna (an opponent of the military conversations that Britain had been having with France), he would ensure weighty support for Foreign Secretary Edward Grey's policy of supporting the Anglo-French entente.

Asquith understood Churchill well, recognizing both his genius and his limitations as a politician. In contrast with the prime minister's "Roman sense of detachment,"[62] Churchill was loquacious and "would in private often develop and air scores of opinions which never matured into conviction or action." Asquith had ample chance to observe Churchill, and concluded that "Winston thinks with his mouth."[63] "His fault," Asquith believed, was "that phrases master him, rather than he them. But his faults and mistakes will be forgotten in his achievement." Asquith recognized Churchill's matchless worth. "He is a wonderful creature," he wrote to Venetia Stanley, "with a curious dash of schoolboy simplicity . . . and what someone said of genius—'A zig-zag streak of lightning in the brain.'"[64] Given the evolution of Churchill's thoughts and interests, it was with delight that he accepted Asquith's offer of the Admiralty and command of the world's most powerful weapon at a time when, according to Sir Edward Grey, "the lights were going out all over Europe."

4

High Office:
War on Land and Sea

Being First Lord of the Admiralty brought joy to Winston Churchill's heart, and between 1911 and 1915 he enjoyed the most fulfilling period of his career—at least, that is, until the unique challenges that faced him in 1940. Barely a decade after leaving the junior officer ranks of the British Army, he was now in command of the Royal Navy. This was the instrument, acknowledged by popular lore and hard military fact, that secured Britain's interests all over the world and made it the foremost political and military power. "For more than three hundred years," Churchill told the Commons in March 1913, "we alone amongst the nations have wielded that mysterious and decisive force which is called sea-power. What have we done with it? We have suppressed the slaver. We have charted the seas. We have made them a safe highway for all."[1] The navy secured the British Isles from invasion and enabled Britain to prevent the movement of an enemy's soldiers or its trade across salt water, the very substance of the Pax Britannica that had settled upon the globe following the decisive victory at Trafalgar in 1815. And it was now at the command of thirty-six-year-old Winston Churchill.

Cometh the hour, cometh the man was Churchill's view on this turn of events. He believed he was destined to play a defining role in British history, and here he was, called to serve his country in the highest military office just as he had developed the conviction that war was likely and Britain's independence imperiled by German expansionism and naval ambitions. His final months at the Home Office had seen this conversion from dashing social reformer to steely strategist consumed by the need to man the barricades. Many found his transmogrification from social crusader scorning rumors of war to apostle of increased military spending difficult to countenance. Politicians are rarely allowed to change their spots despite such pragmatism being crucial to their success. Churchill was doubly condemned, not only as a man who could desert his party, but as a man who could desert his principles. But, as he was to claim, he would rather be right than consistent.

Nevertheless, Churchill was supported by powerful colleagues in the Cabinet who were alive to the German menace, and history has shown that his judgment regarding the international situation was entirely sound. He drew close to Foreign Secretary Grey, who shared his concerns about Germany. The prime minister was in no doubt that the Admiralty needed to emulate the War Office in instituting significant internal reform. Churchill was to be the new broom, Asquith calculating that his robust style qualified him for the job of subjecting the highest-spending department to proper control by politicians and bringing it into line with the gloomy foreign policy assessments most closely associated with Grey. Churchill's view of the world in the three years before war broke out in 1914, and of the Royal Navy's place in it, was crystal clear. As he told the Lord Mayor's Banquet in 1911, "The maintenance of naval supremacy is our whole foundation. Upon it stands not the Empire only, not merely the great commercial prosperity of our people, not merely a fine place in the world's affairs. Upon our naval supremacy stands our lives and the freedom we have guarded for nearly a thousand years."[2]

Violet Bonham Carter captured Churchill's love of the navy and warfare when a guest aboard the Admiralty yacht *Enchantress*, cruising in the Mediterranean in spring 1912:

> As we leaned side by side against the taffrail, gliding past the lovely, smil-ing coastline of the Adriatic, bathed in sun, I remarked: "How perfect!" He startled me by his reply: "Yes—range perfect—visibility perfect—if we had some six-inch guns on board how easily we could bombard . . ." etc. etc.—and details followed showing how effectively we could lay waste the landscape and blow the nestling towns sky-high.[3]

But while reveling in military matters, and chiding himself for being "built" in such a manner that war both fascinated and exhilarated him, Churchill was no warmonger. His own experience of war and the ugly, prosaic nature of death in battle ensured this. "Much as war attracts me," he wrote, "fascinates my mind with its tremen-dous situations—I feel more deeply every year—I can measure the feeling here in the midst of arms [he was at the German army's 1909 manoeuvres] what vile and wicked folly & barbarism it all is."[4] Nevertheless, that was no excuse for not being thoroughly prepared should a rival push things to such a point that war became the only option. Then belligerence, defiance, and preparedness were the only mantles. Churchill held to this formula without wavering, as he was to do later in his career when Nazis and then Communists threatened the peace of the world.

Churchill reveled in the work of First Lord of the Admiralty, fighting for more dreadnoughts and the development of the naval air service, tearing around Britain and the Mediterranean visiting ships, shore establishments, and naval air stations. Whether it was examining the technical elements involved in the procurement of a new shell or conducting the empire's naval business from aboard the thirty-eight-hundred-ton Admiralty yacht *Enchant-ress* (aboard which he spent eight months in his three years as First Lord), Churchill felt hugely fulfilled. He demonstrated his trademark capacity to be involved at all levels of his department's business, and far beyond. On March 26, 1912, he wrote to Clementine that "the electric turrets of the *Invincible* have given so much trouble . . . I had them tested as they have never been tested before—making one gun fire 8 rounds in succession. I stayed in the turret myself to see what happened." Shortly thereafter, he was having himself taken out aboard submarines—"I am getting quite experienced in submarines & the novelty & sense of danger are wearing off. . . . We took the yacht all round the Fleet & the ships looked magnificent. The air is full of aeroplanes, the water black with Dreadnoughts."[5] In his speeches, Churchill made it as clear as possible to the world that Britain would not be outbuilt by any rival power and that an arms race was sheer folly. His speech introducing the naval estimates to the Commons on March 18, 1912, received great applause. In it, he made public a new standard of British naval strength—60 percent above Germany's. The address was a warning to Tirpitz over the heads of the MPs: for every ship Germany added to her navy, Britain would lay down two. But the speech also made it clear that any reduction would be met by proportional reduction and suggested a building "holiday" in 1913. If this were to happen, Churchill said, "The three ships that she [Germany] did not build would therefore automatically wipe out no less than five British potential super-dreadnoughts, and this is more than I expect them to hope to do in a brilliant naval action."[6]

So, with the whirlwind energy for which he was renowned, Churchill set about the Admiralty, innovating, centralizing, interfering, improving, and generally showing the naval world, from top to bottom, that he meant business and did not care if tradition or the top brass were unsettled by his actions. Rigid hierarchy needed to give way to streamlined and intelligent fighting efficiency, and the Board of Admiralty needed to be properly subjected to civilian control. This was hugely important, because Churchill took charge of the Admiralty at a moment of national and international crisis, and of technological and strategic flux. Churchill thought the top ranks of the military were dominated by hidebound, outdated officers to whom the politicians deferred far too easily. Churchill's low

opinion of the upper echelons of the officer corps put him on a collision course with admirals and generals alike. This swelled the ranks
of the anti-Churchill lobby and those prepared to voice their grievances when the going got tough for the overbearing young politician. But this did not deter him. He detested blind veneration of the
military, and the manner in which political masters were expected
to keep out of the business of their nominal military subordinates
goaded him to action. The Admiralty, as he saw it, was hopelessly
out of date in key departments, not least its strategic direction and
leadership, and would be unfit to go to war unless these failings
were remedied.

The admirals used the press, and the naval proclivities of the
king, to try to thwart Churchill's reforms. Often, in these important
prewar years, Churchill encountered "various degrees of naughtiness among the Seals"[7] (the Sea Lords) when he returned from trips
away from the Admiralty. It was quite possible that national survival
depended upon Churchill's ability to shape a more modern navy,
and he longed for the army and navy to be properly subordinated
to civilian politicians and, not surprisingly, saw himself as the most
qualified among them. Asquith, once war had begun, summed up
Churchill's attitude: "His mouth waters at the sight and thought of
K's [Kitchener's] new armies," and asks, " 'Are those glittering com-
mands to be entrusted to dug-out trash bred on the obsolete tactics
of 25 years ago?'"[8]

Churchill's task was formidable. In attempting to reform the navy
from the top down, he took on a huge, powerful, and largely autonomous institution that had not been shaken by defeat in battle and
considered itself exempt from the deliberations of the Committee of
Imperial Defence. His card was marked when he insisted upon the
removal of the First Sea Lord, Admiral Sir Arthur Wilson, because
of his objections to the formation of a Naval War Staff, the central
plank of Churchill's reform program. This was an entirely necessary,
though deeply controversial, move. Illustrating how bad army-navy
cooperation was, and how desperately the forces needed civilian
direction, was Wilson's opposition to the army's plan to transport

seven divisions to France should war with Germany break out: on August 23, 1911, the Admiralty had refused to give an assurance that six divisions could be immediately transported to France if needed. Churchill continued to make bold decisions regarding the command of the navy. When war broke out, he prematurely removed Sir George Callahan as commander of the Home Fleet, replacing him with John Jellicoe, later described by Churchill as "the only man on either side who could lose the war in an afternoon."

Never had a First Lord of the Admiralty taken such hands-on control of the affairs of the navy. Wilson's replacement as First Sea Lord, Sir Francis Bridgeman, lasted little more than a year before Churchill obliged him to retire. Bridgeman had led those resisting Churchill's erosion of the powers of the Sea Lords, objecting to his "peremptory orders" and his practice of sending signals to the fleet without the authority of the boards. Churchill's interference "did him great harm in political as well as naval circles."[9]

Though causing consternation in some quarters, his drive through the Admiralty was met with approval from the other ranks as he continued Admiral Jackie Fisher's policies of improving pay and conditions. Churchill's robust style also won praise among those favoring larger naval budgets, because he was the most insistent minister when it came to arguing his corner in Cabinet and with the Treasury. His belief that the only way to check German expansion was to show that it could never outbuild the Royal Navy led to what Churchill called "polite but deadly" Cabinet arguments over the 1914–15 estimates. His uncompromising demand for a big navy, and his determination to increase British naval superiority over Germany, became the defining aspects of Churchill the politician during these years. He increased annual spending from £39 million to over £50 million. As was always the case with Churchill, qualities that some hated him for were the very foundation of the success that others admired him for. It was a measure of Churchill's journey from social reformer to national guardian that his erstwhile partner, Lloyd George, increasingly became his Cabinet foe, and their friendship, so intense until this point, began to cool. Lloyd George thought that Churchill had been seduced by Grey's "anti-German policy." Responsible as chancellor for limiting the Admiralty's spending, he believed that Churchill's outlook had transformed overnight from little Englander to anti-German warmonger.

Churchill's thirst for innovation was inexhaustible. The Naval War Staff was established at the start of 1912, with divisions devoted to operations, intelligence, and mobilization. He oversaw a major reorganization of the navy; as he told the Commons in March 1912, "The general principle of naval administration to which we adhere—[is] homogeneity of squadrons; simplicity of types and classes; modernity of material; concentration in the decisive theatres; constant and instant readiness for war; reliance upon gun power; reliance upon speed; and, above all, reliance upon 136,000 officers and seamen, the pride of our race."[10] His partnership with Admiral Fisher "produced a great harvest between 1911 and 1913—especially in the field of ship and weapon design."[11]

Importantly, Churchill embraced technological progress at a time of rapid change. He oversaw the fleet's conversion from coal to oil and negotiated the British government's acquisition of a majority shareholding in Anglo-Persian Oil (the future BP); he encouraged the submarine service; he set up a cryptography department that was the forerunner of the Government Code and Cypher School; he introduced a new caliber of heavy gun—the fifteen-inch—ordering a division of five fast battleships bearing them; he encouraged research that contributed to the emergence of the tank as a revolutionary weapon; and he supported with enthusiasm the growth of military aviation and the genesis of the Royal Naval Air Service. As he said in March 1914, addressing a dinner of the Royal Aero Club, "Things are done today which nobody would have thought right or prudent to do twelve months ago or even nine or six months ago."[12] He took up new ideas with enthusiasm and spawned some of his own, from Q-ships to armed merchantmen. Many people sneered at Churchill's fascination with "toys." But as Group Captain Ivor Courtney, one of Churchill's flying instructors, commented, people often saw the importance of them when war came. Critics were then likely to clamor for activity, in contrast to their previous hostility. As a fellow aviator put it shortly after war began, "They have pissed on Churchill's plant [the Naval Air Service] for three years—now they expect it to bloom in a month."[13]

From his final days at the Home Office in 1911, Churchill had been increasingly preoccupied with the need to build a united national front for the clash with Germany that he believed was more than likely to come. He also sought and received Cabinet approval for naval arrangements with France that would enable Britain to withdraw ships from the Mediterranean to home waters in the event of conflict. Between 1911 and 1914, he was often accused of being alarmist, though "he always maintained that it was better to be alarmed before a catastrophe rather than after."[14] As he once put it in the House of Commons, "It is very much better sometimes to have a panic feeling beforehand, and then be quite calm when things happen, than to be extremely calm beforehand and to get into a panic when things happen."[15] He sent letters to the prime minister on all aspects of the fleet and its readiness and supplies, demonstrating his skill at getting lengthy, cogent, well-argued, and informative documents in front of the most important people. It was also indicative of the fact that Churchill believed Asquith had repeatedly promoted him on the basis of their personal correspondence, not just his Cabinet or parliamentary contributions.

The new German naval law of May 1912 confirmed Germany's intention to challenge British supremacy, and this fact slowly sank into the public mind and that of the Opposition. At a meeting of the Committee of Imperial Defence on July 11, 1912, Churchill argued that "the whole character of the German fleet shows that it is designed for aggressive and offensive action of the largest possible character in the North Sea or North Atlantic" and that it was designed for fleet action, not to protect trade routes or colonies. His knowledge of maritime strategy was important in winning the argument to concentrate major vessels in British waters, thus denuding the Mediterranean of sufficient assets to maintain British supremacy there. As he argued, "It should not be supposed that mastery of the seas depends on the simultaneous occupation of every sea. On the contrary it depends upon ability to defeat the strongest battlefleet or combination which can be brought to bear."[16] As he wrote to Haldane in May 1912, "The actual point has been settled long ago by brute force of facts. We cannot possibly hold the Mediterranean or guarantee any of our interests there until we have obtained a decision in the North Sea. . . . It would be very foolish to lose England in safeguarding Egypt."

Owing to the nature of his career, family life had to fit around work, a common enough practice and one made easier by the support of servants and a wife who was capable on the home front. Separation had been a theme in Winston and Clementine's relationship from its first weeks. "My darling I do so want your life to be a full & sweet one. I want it to be worthy of all the beauties of your nature. I am so much centred in my politics that I often feel I must be a dull companion to anyone who is not in the trade."[17] Churchill's engagement with his children was loving but often fleeting. After an evening together, he wrote to Clementine that "I have just seen the PK [Puppy Kitten]. She is flourishing and weighs 10 tons! The nurse says she has written to you about the perambulator. Will you settle what is to be done?" In April 1912, after a flying visit to see the children, he wrote that "both chicks are well and truculent. Diana & I went through the Peter Rabbit picture book together and Randolph gurgled." His immense reserves of energy and interest meant that even in such a lofty position and with such an all-consuming approach to work, he found time for family, hobbies, and flights of fancy. In June 1912, he was taking dancing lessons and suggesting to Clementine that they form a dancing club for their friends in winter.

Churchill recognized the difficulties that his career raised in his marriage and never lost the habit of articulating the depth of his love for his wife and the extent of his reliance upon her. But his work rarely, if ever, suffered because of family constraints. Two letters of October 1913 illustrate the twin pillars of his life. One told Clementine "how lucky I have been—not very gifted where Kats are concerned—I find by right divine the first & best." The very next day, however, he demonstrated his capacity for insensitivity and his obsession with work, blithely reporting on a day spent in aircraft around Sheerness—despite his wife's loathing of his aerial exploits. But it brought out the Unrepentant Toad in him, for he adored flying, and he told her that "it has been as good as one of those old days in the S. African war, & I have lived entirely in the moment, with no care for all these tiresome party politics & searching newspapers, & awkward by-elections, & sulky Orangemen, & obnoxious Cecils and little smugs like Runciman." Clementine hated his aerial expeditions because flight was so dangerous, and Churchill was in fact a senior Cabinet politician, not a stunt man. She did her very best, with various blandishments, to wean him off flying. After he'd confessed to a stint in the air in May 1914, she wrote that she "felt too weak & tired to struggle against it—It is like beating one's head against a stone wall. . . . Goodbye my Dear One—Perhaps if I saw you, I could love and pet you, but you have really been so naughty that I can't do it on paper—I must be 'brought round' first."

Fundamentally, Churchill was aware of his pretensions and was able to get the measure of his own character, even its less appealing facets—even if he made little or no effort to reform. As he wrote to his wife on November 3, 1913, "at times, I think I could conquer everything—& then again I know I am only a weak vain fool." As for the flying, Churchill very reluctantly gave way to his wife, as well as to financial sound sense, given the high cost involved in insuring himself. He moaned to Clementine in June 1914 about the premiums, listing political strain, short-lived parentage, "& of course flying" as reasons why the insurers priced him so highly. On June 6, with some caveats, he agreed to give it up, having "been up" over 140 times and become enthralled by "this fascinating new art."

From 1911 until 1914, Churchill was completely absorbed in naval affairs and matters of national security, though he had occasion to act on the domestic scene when the simmering issue of Irish Home Rule acquired a military dimension. Having become a committed militarist in his new office, his erstwhile bedfellows on the social reform front were left behind, and in consequence, Churchill became isolated from a promising group of admirers and possible followers. This was a shame, particularly when Churchill's reputation (deserved or not) prevented people from understanding his politics. It was clear that with increasing ministerial responsibility, Churchill was becoming more "progressive" on issues such as Irish Home Rule. His experience at the Colonial Office with regard to the postwar settlement of South Africa's problems had provided an excellent object lesson. Reconciliation in South Africa influenced him on Ireland, and he believed that the Irish, as well as the Boers, could "take their place—in a true and indissoluble Union of Empire."[18] In this belief, he not only showed a commendable desire to conciliate and meet the demands of nationalists at least halfway. He also displayed a romantic vision of the British Empire, held throughout his life, that simply did not take account of the opposition to it felt by other people. Speaking in Belfast in February 1912, he tried to square the aspirations of Irish nationalists with the interests of the British Empire: "Would not the arrival of an Irish parliament upon the brilliantly lighted stage of the modern world be an enrichment and an added glory to the treasures of the British Empire?"[19] The fact was that many Irish Catholics, as was the case with the Boers, were, ultimately, irreconcilable, because they were not in favor of British influence in their affairs and did not want to merge their autonomy in what Churchill called "the wider liberties of the British Empire."

Churchill's instinct—that an Irish parliament was the right objective—was clearly correct, even if his hopes of an autonomous Ireland remaining happily within the empire club were not to be realized. When asked in the spring of 1908, "Is Mr. Churchill in favor of Home Rule, meaning an Irish Parliament for the management purely of Irish affairs?" his answer had been, "Yes. Subject to the Imperial Parliament." As First Sea Lord, he toured the country talking about sea power and national security but was also, with the encouragement of the prime minister, the government's main advocate of Irish Home Rule. He was working for an accommodation with the Irish nationalists, particularly at a time when national and imperial unity was so important given the German menace.

Churchill thought his support for Irish Home Rule would revive his liberal credentials. The Irish nationalists, who were key supporters of the Liberal government in the House of Commons, were attempting to cash in on their pivotal parliamentary position by pressing for Home Rule. Churchill's support for Home Rule and his willingness to use the navy to help deal with opponents who acted outside the law enraged Unionists. Churchill ran the gauntlet and visited Belfast in the face of violent protests in January 1912, his life, not for the last time, put at risk by his desire to be on the front line. Clementine bravely accompanied him, and they were greeted by a hostile crowd of ten thousand people outside the Grand Central Hotel. There were further dangers, much closer to home; in the House of Commons chamber, he was struck by the Speaker's copy of the Standing Orders, which drew blood and was thrown by an Ulster MP after Churchill had mockingly waved his handkerchief at the Opposition. The abuse he received over his stand on Ireland was equal to any he ever received, and the damage to his reputation lingered for years.

Determined to ensure that Ulstermen opposed to Home Rule did not hijack the latest Home Rule bill, he ordered the 3rd Battle Squadron to waters off Belfast, in case arms depots were attacked by Ulster Volunteers or in case troops had to be transported from the south to the north. On March 19, 1914, Churchill told the vice admiral commanding the 3rd Battle Squadron to "proceed at once at ordinary speed to Lamlash," while HMS *Gibraltar* and *Royal Arthur* were "to proceed at once to Kingstown Ireland to embark tomorrow 550 Infantry equally divided and to proceed to Dundalk." Two days later, he approved an order to embark field guns on HMS *King Edward VII*, the squadron's flagship. Whatever Churchill's real intent, and although his move received Cabinet approval, he was portrayed as a callous warmonger seeking to provoke the Ulster Volunteers into action that British forces could then smash. Though cast as the villain of the piece, Churchill made it clear that he was standing against "rebellion, organized, avowed, applauded . . . against the ordinary workings of our legislature."[20] The episode appeared to underline Churchill's capacity for finding the wrong way to go about things. While this course of action was considered too soft by some of his Cabinet colleagues, his enemies chose only to highlight the martial aspects of his policy. In reality, Churchill was seeking an honorable path out of the malaise. A conference on Home Rule was summoned by the king in July 1914 and a bill put to Parliament. But then war came, and on September 15, 1914, Asquith announced that the Home Rule bill had been suspended.

WAR

As 1914 unfolded, Churchill remained vigilant regarding the need to prioritize naval construction. He had to fight hard to keep his Cabinet colleagues onside and to secure the funds necessary for building new ships. "I have had another long dose of Winston today and am rather late," Asquith wrote to Venetia Stanley following a crisis over naval estimates.[21] On March 17, 1914, Churchill introduced his naval estimates in the Commons. The *Telegraph* called his two-and-a-half-hour speech "the longest and perhaps the most weighty and eloquent speech to which the House of Commons have listened during the present generation." His message was simple. Other Great Powers were building advanced navies. The empire and the trade of the world and wealth won by Britain over the centuries had to be protected. And this would cost money. "We have got all we want in territory, but our claim to be left in undisputed enjoyment of vast and splendid possessions, largely acquired by war and maintained by force, is one which often seems less reasonable to others than to us."[22]

Churchill relished the prospect of war with Germany—if peace could not be preserved. When on July 28, it seemed as if war might be averted at the last moment, he said moodily to Asquith that it looked as if they were in for "a bloody peace" after all. Venetia Stanley wrote that he had "got on all his warpaint."[23] As war became imminent, Churchill put into effect the Admiralty's war plans. At the Grand Review of the Fleet at Spithead in July 1914, over four hundred Royal Navy vessels of all classes had massed together, the ultimate symbol of British naval power and intent should war come. It was, in Churchill's words, "the greatest assemblage of naval power ever witnessed in the history of the world." On July 28, a letter captured his conflicting thoughts: "Everything tends towards catastrophe and collapse. I am interested, geared up and happy. Is it not horrible to be built like that? The preparations have a hideous fascination for me. I pray God to forgive me for such fearful moods of levity. Yet I would do my best for peace, nothing would induce me wrongly to strike the blow."[24] On this fateful day, as news was awaited from the continent, Churchill strolled in St. James's Park and watched a pair of black swans and their cygnets. Two of the navy's three battle fleets were still at Portland following the Spithead Review, and on the following day, Asquith gave his permission for the First Battle Fleet to move from Portland to its battle station in the North Sea, the "vast concourse of warships," as Churchill wrote, passing "safely through the Straits of Dover without lights on the night of 29 July."[25] "We may now picture this great Fleet," he was later to write in *The World Crisis*, "with its flotillas and cruisers, steaming slowly out of Portland Harbour, squadron by squadron, scores of gigantic castles of steel wending their way across the misty, shining sea, like giants bowed in anxious thought."[26] On July 31, he told Clementine that "at any moment now the stroke may fall," though his letter also touched on domestic concerns, including his consternation that the month's household expenses had topped £175.

Beaverbrook and F. E. Smith were dining with him at Admiralty House on August 1, when they heard that Germany had declared war on Russia. "He was not depressed, he was not elated; he was not surprised. . . . He went straight out like a man going to a well-accustomed job. In fact he had foreseen everything that was going to happen so far that his temperament was in no way upset by the realization of his forecast."[27] As the British ultimatum to Germany expired at midnight on the evening of August 3–4, 1914, Margot

Asquith saw Churchill at Downing Street: "I saw Winston Churchill with a happy face striding towards the double doors of the Cabinet room," she recorded.[28] And who could blame him? While some always found Churchill's relish for war tasteless, it was a quality his country sorely needed in the unprecedented trials that were to come. As he told the National Liberal Club, the government entered into the war "with a full realization of the sufferings, losses, disappointments, vexations and anxieties, and of the appalling and sustaining exertions which would be entailed upon us by our action. The war will be long and sombre."[29] Now that it had come, Churchill relished it. He was exhilarated. A few months into the conflict, Margot Asquith heard him say, "My God! This, this is living History. Everything we are doing and saying is thrilling—it will be read by a thousand generations, think of *that*!"[30] In August 1914, he had the Royal Navy as prepared as possible for a struggle that would probably be a lengthy one. Over a thousand vessels, in ports and on sea lanes across the globe, were under his command. At the center of this unrivaled armada were fifty-three battleships, representing the Royal Navy's superiority over the German fleet.

Now that the moment had come to put plans into action, Churchill did so with zest and excitement. Without fuss, the navy transported six divisions of the British Expeditionary Force to France within two weeks of Britain's going to war. As well as escorting troopships and merchantmen, the navy assumed its time-honored role as a blockade force. By the end of September, 50,000 Indian troops had been safely delivered from Bombay and Karachi to Marseilles, and by mid-October, 25,000 Canadians had crossed the Atlantic without loss. "This was a period of great anxiety to us," Churchill wrote. "All the most fateful possibilities were open. We were bound to expect a military descent on our coasts . . . or a naval raid into the Channel to cut down the transports, or a concentrated submarine attack upon those vessels crammed with men."[31]

Blockade was an effective means of waging economic warfare, though Churchill hungered for more tangible and glorious military achievements, a product of his impatience, his love of the dramatic action, and his weather eye on the annals of history. He was also infected with the naval traditions of his country, the Nelsonian spirit, and the desire to "engage the enemy more closely" at any given opportunity heavily emphasized in schoolrooms and popular literature. This was a weakness on Churchill's part, as the exercise of sea power does not necessarily require brutal engagement with the enemy's battle fleet. Strangling the enemy by blockade and interdicting its merchant shipping was less dramatic, but by guaranteeing safe global communications and contact with the army in France while denying Germany imports and confining its vaunted battle fleet to its home ports, the Royal Navy was doing its job. Churchill was not alone in his hunger for decisive action; it was the core of the navy's tradition and planning, and the navy still had an impractical obsession with attacking Germany's northern seaboards, including those in the Baltic. It also had "unrealistic expectation of a Nelsonian pitched battle that the Germans would offer and lose."[32] The Battle of Heligoland in late August kept the High Seas Fleet cautiously in its harbors, however, glowering at the Grand Fleet across the North Sea.

Churchill's desire to be in control made him more involved in the day-to-day running of the fleet than had been the case with any previous First Lord of the Admiralty, and as the head of the navy, he was associated with failure as well as success. The early months of war brought a series of naval blunders. Matters were not always helped by Churchill's intrusion into the operational sphere or by indifferent staff work. The escape of German battleships from the Adriatic to Constantinople and the bombardment of Hartlepool and Scarborough (December 1914) were bad for the navy's prestige, only somewhat offset by British victories at the battles of the Falklands (December 8, 1914) and Dogger Bank (January 24, 1915). The problem was that in the early months of the war, the Admiralty suffered from some appalling breakdowns of communication, and Churchill's personal involvement with detailed orders sent to fleet units gave him more association with these errors than he need have had. In the operation that failed to catch the *Goeben* and

Breslau, the orders were written in Churchill's own hand. But they were not passed through the War Staff and served to exacerbate the crossed wires of command that enabled these two valuable ships to escape from under the Royal Navy's nose. There were then the orders designed to remove the "live-bait squadron"—a collection of elderly cruisers operating off the German coast—from unacceptable danger. They were enacted too late, and the ships were consequently destroyed, another example of the incompetence of the Naval War Staff and a measure of Churchill's inability to make it fit for purpose. Nevertheless, Churchill's instinctive lust for action was tempered, as the months passed, by recognition that to enforce *inaction* on the enemy was a great strategic achievement in itself.

A key problem was that the Naval War Staff was "too new and inexperienced to be of much use. Its fumbling hand can be traced in most of the navy's early disasters and mishaps."[33] To concentrate power around him, Churchill formed the Admiralty War Group, which met at least once a day and comprised the First Sea Lord, the chief of the War Staff and the secretary of the Admiralty. In Best's opinion, the "system was as efficient an instrument for directing worldwide naval operations as could have been devised in the circumstances." But "when things went wrong, Churchill was in an exposed position and attracted bad publicity."[34] When things went well (meaning nothing much was happening), the public found little to capture its attention. Churchill was involved to an extraordinary degree in the whole management of the war. His actions were closely scrutinized by the train of critics whom he had collected over the years. The Tories and the Tory press hated him and were ready to blame him exclusively for almost anything. Their cause was aided by judicious leaks from Churchill's opponents in the Admiralty. But although short-term setbacks outnumbered successes, what mattered was that the instrument Churchill had done so much to fashion proved, in the long run, invincible.

Churchill's abilities, and his ability to dominate those around him, could have a negative impact. He was simply too persuasive a debater when decisions were being made, and this could allow things to go forward that sterner or better marshaled resistance might have prevented or moderated. As Stephen Roskill puts it, the admirals were at a disadvantage because "they lacked capacity in dealing with so loquacious and argumentative a person as Churchill—namely they lacked the ability to state a case concisely and clearly and then to sustain it against hostile dialectic—an art in which Churchill excelled."[35] This was a problem. Churchill said that "experts should be on tap but not on top." He didn't like being *told* by experts but wanted to be persuaded by them. But there were few people around him who were robust enough to stand before him and get their point across sufficiently, and few political colleagues with sufficient expertise to contribute significantly to policy formulation alongside him.

A theme of Churchill's role in the war was his frequent engagement—or interference—in matters of land warfare, reflecting the fact that he was, after all, a trained soldier and had great confidence in both his strategic acumen and skills in "war direction." Clementine told him off for not confining his activities to the war at sea. Referring to a forthcoming trip to see General Sir John French in France in September 1914, she wrote: "I wish you didn't crave to go . . . you are the only young and vital person in the Cabinet. It is really wicked of you not to be swelling with pride at being 1st Lord of the Admiralty during the greatest War since the beginning of the World." His regular visits to see General French really got under Kitchener's collar. Churchill made unusual decisions based on his belief in his own ability to shape the war and his insatiable desire to be involved and to innovate, even when the scaffolding necessary to support such innovation did not yet exist. He developed what amounted to a private army when he converted the Naval Reserve into the Royal Naval Division, and with this inexperienced force of about fifteen thousand men sought to play a role on land. One of his first opportunities came when Lord Kitchener, fearing Zeppelin raids, asked Churchill to take over the air defense of Britain. He did so gladly and to accomplish the task deployed Royal Naval Air Service squadrons to France, their bases defended by Rolls-Royce armored cars and marines.

A frequent visitor to France and the front line throughout the war, in October 1914 he took over the defenses of the Belgian city of Antwerp with men of the Royal Naval Division. In September the Belgians had appealed for thirty thousand troops, and Kitchener saw a direct danger to Britain if Antwerp were lost. The city was an important coastal point for the Allies to try to hold as they raced the Germans to the sea. Incredibly, for several days Churchill was in sole command of the city, dominating the Belgian king and his ministers as well as senior soldiers and sailors, supervising the disposition of his marines and darting about without fear of shot or shell.

Writing in March 1918, the king of the Belgians said that Churchill's intervention "rendered great service to us" and that "those who deprecate it simply do not understand the history of the war in those early days. Only one man of all your people had the prevision of what the loss of Antwerp would entail, and that man was Mr. Churchill."[36]

Though this action achieved some military advantage, and Churchill was only away for four days, his critics claimed that it confirmed his unsuitability for high office. They described the defense of Antwerp as a pointless adventure when the First Lord should have been concentrating on the affairs of the navy. Some, however, claimed that the five days for which the port was held were of great value to the Allies. It was a move approved by Kitchener and Grey, the ministers for war and foreign affairs, respectively. During the crisis of the moment, in early October 1914, when units needed to be rapidly mustered, the Royal Naval Division was the only unit available, and Churchill's offer to go to Belgium was readily accepted by his colleagues.

Churchill was saddened by the misrepresentation of his efforts at Antwerp. But some defended him. The *Observer* noted that Churchill had been called an amateur. "That happens to be just what he is not. He has seen war; he has written about war; he has studied war."[37] He was more familiar with modern warfare than all his civilian peers, had attended British and European maneuvers annually for years, and was a member of the Committee of Imperial Defence.

The episode showcased his manifest thirst for action, and his occasional lapses of political judgment. He went so far as to telegraph the prime minister to say that he would willingly give up the Admiralty if he could be given high command in the field, and Kitchener was prepared to make him a lieutenant general. Read out to the Cabinet, however, Churchill's suggestion was greeted with what Asquith described as "Homeric laughter."[38] To an extent, this was deserved, the offer demonstrating Churchill's genuine inability to see what it was in him and his behavior that so maddened, amused, and enraged other people. But it also demonstrated his unique qualities. No other politician was as confident as Churchill in his ability to shape the fighting; no other politician was so ready to ignore the opinions of generals and admirals and trust in his own military and strategic abilities.

Nevertheless, the brief campaign served to strengthen the arm of those seeking to portray Churchill as a rash adventurer and attached Churchill's name to military defeat, a connection that was to solidify disturbingly during 1915. Though it might have held up the German advance for precious days—a not inconsiderable benefit—the episode highlighted the Naval Division's lack of training and equipment and ensured that many of them exited the war as casualties or prisoners. It is doubtful whether it was correct, given Churchill's political position, for him to be there and not in London, and offering to give up control of Britain's greatest weapon showed a lack of judgment. Senior naval commanders viewed the escapade with contempt. Asquith and Lloyd George joined the criticism of their wayward colleague, because for them the episode underlined Churchill's impulsiveness and belligerence and weakened their trust in him.

One of the major problems that beset Churchill's Admiralty tenure was the unsatisfactory relationship between senior military figures and their civilian bosses. For too long the tail had wagged the dog, and this continued into the war, notably in the persons of

Herbert Horatio Kitchener and Jackie Fisher. Churchill had already disposed of Wilson and Bridgeman as First Sea Lords. In October 1914, Prince Louis of Battenberg was forced to resign from the position because of mounting anti-German public pressure. To replace him Churchill recalled Admiral Jackie Fisher, who had been First Sea Lord between 1904 and 1910, during which time he earned fame as a major sponsor of naval development and reform, most famously associated with the launch of the revolutionary Dreadnought-class battleships. Churchill held him in unusual reverence and was to continue to do so even after Fisher had nearly ruined him. Thus Churchill acquired, as a close colleague and immediate subordinate, a man of equally domineering personality with pronounced and firmly held views on naval matters and the extra ballast of years of experience and public renown. To make matters more difficult, Fisher rather liked the Kitchener model of political-military fusion and envied his almost supreme authority in all matters relating to the army. Kitchener was in political control of the army as secretary of state for war, a position from which he could dominate his civilian Cabinet colleagues. This was just the type of monster Churchill was intent upon slaying as he strove to subject the military to proper civilian control.

Churchill and Fisher worked well together in many ways, though Fisher found it extremely difficult to accept the extent of his political master's involvement in naval affairs. First Lords were supposed to provide cover and representation at the political level, and let the experts get on with the actual business of deploying fleets and devising strategy. But, as we have seen, Churchill considered himself the best military expert he knew and believed the stakes to be far too great for the higher direction of war to be left in the hands of antediluvian senior officers. It has been argued that during this period, Fisher was at least partly deranged, and his stream-of-consciousness letters, effusive and heavily capitalized ("hortatory, passionate and adjectival," in Roskill's words[39]), certainly lend support to those who make this case. His letters reveal peacock vanity, a need to feel right about everything and to brag about his ability to clip the wings of opponents and exercise a controlling influence over colleagues and peers. His attitude to Churchill veered from an intensity approaching love to jealousy and resentment at his interference. Fisher also bemoaned the fact that Churchill was "always *convincing* me." For his part, Churchill was irresistibly attracted to Fisher, an attraction that was to do him great harm and rekindle concerns about his judgment. The Churchill-Fisher relationship, putting two domineering and stubborn characters head-to-head, was bound to result in fireworks if there were serious disagreements or the war went badly. An attempt to aid Russia and break the stalemate of the Western Front was to do just that.

THE DARDANELLES AND GALLIPOLI

Clement Attlee believed there was "only one brilliant strategic idea" during the First World War, "and that was Winston's; the Dardanelles." In Churchill's words, it was born of the search for an alternative "to chewing barbed wire" on the Western Front. The Dardanelles campaign appealed to Churchill because it offered the prospect of a strategic masterstroke overcoming the Western Front stasis. As he sardonically predicted, "neither side will have the strength to penetrate the other's lines in the Western theatre . . . although no doubt hundreds of thousands of men will be spent to satisfy the military mind on the point."[40]

Despite this, history has cast Churchill as the primary culprit for a military blunder that cost thousands of lives, a great flanking initiative that, tragically, ended in replicating the stalemate of Flanders rather than bringing rapid victories. Churchill's tenure at the Admiralty would have been longer, and far less tarnished retrospectively, had it not been for the Russian government's appeal for support against the Central Powers. This led Lord Kitchener, secretary of state for war and national soldier-hero, to advocate a demonstration by the Royal Navy around the Dardanelles, the narrow, strategically placed strait separating the eastern Mediterranean from the Black Sea. Known to the ancient world as the Hellespont, this stretch of water (forty miles long and between one and four miles wide) separated Asian Turkey and the nearest part of European Turkey, the Gallipoli peninsula.

It was inevitable that Churchill would be interested in such a proposal. It had about it all the elements of "doing something"—and something dramatic and potentially very important—that appealed to both his vision and his restlessness. It also promised significant martial spoils; as Churchill said, "Beyond those few miles of ridge and scrub . . . lie the downfall of a hostile empire, the destruction of an enemy's fleet and army, the fall of a world-famous capital, and probably the accession of powerful Allies."[41] But despite the glimpse of glittering prizes that the prospect of a campaign in this region offered, Churchill was no fool, and he replied that a naval operation was less desirable than one involving both the navy *and* the army, so that territory could be occupied—maybe even including Constantinople—rather than simply having defenses destroyed by naval gunfire. But Kitchener was adamant that no troops were available and again asked that a purely naval operation be considered, and this army-navy dissonance was to be the crux of the disaster that unfolded.

Churchill argued his naval case before the War Council on January 13, 1915, "with great eloquence and forensic skill."[42] The outcome was the order from Asquith to the Admiralty to prepare for a naval expedition to bombard and take the Gallipoli peninsula, with Constantinople as its objective. After this, Fisher began to waver—not about operations in the Dardanelles per se, but because of his concern lest too many ships be taken from the North Sea. On January 28, he put his objections to the prime minister. Asquith decided to carry on regardless. Later that day, Churchill and Fisher conferred, and the Admiral gave his consent for things to proceed (as Fisher later told the Dardanelles Commission): "I went in the whole hog, *totus porcus*."[43]

Thus an ill-made plan was put into operation, once Churchill had checked with the commander of British naval forces in the eastern Mediterranean, Admiral Carden, who believed that it might be possible to force a passage through the Dardanelles using a sufficiently large number of ships. It was hardly an enthusiastic green light, but Churchill had the considered opinion of the local officer commanding. The Admiralty War Group considered Carden's list of requirements and thought they could be met and even exceeded. Churchill now became a keen advocate of the proposal, and though he was later forced to carry far too much of the blame for the ensuing military disaster, it is here that his culpability was most evident. From this moment onward, Churchill's imagination became fixed upon a strategic masterstroke that might knock the Ottomans out of the war and keep wavering nations out of the clutches of the Central Powers, all delivered by battleships sailing through the Dardanelles—shooting up Turkish defenses, and eliciting a revolutionary response in the Ottoman capital itself. Such a prospect was worth considerable sacrifice, but Churchill's enthusiasm overrode more cautious considerations. "I shall be the greatest man in Europe," he said, if the Dardanelles were forced. His enthusiasm steamrollered others into assent.

But no matter how powerful and persuasive an advocate Churchill was, war strategy and government policy were not concentrated in his hands alone; it was a collective Cabinet decision, and Cabinet colleagues (and indeed the head of the navy) could have resigned in protest. It was the War Council that agreed to the minute from the prime minister directing the Admiralty "to prepare for a naval expedition in February 1915 to bombard and take the Gallipoli Peninsula with Constantinople as its objective." It should have been obvious, in Stephen Roskill's opinion, that the navy alone could do neither of these things. The naval advisers had been less keen than Churchill but at this stage were safe in the knowledge that the operation *could be broken off.* The prime minister and other political members of the War Council, understandably, were "dazzled by the possibilities of success" offered by this innovative operation away from the Western Front.

While Churchill might be seen as the driving force behind the attempt and failure to force the Dardanelles by warships, he was

not nearly so closely associated with the dispiriting Gallipoli stalemate that followed and that cost the lives of 46,000 Allied troops.
But, in the public mind, he was. In fact, from March 1915, Churchill
was sidelined by the War Council, as the army took over. While
Churchill was a part of the disaster, its causes lay in the inadequa-
cies of the system of civil-military decision making, the poverty of
strategic thinking, and a general acceptance of very high casualty
rates. Churchill was the "chief instigator of the [naval] campaign
and . . . it was his pressure that prevented the naval attack from
being broken off," though in Roskill's words, "the contemporary
obloquy heaped on his head now seems to have been very harsh
and excessive."[44]

On March 18, 1915, Admiral de Robeck, Carden's replacement,
began the naval attack. It was less successful than had been anticipated, the navy facing particularly unpleasant obstacles in the form
of not only Turkish gun batteries but also minefields. After losing
three battleships, the admiral halted and refused to renew the attack.
Thus the Churchill phase of the operation ended. The War Council
(a committee of the full Cabinet, supported by experts, to which the
Cabinet had effectively delegated responsibility for the war effort)
now decided to mount a combined army and navy operation, an
expeditionary force under Churchill's old friend General Sir Ian
Hamilton arriving on the Gallipoli peninsula on April 25, 1915. It
didn't take long for it to become obvious that the army was pinned
down on small and inadequately defended coastal bridgeheads.
Churchill meanwhile supported the campaign by dispatching
more naval resources. But he was always frustrated by Kitchener's
refusal to send more soldiers, and the two wrangled over the dispatch of the British 29th Division. Kitchener was determined to
minimize the need for land operations and had a low opinion of
Turkish morale. Churchill protested in vain to the War Council:
Kitchener "dominated absolutely at this time," as he put it.[45]

The bombshell for Churchill arrived on May 15, when Fisher
resigned as First Sea Lord. This was just what Churchill's enemies
needed. The knives were out, and the evolving stalemate in the

Dardanelles—not yet a "failure" or a "fiasco" but still ongoing—had sharpened them. Churchill was too closely associated with the campaign to avoid being regarded as its dominant figure, even though the entire Cabinet and the defense chiefs, led by the prime minister, shared collective responsibility. But the connection was easy to forge in the minds of the narrow political elite that ruled Britain and, through the press, in the minds of the general public. The young and bumptious military adventurer had ridden roughshod over the country's senior military men, and the results were there for all to see. This came on the back of a well-developed anti-Churchill narrative—a crime sheet that already bore the names of Tonypandy, Sidney Street, Ulster, and Antwerp. As Sir Henry Wilson put it to Bonar Law, "A man who can plot the Ulster Pogrom, plan Antwerp and carry out the Dardanelles fiasco is worth watching."[46] Churchill had no personal following in the Liberal Party and was the cause of jealousy among Cabinet colleagues, who felt excluded from the Asquith-Churchill-Kitchener triumvirate that appeared to be making all the big decisions about the war. Churchill always maintained that more resolute action—more troops, especially—would have turned disastrous stalemate into glorious victory. "We were separated by very little from complete success," he told the Dardanelles Commission. Fisher, he believed, used uncertainty at the Dardanelles to make a bid for supreme naval power. "Considering that he had agreed to every step taken and had issued every order, it seems to me his conduct was rather treacherous," he wrote.[47]

What transformed a delicate situation into a disaster for Churchill was that the prime minister was about to form a coalition government, his position progressively weakened by military setbacks and the breaking news of the shells shortage (and he himself weakened by news that the love of his life was to marry a close colleague). On May 20, 1915, Sir George Riddell saw Churchill at the Admiralty. "I am finished!" Churchill said. "Not finished at forty, with your remarkable powers?" "Yes, finished in respect of all I care for—waging war, the defeat of the Germans."[48] In forming a coalition (a move Churchill approved of), the incoming Tories made

Churchill's removal from the Admiralty the price of their cooperation, a dread fact that slowly dawned upon him. Thus Churchill
was dumped from the War Cabinet and into the honorific post
of chancellor of the Duchy of Lancaster, an obscure and virtually
powerless ministerial appointment. ("What is a duchy and where is
Lancaster?" a newspaper photo-cartoon had Churchill asking.) His
salary abruptly fell from £4,000 to £2,000 per annum, his reputation in tatters.

Lesser men would not have recovered from this apparent political interment, and it devastated Churchill. His answer was to brood
and expostulate, but not to give in, and to seek redemption and solace through active service and a calming new hobby, painting. His
family and friends worried for him—"I thought he would die of
grief," his wife said. His mother "was in a state of despair at the idea
of her brilliant son being relegated to the trenches."[49] His enemies
viewed his downfall with glee, believing it served him right for his
egotism and overzealous management of the affairs of war rather
than the affairs of state.[50]

Churchill's fall was spectacular. Undoubtedly he was a scapegoat
for Gallipoli, particularly unfairly because his dominant role ended
with the initial naval attack. Kitchener had demanded it, the prime
minister had sanctioned it, and British decision making was governed by the iron rule of collective responsibility. The prime minister was culpable, as primus inter pares, for weakness and inactivity
and for allowing Kitchener to dominate military decision making
(for example, repeatedly blocking conscription, a policy Churchill
knew was inevitable). In the execution of the Dardanelles and Gallipoli operations, once the decision had been taken, the War Office
was responsible for the campaign on land. Admiral Fisher, if indeed
it was the case that he never liked the plan, kept quiet when he
should have spoken up and came later to back it enthusiastically
before withdrawing his support. But Churchill carried the can and,
in the mind of many people, still does.

For some time he withdrew into his family, which had had to
vacate Admiralty House and decamp to Cromwell Road, South

Kensington, to live with Lady Gwendeline Churchill, wife of Winston's brother, who was serving with the army in Gallipoli. At the family's weekend retreat on a farm in Hascombe in Surrey, in "a delightful valley," as Churchill wrote, with a garden that "gleamed with summer jewellery," he first encountered the hobby that was to remain a major recreation for the rest of his life. One June day in 1915, he noticed Gwendeline sketching. This arrested his deep contemplation, and after studying her for a while, he borrowed her brush, and then her son's paint box. He was a quick learner and soon produced a charming study of his sister-in-law in the cottage garden. Violet Bonham Carter saw Churchill at work and wrote that "as he painted, his tensions relaxed, his frustration evaporated. . . . I was suddenly aware that this was the only occupation that I had ever seen him practice [sic] in silence . . . rapt in intense appraisal, observation, assessment."[51]

The question for Churchill's restless mind was what to do next. His sadness and depression were profound, mixed with anger, sorrow, and frustration at remaining in government in a sinecure office shorn of all power to direct the war effort. After leaving the Admiralty, he was still a member of the War Council and the War Cabinet, though his counsel was unheeded. As he put it:

> I knew everything but could do nothing. . . . At a moment when every fibre of my being was inflamed to action, I was forced to remain a spectator of the tragedy, placed cruelly in a front seat. And then it was that the Muse of Painting came to my rescue. . . . I do not know how I should have got through those horrible months from May till November, when I resigned from the Administration, had it not been for this great new interest.[52]

It is easy to see why painting captivated a man so completely possessed by his work as a politician and who found himself out of power and with "long hours of utterly unwanted leisure." "One forgets utterly the work of the past or the worry of the future. . . . I know of nothing which, without exhausting the body, more entirely absorbs the mind." His paintings were characterized by vivid colors, sun and stone, and greenery bursting from canvases capturing country scenes, garden days, and the color of travel, particularly in the Mediterranean.

But despite the superficial distraction of this newfound hobby, he remained wretched at heart. He did not get the Ministry of Munitions position when it became available, remaining resentful and depressed. As he wrote to his brother, Jack, "Is it not damnable that I should be denied all real scope to serve this country in this tremendous hour? . . . Asquith reigns, supine, sodden and supreme." In November 1915, when the government officially abandoned the Gallipoli campaign, Churchill felt obliged to resign his Cabinet position.

Churchill was at a loss as to what best to do. His wife and mother fretted for him throughout the painful months of 1915, Clementine protesting fiercely to the prime minister. As his mother realized, Churchill craved danger in order to ease his own pain. He felt the urge to join the fighting in France, a yearning for catharsis through active service and revulsion at the prospect of sitting idly in the political wings following the Gallipoli debacle. Naturally, Churchill imagined that if he were to get into uniform, his talents would best be employed in a senior position. He hoped for command of operations in East Africa; General French all but promised him command of a brigade (though Churchill thought an entire army a more appropriate use of his talents). The prime minister, however, vetoed this unseemly elevation, which would have seen Churchill promoted from a Territorial Army major to a Regular Army brigadier general. This would have been wrong, even if Churchill's own estimate of his talent was correct: an example of rank nepotism and the advantage of being a member of the ruling elite. But the episode greatly embarrassed Churchill and made him very angry with Asquith, and it was in no small measure Clementine's influence during this period that persuaded him to temper his rage and keep lines of communication open with the man who was, after all, still prime minister. If ever Churchill entered the wilderness, it was surely now.

TO THE TRENCHES

Whatever one's view of Churchill, it can hardly be denied that his decision to give up a position in the British government to go to the lethal environment of the Western Front was a remarkable and unprecedented act of courage. Churchill gave up his government post, and with it the remainder of his government income. He trained with the Grenadier Guards and was given command of the 6th Battalion, Royal Scots Fusiliers. On November 18, 1915, he crossed the Channel to join his pre-1914 yeomanry regiment of the Oxfordshire Hussars, was met on the quay by a car, and taken to GHQ, where he dined with the commander in chief, General French. Though this was a reception based upon his status as a senior politician, he was soon sharing the trenches with the common soldier, observing, as he told the Commons in May 1916, "one of the clearest and grimmest class distinctions ever drawn in this world—the distinction between the trench and the nontrench population."[53] His home was to be "among filth and rubbish" and "graves built into the defenses and scattered about promiscuously," as he told Clementine.[54] Despite the extreme danger of the Western Front, Churchill was not one to suffer discomforts if they could possibly be moderated. He sent letters to Clementine requesting specific items—a periscope, a sheepskin sleeping bag, a leather waistcoat, face towels, sardines, chocolate, and a big beefsteak pie. Brandy, cigars, and a tin bath with copper boiler followed. A "most divine and glorious sleeping bag has arrived," he wrote, "and I spent last night in one long purr!"[55] He took to life in the trenches like a duck to water. "I am very happy here," he wrote to Clementine, "I did not know what release from care meant." On November 23, he wrote that he had "lost all interest in the outer world and no longer worry about it or its stupid newspapers."

It was not, however, to be a release that lasted for long. His letters show that he was still self-absorbed and yearning for a return to political power, and he was not convincing when he wrote of "fate" or of being a small player in an enormous game, especially given that he had struggled so hard to reach the heights of British political life. There had been a lot of speculation about whether Churchill was to get a brigade or a battalion. General French was adamant that he should have a brigade at once; Clementine wrote, "I hope so much my Darling that you may still decide to take a battalion first," ever a brake on her husband's overweening ambition and always seeking to mediate the way in which others would perceive his actions.

Churchill remained bullish, intent on rejoining the political fray as soon as he could. He instructed his wife (in one of his more selfish passages) to "keep in touch with Curzon & others. Don't fail to keep the threads in your fingers. Let me know who you see." He insisted that Clementine marshal her social contacts in order to benefit him, even to the extent of decreeing how she was to conduct herself in the company of certain key individuals. On Asquith: "Make no change except a greater reserve about me & my affairs"; on January 13, 1916, after Clementine had met the maligned prime minister, he complained: "You do not tell me in your letter what the PM said. You only say he said a lot. But I should like a <u>verbatim</u> report"; January 19: "I should like you to make the seeing of my friends a regular business." But then a break in the clouds of ambition and self-absorption the following day: "I wrote a miauling letter yesterday, & I expect the Kat will be flustered by my directives to her to keep in touch with so many people. Do only what comes easily & naturally to you my darling."[57]

He fulminated against Kitchener and Asquith: "My scorn for Kitchener is intense. If they evacuate [Gallipoli] in disaster—all the facts shall come out. They will be incredible to the world. The reckoning will be heavy & I shall make sure it is exacted" (December 8). Churchill cast himself and the actions in which he played a part in a dramatic, almost heroic light. His letters reveal the extent of his hurt, as well as his self-obsession. On December 15, he wrote that "the hour of Asquith's punishment & Kitchener's exposure draws near. The wretched men have nearly wrecked our chances. It may fall for me to strike the blow. I shall do so without compunction." But, at that moment, this wounded beast was a soldier sitting in a muddy trench, no longer a man in power. Meanwhile, the men in power could thwart him, even ignore him; though he felt sure that command of the 56th Brigade was coming his way, Asquith would have none of it.

Despite his unbalanced state of mind at this juncture, Churchill's politically skilled wife encouraged him not to burn bridges and, specifically, in hoping for an eventual renovation of his ministerial career, to write "private interesting friendly letters" to Asquith. Clementine helped Churchill curb his excesses and corrected his sometimes defective political antennae. He appreciated this, even though he never gave up believing that on most things—no matter how they turned out—he was right, and believing that his impatience and impetuosity (while sometimes damaging) were fundamental to his success. On January 7, 1916, he told Clementine that "the beauty and strength of your character, & the sagacity of your judgment are more realized by me every day. I ought to have followed yr counsels in my days of prosperity. Only sometimes they are too negative. I should have made nothing if I had not made mistakes."[57] During this dark period in Churchill's life, he managed to deal with (and limit) the extent of his personal frustration and hurt in order to perform as an officer to the satisfaction of those who served with him. This was all the more remarkable given the frightening and dangerous circumstances. He also retained a vital sense of perspective. On April 10, he added a "pps" to his letter to Clementine: "I must reopen my letter to tell you that quite a good mouse has also paid me a visit just now. I have been watching the little beast reconnoitring the floor of this cave with the utmost skill daring & composure."

While it did not disappear, Churchill's great resentment receded as he knuckled down to soldiering. On February 13, 1916, he reminisced in a letter to Clementine on the time a mere year ago "when all was hope at the Dardanelles & I looked forward to a very wide sphere of triumphant activity. Everything is changed now— only the old block [Asquith] continues solid & supine." Churchill's battalion was soon in the front line and, from an initial reception of suspicion and resentment, he quickly won the confidence and affection of his men. At first, the men were "naturally rather embarrassed at having a kind of large fish in a very small puddle" as Churchill put it, accurately if immodestly, in a letter to his wife on February 10, 1916. They were also, frankly, hostile. A "mutinous spirit" grew when the battalion heard that it was to have Churchill beamed in to run it.[58] Yet, in a flash, Churchill changed morale to an almost unbelievable degree. Winning the affection of his men was no small feat and demonstrated Churchill's ability to get on with soldiers and take his share of discomfort while demonstrating a high degree of personal bravery and genuine concern for the soldiers' welfare. The soldiers were impressed by his indifference to danger and willingness to endure hardship, and he made thirty-six reconnoiters into no-man's-land, "like a baby elephant" roaming at night in the deadly ground between the opposing trenches.[59] Churchill impressed his men by his attention to their welfare, and to detail, such as his dissertation on the laying of sandbags, complete with illustrations. He deserves immense credit for switching from high office to nighttime raids on German trenches, showing rare qualities for a politician and a most impressive ability to adapt and suffer stoically. His battalion was stationed on the French-Belgian border at Ploegsteert (anglicized as "Plug Street"), and some early Churchill paintings record the scenery.

While encouraged by Clementine and friends to stay in the trenches for a suitable period, so as not to give his detractors the chance to label it a tawdry stunt, he was understandably anxious to reenter the Whitehall fray. As he wrote on January 6, 1916, "I do all I can with zest: but I must confess to many spells of emptiness & despondency at the narrow sphere in which I work & the severely restricted horizon." He did, however, very briefly get "his" brigade; in early February 1916, the brigadier was away for a day, and so, as he wrote to Clementine, he was "in command of 5 battalions & 4,000 yards of front." He was still a member of Parliament with political duties to perform. Never for a moment did he give up his appetite for politics and a role in directing the nation's war effort. He was also desperate to clear his name of the stain of Gallipoli.

Even while in the trenches, he found opportunities to return to London and speak in parliamentary debates. Some he won, some he lost, as when he called for Fisher's return to the Admiralty, a spectacular goal of his own. He had learned that there was to be a parliamentary debate on the naval estimates on March 7–8, 1916. His powerful speech wove its magic, growing in force, but the advocacy of Fisher broke the spell, and derision swept the chamber. Churchill was stunned and humiliated by the ridicule that followed and wrote to Clementine on March 13 that "you have seen me very weak & foolish & mentally infirm this week." But he still hankered after "war direction." As he reasoned on March 22, "I have a recognized position in British politics acquired by years of public work,—I cannot exclude myself from these discussions [about the war] or divest myself of responsibilities concerning them." He was, he wrote, "so devoured by egoism," not so surprising a trait for an elite politician to possess, and at least Churchill recognized it.

Clementine, meanwhile, though understanding his ambition and motivation to leave the army and return to the political fray, knew that acting so precipitately would further damage his reputation. She urged him not "to lose your soldier's halo, which if you keep it is unique & different from all the others. . . . You will be held in people's hearts & in their respect. I have no originality or brilliancy but I feel within me the power to help you now if you will let me" (April 6, 1916). Churchill continued to exhort her, not always politely, to help him by keeping in touch with important people. As he wrote four days later, "Now mind in these critical days you keep in touch with my circle." Again, Clementine cautioned him, writing on April 12, 1916, that "the government may not be strong enough to beat the Germans, but they are powerful enough to do you in, and pray God you do not give the heartless brutes the chance. . . . For once I pray be patient."

His speeches often attracted hostile coverage in the press. Even supposed friends such as Lloyd George assented to the substance of the criticisms, if not the withering tone. But Churchill was undeterred, and he had supporters as well as critics. Members of the public had been impressed by his parliamentary protest about the shocking wastage of manpower. He remained a respected and sought-after commentator on the war, developing his reputation as someone who understood its higher direction. While soldiering and remaining in touch with politics and parliamentary business, he also found time to keep his hand in as a journalist, writing, among other things, a column in the *Sunday Pictorial*. Writing newspaper articles earned money and kept his name before the public and allowed him to develop the theme that the higher direction of the war was being sorely mismanaged by a military clique insufficiently subjected to civilian control.

In this period, Churchill made considerable progress in clearing his name and restoring his tattered reputation. In June 1916, the prime minister announced that the papers relating to the Dardanelles would be put before Parliament. He then decided against this "for security reasons." MPs pressed for a full debate, and the government proposed a new select committee. A Commission of Inquiry began work in August 1916 to examine the Dardanelles campaign and published its interim report in March 1917. This made it abundantly clear that Churchill did not deserve his scapegoat tag (and enabled him, as he put it, to become "the escaped scapegoat") and that he had not been the principal author of the fiasco. The main criticism fell upon Asquith for his lack of clear direction and his failure to call a War Council meeting for a two-month period between March and May 1915. It highlighted the confusion surrounding the respective roles of service chiefs and Cabinet ministers. In scrutinizing the role of experts advising the War Council, the inquiry found that the "functions of the experts were differently understood by the experts themselves and the ministerial members of the War Council."[60] What this meant was that those naval experts who had reservations about the operation should have spoken up forcefully, though they had not thought it their place to do so. The inquiry asked Sir Arthur Wilson if, "in representing the opinion of the Admiralty to the War Council on 13 January and 28 January," Churchill reflected "these unfavourable opinions." Wilson answered: "No, I think he rather passed them over. He was very keen on his own view." Churchill protested: "No one ever said 'This is a thing you cannot do.'"

The inquiry concluded on this issue that:

> We have not the least doubt that, in speaking at the Council, Mr. Churchill thought that he was correctly representing the collective views of the Admiralty experts. But, without in any way wishing to impugn his good faith, it seems clear that he was carried away by his sanguine temperament and his firm belief in the success of the undertaking which he advocated. Although none of his expert advisers absolutely expressed dissent . . . Mr. Churchill had obtained their support to a less extent than he himself imagined. . . . Other members of the Council, especially the Chair [prime minister Asquith], should have encouraged experts to give their opinions, should have insisted upon it.[61]

As 1916 unfolded, Asquith's government foundered, culminating in the disastrous Somme offensive. Churchill urged the government to revamp the nation's war effort, adding to its troubles. With Asquith's administration divided over conscription and on its last legs, Churchill was anxious to be in London with his finger on the political pulse. He spoke in the secret session of Parliament on April 25 but was recalled to his battalion two days later. Fortunately for Churchill, in May 1916, his battalion was amalgamated with another, and his role as a battalion commander therefore became redundant, the senior battalion commander by rights taking over the merged formation. His post having ceased to exist, he could now leave the army honorably. In the meantime, he hoped that Asquith's government would fall and was buoyed by the prospect of a proposed alliance with Lloyd George and Bonar Law that would see his return to high office.

But what Churchill did not appreciate was the strength of opposition toward his return to government. As Lloyd George observed, some Conservatives felt more strongly about Churchill than they did about the kaiser. Churchill was yet to grasp the visceral hatred toward him in certain quarters of the Tory party and how impossible it was—even for a powerful man such as Lloyd George—to overcome their objections. When Asquith was replaced as prime minister by Lloyd George in December 1916, at the head of a coalition containing both Conservatives and Liberals, Churchill was excluded. This was a shock to him, and he felt betrayed by his old friend. Time weighed heavily: "One is quite powerless as far as war is concerned. . . . I am simply existing."[62]

Despite his peripheral position, Churchill was still a very highly regarded figure and was even called upon by the First Lord of the Admiralty, Arthur Balfour, to prepare a statement for public release following the Battle of Jutland, partly in the hope of keeping him friendly toward the government, partly to employ his unrivaled skill with words. Lloyd George was not deliberately trying to exclude Churchill, but he was not prepared to ruin his first term as prime minister (which rested upon a delicate alliance with the Conservatives) for the sake of including him. Though Churchill was crestfallen over his omission from office, Lloyd George fully recognized his abilities and was also concerned lest a resurgent Churchill, already scoring points as a parliamentary and press critic of government war strategy, become the focus of a new opposition to the government. This had its own logical momentum. Better to invite him in, thereby boosting the coalition's Liberal credentials and harnessing a talent that, if mishandled, might be used in opposition.

Churchill was instrumental in calling a secret session of Parliament in May 1917, in which the state of the war was fully debated. He spoke authoritatively about the need to avoid a repeat of the disastrous Somme offensive of the previous year and said that there should be no premature offensive, arguing that the war situation was bleaker than generally acknowledged. "We ought not to squander the remaining armies in France and Britain in precipitate offensives before the American power begins to be felt on the battlefields."[63] The debate showed Churchill to be the outstanding man among the government's critics and an expert on the higher direction of war, and Lloyd George sought him out in the Commons bar afterward, asking him to lunch a few days later. Soon he was relying on frequent advice from Churchill and moving delicately among the Tories to try to engineer Churchill's return to government. But resistance remained potent. As Lord Esher wrote, "The power of Winston for good and evil is, I should say, very considerable. His temperament is of wax and quicksilver, and this strange toy amuses and fascinates L. George, who likes and fears him."[64]

RETURN TO GOVERNMENT

Churchill's path was smoothed by publication of the investigation into the Dardanelles. In the face of fierce Tory opposition, Lloyd George restored Churchill to the Cabinet, appointing him minister of munitions in July 1917. The Tory *Morning Post* commented archly that "although we have not yet invented the unsinkable ship we have discovered the unsinkable politician."[65] But the fact was that Churchill's unique attributes made him a desirable political commodity. Sir Maurice Hankey's assessment was that though he might be rash, his courage and inspiration made him a tower of strength.

While of vital importance to the war effort, Churchill's ministerial position entitled him to a seat in the Cabinet, but not access to the inner sanctum of the War Cabinet. It was this fact, indeed, that had overcome the opposition of the most important Conservatives to Churchill's return. Even so, a hundred Conservative backbenchers signed a motion objecting to his appointment. His new ministerial position meant resigning his parliamentary seat and fighting a special election in Dundee, a campaign combined with the urgent work of his ministry that saw Clementine address many meetings in her husband's stead, helping him toward a handsome victory at the polls. He was back in government and back in the business of war direction in which he reveled.

The headquarters of Churchill's new ministerial empire was the Metropole Hotel on Northumberland Avenue off Trafalgar Square. It presided over twelve thousand officials (rising to twenty-five thousand by the end of the war) and approximately two and a half million factory workers. It was, in his words, "the biggest purchasing business and industrial employer in the world." Its job was to make the bombs and guns that serviced the fighting men of the British Empire all over the world. The ministry had been created to rectify the faults in British industry and war coordination that had led to the "shells scandal" of 1915 and to ensure plentiful supplies of munitions and prioritization in the production of weapons. Managing such a gigantic organization, and driven by the overriding need to defeat the enemy, Churchill realized that radical new methods of organization and industrial relations were called for, an experiment in "war socialism" that was to stand him in good stead during the next war.

Churchill's appointment was greeted by some hostility within the ministry, though his opening address to his new staff saw "the atmosphere changed perceptibly . . . those who came to curse, remained to cheer."[66] As he had done at the Admiralty, Churchill began his tenure by reorganizing the ministry's higher management, reducing fifty subdivisions to a more streamlined ten and instituting a daily council that decided upon policy and took decisions based on a cross-departmental awareness of priorities and demands. There were areas of overlap and tension that Churchill could not easily smooth out, most noticeably involving the Admiralty, which was responsible for its own weapons procurement and therefore a competitor for industrial resources. To ease tensions within the various organizations and industries working toward the common goal of victory, and to promote efficiency, a War Priorities Committee of the War Cabinet was set up under the South African prime minister, Jan Smuts. Trademark work habits soon emerged—on August 3, 1917, for instance, Churchill asked for detailed information about the tank program "on a single sheet of paper,"[67] and it wasn't long before Cabinet colleagues were bristling at his intervention in their departments' affairs.

The job of minister of munitions thrust Churchill back into the turbulent waters of labor relations. The demand for war material meant that the bargaining power of the workers increased dramatically, their ability to impact war policy through strikes growing stronger in a time of industrial warfare. Churchill spent a great deal of his time visiting industrial sites across Britain, as well as making frequent visits to France. He was able to indulge his love of France and his desire to be close to the action, and to meet firsthand with those responsible for using the equipment his ministry was producing. The commander in chief, General Haig, placed the Château Verchocq at his disposal during these visits. On one such occasion, he witnessed the ceremonial entry of British troops into Flanders. As minister of munitions, he provided for a great expansion of the Tank Corps and the Machine Gun Corps, increased the number of aircraft in France, and encouraged the development of mustard gas. Haig thought that through these visits, "Winston means to do his utmost to provide the army with all it requires, but at the same time he can hardly stop meddling in the larger questions of strategy and tactics."[68] But Churchill's belief in the futility of a further major offensive in 1917 proved to be correct—while Haig had every confidence in Passchendaele.

Churchill's department was also responsible for delivering vast quantities of material to American forces fighting in France. During his tenure, 164 heavy guns, 1,500 trench mortars, 300,000 grenades, 11 million rounds of ammunition, 4,553 lorries and ambulances, 2,219 motorcycles and bicycles, 811 cars, and 452 airplanes were supplied. His fertile mind conceived and supported technological advances and constantly searched for solutions to problems such as the threat of land mines to tanks. Sometimes criticized or pooh-poohed, such thinking and ceaseless interest was vital, and his "crude ideas," as he wrote, were "only intended to excite the scientific mind and lead to the production of definite solutions!"[69] He welcomed the arrival of soldiers from America, a country he considered a "mighty champion at the other end of the world" that had "restored to us the fortunes of the war,"[70] building in his mind ideas of Anglo-American union that were to grow to full maturity in the 1940s and 1950s.

In terms of war strategy, Churchill was a convinced 1919 man. He believed that during the course of that year, the vastly superior Allied resources then coming onstream would bring victory, and that until then the Allies should adopt a more defensive posture—and avoid any more offensives involving mass bloodletting for the sake of limited territorial gains. Though Lloyd George dissented from this view, he acknowledged the regard in which Churchill was held in military circles and sent him to France to coordinate action with Clemenceau when the German offensive of spring 1918 nearly undid the Allies. During these critical weeks, Churchill performed an important steadying role and exhorted his ministry to labor intensely to replace heavy weapons losses. In France, he conducted business using his creative knowledge of the French language.* As late as the summer of 1918, Churchill, like many others, believed that the war had at least a year to run. The trick was to allow superior Allied resources to come into play and to avoid catastrophic defeat in the meantime. As he wrote from France on August 10, 1918, "Today I have been working at GHQ on shells. [We] hope to 'catch up' with the Germans next year."

When the Allied counteroffensive proved successful, Churchill wrote to Haig: "I am so glad about this great and fine victory of the British Army. It is our victory, won chiefly by our troops under a British Commander, and largely through the invincible tank which British brains have invented and developed."[71] On August 8, he had written to Clementine from France that "the events which have taken place in the last 3 days are among the most important that have happened in the war. . . . The tide has turned!"[72]

Given the disaster of the Dardanelles and its impact upon Churchill's career, by the end of the war a remarkable turnaround in

---

* Churchill spoke French better than the vast majority of Britain's twentieth-century prime ministers and senior politicians. Yet his forays into the language are often used to poke (usually affectionate) fun at him and augment the "schoolboy" aspect of his character.

his fortunes had been achieved. He had developed an even thicker political skin and perhaps shed some of his restlessness, without losing any of his fight. On September 15, 1918, he wrote that he was thoroughly "contented with my office. I do not chafe at adverse political combinations, or at not being able to direct general policy. I am content to be associated with the splendid machines of the British Army, & to feel how many ways there are open to me to serve them."[73] Siegfried Sassoon met Churchill in September, at Churchill's request. Churchill talked and talked, pacing his office with his cigar, soon addressing, Sassoon realized, not him but "no one in particular." "It had been unmistakeable that for him war was the finest activity on earth."[74]

His new ministerial absorption, together with the opportunities to travel overseas, was not particularly good for Churchill's home life. The Churchill family had moved out of their London home at 33 Eccleston Square in 1918 and spent some time squatting in various homes, which bothered Churchill (who often elected to stay in his ministerial hotel) less than his wife. In the spring of 1917, they had also taken Lullenden, a ramshackle Tudor manor in Sussex, in order to get away from potential German air raids and as a country seat. This was something that both Winston and Clementine desired, though the house was sold in 1919 as the Churchills' finances again proved troublesome. Clementine chided her husband for spending too much time in France when his job also required constant attention at home. As she told him in October 1918: "Darling do come home and look after what is to be done with the Munition Workers when the fighting really does stop. Even if the fighting is not over yet, your share of it must be, & I would like you to be praised as a reconstructive genius as well as for a Mustard Gas Field, a Tank juggernaut & a flying Terror." In reprimanding him for his desire to spend time overseas when his presence was needed at home, Clementine was also censuring him for making too little time for his family. As she wrote after an unusually long silence: "No letter—I just think you are a little pig. 'What can you expect from a pig but a grunt?', says the adage—But I haven't even had a grunt from mine."[75]

Churchill learned a great deal about war leadership in the last years of the war, which was to stand him in good stead when he became prime minister in 1940. In Churchill's mind, Lloyd George's tenure demonstrated the need to provide dynamic leadership, to inspire the public and one's colleagues, and to streamline the machinery of government in a situation of total war that encouraged the growth of bloated and unwieldy ministries and industrial and administrative structures. The First World War experience also demonstrated to him the value of a small and supreme War Cabinet drawing its strength and legitimacy from cross-party composition. The quest for government effectiveness in this period also confirmed Churchill's belief in the need to remain in constant contact with Parliament in order to receive sanction for strategic direction and to explain policy decisions and military operations. Finally, the conduct of the Lloyd George administration taught Churchill the merit of appointing people from outside of politics to key political jobs.

"Our country had emerged from the ordeal alive and safe," Churchill wrote of the armistice, "its vast possessions intact, its war effort still waxing, its institutions unshaken, its people and Empire united as never before. Victory had come after all the hazards and heartbreaks in an absolute and unlimited form."[76] Two weeks after the armistice that ended the First World War, Parliament was dissolved, and in an atmosphere of patriotic fervor, the "coupon election" took place. Swimming somewhat against the tide, Churchill spoke out against harsh measures being forced upon the vanquished enemy, a manifestation of his liberal and forward-looking political beliefs. This was typical of the man, more compassionate than his peers, though his resolution in conflict has led consistently to him being misrepresented as a warmonger. He was adamant that Germany had to be utterly defeated—"Germany must know she is beaten; Germany must feel she is beaten"[77]—but once the victory had been won, compassion and healing were the things most needed.

5

Home and Colonial:
New Nations, Strikes, and Gold

As the general election of December 1918 took place, the Churchill family spent Christmas at Blenheim. It had been a good year for Churchill. After restoring his political fortunes following the Gallipoli debacle and rejoining the Cabinet's inner sanctum, over a decade of continual high office opened up before him. It was to see Churchill grapple with the thorniest problems of imperial rule and national economic policy as nationalism became a clamant call around the world and as postwar economic trends pointed toward the "great depression." This was to be a remarkable period for Churchill, during which he continued his post-Gallipoli restoration and again—incredibly—managed to switch political party without emasculating his ministerial career, though inevitably swelling the ranks of those who found him intolerable. He also sustained his position as a distinguished writer and journalist able to command terms as lucrative as any writer of the day.

Lloyd George's coalition won a massive electoral victory. Churchill, like many others, had chosen to cling to the coalition after the war had ended. Bonar Law, the Tory leader, was the mainstay of the coalition while the prime minister busied himself concluding the various peace treaties, requiring his absence from London for long periods. Churchill remained a prominent member of the government. In his mid-forties, he was remarkably young to have enjoyed such political longevity and attained such seniority. He had already proved himself the greatest political survivor of the twentieth century, and this was long before either his "finest hour" or his last hurrah as prime minister in the 1950s. Yet the political landscape in which he had been immersed since childhood was shifting all around. Social developments at home were unprecedented; Britain's position as primus inter pares overseas was increasingly challenged by the rising power of America and Japan; and from below, the peoples of the world's greatest empire sought either to shake off the imperial yoke or to renegotiate their position within an increasingly egalitarian Commonwealth. With regard to the various peace treaties that formalized the cessation of hostilities in Europe, Churchill advocated magnanimity toward the vanquished, putting him at odds with the majority of his colleagues and his constituents. Even while it was in progress, he believed that the peacemaking was being poorly handled and that Versailles contained within it the seeds of future conflict, indeed that it represented a mere break in what would transpire to be a thirty-year war. During the interwar years, he came increasingly to believe that the British political elite was throwing away the victory won so notably by the British Army and its allies in 1918 and progressively losing the will to lead and to defy wicked regimes.

As Churchill journeyed from London to Blenheim in late December 1918, he had pondered Lloyd George's offer of government office. His reply favored a return to the Admiralty, but by that time, things had already moved on in the prime minister's mind. Thus Churchill was given the War Office with the new Air Ministry attached, his seventh (and eighth) office of state. Predictably, sections of the press deplored the appointment. The *Morning Post* said this "brilliant and erratic" man "would make a mess of anything he undertook. Character is destiny; there is some tragic flaw in Mr. Churchill which determines him on every occasion in the wrong course."[1] The work of both ministries, given the recent cessation of hostilities, revolved around demobilizing the swollen ranks of the military and managing its return to peacetime duties. Mutinies were in the offing, morale plummeting as men waited impatiently to go home. Churchill had to convince the prime minister, absorbed with the peacemaking in Paris, that the government faced an emergency situation. A new army demobilization plan was in place within two weeks of Churchill's assuming office on January 10, 1919, based upon the length of a man's service, his age, and the number of times he had been wounded. It was widely perceived to be fair, and morale improved. Churchill was then able to get on with the business of returning Britain's military establishment to its peacetime shape, reducing an army of 3.5 million to a volunteer force of around 200,000 men and organizing several armies of occupation amounting to a million or more men. It was a delicate balancing act, because, as Churchill knew, if the army was run down too much, European security would suffer; while colleagues might demand a "peace dividend," the security of Britain's global interests in an unsettled world remained the paramount duty of government.

WINSTON AND THE BOLSHEVIKS

Throughout the 1920s, Churchill excelled at handling political emergencies. A major focus of Churchill's activities in the early postwar period was British intervention in the Russian civil war, and it dominated his time at the War Office. He was determined to block the prospect of a Bolshevik future for the empire so recently deprived of its monarchy and forced into a humiliating peace with Germany. In fact, he wanted "to strangle Bolshevism at birth," as he put it, and sought to do so by supporting the "White" Russian forces against the "Reds." As early as November 10, 1918, he told the War Cabinet that it was necessary to build up the German army "for fear of the spread of Bolshevism"[2] (presaging his concerns in spring 1945 that it might soon be necessary to rearm the Germans to meet the emerging Soviet menace). His stance on Bolshevism was unequivocal: "In Russia a man is called a reactionary if he objects to having his property stolen, and his wife and children murdered."[3] As he said on April 11, 1919, "Of all the tyrannies in history the Bolshevist tyranny is the worst, the most destructive, and the most degrading. It is sheer humbug to pretend that it is not far worse than German militarism. . . . The atrocities by Lenin and Trotsky are incomparably more hideous, on a larger scale, and more numerous than any for which the kaiser himself is responsible."[4] This was a theme he returned to three decades later. Speaking in January 1949, he told the Commons: "I think the day will come when it will be recognized without doubt, not only on one side of the House but throughout the civilized world, that the strangling of Bolshevism at birth would have been an untold blessing to the human race."[5]

British forces had been engaged within Russia's borders since before the end of the war. On the subject of Bolshevism and Russia (as on numerous other subjects), Churchill could sound like a stuck record, more likely to turn listeners off than on. But this is an unavoidable pitfall for politicians of longevity, and at least Churchill had the power of his convictions to keep banging away at issues he held in passionate regard, and with the benefit of hindsight, it is possible to say that on most of the big issues, Churchill had it right—including his verdict on the nature of the regime born in Russia in 1917 and taken to new levels of inhumanity under Stalin. Churchill thought that the British public might change its mind if it was made clear that the Bolsheviks were conducting mass atrocities.

In the immediate post–First World War years, however, an exhausted Britain cared little about Russia and had no stomach for such an endeavor. This determined Britain's role, which proceeded to be both inglorious and ineffective, though no great damage was done to Churchill's reputation. Indeed, it did quite a lot to resurrect it in right-wing circles while arousing the hostility of many on the left, perpetuating the myth of Churchill as the hammer of the working class. The *Morning Post*, for so long a withering critic, swung back in Churchill's favor, while the left-wing press regurgitated his past crimes, and the Labour Party's distrust increased. Churchill's Russian policy was based squarely upon the belief that Russia under the Bolsheviks was a greater threat to world peace than the kaiser's Germany had ever been and that it threatened revolution throughout Europe. He railed against the "foul baboonery" of Bolshevism and the chasm separating communist rhetoric from actual practice. Churchill's revulsion stemmed in part from his dislike of change and his regret that the world in which he had grown up had been fundamentally altered. "What a disappointment the Twentieth Century has been," he wrote.[6]

But employing large British forces to help smash Bolshevism was simply not practical politics at the time. The public and the army were hostile to the prospect of large-scale intervention in Russia. Though Churchill might see in Bolshevism a threat far greater than almost anyone imagined, for most people it was a cloud not even descried on the horizon. Added to this was the popular idea that Bolshevism was an ideology that could uplift the workers, seen by many as a paragon of hope to be nurtured rather than charged down by British bayonets. Though Churchill urged robust intervention, the Americans opposed it, but he did manage to garner support for an inter-Allied war scheme that even had President Wilson's tepid assent. Churchill's success in drumming up this inter-Allied support both surprised and irritated Lloyd George. The prime minister deplored the fact that Churchill was "mad for operations in Russia." "The problem with Winston," he wrote, "is that he's always taking action. *He will insist on getting out his maps.*" The prime minister had thought Churchill would be safe at the War Office, "but was he? Before I could look around, he's got out his maps of Russia and we are making fools of ourselves in the Civil War."[7] Bonar Law referred testily to "Winston's nonsense" about Russia, and this summed up the attitude of the prime minister and most of his colleagues. Lloyd George was compelled amid the postwar ruins to give priority to the way the world *was* rather than the way that it should be. From this point of view, having a senior and very vocal Cabinet colleague arguing for leniency in dealing with the Germans while warning of the menace of Russia was unhelpful.

Politically, Lloyd George and Churchill were drifting apart—Lloyd George toward a rock on which he would be marooned without political support, Churchill toward a tempestuous reunion with the Conservatives that would lead him toward the two highest offices of state. Winston's "carry on regardless" policy toward Russia was largely based upon a disregard, or misunderstanding, of the level of support that existed for the Bolsheviks. There was no public appetite for Churchill's policy of backing General Denikin and the White Russians, and the public feared another major international conflict. This would eventually lead Lloyd George to conclude that Churchill was best away from the War Office. Thus, in February 1921, Winston would be shunted sideways to the Colonial Office, where the responsibilities were again global, but confined to parts of the world painted red on the map.

AIR MINISTER

While serving as secretary of state for war from January 1919 until February 1921 (and as colonial secretary from February until April 1921), Churchill was also in charge of the fledgling Air Ministry. This was not to everyone's liking, and Clementine wrote on March 9, 1919: "Do you not think it would be better to give up the Air. . . . It would be a sign of real strength to do so, & people would admire you very much. It is weak to hang on to 2 offices. . . . After all, you want to be a Statesman, not a juggler." The undersecretary for air went so far as to complain to the prime minister that the infant Royal Air Force (RAF) suffered because of the many calls upon Churchill's time. Churchill firmly rebuffed such claims, retorting that it was important to have a combative figure with proven military credentials at the helm. He had been an apostle of air power since its inception and now enthusiastically took up the arguments of Sir Hugh Trenchard, the chief of the Air Staff, proclaiming the RAF's fitness for "sky policing" imperial troublespots at a fraction of the cost of the army. The RAF had demonstrated its potential in this direction by providing Britain's presence in Somaliland and the new imperial acquisition of Iraq. Together Churchill and Trenchard argued the case for the continuation of an independent air force, and success in imperial policing gave them concrete examples of efficiency and cost-effectiveness on which to build their case and keep the RAF out of the clutches of the two established services.

The association of Churchill's name with the use of poison gas dates from his time at the Air Ministry. Gas had been widely used by both sides in the war and was seen as an efficient tool in imperial policing. Its use by the postwar air force is sometimes held up as an example of Churchill's supposed callousness. But, notwithstanding changing attitudes, his position needs to be more clearly stated. The gas he was interested in for colonial policing was tear gas, not mustard gas intended to kill and maim. Contrary to some interpretations, in colonial policing, Churchill evinced sensitivity to the rights and wrongs of the use of force, even among so-called subject peoples. There always had to be discrimination and legality in the use of force, he claimed, and he advocated courts-martial for any RAF personnel alleged to have fired on women and children in Iraq. His views were relatively enlightened for his time, though of course problematic when considered from the distance of a hundred years. He believed in the rule of law as a protection to individuals' rights and as a foundation of Western civilization. He also believed in Britain's role as a great nation and in the importance of its empire for British security and for the benefit of its inhabitants. At this time, he spoke out strongly against the events and decisions that led to the Amritsar massacre, believing that the episode had a deleterious effect on British rule.

Churchill's performance as air minister has been criticized because of his lack of sustained focus on the job. This is particularly true in the realm of civil aviation, where not enough nurturing took place, especially given the desire of the Treasury for retrenchment in this period. Churchill's attitude toward civil aviation stemmed from the common dislike of state intervention in private enterprise and a desire to let an industry that had been forced to grow up by war find its own way. As far as Churchill was concerned, beyond legislating and helping to finance infrastructure, there should be no subsidies to airline companies. "Civil aviation," as he put it, "must fly by itself, the Government cannot possibly hold it up in the air." But this starved a fledgling industry of necessary support, according to one historian, and "for two crucial years after the war, Churchill's parsimony, negligence and disinterest meant that British aviation lost opportunities close to home and in the Empire . . . and lost forever its one chance to lead the world in air transport development."[8]

COLONIAL AFFAIRS: THE MIDDLE EAST AND IRELAND

The Middle East was a region of pressing importance for Britain, given its new territorial responsibilities there and the area's continuing strategic significance. Up until this time, a hodgepodge of "British" institutions had been involved in the region's affairs. The India Office, signifying the subcontinent's role as the leading "British" agency in the Tigris valley, had overseen the affairs of Iraq and relations with Persia; Palestine, with its delicate racial dynamics, was a preserve of the Foreign Office, while the other Arab territories newly conquered from the Turks came under the wing of the Colonial Office. Churchill suggested that all should now come under the Colonial Office. Lloyd George agreed and promptly asked him, on New Year's Day 1921, to take over that office (retaining also the Air Ministry). This was just the kind of opportunity that appealed to Churchill, as Lloyd George well knew. It gave him a chance to play kingmaker and to enter his name in the annals of history at a time when new kingdoms were in the making.

Churchill's change of job meant a return to the buildings of the Colonial Office in Downing Street (opposite Numbers 10 and 11) where he had served under Lord Elgin in his first government appointment. Churchill's new office allowed his fertile imagination to wander over Britain's vast imperial estate once again. Writing from his bed in Cannes in December 1921, he pictured Clementine far away, and "far beyond that again in outer circles of darkness ranges the wide colonial Empire and the Emerald Isle." On February 3, 1922, he wrote that "these tasks & the Arabs & the Kenya folk & the Ishmaelis for Iraq & Palestine have kept me busy."[9] This was Britain's "moment in the Middle East," the beginning of the brief period in which Britain was master in this strategically vital region. Churchill fully appreciated the significance of this moment and was very interested in supervising this latest phase of British imperial expansion. The Middle East was one of the most difficult regions of the world in which to formulate imperial policy, and many contested Britain's right to be there in the first place. Churchill's instinct was to streamline the various strands of British Middle Eastern policy, and one of his conditions when accepting the Colonial Office was the creation of a Middle East Department within it. Naturally, this change irritated some, the Foreign Office seeing it as a bid by Churchill to make himself "an Asiatic Foreign Secretary."[10]

The Middle East was central to British world power, the "swing door" of imperial communications and the defense of India, source of the oil on which the Royal Navy and the British economy rested, and a location from which to influence and pressure rivals. After centuries of British growth in the region, it supported a hodgepodge of competing imperial interests. Though all allegedly on the same "side," the India Office, the Foreign Office, the Colonial Office, the War Office, the Admiralty, and more recently, the Air Ministry all had a say in Middle Eastern policy and usually had their own distinct agendas to pursue. In these early postwar years, Middle Eastern affairs were more fluid and complicated than ever before, because Britain's stake in the region, and its territorial footprint, had undergone a remarkable growth owing to the defeat of the Ottoman Empire and the division of its erstwhile domains. As the primary Allied power in the region, operating from its Egyptian stronghold, Britain emerged with the lion's share of the spoils—Iraq, Palestine, and Trans-Jordan—and the political headaches that went with them.

Churchill's primary task was to make arrangements for supervising Britain's growing territorial portfolio between the Sinai Desert and the Persian Gulf. His first major step was to tour the region, appointing Middle Eastern allies through whom Britain would rule its new Arab domains. The centerpiece of Churchill's visit was a meeting of imperial and indigenous potentates in Cairo. This durbar cum conference, held in March 1921, had considerable significance for the entire Middle East and displayed Churchill's mastery of detail. Egyptian nationalists timed public demonstrations to coincide with Churchill's arrival, demanding that Britain leave their homeland. Security was a key concern, as Churchill's life was at risk: his party was stoned on arrival in the Egyptian capital, and his bodyguard remained constantly on the alert and needed occasionally to use his fists. After the murder of Field Marshal Sir Henry Wilson by the IRA in London in June 1922, Churchill was deemed to require the protection of three detectives while visiting the high commissioner, Lord Allenby, King Faud, and various RAF stations.

The future of Iraq was uppermost in Churchill's mind, and the upshot of his visit was that Feisal was appointed king, with Britain retaining significant base rights in the former Ottoman province. This guaranteed Britain control, at a knockdown price, of the land bridge linking Europe and Asia, as well as securing its oil riches. It was a move designed to secure influence and cut costs. As he wrote, "We are paying eight millions a year for the privilege of living on an ungrateful volcano out of which we are in no circumstances to get anything worth having—except, of course, for the oil."[11] Churchill's view of what Britain was building in Iraq is revealing, for it contains within it a statement of the aims of both sides—influence in a sensitive strategic region for the British, independence for the Iraqis—competing aims that were to prove ultimately irreconcilable, as in Ireland and South Africa and many other parts of the world as the twentieth century progressed. "Our object and our policy," he told the Commons in June 1921, "is to set up an Arab Government, and to make it take the responsibility, with our aid and our guidance and with an effective measure of our support, until they are strong enough to stand alone, and so to foster the development of their independence as to permit the steady and speedy diminution of our burden."[12] The trouble with such arrangements was that the extent of external involvement, and the timing of its withdrawal, was always disputed by the external power and internal political leaders aspiring to greater measures of control themselves.

Churchill's visit to the Middle East meant that the government's policy for the region was clearly enunciated for the benefit of all interested parties, whether they agreed with it or not. In attempting to resolve the thorny problems associated with Palestine, Churchill left Cairo for Jerusalem, where he met High Commissioner Sir Herbert Samuel. Churchill, a pro-Zionist, reiterated Britain's wartime promise of a national home for the Jews and saw at first hand Arab hostility toward them. He negotiated with Emir Abdullah, soon to be installed as Hashemite ruler of the former Ottoman province of Trans-Jordan. The major objective of his policy in the region was to create the infrastructure of indirect rule that would allow Britain to cut its commitments there while retaining its influence and protecting its interests. Whatever criticisms may be directed at Churchill's policy in the Middle East, it proved extremely durable, given the region's political volatility, and formed the basis of Britain's position in the region until long after the Second World War. In reaching a settlement in the Middle East, Churchill made good use of his experts. Though his urge to go to the region and hold court attracted the usual criticism, the failures of the Cairo conference were collective and reflected British policy, not Churchillian diktat. The intractable problems of the region—of Iraq and Palestine, for example—form pinheads on which statesmen continue to dance.

In June 1920, Lloyd George had appointed Churchill as chairman of a Cabinet committee on Ireland, and this involved him in the birth of an independent Ireland for the first time since English expansion under the Tudors and Stuarts. With the war over, it was clear that the situation in Ireland was no closer to being resolved. Increasingly militarizing the problem did not appeal to Lloyd George, though he did choose to increase the size and power of the police as a robust response to IRA activity, leading to the deployment of the Auxiliaries and the Black and Tans. It soon became clear that martial law was not improving the situation, and Churchill was convinced that this path could not be continued. His involvement with Irish affairs, which had started before the First World War, drew him closer to the heart of the coalition government than he had ever been, particularly as Ireland was returning to the center of the political agenda. His wife pressed him to work toward a settlement, exhorting him to "use your influence now for some sort of moderation or at any rate justice in Ireland." Once it had been decided to negotiate, he was prepared to use force as a last resort but urged both sides to make concessions.

For many decades, Ireland had been Britain's most intractable colonial issue, a thorn in the side of Westminster politicians, given the salience of the Home Rule issue since the mid-nineteenth century and the presence of large number of Irish MPs in the Commons. As Churchill had been the public face of Asquith's prewar Irish policy, so he was to the fore in Lloyd George's, and this meant dealing with a new and much more ferocious political enemy—Sinn Fein and its military wing, the Irish Republican Army. There was a dramatic turnaround in Britain's policy toward Ireland in 1921, when Lloyd George switched from suppressing the IRA to a policy of reconciliation, moving toward a truce that came into effect in July 1921. Churchill maintained a steely tolerance of the more unpleasant aspects of war and prepared to meet the IRA's challenge with uncompromising force. In this way, Churchill helped provide the political nerve needed to deal ruthlessly with the IRA and to force its leaders to the negotiating table.

In October 1921, Lloyd George convened a meeting at Downing Street involving Sinn Fein leaders and members of the Cabinet. The main British demands were that Ireland must remain in the British Empire; that Irish ministers should swear allegiance to the Crown; and that the Royal Navy should retain the use of certain strategically positioned Irish ports. Tough face-to-face negotiations ensued, during the course of which Churchill developed a respect for the Irish leaders Michael Collins and Arthur Griffith and an understanding of the dynamics of their position. In particular, the relationship he forged with Collins helped lubricate the negotiations. After weeks of talking, an agreement was reached, spurred by Lloyd George's threat to resume the war—his "take it or leave it" offer of December 5—and a new Dominion, the Irish Free State, was born.

As colonial secretary, it fell to Churchill to translate the agreement into practice, overseeing what was an early act of twentieth-century decolonization. Leading the government's defense of the Irish treaty in the Commons, Churchill gave a masterly performance and subsequently did his best to see that the agreement worked, showing commendable restraint on several occasions. In the Commons, during the reading of the Irish Free State Bill in February 1922, Churchill memorably caricatured the place of Irish politics in British life. He began by summarizing the momentous, world-changing events of the First World War. But when the war ended, he continued:

> As the deluge subsides and the waters fall short we see the dreary steeples of Fermanagh and Tyrone emerging once again. The integrity of their quarrel is one of the few institutions that has been unaltered in the cataclysm which has swept the world. That says a lot for the persistency with which Irishmen on the one side or the other are able to pursue their controversies. It says a great deal for the power which Ireland has, both Nationalist and Orange, to lay their hands upon the vital strings of British life and politics, and to hold, dominate, and convulse, year after year, generation after generation, the politics of this powerful country.[13]

Churchill dealt skillfully with these issues, but his ambitious nature craved higher office. Upon his return to England from the Middle East in the spring of 1921, he had been disappointed not to secure the position of chancellor of the Exchequer when Lloyd George shuffled his Cabinet (a reshuffle that divested Churchill of responsibility for the Air Ministry). Remaining at the Colonial Office, with the pressing issues in Ireland and the Middle East under control for the time being, a lack of funds frustrated Churchill's desire for economic development in imperial domains such as East Africa, mundane obstacles obscuring his visions of grandiose progress. Unable to write bold headlines, he found little glory in pronouncing on issues such as New Hebridean governance and the limitation of Indian immigration into Kenya.

THE END OF THE COALITION AND RETURN TO THE TORY FOLD

The year 1922 saw a steady erosion of both the government's reputation and the popularity of the prime minister. His handling of the Irish question and the Chanak crisis, his stance on Russia, and postwar economic difficulties sapped the Conservative support on which Lloyd George's administration rested, while enhancing support for the Labour Party. As far as Churchill was concerned, while he supported the coalition, he was increasingly at odds with Lloyd George's leadership, and the prime minister suspected that Churchill was working toward a right-wing coalition under Austen Chamberlain. Churchill was still vying for new ministerial appointments, at this time showing enthusiasm for the creation of a new Ministry of Defence to supersede the Admiralty, Air Ministry, and War Office. He also retained his interest in coalition, as opposed to single-party, government. Fearing the rise of the Labour Party, he was keen on the formation of a new coalition to fight it, believing that old-fashioned Conservative-Liberal political designations were redundant. "Liberalism," he pronounced, "is the greatest form of Conservatism." But the Conservatives withdrew from the coalition, Lloyd George resigned, and Andrew Bonar Law, the Conservative leader, became prime minister after a general election in November 1922. Churchill lost his seat in this election and was not to regain it for two years, leading to a very unsettled period in his life. Finishing fourth and having developed appendicitis, "I found myself without an office, without a seat, without a party and without an appendix."

His illness had prevented him from campaigning, though he did make an appearance in Dundee on Armistice Day, wearing his eleven campaign medals.

The election weakened the Tories, but rather than boosting the waning Liberal Party, it brought ever closer the likelihood of the first Labour government in history, a prospect that Churchill deplored with all his instinctive fear of "socialism." Without a seat for the first time in twenty-two years, Churchill was looking for the right moment at which to rejoin the Conservatives. The election had wiped out the Liberals as a party of government. He spent the winter on the Riviera and remained in the south of France painting, writing, and lobbying until May 1923. For six months after the election Churchill was out of the public eye as a politician, and his writing again came to the fore. In January 1923, he finished the proofs of the first volume of his book *The World Crisis*. "We have reached the moment when one must say, 'As the tree falls, so shall it lie,'" he said as he delivered the final proof.[14] Running to five volumes and nearly a million words, it was his record of the First World War: "A contribution to history," he wrote, "strung upon a fairly strong thread of personal reminiscence."[15] Its style was superlative, and the work offered a vivid account of a war about which the public still knew little, at once intricately informed and constructed on a grand scale. He was also working on his autobiographical *My Early Life*. He would compose his works standing up at a sloping desk, or sometimes in bed. *The Times* serialized the first volume of *The World Crisis*, an event that caused the prime minister to complain that Churchill's account breached his oath as a privy councillor, eliciting a vigorous defense from Churchill.

The new government didn't last for long, and in May 1923 Bonar Law resigned. Coalitions were out of fashion, and the familiar pattern of party politics once again came to the fore as the two main political parties found a cause upon which to resume traditional party hostilities. Stanley Baldwin, the new Tory leader, announced his intention to introduce protective tariffs on manufactured imports as a remedy for unemployment. This led the Liberals to reunite under the banner of free trade. Churchill took up the free-trade cudgels and threw in his lot with the Asquithian Liberals but was beaten at a special election in Leicester West by a Labour candidate. Parliament was dissolved in November 1923 and an election held the following month. The Labour Party won, resulting in the first-ever Labour government, which took office under Ramsay MacDonald (a man with "the gift of compressing the largest number of words into the smallest amount of thought") in January 1924.

Churchill believed that the Liberal Party was no longer capable of standing in the way of the rise of the Labour Party. An alliance with the Conservatives was, therefore, essential. "I am a Liberal, opposed to the official Liberal leaders on account of their putting socialists into power. I am a Liberal working shoulder to shoulder with the Conservatives in a national emergency." In early 1924, Baldwin renounced his party's protectionist pledge, thus removing for Churchill the last serious obstacle to rejoining the Tories. Moving ever further from the Liberal Party, Churchill stood for Parliament in a March 1924 special election in the Abbey division of Westminster, campaigning as an "independent anti-socialist." He was assisted by the young Brendan Bracken and chorus girls from Daly's Theatre, who addressed envelopes as Churchill inveighed against the perils of socialism. He failed to beat the Conservative candidate by a narrow margin of forty-three votes, his third electoral defeat in a row and one that had him tramping up and down the hall "head down, body lurching, like a despairing animal" as the results came in. Nevertheless, though he had opposed an official Conservative candidate in this special election, it moved him closer to the party that he was soon to rejoin.

Churchill was adopted as a "constitutionalist" candidate for Epping, where he fought the 1924 general election, campaigning with his usual vigor. His speeches were widely reported and welcomed by Baldwin, and he won by a majority of nearly ten thousand votes. Returning to the Conservative Party, he was predictably accused of opportunism but had been genuinely appalled at the Liberals' weakness against the Labour government and the "socialism" he so hated. Throughout his career, Churchill was never afraid to change his mind: "A man who doesn't change his mind with new evidence is no use,"[16] as he told Lord Moran. This agility was tempered by many continuities and consistencies in the causes and policies he advocated throughout his lengthy parliamentary life. As soon as he had reentered the House of Commons, Churchill contemplated a return to high office, based upon his public performances and the fact that he represented many alienated Liberal voters who were now finding a home in Conservative circles.

When Neville Chamberlain turned down the Treasury, Churchill was offered this highest of Cabinet positions, an offer he accepted with tears in his eyes. Soon he was dusting down the robes his father had worn when he occupied the office, which had been wrapped in tissue paper and camphor for forty years. Churchill's appointment was opposed by Tories such as Leopold Amery and numerous backbenchers. Over the next few years, however, many of these backbenchers came to look to him for leadership, and for the first time he began to attract a parliamentary following. This was a dramatic rebirth for Churchill, though one that reflected the fact that he was probably the ablest, and certainly the most experienced, politician of the day.

As chancellor, Churchill's propensity to involve himself in the affairs of other government departments reached new heights. His colleagues dreaded his interdepartmental interrogations and initiatives. As Neville Chamberlain put it, "Winston is a very interesting but d--d uncomfortable bed fellow. You never get a moment's rest and you never know at what point he'll break out."[17] Haldane put it even more succinctly: working with Churchill was like arguing with a brass band. Churchill, rather remarkably, given the vagaries of his extraordinary career to date, was at one remove from the summit of British politics. He was where he loved to be. As Clementine wrote, "You are having an anxious but thrilling & engrossing time with power & scope which is what the Pig likes."[18] "Pig" liked it so much, in fact, that he desired a metamorphosis, telling Clementine that he was "tired of being a 'Pig'" and "wished to become a 'Lion.'"

GOLD AND THE EXCHEQUER

So Churchill came to reside at Number 11 Downing Street. Here he would usually work in the later part of the mornings, having begun the working day from his bed at home. He saw a lot of Baldwin, because his custom was to leave Number 11 by way of Number 10. Churchill's prestige with the prime minister made him a powerful force in the government, regardless of his recent defection from a rival political party. As chancellor, Churchill displayed no shyness despite the unfamiliar nature of the business, and he refused to unquestioningly accept the opinions of those with long-standing specialist knowledge. Other men would have been daunted; Churchill plunged in, a volcano spewing ideas and memoranda in all directions. He challenged Treasury orthodoxy and the advice of its officials and was prepared to fight at dinner parties and in committee meetings with those whose advice other chancellors would meekly have followed. He harried experts with lengthy counterarguments as policy was formulated—"Forgive me adding to your labours with these Sunday morning reflections," he typically began an inquisitorial missive to one of them.

Churchill made his first Budget Day speech in 1925 and throughout his tenure at the Treasury reveled in the tradition and publicity surrounding the event. His Budget Day speeches were delivered with a sense of occasion and prepared with his customary meticulousness (the 1928 speech ran to over fifteen thousand words, hammered out at Chartwell). As he left 11 Downing Street in frock coat and top hat, showing the famous red dispatch case, he would walk with his family to Parliament, surrounded by the public and the press. His first speech, which lasted for two and a half hours, was a "masterly performance," according to Neville Chamberlain. He announced tax reductions, a contributory scheme of pensions for widows and orphans, and the lowering of the pension age from seventy to sixty-five. As chancellor, Churchill was able to dominate the House with his oratory.

While rightly renowned as a speaker, he was not expert in all fields of the art. He prepared speeches laboriously in advance, but if the mood of a meeting or a House of Commons session was not with him, he was not flexible enough to ad-lib, and his guns could be spiked. Moreover the qualities of the platform orator were becoming less important as the significance of lengthy parliamentary or election disquisitions declined, with speeches becoming shorter and attention spans waning. Showing his ability to move with the times while apparently impersonating a dinosaur, Churchill was aware of the growing power of radio and sought to manipulate it, ahead of many of his peers, and attempted to change his speaking style to remain in tune with changing public tastes.

Churchill's first big decision as chancellor was whether to return to gold at the prewar rate, a move the Bank of England had coveted ever since the end of the war. Most economists argued that a return to gold at prewar rates would drive down inflation and restore stability. But Churchill was not an uncritical champion of the principles of classical economics. The return to the gold standard, far from being a blow deliberately aimed at the working classes on behalf of the owners of the "means of production," was an attempt to protect home industries by making them more efficient. A committee appointed in 1924 by the Labour government had reported unanimously in favor of a return, despite the adverse comment of the economist John Maynard Keynes (who was prompted to pen the famous tract "The Economic Consequences of Mr. Churchill"). By the following year the governor of the Bank of England and Treasury officials were keen to expedite the return. In January 1925, however, Churchill had serious second thoughts following criticism of the policy in the *Daily Express*. The governor of the bank, Montagu Norman, and other leading economists and Treasury officials had to paddle hard to counter this opposition. A clutch of former chancellors supported the return to gold, Keynes remaining a lone voice in opposition. The battle over the gold standard dragged on for two months. Churchill's decision to return to gold, which later in life he came to regard as his greatest mistake, was supported by both the other main political parties as well as the Bank of England and the Treasury.

Aside from the issue of gold, Chancellor Churchill needed to wield the ax on government spending. He was unable to make immediate cuts in military expenditure, and existing plans for the RAF and the navy anticipated spending increases. So Churchill told Baldwin that something had to be done to keep military estimates down. This, of course, provided ammunition for Churchill's opponents, as the spectacle of the former "we want eight" dreadnoughts champion arguing for military cuts offered an attractive contrast and led later historians to emphasize Churchill's role in Britain's interwar disarmament. The reality at the time was that Churchill's desire for retrenchment reflected nothing more than the inevitable cut and thrust of democratic politics and the fact that the international atmosphere of the 1920s was very different from that prevailing in the 1930s. It also reflected Churchill's entirely sound assessment that a major world war was unlikely for the foreseeable future, and it logically followed that cutting military expenditure was not tantamount to a desertion of the government's duty to protect Britain and its interests around the world. Adopting the "ten-year rule" that had already been established was not a gross dereliction of duty, but "a perfectly reasonable prognostication" which "in fact proved fairly accurate."[19] This was the age of Locarno, not of Munich, and prophesying doom from the vantage point of hindsight is a singularly profitless enterprise, though one that holds a strange attraction for historians. With Germany vanquished and Japan an ally, the British Empire appeared to be secure. An attempt to see off New York's challenge to the City of London as the world's financial center, therefore, seemed like a reasonable target.

The service departments were the ones who found Churchill most implacable as chancellor. He battled with the Admiralty over the 1924–25 and 1925–26 estimates, asking, "Why should there be a war with Japan? I do not believe there is the slightest chance of it in our lifetime," as he attempted to curb their spending.[20] Some contend that he disarmed the navy, though this fails to take into account the vicissitudes of democratic politics and the inability of politicians to predict the future or stop economic tidal waves in their course. In the case of the Singapore naval base, the problems had as much to do with interservice rivalry as with interwar parsimony. What is more, the naval budget actually rose while Churchill was chancellor, from £105 million in 1923 to £113 million in 1929. Any chancellor in the mid-1920s would have sought significant cuts in military spending. Churchill thought the prospect of war with Germany or Japan was remote and argued against the proposed creation of a fleet to be based at Singapore, the reverse of his position when Labour had talked along similar lines when in power. Eventually, Baldwin decided the matter, accepting the need for new ships, though reducing the size of a new class of cruisers and making other economies. Churchill's battles with the Admiralty, the department for which he had demanded ever-increasing resources in the run-up to the First World War, led to many bruising encounters. Unlike the other two services, the navy was used to being given pretty much whatever it asked for, though it faced a formidable cost-cutting opponent in Churchill. As the First Sea Lord, the Earl Beatty, put it, "It takes a good deal out of me when dealing with a man of his caliber with a very quick brain."[21]

One of the most unfortunate elements of 1920s defense cuts was the weakening of the Royal Navy in the Far East. Because adequate ships were not forthcoming, unreasonable expectations were piled onto "the Singapore strategy." The strategy, intended to protect the eastern empire, deter Japan, and develop an alliance with America, came unstuck when Britain faced the worst possible scenario of fighting Germany, Italy, and Japan simultaneously. But there was little alternative for the British government in the 1920s when, after a period of total military mobilization, the electorate insisted upon peace and the prioritization of social issues at home rather than building defensive castles in oriental skies. In the mid-1920s, the grave challenges that were to beset Britain and the empire in the 1930s were far off, if discerned at all. Disarmament and collective security—trusting to naval limitation conferences and the League of Nations—were the preferred methods of dealing with potentially troublesome foreign powers.

Churchill remained an influential contributor to European and international developments. From an early juncture, he recognized the problems the League of Nations faced in trying to deliver international security—"How can the League of Nations accomplish anything without a Navy & an Army behind it?" he asked.[22] At negotiations on international war debts in Paris in January 1924, he achieved a widely admired settlement and was a force behind the Locarno guarantee of European frontiers, which brought Germany in as a signatory and equal partner, part of the process of rehabilitating Germany, of which Churchill was a vocal proponent.

Given Churchill's association with the concept of an "English-speaking world" and the transatlantic alliance, it is interesting to note that in this period he criticized the land of his mother's birth, perceiving how America was seeking to supplant British power. In 1928, Herbert Hoover won the American presidential election. Churchill thought it bad for Britain—"I feel that this is not good for us. Poor old England—she is being slowly but surely forced into the shade."[23] After outgoing president Calvin Coolidge's Armistice Day speech of 1928, in which he vented his anger at British naval policy and openly called for American naval superiority, Clementine wrote that it made her "blood boil" and that "it should be learned by everyone over here so that we shall thoroughly grasp what the Swine think and mean."[24] Churchill agreed, writing that "my blood boiled too at Coolidge's proclamation. Why can't they let us alone? They have exacted every last penny owing from Europe: they say they are not going to help: surely they might leave us to manage our own affairs."[25] On the same day, Clementine, contemplating Churchill's next ministerial position, wrote, "I think it would be a good idea if you went to the Foreign Office. But I am afraid your known hostility to America might stand in the way—You would have to try & understand & master America & make her like you."

THE GENERAL STRIKE

Given the prevailing economic climate in Britain, as Chancellor Churchill had no choice but to demand economy in government expenditure. The main problems afflicting the British economy were not financial but revolved around excessive capacity in the staple industry sector. The increased value of the pound after the return to gold detracted from Baldwin's industrial policy, making things more difficult for the traditional export trades, especially coal.

Like other staples, the British coal industry was in a state of structural decline, and trouble between employers and miners loomed large in the mid-1920s. Once again, Churchill was to find himself at the center of a national storm. At the end of June 1925, the mine owners served notice: wages would have to be reduced and working hours increased if the industry was to keep going. The Miners' Federation prepared for a national strike to oppose these draconian moves. The entire nation's workforce then became involved when the Trades Union Congress (TUC) was called upon, and the prospect of a general strike loomed. The government, watching uneasily, announced a temporary subsidy and hoped the two sides would come to some agreement.

Churchill, like the prime minister, but unlike some Cabinet colleagues, sympathized with the miners' plight. His prestige in Baldwin's eyes gave him a more prominent role during the strike than was perhaps necessary or wise. The budget of April 1926, another personal triumph for Churchill, occurred just as the subsidy supporting the status quo in the coal industry came to an end, and the prospect of a general strike reappeared. There was stalemate in the coal districts, and the TUC prepared for a national strike. On the evening of May 2, the Cabinet voted unanimously to break off negotiations with the General Council of the TUC, and the threatened strike began.

The chancellor's conduct during the strike has come to form part of the Churchill mythology. Because he chose—once hostilities had been declared—to prosecute the campaign against the strikers with resolution and military precision, he was castigated as a heartless, trigger-happy enemy of the working man. In fact, he was more in sympathy with the miners' plight and did more to ameliorate their suffering than any of his colleagues. He firmly believed that robust action would end the strike soonest and limit the potentially catastrophic damage to the national economy, his first priority as chancellor. Churchill also saw the strike as a potential threat to con-stitutional government and throughout its duration distinguished sharply between the constitutional issue and the dispute in the coal industry. Of course, there was more to it than this, for Churchill found the opportunity in the rarefied atmosphere of a national crisis to indulge his passion for hands-on involvement. The strike brought out his martial instincts, which exasperated those around him. As Neville Chamberlain wrote, "He simply revels in this affair, which he *will* continually treat and talk of as if it were 1914."[26] Yet while Churchill's bellicose stance confirmed the prejudices of his opponents and reaffirmed the antipathy of the Labour Party, just like his position on Bolshevism, it pleased many Conservatives.

During the strike, Churchill took special interest in the creation and production of a government mouthpiece, the *British Gazette* newspaper. Given that the newspapermen had joined the strike, the government needed a method of reaching the people, and the paper achieved a record circulation of over two and a half million. Though J. C. C. Davidson, a junior minister, was in charge of the paper, Churchill saw it as an extremely effective weapon against the strik-ers and wrote for it with gusto. Davidson found some of his more explosive pieces unprintable. Exasperated, he wrote that Churchill "thinks he is Napoleon, but curiously enough the men who have been printing all their life in the various processes happen to know more about their job than he does." Davidson effectively summed up the qualities that made Churchill a frustrating colleague: "If I had a mountain that wanted to be moved, I should send for him at once. I think, however, that I should not consult him . . . if I wanted to know where to put it."[27] Churchill's enthusiasm for using the armed forces to intimidate the strikers also had to be curbed by his col-leagues, though he was put in charge of a subcommittee overseeing

Territorial Army volunteers in an unarmed police reserve. Characteristically, Churchill produced a comprehensive plan of action that would have allowed this force to be deployed in the event of the regular police being stretched beyond capacity.

Despite his penchant for robust action, Churchill was thought soft by some of his colleagues because of his desire to offer an olive branch to the strikers; "ready to agree to anything," as the minister of labor put it. The restraining hand of the prime minister was applied in negotiations with the miners, lest Churchill give away too much. Churchill's actions, at least in part, were motivated by a mounting concern about the damage to the economy, and he was prepared to offer all sorts of terms and conditions in order to end the strike. By the end of September, Churchill was in the backseat as Baldwin returned from holiday. From October to November 1926, Churchill became a prisoner of the prevailing views of his Cabinet colleagues, who much preferred victory for the mine owners to a negotiated settlement. He was a lone voice in Cabinet arguing the miners' cause. Though the general strike petered out, the dispute in the coal industry lingered on, with very little attempt by Baldwin to resolve it. Eventually the bitter economic realities forced the men back to work.

Churchill's 1927 budget recorded a worrying deficit caused by the strike. But in his budget speech he proceeded to pull a series of rabbits from the hat, finding money without resorting to unpopular and vote-losing retrenchments and taxes. Churchill subsequently fought hard to assist industrial recovery and ameliorate the state of depression settling over the staple industries. He also showed his long-standing concern for social welfare in measures like the increase in children's allowance on income tax (1928)—an example, as he put it in Parliament, of the government "helping the producer."

1929: OUT OF OFFICE

Clementine, Randolph, and Diana were all involved in Churchill's campaign for the 1929 general election, in which he held his Epping seat. The Labour Party, however, made significant gains, and

Baldwin was obliged to resign, ushering in Ramsay MacDonald's second Labour government. Thomas Jones, deputy secretary to the Cabinet, described Churchill on election night 1929, which he spent at 10 Downing Street. He kept "score as results came in, sipping whisky and soda, getting redder and redder, rising often and going to glare at the machine . . . hunching his shoulders, bowing his head like a bull about to charge. As Labour gain after Labour gain was announced, Winston became more and more flushed with anger . . . and behaved as if any more Labour gains came along he would smash the whole apparatus. His ejaculations to the surrounding staff were quite unprintable."[28]

The departure from office which followed this defeat allowed Churchill to redirect his energies, though for far longer, as it turned out, than he would have wished. His quite incredible portfolio of nonpolitical activities, pastimes, jobs, and hobbies now came to the fore. The major writing project he embarked upon was the life of his ancestor the 1st Duke of Marlborough. Adopting a practice that was to become common in the preparation of his great works, Churchill employed a part-time researcher, Maurice Ashley, and a couple of former naval officers advised him on the maritime aspects of the campaign.

In 1929, a Churchill delegation—Jack, Randolph, and Winston—embarked on a three-month visit to North America aboard the *Empress of Australia*, part holiday, part lecture tour. Tonsil problems prevented Clementine from accompanying them. On the voyage out, Churchill spent hours writing articles from his grand cabin suite and reading into his Marlborough book. He also spent hours inflicting "most cruel defeats" upon Jack at bezique, the early-nineteenth-century French card game. At one point, a bottle of 1865 brandy was required to help him overcome the news from home that the new Labour government had dismissed Lord Lloyd as high commissioner in Egypt. Leopold Amery, also on board the *Empress of Australia*, offered an interesting insight into Churchill's political thoughts at the time: "He was of the opinion that the caliber of politicians had declined. He felt that he had had a good political innings, and that there was little hope of his ever becoming Prime Minister." It was a sound assessment, given the causes Churchill was to champion during the coming decade and the wariness with which leading politicians viewed him. As the 1930s began, Churchill appeared to have peaked as a politician. The general consensus of opinion was that he was uniquely talented, even a genius perhaps, but had major faults that diminished his potential as a politician. He was not a team player, was unreliable and even disloyal, and his judgment could be poor as the appeal of risk and danger trumped discretion.

A British Parliamentary Association reporter met Churchill off the ship on August 12, 1929, and he cashed in on his visit with a series of articles in the *Telegraph* entitled "Impressions of America." Once in Canada, the luxurious Canadian Pacific Railway conveyed the Churchills across the vast Dominion. Churchill had a special saloon cabin with double beds, an observation room, and a dining room, carriages placed at his disposal by Mr. Schwab of the Bethlehem Steel Corporation. He traveled to Montreal, writing to Clementine of the luxury of the carriages and their short baths—though he reported that "by lying on one's back with one's paws in the air, a good dip can be obtained."[29] Churchill was charmed by his reception in Canada and even talked of moving there and starting a new life.

After nearly a month in Canada, Churchill headed to America. Here he visited California, met Charlie Chaplin at the MGM studios, called upon President Hoover, toured Civil War battlefields, and found ways to overcome the strictures of Prohibition. From Santa Barbara, he wrote to Clementine on September 19, 1929 that he reckoned they had over £21,000 coming in. But such rosy assessments were soon dashed, as the Wall Street Crash decimated his personal investments. Churchill was in New York on October 29—Black Tuesday—which precipitated the Great Crash. He had speculated on the New York stock market, and lost over £10,000. He returned to Britain on October 30. With Churchill out of government and facing financial difficulties, dust sheets appeared at Chartwell, and he took up his pen with frenzied energy, writing articles and columns wherever he could find an outlet. Only his office was left habitable in the house, and the small house in the Chartwell grounds, Wellstreet Cottage, became the family's "slump haven." Nineteen thirty was for the Churchill family an unusually sedentary, stay-at-home year, which the children loved.

Churchill's visit to America was important in developing his thinking about Anglo-American relations and their significance in international affairs. During the 1920s, his enthusiasm for America had waned because of evidence that it was trying to diminish Britain's power while augmenting its own. America's uncompromising attitude to British war debt irked him, especially as Britain was owed nearly twice as much by other allies as it owed America (like his attitude toward the miners, Churchill was more sympathetic to the debt relief of European countries that owed Britain than were his Cabinet colleagues). Churchill viewed America's insistence upon naval parity with Britain as a tactic designed to give it significant influence on British policy. He was right to be worried, though the 1929 visit converted Churchill into an enthusiast for the extension of American power around the world, a second pillar of the "English-speaking world" with which he was to become fixated. Herein lay the dilemma at the core of Britain's relations with America: America did not see things in such terms and was always less enthusiastic about a "special relationship"—a phrase pioneered by Churchill—and alliance with the British Empire–Commonwealth. It was, indeed, attempting to supplant British power with its own. And soon Britain was to become dependent on American power for its own security.

FAMILY AND PERSONAL AFFAIRS

During the First World War, and for long stretches of the 1920s, Churchill was too busy to see much of his family. But Clementine was a politician's wife and knew what to expect. Trips together, to the theater for example, were rare, and Churchill's circle of friends, never large, contracted. When he was able to spend time with his family, he remained an engaging father, playing gorilla with the children in the garden, making tree houses and encouraging them to participate in dinner table conversations about politics and current affairs. He took less exercise than in the past, playing the occasional game of polo (for example, for the Commons versus the Lords), though he played his last game in 1927. Infrequently, Churchill monitored "lifestyle" matters, such as body weight and alcohol consumption, but he remained a reluctant convert. "Not for Pig" was his assessment, in a letter to Clementine, of the news that his great friend F. E. Smith had given up all alcohol except cider.*

Churchill's character developed along its set course. In 1921, A. G. Gardener wrote that he "doesn't want to hear your views. He does not want to disturb the beautiful clarity of his thought by the tiresome reminders of the other side."[30] His writing continued to serve his personal rendition of history—though of no lesser value to the historian because of this—his multivolume *The World Crisis* having as one of its major themes the desire to set the record straight regarding Churchill's tenure at the Admiralty, a work famously described by Balfour as "Winston's brilliant autobiography, disguised as a history of the universe."[31]

The 1920s were years of considerable upheaval in the personal life of the Churchill family. There were regular house moves; in 1920, they took 2 Sussex Square, north of Hyde Park. Typically, while Clementine grappled with the move, Churchill was boar-hunting and painting at the Duke of Westminster's estate in the south of France. The fact that he remained undiminished as a politician and writer showed immense reserves of strength. Churchill had an ability to maintain bulkheads between the competing spheres of his life— not, for example, allowing bereavement, a downturn in political fortunes, withering press criticism, or financial concerns to ruin his family life or his career as a writer. It is an ability that very few people possess, founded, possibly, on egocentrism.

---

* In 1936, Lord Beaverbrook offered to bet Churchill £2,000 that he couldn't remain teetotal for the year. Churchill declined, opting instead for a bet of £600 that he could survive the year without drinking brandy or any undiluted spirits.

One brief period in the early 1920s brought not only the death of his mother, but also the suicide of Clementine's brother, plus the death of his manservant Thomas Walden. Jennie Churchill's life in the postwar years had reflected the country-house party lifestyle of the upper classes, as well as the social whirl of the 1920s. By then in her sixties, she was still a well-known hostess and partygoer. She met Ravel, Conrad, Stravinsky, Picasso, and Delius. Though she was sixty-seven, her joie de vivre was undiminished, but in June 1921 she fell down the stairs while wearing high-heeled shoes. Gangrene set in, an amputation was performed, and she entered a coma before Winston and Jack could arrive at her bedside. She died on June 29, 1921. As Churchill wrote to the Duke of Connaught, "She looked beautiful yesterday in her coffin. Since the pangs of the morning thirty years had rolled from her brow and one saw again her old splendour."[32] She was laid to rest alongside her husband, Randolph, in the churchyard at Bladon.

For themselves, Churchill and Clementine remained a loving couple, though often apart. On January 4, 1922 Churchill wrote from Cannes that "I have been thinking so much about you & worrying over your health." He returned on January 7, though before the month was out, Clementine, pregnant once more (with her last child, Mary), was off to Cannes. The couple stoically endured the tragedy of their three-year-old daughter, Marigold, dying of septicemia in the previous April. Clementine suffered bouts of ill health; she was knocked over by a bus on Brompton Road in June 1927, and in the following February was gravely ill with a mastoid problem requiring two operations in the space of ten hours at 11 Downing Street. What is more, she was often worried about domestic and family matters. Though Churchill told her not to fret, and that "servants exist to save one trouble,"[33] she was one of life's worriers. Churchill, too, had his bouts of depression, though the famous "Black Dog" was clearly a beast that drove him to new heights of endeavor. More is made of Churchill's depressive tendencies than they deserve. They did not rule him or warp his judgment. Overemphasis upon the "Black Dog" reflects the common tendency to view and assess Churchill in a manner in which one would not view or assess other human beings, perhaps an inevitable penalty of greatness. Toward the end of his own life, Brendan Bracken offered Lord Moran some penetrating insights about Churchill. He said that Churchill had great success at controlling his fears, which was sometimes mistaken for recklessness. He noted the strain of melancholy that had afflicted the Marlborough line, and how in Winston's case it had been offset by the robustness of the Jeromes. A man who, especially as he aged, could sit in silence for hours—like a trance, Bracken said—liked to surround himself with buoyant people.

Churchill often had to worry about money, but his personal fortunes rose when he inherited the Garron Tower estate in Northern Ireland from his grandmother. Its sale allowed the purchase of Chartwell in Kent in September 1922, a property that Churchill had viewed and fallen in love with the year before. Though it was only twenty-four miles from Westminster and the heart of the empire, it stood in an idyllic rural setting, surrounded by sweeping views of the English countryside. For some time, the Churchills had wanted a country house, having sold Lullenden in 1919 for financial reasons. But Clementine, practical as ever, wanted to become a country lady on the right terms. As she wrote to her husband in July 1921, "I long for a country home but I would like it to be a rest & a joy Bunny not a fresh preoccupation." Purchased for £5,000, Chartwell, with its age and rural location, satisfied Churchill's sense of English history, though it took many years to become the leisurely abode that Clementine wished for. This was because it required substantial, and expensive, renovation. Nevertheless, the fact that it was so far from being the finished article satisfied Churchill's instincts to build, plant, and design his own landscape in which to live. It was to become a huge financial drain, however, as Clementine recognized from the start that it would be, indicated by the fact that Philip Tilden was immediately commissioned to rebuild the house (Lutyens and Baker, the two most famous architects of the period, being unavailable).

At Chartwell, Churchill spent many decades improving the buildings, erecting new cottages and walls, excavating lakes and gardens, and experimenting with pigs and chickens. Animals played an important part in Churchill's life, from Australian black swans to golden carp, racehorses, marmalade cats, and poodles. He loved playing the farmer and gardener, reporting to Clementine on events such as "a minor catastrophe in the pig world"[34] and planting Japanese azaleas, Britannia rhododendrons, and white magnolias. Showing his capacity to engage deeply with whatever he turned his attention to, he took delight in building and furnishing his home. On July 22, 1922 he wrote a "dissertation on dining room chairs" as a guide to their purchase. "The Dining Room chair has certain very marked requisites," he began, declaring that there should be twenty, comfortable and with arms. Though Chartwell was purchased in 1922, the family did not properly move in until 1924. As their daughter was to write, "I think it most significant that Clementine was not there at a moment when most women would feel their presence absolutely necessary."[35] Instead, Churchill reported on these first Chartwell days in letters—"I drink champagne at meals & buckets of claret and soda in between."[36]

Chartwell was to witness a procession of Churchillian fads, fancies, hobbies, and business ventures over the ensuing forty years. He indulged in extensive stockbreeding, as well as creating lakes and buildings, turning his own hand to bricklaying in the construction, for example, of Chickenham Palace, a large brick hen house. He bought up surrounding farms when funds allowed and wrangled over bills with builders and plumbers. He pored over lawnmower catalogues before making a purchase, imported black swans, and attempted to introduce new varieties of butterfly. He planted roses and dabbled in commercial market gardening. He stocked his lakes with carp, lionheads, catfish, and golden comets, bred English Shorthorn cattle and Swedish Landrace pigs. New livestock arrivals he toasted with sherry and maintained that it was wrong to eat an animal one had said "Good Morning" to.

During the 1920s, painting intensified as a pleasure and release for Churchill. He even wrote about it, articles on "Painting as a Pastime" appearing in the *Strand Magazine* in 1921 and 1922, netting the princely sum of £1,000. Clementine had counseled caution—"I expect the professionals would be vexed & say you do not yet know enough about Art." But the lure of the money prevailed, and the articles were a great success, Churchill explaining how painting had first come to him and the many pleasures associated with brush and canvas. His paintings varied considerably in this period. Following the death of Marigold, he retreated with his family to Lochmore in the Scottish Highlands, where painting brought him solace. "Happy are the painters," he wrote, "for they shall not be lonely. Light and color, peace and hope, will keep them company to the end, or almost to the end, of the day." It was very much Churchill's practice, in the aristocratic tradition, to visit the country homes of friends and colleagues. Trips to such "paintatious" places (as he called them) often led to new canvases. Venues included Colonel John Astor's home, Hever Castle in Kent, where the colonnaded Italian garden captured Churchill's artistic attention, and Breccles in Norfolk, home of Clementine's cousin, where he painted the wooded gardens. In 1927, he stayed with King George V at Balmoral, where he worked from a painting of the churchyard of St. Paul's Cathedral. He painted on his regular jaunts to the French Riviera, attempted the pyramids when visiting Cairo, and took his paints to America and Canada's Rocky Mountains. When at home and the weather inclement, he resorted to still-life studies of fruit, bottles, and glassware collected by the children, or blooms from the magnolia that Clementine had planted beneath his window.

Wherever he went, even on official visits, the full paraphernalia of the painter went, too. In 1925, he showed a painting anonymously at an amateur art exhibition in London. The judges awarded *Winter Sunshine, Chartwell* first prize, though one of them, Sir Joseph Duveen, at first refused to believe it was the work of an amateur. Observing Churchill painting at Lympne near Folkestone, a friend captured the extent of his concentration: "He was completely absorbed . . . wearing his immense sombrero of light felt. . . . Four sketches were drying in the sun, propped against the feet of the easel. He was now slashing the fifth canvas, almost throwing the paint on; he was sighing, almost out of breath with the effort of expressing his feelings."[37]

6

Man of Kent:
A Frenzied Unemployment

In the 1930s, Winston Churchill had no sense of the inevitability of war, no prescient inkling that the time and the hour were close at hand when he would be called upon to lead the nation. Though Churchill, along with many others, subsequently cast the years leading to his "finest hour" in a golden light, the decade had neither the consistency nor the continuity sometimes ascribed to it, and accounts that highlight Churchill's activities and portentous pronouncements are devoid of proper context. Before the heroic War Leader coming to his country's aid in its moment of greatest peril, the Churchill myth-history would have it, came a decade in which the Great Sage prophesied from the wilderness and was ignored. But while Churchill's political activity, especially his consistent warnings about Germany, were a major theme of the decade, there were a myriad other things going on in the 1930s—it wasn't all about a world waiting patiently to stumble into catastrophic conflict. Beyond the politics, wilderness or no, the 1930s was a very successful decade for both Churchill the writer and Churchill the artist. He remained one of the nation's most powerful politicians and, for the first time, a leader of mass movements. He also developed his portfolio as a stockbreeder and beekeeper.

For much of the 1930s, Churchill believed that Britain was not directly threatened from the continent, and even when the German menace became clear to him, he perceived no serious threat from Italy or Japan, the latter a notable Churchillian blind spot. On September 15, 1937, he wrote in the *Evening Standard* that "major war is not imminent, and I still believe there is a good chance of no major war taking place in our time." But his whole stance was based upon the notion that war would be far less likely if Britain were properly prepared to fight and prepared to deal robustly and consistently with potential enemies. such as Germany.

During the second half of the decade, Churchill's concern about the menace of German resurgence grew, as did the force of his warnings that all due preparation was needed. Churchill was the most prominent British politician who simply refused to see the appeasement of Germany as a sensible policy (though he supported measures that amounted to the appeasement of Italy and Japan). As early as 1932, Churchill was raising the alarm with regard to the Nazis. "He understood what Hitler meant by the Versailles grievances but something, probably just brilliant intuition, told him that Hitler had much more in mind than the mere redress of them."[1] Much of what Churchill achieved during the 1930s, including the foundations of his claim to be a national leader in 1940 despite severe opposition, depended upon his isolation and independence from the government, as well as the accuracy of his predictions. For when the time came, he could legitimately claim to bear no responsibility for British foreign and defense policy during the so-called appeasement years. He could appear instead as a new broom, renowned for his pugnacity and just the man to call time on the follies of appeasement and show Hitler a line in the sand with John Bull standing four-square behind it.

It has often been remarked that some of Churchill's other salient activities during the 1930s diminished the potency of his calls for serious preparation in the face of German expansionism and militarism. In particular, his role in opposing reform in India and in supporting King Edward VIII during the abdication crisis are widely seen to have demonstrated his poor judgment. But it would transpire that Churchill's argumentativeness and willingness to crusade for lost causes was also a boon for democracy and civilization. For much of the decade, however, these traits were regarded as a source of national inconvenience warranting ridicule. While his stance on India or the abdication might have augmented his reputation for poor judgment and belligerence, his lonely stand on Germany and rearmament had immeasurable significance for his country's future independence.

In 1929, Churchill had said that he quite relished the prospect of a period out of government, as it would offer a chance for him to show his mettle as an Opposition spokesman. Two years later, his wish was granted, though his spell as an Opposition front-bencher soon came to an untimely end and ushered in almost a decade in which he held no major office and wielded no governmental or party power. After the Conservatives lost office in 1929, and after Churchill had subsequently fallen foul of his party's leadership following marked differences of opinion, the sensible money would have been on his career as a national and international politician being over. This would almost certainly have been the case if the 1930s had not witnessed the most severe international crisis in history. The threat to British survival posed by the European dictators called for a type of political animal that democratic politics was simply not designed to produce. Thankfully, a man of talent, bellicosity, and strategic vision was waiting in the wings, a descendant of Marlborough.

But this is to anticipate. The 1930s were presented by Churchill, as he subsequently sought to design the historical architecture of his own life and of the twentieth century, as "wilderness years" in which he was forced from the citadel of power. In the wastelands beyond, he roamed alone, a soothsayer foretelling doom as the world sleepwalked toward the abyss. But Churchill barely had a moment to spare during this period, such were the calls of both his political duties and his manifold activities beyond. Contrary to the myth, his influence remained considerable, and he remained close to the center of British political life, his leadership sought and his voice listened to. He had still to perform his duties as a member of Parliament and a noteworthy commentator on national and international events. There were then the calls of his historical and journalistic pursuits, many of these aimed at restoring fortunes damaged by the Wall Street Crash, the continuing drain of Chartwell, and the need to secure the future of his children. On top of all this, there was his painting and the bucolic home pursuits that enriched his life and so burnish his historical image. If the decade was a wilderness, it was a surprisingly fertile one.

Throughout the 1930s, Churchill kept up a steady assault on the policies of the government, voicing criticisms and sponsoring and leading pressure-group movements that indicated the health and vitality of a democratic state. All the time fostering networks of support, Churchill variously spoke out about political developments in Britain's Indian empire, the threat posed to British security by the air forces of hostile powers, and the growing menace posed by Nazi Germany and the flawed nature of the government's policy in attempting to meet it. Much of Churchill's fire during the 1930s came from his belief that Britain was getting soft and failing to live up to the expectations placed upon it as the foremost international power. He had been deeply disturbed during his visit to America in 1929 by the common assumption that Britain was in decline. Though with hindsight, it might be said that the rot had set in and Britain was no longer powerful enough, unilaterally, to defend its far-flung interests or to act alone as the world's policeman, Churchill set himself to defy such notions. This defiance was to take him to Number 10.

Churchill's vigor was also inspired by a desire to prevent the 1920s and 1930s being dominated by what he considered "lesser" politicians. Always prone to nostalgia, Churchill believed himself to be one of history's great captains, though by the 1930s, it seemed as if the political giants had tamely yielded the ship of state to men like Baldwin, MacDonald, and the plebeians of the left. But Britain's proud international position was not to be frittered away by such pygmies, one of the sentiments that determined him to take up the cudgels over Indian reform. While the age of nineteenth-century-style imperialism might have passed, and new political forces were afoot, Churchill hardly thought that an era in which fascism was triumphing in many parts of the world was a good time for Britain to be divesting itself of empire and its manifold responsibilities around the world. In short, Britain would be unwise, as well as negligent, if it were to lose India just as it was about to engage in a global struggle for national and imperial survival. Moreover, Churchill clung resolutely to a Whig conception of Britain's role as the light of world progress.[2]

THE TORIES AFTER ELECTORAL DEFEAT

The Conservative Party was divided following its electoral defeat in 1929. Facing the fallout from depression and financial crisis, groping for a way forward, some argued forcefully for a serious program of tariff reform leading to widespread protection. Lords Beaverbrook and Rothermere launched a "United Empire Party" to try to persuade Baldwin along this path. This naturally concerned Churchill, who had only been able to return to the Conservative Party after it had forsaken such an unequivocal position in the protection-versus-free-trade debate. But in October 1931, Baldwin finally accepted a policy of levying tariffs on all imported manufactures. Churchill wavered in his convictions. With unemployment spiraling, even significant sections of the Liberal Party (the great champion of free trade) moved behind the cause of protection. Eventually Churchill also succumbed. He pledged himself to support tariff reform, even to the point of accepting tariffs on food imports, a free-trade shibboleth. In Parliament he vigorously attacked Labour and maintained his reputation for repartee. As he said after a long speech by Labour MP William Graham, "He spoke without a note, and almost without a point."[3]

In the October 1931 election, Churchill doubled his majority, and the Conservatives won handsomely, though a national government under Ramsay MacDonald took office. Churchill was far too loathed by Labour to even be considered for office and his age-old opposition to the Labour movement was more important than his right-wing views on India in excluding him from power in the coalition governments that dominated the 1930s. It was not, as is widely held, his resignation from the Tories' embryonic "business committee" (today's shadow cabinet) following a speech on India in the Commons in January 1931 that estranged Churchill from the Tory leadership. To say that Churchill "resigned" from the business committee—a low-key affair established only in March 1930—is putting it rather strongly, and this minor event did not represent an irrevocable breach with the Tory front bench.

There were real enough differences nonetheless. Churchill had been bothered by Baldwin's support of the Indian political advances proposed during the Labour government's tenure of office. News of Viceroy Lord Irwin's offer of Dominion status to India, received as he returned to Britain from New York in October 1929, had electrified Churchill. He was concerned about Britain's status in the world, not just events in India, and was by no means alone in worrying about how to ensure Britain's position and deal with rising nationalism in India and elsewhere.

Consequently, the pattern for the 1930s was set. While Churchill continued to function as an MP and a political loose cannon, his time was occupied by private and nonpolitical pursuits. He researched the biography of the 1st Duke of Marlborough and seldom attended the Commons. In November 1931, the last volume of his war memoirs appeared (*The Eastern Front*); lecture tours were undertaken; and continental painting holidays and cruises were manfully endured. Chartwell, painting, writing, farming, building, holidaying—all of these things were as important to the Churchill of the 1930s as were politics, all important features of a many-layered and richly textured life. Though now an older dog, he could still learn new tricks and even attempted to change the way he delivered

Blenheim Palace (above)

January 1884: Jack, Jennie and Winston Churchill

Churchill as a schoolboy
at Harrow, aged thirteen

The Boer war: Churchill aboard a steamer at Durban, 1899, war
correspondentfor the Morning Post and combatan

In formal dress uniform

The young politician: Churchill in 1904, shortly
after he left the Conservative Party for the Liberals.
Note the picture of Lord Kitchener behind him

Churchill and Kaiser Wilhelm
at military exercises in the years
before the First World War

September 1915:
Churchill speaking
at the opening of the
YMCA hostel for
munitions workers,
Enfield, Middlesex

March 1924: Churchill and
Clementine at the by-election in the
Abbey division of Westminster

February 1928: Building a wall at Chartwell with daughter Sarah

January 1932: Churchill on the
move after a bout of typhus

February 1939: Churchill at his specially
designed standing desk, Chartwell

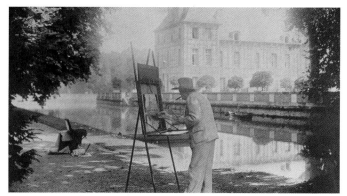

January 1937: Painting the Château de St George in Normandy

January 1942: Churchill addressing the 4th Hussars, his old regiment, in Egypt

November 1942: The famous "V" sign

December 1943: The Bermuda conference. French Premier
Joseph Laniel, President Eisenhower and Churchill

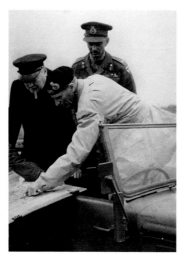

July 1944: Churchill poring over a map with General Bernard Montgomery

December 1944: Crossing the Rhine

July 1945: Churchill sitting on a chair from Hitler's chancellery amidst the ruins of Berlin, surrounded by Russian soldiers

October 1947: Churchill and
poodle at Chartwell

Riding in the Old Surrey and Burstow
Hunt at Chartwell Farm, 1948

Churchill with his Foreign Secretary and heir apparent, Anthony
Eden, returning to Downing Street in September 1954

February 1959: Churchill is taken out to Aristotle Onassis's yacht, Christina O, while on holiday in Morocco

The funeral cortège passes the Houses of Parliament

January 1965: The queue in Bladon, waiting to enter the churchyard of St. Martin's to see Churchill's grave

speeches (altered "largely under Randolph's tuition" so that, as he told Clementine in April 1935, he could talk to the Commons "with garrulous unpremeditated flows. . . . There is apparently nothing in the literary effect I have sought for forty years!").

On December 5, 1931, Churchill, Clementine, and Diana embarked on the liner *Europa* for a tour of North America, during the course of which he intended to deliver forty lectures. The trip was designed to gross over £10,000 and recoup the losses sustained in the 1929 crash, as well as to provide a holiday. His main lecture theme during this trip was to become a familiar one, central to Churchill's activities as an international statesman: he espoused the cause of Anglo-American unity and the mutual interests of the English-speaking peoples, meaning the British Commonwealth and empire and America. This American angle of vision, this advocacy of a "special relationship," was to be a distinctive theme of his politics for the rest of his life. The trip was interrupted when Churchill was knocked down by a car on Fifth Avenue in New York, an accident that put him in hospital for eight days and prevented him from returning to England until March. After leaving the hospital, he continued with a reduced lecture tour and then sailed for the Bahamas aboard the liner *Majestic* to recuperate, staying at Government House. He returned home to find a £2,000 Daimler waiting for him alongside the platform at Victoria, a gift from American and British friends.

INDIA

It was upon the relatively minor issue of political reform in India that Churchill risked impaling his political career. At first, his opposition to the government's proposed India reforms looked as if it might provide a significant fillip to his political standing. On February 26, 1931, he wrote that there had been a great change in the political position in the last six weeks: "Every speech I've made and step I've taken has been well received beyond expectations."[4] This apparent change in fortunes was largely due to his first speech on the issue of political reform in India.

As a reward for its support during the First World War, India had been promised Dominion status at some future date. So the course was already set for its political advancement along the road toward self-government as enjoyed by the "white" Dominions. Of course, from that point on, Indian nationalists pushed hard for the announcement of a firm timeline. In 1928, Sir John Simon was appointed to head a committee to plan constitutional advance and provincial self-government, the latter an important concession in any likely reform package devolving power at the level of the province to Indian legislatures, while Britain retained control of the all-important central government functions of finance, defense, and foreign policy. Simon's commission was boycotted by the Indian National Congress, for whom the proposals did not go far enough.

In order to try to establish better relations with the powerful nationalist party, Lord Irwin believed it necessary to demonstrate London's continuing commitment to the goal of Dominion status. Soon after the release of Gandhi, Nehru, and other Indian National Congress (INC) leaders from prison, Gandhi met the viceroy at Government House, and civil disobedience was suspended in return for government concessions. This appalled Churchill, who found it "nauseating" to see "a seditious Middle Temple lawyer, now posing as a fakir of a type well-known in the East, striding half-naked up the steps of the Viceregal Palace."[5] During Gandhi's visit to London for the Round Table conference, Lloyd George spent hours curled up on a sofa with him and rated him the most brilliant man he had ever met, whereas Churchill fulminated. At the conference, the Indian delegates demanded an all-India federation as opposed to immediate Dominion status. Churchill's view was that a weak viceroy had been bounced by Gandhi into believing that a few half-baked, well-educated urban agitators represented the views of 365 million Indians. His opposition to India's political advance was stentorian. One of the main pegs upon which it hung was Churchill's concern for the "untouchables." As he said in the Royal Albert Hall on March 18, 1931:

To abandon India to the rule of the Brahmins would be an act of cruel and wicked negligence. It would be a shame for ever for those who bore this guilt. These Brahmins who mouth and patter the principles of Western Liberalism, and pose as philosophic and democratic politicians, are the same Brahmins who deny the primary rights of existence to nearly sixty million of their own fellow-countrymen whom they call "untouchable," and whom they have by thousands of years of oppression actually taught to accept this sad position. . . . They consider themselves contaminated even by their approach. And then in a moment they turn round and begin chopping logic with John Stuart Mill, or pleading the rights of man with Jean-Jacques Rousseau.[6]

This was one of the central planks of Churchill's opposition to India's advance to Dominion status: that it should not be granted to a country that branded sixty million people "untouchable." Churchill was opposed to moves toward Dominion status under present conditions in India, believing that the political elite was completely unrepresentative of the subcontinent's enormous population, and that only British rule could prevent its racial and religious divisions spilling into open violence. What mattered most to Indians, he believed, was good government rather than self-government. As he famously described it: "India is not a country or a nation: it is rather a continent inhabited by many nations. . . . It is a geographical abstraction. . . . Such unity of sentiment as exists in India arises entirely through the centralized British Government."[7] He summed up his beliefs regarding India in a letter to Clementine on New Year's Day 1935: "Imagine what will happen to India when sagacious, scientific, incorruptible direction is withdrawn!" Later that month he told her about the start of his India campaign in Parliament. "I am about to begin my very hard fight in the House about India. The odds are very heavy against us. But I feel a strong sense that I am doing my duty, & expressing my sincere convictions."[8] Clementine was off on a komodo-dragon-hunting cruise to the Sunda Islands aboard Lord Moyne's yacht. During her absence, Churchill missed her immensely and sent her regular "Chartwell Bulletins" in which animals, India, the "increasingly sombre" German situation, and children were reported upon—Randolph's "scrubby" beard, Mary's whooping cough—causing him to liken children to "live bombs" liable to go off at any moment.

Churchill had long been disturbed by the signs of imperial dissolution signified by a succession of independence treaties, even if the independence granted had been impaired by continuing British military presence (Egypt, Iraq) or the veneer of imperial unity preserved by membership of an emerging "Commonwealth" (Ireland). Thus, despite his own role in negotiating it, he thought that the Irish Treaty of 1921 was at the extreme margins of acceptability in its concessions to nationalism. He had been determined to retain base rights for the Royal Navy in Ireland and was outraged by the government's decision in 1938 to give them up (with reason, as the difficulties in defending the Western Approaches without Irish bases during the war were to show). He had also opposed the granting of a form of independence to Egypt in 1922, a concession calculated to head off nationalist opposition to the British occupation while securing Britain its cherished base rights in Alexandria and the Suez Canal Zone. Speaking in the debate on Egyptian constitutional reform in December 1929, Churchill had told the Commons:

> Once we lose confidence in our mission in the East, once we repudiate our responsibilities to foreigners and minorities, once we feel ourselves unable calmly and fearlessly to discharge our duties to vast helpless populations, then our presence in those countries will be stripped of every moral sanction, and resting upon selfish or military requirements, it will be a presence which cannot endure long.[9]

Thus it was no surprise that Churchill opposed similar moves in India. He realized, unpalatable truth though it may have been, that the nature of imperial power was the rule of one group over another. It was all very well managing imperial decline by co-opting indigenous elites and effectively power-sharing. But it was a doomed strategy, nonetheless, and could lead only to dissolution. Churchill sensed keenly Britain's loosening grip on its empire. He believed that Britain had a right to be in India because it had conquered it—a position that became more and more difficult to sustain as the twentieth century progressed—and that self-respecting powers did not give up what they held if they wanted to remain great.

Churchill claimed to have special knowledge of India, though he was subsequently condemned for holding completely outdated views and therefore espousing unrealistic policies. He had "studied" the caste system and lived in India for four years and knew something of the ethnic makeup of the subcontinent and the role of the princes. His firsthand experience, however, had been confined to the rarefied atmosphere of the late Victorian junior officer: the mess, servants, polo, and exclusive European society. Ramsay MacDonald remarked upon Churchill's antiquated understanding of the relationship between the imperial center and the colonial peoples over which it ruled. Baldwin accused him of backwardness and insensitivity toward India's legitimate aspirations, aspirations the British had directly encouraged. Though it might be claimed with hindsight that he had a sound grasp of the likelihood of Hindu-Muslim violence should the British leave, he had no real understanding of the strength of Indian nationalism by the 1930s and was wrong to perpetuate the justificatory myth that the leaders of the INC were nothing more than self-serving lawyers and doctors with no popular support behind them, denying the forces of nationalism that were beginning to engulf European colonial empires throughout Asia.

Beyond the Tory right, his position attracted little support in the Commons and renewed all the old suspicions about his lack of judgment and reliability. Even those who agreed in principle with his point of view thought his actions played into the hands of Indian nationalists. But this was just one more example of Churchill's doing what he thought was necessary with scant regard for the political consequences. Though keen to find an issue that could serve as a platform for political revival, he was not, as some suspected, attempting to rival Baldwin for the Tory leadership (though he continued to josh him; in the Commons in May 1935, he said that "in those days Mr. Baldwin was wiser than he is now; he used frequently to take my advice.")[10] Baldwin was a regular butt of Churchillian humor—as Churchill said of him the following year, "Occasionally he stumbled over the truth, but hastily picked himself up and hurried on as if nothing had happened.")[11] Rather, Churchill was convinced that the situation in India thoroughly justified raising the alarm. Churchill's departure from the business committee freed him to rally support among like-minded people beyond Westminster and Whitehall. He thus became a leading figure in the "Indian Empire Society," formed to resist precipitate constitutional advance. Churchill's position meant he was widely identified as the leader of a group of about sixty MPs on the Tory right who were also opposed to the government's India policy. These were the very Tory diehards who had previously most loathed him. Now, indicating the unpopularity of his position among mainstream politicians, Churchill was the only senior figure prepared to champion their cause. But his stand on this issue alienated such supporters as Duff Cooper, Eden, and Macmillan, as well as a great deal of public opinion.

Despite being out of government and off the Conservative front bench, Churchill was not a lonely figure bereft of support or sympathy. His stance on India turned him into a national crusader, and the respect accorded to his continuing political vitality, plus his longevity as a senior statesman and powerful orator, meant that even those who held high office did not wish to spurn him. A Joint Select Committee of both houses of Parliament was formed to report on the white paper proposals for Indian reform in 1933. A Commons debate on the committee's report resulted in an overwhelming endorsement. Churchill attacked it, and the civil service, but was embarrassed by his failure to have mastered the detail contained in the report, leaving him "painfully exposed" before the Select Committee. In the debate, he claimed that promotion in the Indian Civil Service was dependent on a man's supporting the reform program. When challenged on this point, he was unable to substantiate his claim. While the committee had been deliberating, Churchill had been to the fore in marshaling opposition in the country, though converting it into effective parliamentary opposition proved very difficult.

Given the gathering economic crisis affecting the global economy, India was not a subject that commanded widespread popular attention, and because Churchill felt deeply about it, it did not follow that others did so, too. But some powerful people did. Esmond Harmsworth, son of Lord Rothermere, agreed with him on India, so much so that he published his views in the *Daily Mail*. The *Morning Post* also supported Churchill's position. He tried to rouse the passions of Lancashire over the issue of textiles, as India had imposed tariffs on cotton manufactures from Britain. Despite manifold setbacks, Churchill was invigorated by a good old-fashioned political scrap, which involved tub-thumping up and down the country and engagement with a new set of political bedfellows. Though the government had little trouble from the Opposition, Churchill's India crusade represented a significant challenge to the coalition and to Baldwin's position as Tory leader. In the short term, however, it was to be Churchill's reputation and position that suffered the most, because he was simply unable to generate sufficient support or interest for his cause. Once the India Act had been passed in June 1935 (the month in which Baldwin succeeded MacDonald as prime minister), Churchill knuckled down to supporting his party. He also continued to enjoy life; in late 1934, he embarked on a Mediterranean cruise aboard Lord Moyne's yacht, visiting Lebanon, Syria, and Palestine and flying to Cairo.

On India, Churchill found himself at the apex of several alliances as he berated the government for "throwing away our conquests and our inheritance."[12] Churchill and the Tory diehards mounted an impressive challenge to the seemingly impregnable national government—so it might be suggested that Churchill's renegade activity was not the strategic blunder it is often presented to have been. The India issue, as has been seen, was not the reason for his exclusion from government; the campaign actually resurrected his claim to be in the Cabinet, and the support garnered in this campaign joined him in the new crusade to get Britain to rearm in the face of the German threat. "Far from being destroyed over India, he was still an indomitable obstacle in the way of the direction in which Baldwin and his government had hoped to travel. Furthermore, on the defense of the realm, Churchill was making his stand on an issue even closer to the hearts of committed Tories."[13] India did not weaken his ability to make the rearmament case, and the campaign for air parity was a triumph within the Tory party, the forum that mattered most. As the 1930s wore on, Baldwin decided not to recall Churchill to government, not because he was unpopular, not because of India, but because he might become too strong.

CHURCHILL AND THE RISE OF HITLER

A fundamental fact of 1930s politics is that Churchill's "judgement on Hitler was sounder than the dozens of European pilgrims to Berlin and the Berchtesgaden."[14] Churchill's misgivings about Germany dated from very early in the decade, predating Hitler's accession to power in 1933. He had visited Bavaria in 1932 in order to tour the battlefields trodden by the 1st Duke of Marlborough. As well as contracting paratyphoid, he was disturbed by the spirit of militarism he observed, which he described in the Commons in November 1932 as "bands of sturdy Teutonic youths, marching through the streets and roads of Germany, with the light of desire in their eyes to suffer for the Fatherland."[15] From this point on, Germany's card was marked in Churchill's mind—and Churchill was soon to become viewed in Germany as an enemy of its "rightful" progress as a major power. Given his concerns about Germany, it was logical for Churchill to oppose the general policies of disarmament that were pursued under the leadership of Ramsay MacDonald. While by no means decrying "collective security" (a contemporary buzz term and political movement too popular to work against), he argued strongly against placing all the eggs in one basket and hoping that others would do the same, seeing in this a crashing naivety as to the nature of international affairs.

Churchill also realized how the advent of air power had transformed the strategic situation; "this cursed, hellish invention and development of war," he said in the Commons in February 1934, "has revolutionized our position. We are not the same kind of country we used to be when we were an island, only twenty years ago." He went on to argue that it was inconceivable that Britain should delay establishing "an Air Force at least as strong as that of any Power that can get at us."[16] He struck an uncompromising sense of urgency. In March 1934, he implored the House to realize that "this *is* the stage [at which to increase the air force]. The turning point has been reached. . . . The scene has changed. This terrible new fact has occurred. Germany is arming—she is rapidly arming—and no one will stop her."[17]

Churchill had denounced Hitler's regime as soon as it attained power in 1933 and railed against its "pitiless ill-treatment of minorities." He never fell for Hitler's blandishments and empty reassurances about the reasonable claims of German foreign policy. The renaissance of German militarism led Churchill to appreciate the towering importance of the French army and the Royal Navy, the key instruments in any plan to contain German power. But Churchill's warnings about Germany met with little favor in either the Commons or the country. There was no interest in visions of future war, and there was an obsession on the left with collective security, not rearmament. Both in Britain and France, the public were "keener on hearing what Hitler said about peace than what Churchill said about war."[18]

In 1933 Churchill called for the scrapping of the ten-year rule. He condemned government attempts at the International Disarmament Conference in Geneva to reduce Britain's and France's armed forces to the level of Germany's and also condemned the concessions made in the Anglo-German naval agreement of 1935. He firmly believed that diplomacy had to be backed up with credible force. His main political activity in 1936 was trying to align support for the League of Nations with support for British rearmament, a belt-and-braces approach calculated to appeal to the doves as well as the hawks. As he put it, "Some people say: 'Put your trust in the League of Nations.' Others say: 'Put your trust in British rearmament.' I say we want both. I put my trust in both."[19] By this time, Churchill was convinced that nothing was more important than restraining Germany. Action through the League, he believed, was the way of getting the disparate forces of right and left assembled.

The Focus group, started in 1936, was central to this enterprise, a sort of luncheon club supporting the view that Germany must be dealt with from a position of strength, drawing its members from all political parties. It advocated a foreign policy based on the League of Nations and collective security involving Russia. The Focus group wanted to attract genuine support from the left, hence its emphasis on the League and collective security and its pacifist overtones. It held public meetings and produced research papers. While the Focus group emphasized the prevailing hope that collective security could secure world peace, it was against disarmament. In Churchill's mind, though the League was a useful adjunct, it could never be a substitute for balance-of-power diplomacy, and the military force that gave it substance.

It was crucial to Churchill's cause that he strike this mollifying tone. At the 1935 general election, Baldwin had promised rearmament but also to do all he could to ensure that the League and collective security worked. There was no appetite in the country for belligerence, and both the prime minister and Churchill had to tread warily. Many in the Labour Party and on the left firmly believed that any kind of rearmament brought war closer; the message that war was coming anyway and that preparation was likely to be a matter of national survival was not a welcome one. This attitude frustrated Churchill, and he chided the House for not taking the dangers facing the country seriously. He also believed that the government had misled Parliament and the country regarding the relative strengths of the RAF and the Luftwaffe, and that there was too much talk and not nearly enough action, too much wishful thinking and precious little engagement with the harsh realities that threatened Britain's independence. "Nourish your hopes, but do not overlook realities," he counseled Parliament at the end of May 1935. But few were for acting.

Churchill thought that Britain's political elite was destroying Britain's Great Power inheritance because of its failure to lead. He deplored the "unwarrantable self-abasement" he saw around him. The world, he told Clementine, "seems to be divided between the confident nations who behave harshly, and the nations who have lost confidence and behave fatuously."[20] "We cannot afford," he told the Commons in October 1935, "to see Nazidom in its present phase of cruelty and intolerance, with all its hatreds and all its gleaming weapons, paramount in Europe."[21] While not wishing to criticize it out of hand, he was distrustful of the whole "League of Nations" mentality as a solution to the world's troubles. Germany, "now the greatest armed power in Europe," was unlikely to be tamed by talk alone. As he wrote in December 1935, "The more I think over the European Affair, the more I fear for our future—feebly armed & in the heart of every quarrel!"[22] Unfortunately for Britain and its extensive global interests, the trouble didn't end in Europe; as Churchill noted in January 1936, while Germany caused problems in Europe, Japan was seeking more provinces of China, presenting the problem of two "predatory military dictatorship nations."

Churchill strove tirelessly to warn the British people of the true extent of the menace posed by the dictators, and to exhort the government to do all in its power to meet it. He launched devastating attacks on the Baldwin government in 1936, chiding it for dithering when resolute action was the only possible course to be pursued: "His Majesty's Government were very slow in accepting the unwelcome fact of German rearmament," he said in November 1936 in a lengthy speech chronicling in minute detail the failure of the government to get to grips with the problem and the still extant unpreparedness in Britain's military structure—reserves not up to strength, a lack of modern weapons in the army, the backwardness of Britain's tank doctrine and equipment, the limits of Britain's strength in the air:

> Owing to past neglect, in the face of the plainest warnings, we have entered upon a period of danger greater than has befallen Britain since the U-boat campaign was crushed. . . . The era of procrastination, of half-measures, of soothing and baffling expedients, of delays, is coming to its close. . . . I have been staggered by the failure of the House of Commons to react effectively against those dangers. . . . I say that unless the House resolves to find out the truth for itself it will have committed an act of abdication of duty without parallel in its long history.[23]

"Europe, and it might well be the whole world, is now approaching the most dangerous moment in its history," he rightly claimed in November 1936. "If it is true, as the prime minister stated last week in a deplorable utterance, that 'democracy is always two years behind the dictator,' then democracy will be destroyed."[24]

During these crucial years of activity aimed at preparing Britain for war, Churchill kept his eye on developments in France, visiting regularly and spending time with senior politicians and generals, meetings often arranged through the good offices of the British Embassy. On a short holiday to Normandy, for example, he met General Georges; on a trip to Marrakech, he was visited by the French general in command of the large North African army. He was a great believer in the power of the French army and in 1936 watched its maneuvers. Churchill was highly valued in France, despite being out of office, a fact reflected by the favorable treatment he received during George VI's state visit to Paris in July 1938. On his way to the Riviera at the beginning of 1939, he stopped off in Paris again, where he lunched with Reynaud, the minister of finance, and met the British ambassador, the sometime premier Léon Blum, and General Georges. Back in Britain, while Churchill was out of office, he was certainly no outsider, even though the myth-history of the interwar years often portrays him as such.

ABDICATION CRISIS

There were, as ever, lapses in Churchill's political fortunes and moments when it seemed as if he'd done a Lord Randolph and shot himself in the foot. One such episode, which gravely threatened Churchill's credibility, was the position he adopted over the abdication of King Edward VIII in 1936. Churchill had wept upon hearing the king's abdication speech. He considered himself a friend of the king and a royal counselor of some pedigree and believed that the crown was hereditary and could not simply be given up. In the summer of 1935, he stayed at Blenheim with the king, Wallis Simpson, her then husband, and Duff and Diana Cooper, a suitably raffish, upper-crust set. His support for the king in the following year, when the latter wished to marry the now divorced Mrs. Simpson, badly affected Churchill's growing reputation and the work being done by the Focus group in sounding the klaxon with regard to Germany and the need for rearmament. Churchill believed that the king would get over Mrs. Simpson, failing to realize that he had made up his mind. With Baldwin's knowledge and consent, Churchill supported him, hoping to buy time. Many considered his stance very ill advised, and Neville Chamberlain resolved not to offer Churchill a government position when Chamberlain became prime minister in May 1937. Churchill, all on his own, appeared to be making short work of squandering the support he had gained. Such was the hostility to him that many believed his political career was finished. Clementine profoundly disagreed with her husband's stance on the abdication, recognizing the political calamity he was courting. Churchill was dumbstruck by the hostility in the House when, on December 7, 1936, he begged that no "irrevocable step" be taken regarding the issue of the king's proposed marriage. In Harold Nicolson's words, the reception of the speech represented an "utter defeat." Robert Boothby compared him to a dog being sick on the carpet, only Churchill had been sick "right across the floor" of the house.[25] Some of Churchill's enemies attributed his actions to hostility toward Baldwin, though this was not true. His stock with the new king, George VI, soon rose because Churchill was one of the few who supported him in blocking the conferment of the title "Her Royal Highness" upon Mrs. Simpson. In May 1937, the king wrote him a letter of thanks, which Churchill considered a great tonic, for it appeared in the eyes of many as if the abdication issue had finished him.

THE DEFENSE OF THE REALM

The key theme of Churchill's political career in the 1930s was his championing of rearmament and sufficiently strong air defenses in the light of the threat posed by a resurgent Germany. He considered it, later in life, to be one of the core aspects of what he termed his "life-work." In this he was supported by his friend and colleague Professor Lindemann, who had convinced him that there was a lack of scientific research on air defense. In the 1930s, much of the concern surrounding defense related to the growing potency of air power. Baldwin's succinct phrase of 1932—that "the bomber would always get through"—had become a truism as well as a strategic maxim. It logically followed that in a future European war, there was every prospect of mass civilian casualties caused by incendiary bombs and even gas bombs rained down upon British cities. This created vulnerability unknown in any previous conflict, the immunity afforded by Britain's island status, and the sure shield of the Royal Navy no longer being enough to guarantee security. On July 30, 1934, Churchill described London as "the greatest target in the whole world, a kind of tremendous, fat, valuable cow tied up to attract the beast of prey."[26] Hence the panic when it was learned that the RAF was weaker than thought. The German air force was a dagger pointed at what Churchill described as the "heart of the British Empire." As well as publicizing the urgent need to improve the country's air defenses, he emphasized the need to build up the RAF's strength as an attacking force, and this, given the prevailing wisdom about air power at the time, meant building bombers.

Churchill argued with Baldwin over the official figures relating to the strength and projected strength of the RAF. Churchill's carping on this subject was not wholly unwelcome to the government, for by this time Baldwin was convinced that Churchill's prognosis regarding Germany was correct, though as head of government he had to be careful not to be seen as alarmist or belligerent. Churchill's endeavors, therefore, were a useful way of getting the peace-hungry public to realize that rearmament and war were topics that could not be dealt with by burying one's head in the sand. The battle for adequate air defenses effected something of a rapprochement between Churchill and the government, though as is now clear, neither Baldwin nor his successor, Neville Chamberlain, had any intention of taking Churchill back into government unless they could really not help it. Nevertheless, dangling the prospect of a return to government before Churchill proved to be a useful technique for both of them.

Churchill kept up his assault, repeating the same simple message. As he told the Commons in October 1938:

> The sole method that is open for us to regain our old island independence is by acquiring that supremacy in the air which we were promised, that security in our air defenses which we were assured we had, and thus to make ourselves an island once again. That, in all this grim outlook, shines out as the overwhelming fact. An effort at rearmament, the like of which has not been seen, ought to be made forthwith, and all the resources of the country and all its united strength should be bent to the task.[27]

As a result of their work and the government's attitude toward it, both Churchill and Professor Lindemann were co-opted onto a new committee looking at air defense. The air minister had asked for Lindemann's views, and the committee was established under Sir Henry Tizard. Lindemann promptly exposed the more dislikable qualities for which he was known, demanding a body with direct access to the Committee of Imperial Defence. Churchill appealed to the prime minister along the same lines. The result was the creation of the Air Defence Research Committee. These committees were instrumental in providing Britain with radar cover against enemy aircraft by the time the Second World War commenced. Involvement also gave Churchill valuable knowledge that aided his understanding of the technicalities of aerial defense during the Battle of Britain.

In such ways, Churchill remained an important national figure in touch with official circles, not a spurned soothsayer wandering in the wilderness. He was a friend of important government ministers, and his advice was sought, though less frequently than it was offered. His continental holidays also afforded him access to ministers—in the south of France, for example, he saw a good deal of Anthony Eden (and formed what was to be a lasting impression about his limitations: when Eden was appointed foreign secretary in December 1935, Churchill wrote that the appointment "does not inspire me with confidence. I expect the greatness of his office will find him out").[28] He held countless meetings and lunches and engaged in voluminous correspondence with central government figures. Shortly before the First Lord of the Admiralty, Duff Cooper, resigned in protest over Chamberlain's Czechoslovakia policy (October 1938), Churchill had visited him and denounced the prime minister's actions. He suggested that Germany be told that war would follow should Hitler set foot in Czechoslovakia. To make such a threat credible, Churchill claimed, Britain would need close collaboration with Russia. He constantly returned to the point that Hitler would not be stopped by empty threats; military might had to be thrown into the balance.

Though critical of the government, Churchill supported its efforts to rearm, and his involvement with the Air Defence Research Committee led him to believe that his breach with Baldwin was healed, to such an extent that he was disappointed not to be brought back into government. There were growing calls for this to happen, coming from various quarters. All in all, as the decade developed, Churchill was immensely busy on numerous fronts. As he wrote in July 1937, "I am overwhelmed with work. Three days HofC last week: the new book in its final birth throes: articles, & always Marlborough: & now ahead on Tuesday next another debate on Inskip's salary. I really don't know how I find all that I need, but the well flows freely: only the time is needed to draw the water from it."[29] His energy and capacity for work were undiminished. As he recorded a few weeks later, "I am working night & day and the progress on M is enormous—I have done nearly 20,000 words this week alone."

The most dramatic parliamentary action of the period surrounded the so-called appeasement policy pursued by Neville Chamberlain, who succeeded Baldwin as prime minister in May 1937 (Churchill seconding his nomination as party leader). Eden's resignation from the government in February of the following year signaled a new offensive against the government's policy. When Eden and Cranborne announced their resignations to the House of Commons, Churchill cheered so enthusiastically that a livid scar originating from his American motor accident blazed on his forehead. Churchill did not just blame Chamberlain and his government for the appeasement of Germany, but also their predecessors in the early 1930s. As he wrote on January 10, 1938, the problem took root in the years 1932 to 1935, "when Ramsay, Baldwin and Simon would never make friends with Germany, nor prevent her rearming. A thousand years hence it will be incredible to historians that the victorious Allies delivered themselves over to the vengeance of the foe they had overcome."[30]

Having annexed Austria in March 1938, a year later Hitler invaded the rump of Czechoslovakia, sparking great revulsion in Britain. Churchill turned his attention to forming a European security alliance. He urged the creation of a Grand Alliance and the issuing of strong statements of condemnation and warning from Britain, France, and Russia. Such an alliance, resting "upon the Covenant of the League of Nations," might "even now arrest this approaching war."[31] There were shouts in the Commons for his immediate return to Cabinet, the great warrior-statesman saluted once more as the prospect of war loomed. But within the Cabinet, the old fear that he would dominate remained. As prime minister, Chamberlain liked to exert much stronger control than had been the case under Baldwin. There were also those in the House who were unimpressed by Churchill's parliamentary interventions during this period. George Lansbury complained of his habit of walking in, making his speech, and walking out, leaving "the whole place as if God Almighty had spoken."[32] He also received criticism from his constituency because of his views on the European situation and his criticism of the government. He voted with the Opposition on November 17, 1938, on a motion for the creation of a Ministry of Supply, the first time he had voted against the government (as opposed to abstaining) since the India Bill in 1935.

Showing how far removed from government policy his views were, Churchill advocated turning over sectors of the economy to war production. Chamberlain, with sound economic logic, believed this would be financially ruinous and that war could be prevented, and was desperate to avoid any suggestion that Britain was adopting a warlike, or defensive, mindset. Appeasement was the order of the day. But as events were to show, Churchill was right—Hitler was unstoppable, and the British would have to devote their lives to war in order to overcome him. As he said in the House in March 1938, "For five years I have talked to the House on these matters—not with very great success. I have watched this famous island descending incontinently, fecklessly, the stairway which leads to the dark gulf."[33] There is no doubt that Churchill did all that he could to prepare the country for war, warning again and again, providing the most informed and detailed arguments to support his case, always seeking to get the British people and their leaders to face the facts. As he told the Commons in his lengthy and excellent speech damning the Munich Agreement, "We are in the presence of a disaster of the first magnitude which has befallen Great Britain and France. Do not let us blind ourselves to that. . . . We have sustained a total and unmitigated defeat. . . . Do not suppose that this is the end. This is only the beginning of the reckoning. This is only the first sip, the first foretaste of a bitter cup that will be proffered to us year by year."[34] With his unique transatlantic sensors, at this moment of impending disaster Churchill reached out to the people of America. In a radio broadcast in October 1938, he praised their percipient view of the emerging European crisis but warned them that it would affect them, too: "We are left in no doubt where American conviction and sympathies lie: but will you wait until British freedom and independence have succumbed, and then take up the cause when it is three-quarters ruined, yourselves alone?"[35]

With hindsight, it is clear that Churchill's most valuable asset over the crucial winter of 1938–39 was his isolation. The position of wise counselor spurned augmented his appeal to those opposed to the government's policy. But at the time, Churchill rued his powerlessness. Despite this, and the fact that in the eyes of people such as Harold Nicolson he was "becoming an old man," the fire remained. Churchill continued his frenetic activity, using the Focus group, public and private meetings, and personal letters. In the summer of 1938, his regular columns in the *Daily Telegraph* added power to his point of view. In that year, alarm mounted as the Czech crisis unfolded and the fleet was mobilized. Given the situation, Churchill canceled what would have been a lucrative American lecture tour because he believed the situation in Europe was so grave. Though there were calls for him to be readmitted to the Cabinet, this was by no means the overwhelming desire of the House. At the time of the Munich Agreement (September 29, 1938), most Tories still shunned him, as did the Opposition, and loyalty to Chamberlain remained solid. But Churchill and his growing band of supporters viewed the Munich Agreement as an act of shame. In the post-Munich vote on the Liberal motion calling for the creation of a Ministry of Supply, Churchill appealed to fifty Tories to join him; two did. He was criticized for attacking the prime minister, who made a memorable reference to Churchill's lack of judgment. But Churchill paid Chamberlain out. Chamberlain said that Churchill had "many brilliant qualities," but if anyone were to ask him if he had good judgment, "I should have to ask the House of Commons not to press me too far."[36] Churchill's retort: "I will gladly submit my judgment about foreign affairs and national defense during the last five years, in comparison with his own."

Churchill spent Christmas 1938 at Blenheim. Early in the new year, he wrote a series of letters advising Chamberlain, who did not welcome Churchill's barrage. As he wrote to his sister, "Churchill the worst of the lot—telephoning almost every hour of the day. I suppose he has prepared a terrific oration which he wants to let off."[37] Mussolini added to the sense of impending crisis when he invaded Albania on April 7, 1939. Calls for Churchill's return to government mounted. Still he kept up his criticism of the government's handling of affairs. He ridiculed the fact that trenches dug in London's parks had filled with water, requiring guards in order to prevent people from drowning in them. There was muddle in the air raid precautions and a complete absence of drive and leadership. Chamberlain, he wrote to Clementine, didn't know "a tithe of the neglects for which he is responsible."

At this time, Churchill was unique in his ability to communicate, not only to informed observers but also to the general public, that he knew what to do and had both the confidence and resolve to do it. His hope of returning to government was becoming increasingly realistic. He even felt that, given the extraordinary circumstances, he might have a chance of becoming prime minister. He was clear, however, that if he were to be offered the job, he would only accept if he were afforded powers "such as they have not dreamed of according." Harold Macmillan recalled a visit to Chartwell at this time. He found Churchill thoroughly caught up in the momentous events that were unfolding. He bustled around searching for maps, demanding to know the dispositions of the fleet, and surrounded himself with phones and secretaries. "I shall always have a picture of that spring day and the sense of power and energy, the great flow of action, which came from Churchill, although he then held no public office. He alone seemed in command, when everyone else was dazed and hesitating."[38] Churchill was marshaling his toy soldiers again and sensing the return of war.

The mounting problem for Chamberlain was that after Munich, he depended on the agreement delivering tangible results and halting the march toward war. But it did not. *Kristallnacht* soon followed, and Hitler's European ambitions remained undimmed, though in the spring of 1939, Chamberlain felt things were improving and his policies for dealing with the dictators yielding results. But if the government's policies were to fail, it increasingly seemed as if Churchill was the only politician advocating an alternative approach. The German occupation of Prague in March 1939 buoyed Churchill's stock as much as it diminished Chamberlain's. Then Chamberlain guaranteed the integrity of Poland, drawing a line in the sand.

Halifax and the Foreign Office were moving away from Chamberlain's policy, convinced now that Munich had only bought time and that war was coming. Events were working in Churchill's favor, and with regular information coming from Halifax, the king was also moving toward acceptance of the position represented by Churchill and Eden. Churchill had become a beacon of resistance and reason. As General Ironside wrote after a visit to Chartwell, Churchill was "full of patriotism and ideas for saving the Empire. A man who knows you must act to win. You cannot remain supine and allow yourself to be hit indefinitely. Winston must be chafing at the inaction. I keep thinking of him walking up and down the room."[39] Chamberlain, who had some of Churchill's telephones wiretapped, concluded that the best way of keeping him quiet was to dangle the prospect of a return to the Cabinet before him. In August 1939, while Chamberlain went fishing in Scotland, Churchill inspected the Maginot Line, voicing concern about the prospect of a German tank advance through the Ardennes, bypassing the defensive bulk of the line.

BEYOND POLITICS

Churchill's life in the 1930s appears less rarefied than popular mythology would have it if one considers his manifold activities beyond the political sphere. They provide vital background to his famous political endeavors. Even in the fateful year of 1938, he was absorbed in the construction of a cottage and the writing of his celebrated biography of the 1st Duke of Marlborough. Since August 1, he had been on a regime of two thousand words a day, only traveling to London for the occasional parliamentary debate ("200 bricks and 2,000 words a day" was a Churchill maxim when under full steam at Chartwell). He was living, he wrote, a life of "unbroken routine at Chartwell." As well as writing, bricklaying, and pig breeding to occupy his time, there were honorific positions such as the chancellorship of Bristol University. With no official national political responsibilities, there was more time for painting, too, and about half of Churchill's known works were produced during this decade. His writing was just as prolific, including numerous books and a massive output of articles. In 1930 alone, for instance, he wrote forty newspaper and magazine articles, over half of them for the *Daily Telegraph*. His press output for 1937 comprised sixty-four articles, thirty-three of them for the *Evening Standard* (a contractual arrangement terminated by Beaverbrook in 1938, when their political views diverged). With a seemingly limitless capacity for work and activity in disparate fields, Churchill even started converting classic novels and plays into newspaper articles. Authors abridged and repackaged include Shakespeare and Tolstoy. He was paid £300 per story; Eddie Marsh, his assistant, got £25 a piece for doing the donkey work. Churchill was never ashamed to write purely for money, subcontracting research assistance, as for his major historical works. His journalistic ventures included things like "Great Bible Stories Retold by the World's Best Writers" for the *Sunday Chronicle*, and in early 1936, a series of articles for the *News of the World* on "Great Men of Our Time," which became a book the following year entitled *Great Contemporaries*.

This was all remarkably lucrative work when added to the advances and transatlantic rights and royalties on his books, making him the most highly paid English author of his day. His major study of the origins and course of the First World War, *The World Crisis*, has been admired for its architectural power as well as its revelation of the thoughts and actions of a senior government minister intimately involved in the conflict. *My Early Life* appeared in 1930, a study in which the days of his youth were presented very much as a distant, dead epoch. It was written in order to pay the taxman, though it turned out to be one of his most admired works, with its endearing self-satirizing tone. In 1932, he accepted an advance for *A History of the English-Speaking Peoples*, another massive work, though one that was to be delayed by the war and not see publication until the 1950s (his history of the war taking priority when hostilities ended). In 1938, he published a series of speeches he'd given warning of the dangers of European and American unpreparedness in the face of the Nazi threat, called *Arms and the Covenant* in Britain and *While England Slept* in America.

To achieve all this, Churchill embarked on what became a lifelong practice—hiring help to write books. For *Marlborough* he recruited Maurice Ashley, a recent first-class graduate from Oxford, paid £300 a year for part-time research assistance. He also employed a colonel as military adviser. The contract for the biography of Marlborough, signed in 1929, was worth £10,000. In writing it, he was granted extensive access to the Marlborough papers at Blenheim by the 9th Duke. By the summer of 1933, he had produced 200,000 words and written 308 letters relating to the project. When *Marlborough* appeared in 1933, it was to critical acclaim. Importantly for Churchill's reputation, it was generally well received among professional historians. Such a detailed study of the life and times of the 1st Duke of Marlborough also helped develop Churchill's education concerning grand alliances and the interactions of political leaders and military commanders.

Despite all of this revenue-generating activity, keeping the Churchill family in the manner to which it was accustomed was a very expensive business. Chartwell was Churchill's aristocratic domain, and it cost money with its five reception rooms, nineteen bed and dressing rooms, nine indoor servants, nanny, two secretaries, chauffeur, three gardeners, bailiff, groom, and heated outdoor swimming pool. After a time without a London base, in 1936

Churchill also acquired a flat in Pimlico. For much of this period, he was badly in debt, adversely affected by vicissitudes such as the Wall Street Crash and the cancellation of Beaverbrook newspaper contracts. Capital losses caused by recession led to Chartwell being put up for sale, though Churchill was bailed out by Sir Henry Strakosch, who took over his American shares at the value he had paid for them (and upon his death in 1943 left Churchill £20,000).

In the 1930s, Chartwell was one of the most important houses in the world. As the meeting place of Churchill and his circle of friends, advisers, and clandestine informants, it became a major center of resistance to the Nazis. Here the group developed a viable alternative to the policy of the British government, supplied with intelligence from both inside and outside Parliament, and prepared the way for Churchill's accession to the premiership. Approaching sixty-five, an age when most people retire and begin to lead quieter and more sedentary lives, Churchill was still in fifth gear, operating across a vast range of activities, from statesmanship to stockbreeding. His capacity to fit it all in, and to do so many things so very well, is what marked him out as unique.

Churchill's love affair with the continent continued during this period. Lavish foreign breaks in smart hotels or châteaux, where Churchill sought to recharge his batteries and draw vitality and cheer from friends and associates, occurred in places such as Aix-les-Bains, Biarritz, and Cannes. Sometimes he stayed at the Riviera château of actress and socialite Maxine Elliott, painting at nearby Saint-Paul-de-Vence. Baldwin amusingly recalled staying with Winston at Aix-les-Bains in 1934. "He had never seen Mont Blanc, so he was going there, letting the mountains have a peep at him." Churchill indulged another of his favorite pastimes, cruising in the Mediterranean aboard Lord Moyne's yacht, painting Greek temples and the battlements of Rhodes. In 1936, he visited Tangier and Marrakech with his paints, as well as Knebworth as the guest of Lord and Lady Lytton. In January 1939, he visited Antibes on what was to be his last proper holiday for some time. Despite his evident enthusiasm for painting, he had a pleasingly modest opinion of his talents, which led him to refuse Sir John Lavery's request for a picture to exhibit at a "Sea Power" exhibition. He did not think he had painted anything good enough.

At the root of Churchill's frenetic activity remained the love of his wife, which was as ardent as ever. He was quite often alone; she was off cruising in 1934 with Lord Moyne in the Dutch East Indies, and in November 1938 she was in the West Indies with a commission reporting on conditions in the British colonies. Churchill missed her terribly during these absences. "Do you love me?" he wrote. "I feel so deeply interwoven with you that I follow your movement in my mind at every hour & in all circumstances."

Churchill sat in the Commons on the fateful day, September 3, 1939, when Europe once more descended into war. It was a day remembered in popular memory for its late-summer sun, the sound of suburban lawnmowers, and the aroma of Sunday lunch, an image of homely normality providing a sharp contrast to the violation signaled by Chamberlain's doleful radio broadcast announcing that, despite all his efforts, Great Britain was at war with Germany. Shortly after the news came over the airwaves at eleven o'clock, an air raid siren sounded, and with Clementine at his side Churchill went onto the roof of their Pimlico flat and saw a barrage balloon rise into the sky. They made their way to the nearest communal shelter, equipped with a bottle of brandy. The sense of having embarked upon a noble struggle suffused Churchill's mind as he attended the Commons meeting later that day:

> As I sat in my place, listening to the speeches, a very strong sense of calm came over me. . . . I felt a serenity of mind and was conscious of a kind of spiritual detachment from human and personal affairs. The glory of Old England, peace-loving and ill-prepared as she was, but instant and fearless at the call of honor, thrilled my being and seemed to lift our fate to those spheres far removed from earthly facts and physical sensation.[40]

Later, the prime minister Neville Chamberlain summoned him for a conversation.

7

War Machine: The Management of Global Conflict

"WINSTON IS BACK." This was the signal the Admiralty transmitted to the Royal Navy's vast network of warships, air stations, and shore bases scattered from Bermuda to Shanghai when Chamberlain brought Churchill back into the Cabinet after an absence of over ten years. Twenty-five years after resigning as First Sea Lord in 1915 following the Dardanelles debacle, Churchill had returned to his first true political love—stewardship of the mighty navy upon which the British Empire's security rested. "So it was that I came again to the room I had quitted in pain and sorrow almost a quarter of a century before. . . . Once again we must fight for life and honour against all the might and fury of the valiant, disciplined and ruthless German race. Once again! So be it!"[1]

A global network of sea lanes, and the ability to move resources of food and raw materials as well as troops from one part of the world to another, remained as important as ever to Britain and its empire. Their security depended upon the Royal Navy, "unsurpassed in the world and . . . still the main bulwark of our security," as Churchill described it.[2] The Germans no longer had a High Seas

Fleet, and the disparity between the two rival navies was greater than it had been in 1914. But there was one branch of naval warfare in which the Nazis had invested heavily—submarines—and this was to threaten the independence of the British Isles as never before. Together with the advent of air power, the measures by which national strength and national vulnerability were calculated had shifted dramatically. Yet the navy's work in keeping Britain in touch with its colonies and trading partners overseas, in blockading enemy shores and defending those of Britain, and in enabling the movement of troops and military resources around the world remained as important as ever. The navy remained Britain's shield against invasion and essential to Britain's prosecution of military operations overseas, whether across the Channel in France or on the other side of the world in Burma and Hong Kong.

Chamberlain asked Churchill to join his government on September 1, 1939, though it was not until September 3 that it became clear Churchill was to be given the Admiralty and a seat in the newly formed War Cabinet. "This is not a question of fighting for Danzig or fighting for Poland," he told the House on that memorable day. "We are fighting to save the whole world from the pestilence of Nazi tyranny and in defense of all that is most sacred to man."[3] Immediately upon joining the Cabinet, Churchill unleashed a fusillade of ideas and commandments across his own and other government departments, showing the energy and innovation that was to be an inspiration to his countrymen and should have brought fire to the bellies of his less convinced political peers. Right from the start of the war, Churchill's clarity of vision and confidence marked him out as unique, as did his pronouncements, which were simple, dramatic, realistic, and all embracing.

Yet he remained in this initial phase of the war an outsider with no discernible power base, and long memories of personal and party wrangles—and the failure by many to grasp the horrifying significance of events unfolding in Europe—meant that he was still regarded with suspicion and even contempt. Friends, including Brendan Bracken and David Lloyd George, had advised

Churchill not to join Chamberlain's government if invited to do so, but Churchill could not resist the call when it came. Chamberlain remained very much the ringmaster, Churchill his reluctantly appointed probationer. This did not prevent him from getting stuck in, and thirteen letters to Chamberlain in the first six weeks of war demonstrated Churchill's trademark habit of allowing all around him the benefit of his advice.

Churchill set about the Admiralty with unrestrained gusto. He organized weekly dinners to get to know his staff and other relevant people, a trick that was repeated later in the war when plans for the invasion of France were gathering pace. At Admiralty House he created an Upper War Room with maps of all shipping movements and throughout the war was followed all over the world by his maps and the naval officer who kept them up to date. He did what was necessary to ensure merchant ships were well protected and employed in convoy, remembering what had transpired in the previous war. He ordered that all ships should have radar fitted and all merchant ships be armed. Reveling in a constant flow of information, Churchill established a Statistical Department under his trusted friend Professor Lindemann, which yielded a ready stream of the most up-to-date information about all aspects of the Admiralty's business. Like his love of big maps, this innovation gave Churchill a comprehensive picture of all Admiralty activity around the world (a system later taken with him to Number 10 and applied across the range of government activity). On September 14, 1939, he toured the Home Fleet, setting out his stall as a First Lord determined to spend as much time as possible visiting naval installations across the country, seeing what was going on and letting others have a look at him.

His chief dictating secretary wrote that "when Winston was at the Admiralty the place was buzzing with atmosphere, with electricity. When he was away on tour, it was dead, dead, dead."[4] He had the confidence to override the naval opinion of admirals while never disdaining their advice and constantly sought a daring role for the navy, which, given the essentially unspectacular nature of some of its core roles—convoy escort and blockade—was not entirely realistic. Churchill considered several harebrained schemes, like sending a force into the Baltic, quashed with some difficulty by the First Sea Lord, Admiral Sir Dudley Pound. But genuine knowledge, robust leadership, and a fertile mind are qualities never to be despised in leaders pursuing national survival. Even if some of the ideas were stinkers, most were not, and there were sufficient talented and powerful people surrounding Churchill to ensure that, on the whole, Britain's strategic decision making throughout the war was of a very high quality, and innovative ideas were developed. Stephen Roskill avers that Churchill's return to the Admiralty "was warmly welcomed throughout the navy." He "invigorated the whole administrative machinery of the department and made his personality felt far and wide."[5] But, on the more negative side, Roskill claims, he "diverted to fruitless schemes manpower and materials which were sorely needed for more conventional purposes."

Churchill's attention to detail showed no sign of waning, though it was sometimes based on smoke-and-mirrors tactics. His ability to seize upon a detail and pursue it suggested omniscience on his part and might imply an absence of knowledge or attention on the part of others, putting them on their mettle. At Scapa Flow, for example, Churchill noticed that there were no gulls fussing around the dummy warships, meaning they were unlikely to fox German reconnaissance flights. "Pray tell me why . . ." was a familiar opening to a Churchillian enquiry about some relative minutiae, often accompanied by a request to summarize the situation on a single piece of paper. This in itself was important; while Churchill was renowned for not being a good listener, his wife advised those seeking to get through to him that he always took note of things put in writing. He also directed that no decisions from him be considered valid unless expressed in writing. In the opinion of Sir Ian Jacob, military assistant secretary to the War Cabinet and deputy to General Ismay, Churchill's pursuit of detail across a very wide spectrum could come across as a lack of confidence in his colleagues and military commanders, a few of whom "never recovered from the initial shock of exposure" to his attentions.[6] But it kept people on their toes at a time when keeping up to the mark was absolutely crucial. Churchill was well known for using knowledge of a particular detail, or a well-marshaled half-truth, to get his own way while pooh-poohing the schemes of others. Attlee explained how this might be done:

> Now and again he would pick up a document with which he wasn't familiar, and ask questions in the tone of a man who had read the whole thing through several times, and discovered the critical weakness in it. "What about *this*!", he would say, glowering around the room. Sometimes we would have to point out to him that the passage he quoted was followed by its refutation and was not a recommendation. If he was in the mood, quite unabashed, he would try another. Or again, he might ignore our observation, and hold forth for ten or fifteen minutes about something that no longer existed. . . . We used to let him get it off his chest, and not interrupt—indeed, it was extremely difficult to interrupt him because not only had he no intention of stopping, but frequently he had no intention of listening. His monologues sometimes went on for very long periods indeed.[7]

His capacity to focus on detail was very important. Norman Book said it was like a searchlight sweeping round: no one knew when it would settle on them, "So everyone worked like blazes."[8] His greatest war-winning virtue, according to Jock Colville, was his "capacity for picking out essential things and concentrating on them."[9] In the first faltering weeks of war, Churchill's pedigree as a leader was displayed to the nation. On September 26, 1939 he spoke from the dispatch box for the first time in a decade and cast a rousing spell over the House with a fast-moving account of the war at sea. This was followed by a worldwide radio broadcast in which he summarized the war to date. Though the speech included statistics biased in Britain's favor, it provided authoritative information prized by the listening public. Harold Nicolson praised a "really amazing" speech that had sounded "every note from deep preoccupation to flippancy, from resolution to sheer boyishness. One could feel the spirits of the House rising with every word."[10] Winston's tour de force came after Chamberlain had made "his usual dignified statement." The contrast was apparent for all to see. Though diminished, Chamberlain remained powerful and solidly supported in Parliament, but in elite political circles, opposition to Churchill was evaporating. As the Earl of Crawford, a long-term opponent, put it, "He remains the only figure in the Cabinet with the virtue of constant uncompromising aggressive victory." In his speech on the first month of war, Churchill demonstrated his oratorical skills. "The British Empire and the French Republic have been at war with Nazi Germany for a month tonight," he said. "Poland was overrun by the two Great Powers which have held her in bondage for 150 years but were unable to quench the spirit of the Polish nation. The heroic defense of Warsaw shows that the soul of Poland is indestructible and that she will rise again."[11] He forged a link between Britain and the Polish people, their heroism and history. This kind of flourish was central to his speeches and was a skill that few politicians possessed. In his speeches, he would give basic information as well as detail—reporting on destruction wrought by mines, praising the work of the submariners, or singling out the salvage service that had retrieved a million tons of shipping. This gave a great sense of inclusiveness. He reviewed the war situation in Europe, but also in distant places such as Africa, Iran, or South Asia, reassuring the British public that we are "still masters of our fate." He had an extraordinary "ability to magnify the chances of success while minimizing the possibility of failure."[12]

Churchill's new Cabinet colleagues sought to temper his public pronouncements, especially as he tended to drift far beyond his Admiralty brief and speak as if he were laying out official government policy with regard to the wider war effort. But Churchill resisted any form of censorship even when it was proposed that Sir Samuel Hoare "oversee" his public utterances. A radio broadcast in mid-October 1939 strayed significantly beyond Admiralty turf and onto general policy, allowing Churchill to make (apparently on behalf of the whole government) an unequivocal statement for fighting on regardless, ruling out any possibility of a negotiated peace, which was far from being the unanimous position of all his colleagues. In January 1940, he attracted the ire of the Foreign Office when he said that without Britain and France, the smaller states of Europe would be divided between the "similar barbarisms of Nazidom and Bolshevism." He was, of course, right, though it pained people to hear things so starkly stated, and at the Foreign Office, Halifax (one of those Christians who should have been thrown to the lions, according to Churchill) gathered a sheaf of adverse press comment from the "tiresome neutrals" with whom it was his job to deal. In March, in an unequivocal and belligerent address broadcast by the BBC, Churchill said that "thoughtless, dilettante, or purblind wordlings sometimes ask us: 'What is it that Britain and France are fighting for?' To this I answer: 'If we left off fighting you would soon find out.'"[13]

In terms of the navy's activities, Churchill showed his characteristic impatience, yearning for dramatic victories with which to capture the public imagination. Yet the navy was well prepared for the less spectacular but vital job of blockading Germany and protecting Britain's far-flung trade arteries. Those moments of naval drama that did come to the public's attention tended to be entries on the wrong side of the ledger. The destruction of HMS *Royal Oak* (October 1939), at anchor in the Home Fleet's defended base at Scapa Flow, cost over eight hundred lives and showed that even "impregnable" bases could be breached by daring and skillful U-boat commanders. The carrier *Courageous* was lost in the Bristol Channel with over five hundred lives (September 1939). Such losses were an inevitable consequence of the size and visibility of the Royal Navy, the unrivaled extent of its global tasks, and the potency of the enemy. But they were galling nonetheless.

On the plus side, there were dramatic fillips to morale and battered national pride as well, such as the sinking of the battleship *Graf Spee*, run to ground and forced to scuttle off Montevideo, and the rescue of British prisoners of war from the *Altmark* as a result of a daring raid in Norwegian waters. Churchill cast such victories in a dramatic and even a romantic light, speaking of Britain's naval heritage stretching back to the days of Elizabeth I and Sir Walter Raleigh and the continuing globality of British maritime power and endeavor in a struggle of good against evil. Despite intense activity at sea, however, this period of the war gained the misnomer "phony war," referring to the apparent inactivity that followed the declaration of war in September 1939. It was a misnomer because although some elements of the British military might not have been doing much that was visible, other elements (such as the navy) were extremely active. Alliance diplomacy, war production, and logistics were spheres of constant activity during this period, as was the commitment of troops and RAF squadrons to the defense of France. Furthermore, it was only abject European paralysis in the face of Germany's diplomatic and military thrusts that allowed this period to appear "phony": in reality, it was as "phony" as the moment before a tiger pounces upon its prey.

THE NORWEGIAN CAMPAIGN

Churchill was full of schemes, which he argued for with his customary conviction. As usual, some of the seed he scattered fell on fertile, some on stony ground; and while it could be extremely exasperating for his colleagues, as Clement Attlee remarked, this fertility "kept us on our toes." Some of the schemes verged on brilliance; others came straight from the mad professor's laboratory. But overall, Habbakuk—the plan to use icebergs as aircraft carriers—was more than canceled out by the brilliance of Mulberry, the floating harbors that made the D-Day landings possible and that Churchill enthusiastically sponsored, as he did many other new "toys," from sticky bombs to Hobart's "funnies" ahead of the Normandy landings. He bombarded the Cabinet with ideas—to mine the Ruhr, to take resolute action in Norwegian waters, to operate in strength in the Baltic. A particular favorite was the desire to cut the Germans (and indeed the Russians) off from supplies of Swedish ore. Churchill became the leading proponent of this plan in the extended Cabinet wranglings that were to follow.

Churchill and the Admiralty had long made plans to act on that side of the North Sea, but it was some time before the War Cabinet granted permission to enact one of them. Thus was born the Norwegian campaign, designed to stop Germany importing iron ore from Sweden, though it was badly planned and executed, betraying inept British strategy not helped by Churchill's influence and constantly changing plans. The plan was to mine Narvik, the most important port, though at that very moment Hitler dispatched troops to seize it and the other main ports. While British ships bested German ships in the fjords (leading to crippling losses that diminished the Kriegsmarine's chances of success in Hitler's planned invasion of Britain), British, French, Norwegian, and Polish troops failed to dislodge their German opponents in the vicinity of Trondheim, and German fighters dominated the freezing skies above. So the campaign failed, and a gallant attempt to take Narvik—briefly successful—led to a coastal evacuation that presaged the much larger operation that took place at Dunkirk only weeks later, the first in a series of British evacuations expertly managed by the navy but of little help in winning the war.

The Norwegian campaign showed Churchill in full spate, closely engaged in strategic and tactical decisions and with his fingerprints all over the operation, taking a larger share of the blame than was properly his own (or that he should have allowed himself to carry). The campaign also revealed the muddled machinery for interservice cooperation and determined Churchill to create dedicated combined-operations capabilities. This became a significant innovation; with Britain and its allies having been shut out of Europe (and later out of much of Asia, too), conducting coastal raids and amphibious attacks became a prominent activity.

When the Norway campaign got under way in spring 1940, it had looked as if the situation was up for grabs both at sea and on land. This was why the War Cabinet's Military Co-ordination Committee, which Churchill chaired following the resignation of

Lord Chatfield in April 1940, decided to land troops in the vicinity of Trondheim. The committee was part of the clumsy war machinery in place under Chamberlain, intended to advise the prime minister and Cabinet. This particular decision of the committee was made in the absence of Oliver Stanley, the minister for war, who complained to Chamberlain. The prime minister was persuaded that he himself should chair the committee as the ultimate Cabinet authority, though the campaign as a whole was to demonstrate that Chamberlain was not able to provide the degree of war direction necessary. Churchill's powers were soon enhanced, and the war-fighting machinery of government improved, when he returned to chair a newly empowered Military Co-ordination Committee. It now had direct access to the Chiefs of Staff Committee (the three most senior British officers) and its own staff, headed by Major-General Hastings "Pug" Ismay. This was an important step toward the concentration of war-directing power in the hands of one individual, which would mature when Churchill became prime minister.

Despite mistakes on Churchill's part, the Norway campaign did little to diminish the sense that he was head and shoulders above his Cabinet colleagues. Operations in Norway led to mounting public dissatisfaction with Chamberlain's government. The campaign had been plodding rather than innovative and fluid, showing the paucity of British (and French) strategic thinking and operational art, as well as poor cooperation between the army and the navy. It offered invaluable lessons about the necessity of adequate air cover if land operations were to succeed. Much of the blame rested with Churchill, though at a superficial rather than a fundamental level: Britain's strategic posture and conduct was the responsibility of the government that had taken Britain to war and that had prepared (or not prepared) Britain to face a war with Germany. Chamberlain and his colleagues had been in power since 1931, and blame for the situation in which Britain found itself naturally attached to them, not to the erstwhile exile Winston Churchill. Nevertheless, even Churchill was to consider himself fortunate for escaping blame for the Norwegian fiasco, which rather than damaging him was to elevate him to the premiership.

Framed against a growing atmosphere of national failure and retreat, the Commons debate, or rather inquest, on the Norway campaign began on May 7, 1940. Churchill spoke eloquently and pugnaciously in defense of the government's actions, ("Let pre-war feuds die; let personal quarrels be forgotten, and let us keep our hatreds for the common enemy") but Lloyd George admonished him not to convert himself into an "air-raid shelter to keep the splinters from hitting his colleagues" (meaning the "failures" Chamberlain, Hoare, and Simon).[14] It was, according to Roy Jenkins, "the most dramatic and the most far-reaching in its consequences of any parliamentary debate of the twentieth century."[15] "Everywhere the story is 'too late,'" lamented Clement Attlee, leader of the Labour Party. It was during this debate that Leopold Amery made his most famous contribution to British political life, telling Chamberlain that "in the name of God," he should go. In the subsequent vote, the government's majority of 213 was cut to 81, a wounding margin conveying the sense that Britain was losing the war and that better leadership was urgently needed. Just over a day after this vote, Hitler invaded Western Europe, ending anything that had been "phony" about the war and precipitating a period of dramatic crisis. Thus began the "five days in London," in which the fate of Europe hung in the balance, and it was decided that Winston Churchill would lead the nation and the anti-Fascist world, and that there would be no surrender.

Chamberlain, who during his speech had said that Churchill was to be authorized on behalf of the Military Co-ordination Committee to give direction to the chiefs of staff, realized that a coalition government was now unavoidable, seeking to broaden the base of his government and move toward the kind of cross-party coalition that had served Britain well in past crises. But key opposition figures refused to serve under Chamberlain, most notably Clement Attlee. The writing was on the wall for the weary, sick politician whose name remained associated with "appeasement" and whose demeanor as a war leader lacked conviction. He decided to resign.

PRIME MINISTER

On May 9, Chamberlain summoned Churchill for a consultation about the choice of a successor. Churchill demurred when asked to comment on the suitability of Lord Halifax, biting his tongue on the premeditated advice of Kingsley Wood. Halifax, also present, eventually said that as a peer, and therefore not a member of the House of Commons, it would be almost impossible for him to take the job. In any case, it was quite clear that it was a job he did not want in a moment of supreme national crisis. His decision was tempered by a belief that he would remain close to the center of affairs and could act as a restraining and guiding influence on Churchill. There was also the distinct possibility that a Churchill government would not last long and that Halifax could then emerge to pick up the pieces. In contrast to Halifax, Churchill relished the prospect of becoming prime minister. He believed in his destiny and that Britain could not lose.

Thus it was that almost by default Winston Churchill reached the summit of British political life. No other combination of circumstances could have removed the seemingly insuperable obstacles that barred the way to this aging leviathan, this political Methuselah, becoming the king's first minister. But in the exceptional circumstances of 1940, the obstacles had evaporated like the morning mist. His rivals and detractors stood aside or ceased to matter. Even the pro-Labour *Daily Mirror* called him "the most trusted statesman in Britain." This was a remarkable turnaround, caused by the simple fact that now his country—it is not an exaggeration to say the world—needed the unique range of talents that his constitution, personality, and experience had caused him to possess. His message in these crucial days was simple and communicated to the whole nation and beyond:

We have before us an ordeal of the most grievous kind. We have before us many, many long months of struggle and of suffering. You ask, what is our policy? I can say: It is to wage war, by sea, land and air, with all our might and all the strength that God can give us; to wage war against a monstrous tyranny. . . . You ask, what is our aim? I can answer that in one word: It is victory, victory at all costs, victory in spite of all terror, victory, however long and hard the road may be; for without victory, there is no survival.[16]

Having reviewed the gravity of the situation in this prime minis-terial broadcast of May 13, 1940, he concluded: "But I take up my task with buoyancy and hope. I feel sure that our cause will not be suffered to fail among men. At this time I feel entitled to claim the aid of all, and I say, 'Come then, let us go forward together with our united strength.'"[17] Churchill's speeches at this time had a major impact. As Enoch Powell put it, "My impression is that Churchill was aiming exactly right, that he was talking to those who were predisposed to see the situation as he was presenting it to them, a situation where one at least had the advantage of having clarified the nature of the danger, having almost maximized the nature of the danger, and yet of a degree of confidence that one would survive it."[18] In 1940, Churchill didn't flinch. He told it as it was, "convinced that people would respect the truth and respond with fortitude."[19]

It is worth reflecting on Churchill's speeches. He savored the English language, the opulence of words, and loved "to ambush the unexpected word or phrase."[20] His orations recorded simple narrative accounts of the progress of the war, *tours d'horizon* of the military situation, and dwelled on themes such as resistance, defiance, the importance of the Atlantic lifeline, the need to pro-tect small states, the significance of sea power, and the importance of unity. He was a master of effective communication. One of his practices, as he told the future King Edward VIII, was to drive home his main points. "If you have an important point to make, don't try and be subtle or clever. Use a pile driver. Hit the point once. Then come back and hit it again. Then hit it a third time."[21] Harold

Nicolson ascribed "his mastery of the House" to "the combination of great flights of oratory with sudden swoops into the intimate and conversational."[22] He rhetorically involved America in the
war on Britain's side long before it became a belligerent. Churchill's
speeches in the late 1930s and the early months of the war became
so famous not just because of what he said, but because no other
public figure offered the people an explanation of what was happening and why. He understood what a huge mind shift the public had
to go through in order to brace themselves for the horrors and the
tedium of a lengthy war.

Though he was a master of repartee and conversation, Churchill
was never a natural when it came to extempore public speaking. He
had an unusual, to some unattractive, voice. He struggled to overcome a lisp and a stammer, consulting voice specialists, practicing in
private and choosing appropriate words. Churchill's speeches were
meticulously prepared; his first major Commons speech had taken
six weeks to perfect. A problem with this kind of public speaking
was that if circumstances did not favor the big, prepacked set piece,
a speech could fall wide of the mark, as was also the case if the mood
of a meeting or a Commons session was against him. Churchill
recognized that dramatic set pieces were not always suited to the
intimate and conversational atmosphere of parliamentary debate.
As he wrote to Clementine, "It is astonishing what goes down in
these days of mass politics. One thing is as good as another. All
the old Parliamentary drama & personal clashes are gone—perhaps
forever." Sometimes the argument was lost in the show, and while
people might admire his words and phrases, they might not be at all
swayed by his message. As Rab Butler put it, whereas Churchill was
profoundly moved by his own words, others were not.

Churchill's speeches and their effectiveness changed over time.
As a young minister, he was renowned for the command of detail
shown in his parliamentary speeches. Later on, his budget speeches
were widely praised; yet by the 1940s and 1950s. his speeches lacked
detail, and in the age of the mass electorate, his grandiloquent style
lost some of its appeal. Whereas his famous speeches of the war

years had usually been exquisitely appropriate and aimed at a receptive audience, his election speeches of 1945 appeared out of tune.

Nevertheless, he was one of the greatest British orators of all time, and his wartime speeches deserve their renown. As Lord Tweedsmuir noted, "Some speeches rank as deeds," and Winston Churchill was the master of this form of communication.[23] His faith in his ability as a war leader, and the relish with which he approached the task, made him utterly unique. The contrast between him and all other senior British politicians was marked. Chamberlain despised the role—"How I loathe and hate this war. I was never meant to be a War Minister," he wrote.[24] Churchill, on the other hand, relished it. Harold Nicolson caught the contrast between the two men, observing them on the Commons front bench on September 26, 1939, the one "dressed in deep mourning," the other "looking like the Chinese god of plenty suffering from acute indigestion."[25] After turning down Churchill's offer of a Cabinet position because he could not face sitting around the Cabinet table with Chamberlain, Lloyd George wrote that "Winston *likes* war; I don't."

Winston Churchill became the nation's leader and champion because of extraordinary times in international affairs and because Britain faced defeat and occupation by the forces of an evil foreign power. His elevation was aided by his character and reputation—for so long, brakes upon his political ascent—and even by the way he looked and the way he dressed, as distinctly Victorian and aristocratic habits blended with the eccentric, the theatrical, and the unconventional. The cigar (a spare case, along with his National Registration Card and gas mask, was carried around by his bodyguard) was his most famous prop, but there were others, including hats and uniforms, the "V for Victory" sign, and Pol Roger champagne.

Churchill, like Hitler, became a historical colossus because of the Second World War. But Churchill did not win the war single-handedly, and though he may have personified traits the British liked to think they possessed in abundance—resolve, defiance, and pluck—he was the democratic leader of forty-five million Britons, not their god. Winston Churchill was no superman, though because of the Second World War, many readings of the historical runes have sought to portray him as such. This has unnecessarily exacerbated the division between Churchill supporters and Churchill detractors: too much hagiography surrounding Churchill the war leader has surrendered ground cheaply to his enemies as they seek to show in detail how the man often failed to measure up to his inflated billing.

The apparent energy and ubiquity of Winston Churchill during the Second World War, and in its historical memory, is staggering. He appears everywhere, interested in every minute facet of the conflict, his image and his voice dominating popular memory. His name is everywhere, too: "Winston Special" convoys, Churchill tanks, "Churchill aerodromes" (the Japanese name for captured airfields in Malaya), Churchill films (such as the 1941 *Churchill's Island*), a Winston Churchill Bridge on the island of Rodrigues, iconic photographs in newspapers and international magazines, souvenir prints, mugs, and buttonholes. Churchill became, among many other things, an unlikely pinup. His boundless energy and appetite for work, his bloody-minded stamina and incessant desire to involve himself in other people's business—here a divisional commander positioning his tanks, there a scientist searching for a technological breakthrough, or a Cabinet colleague minding his departmental business—amplified his role in the Second World War, as it had in the First. His faults now became his chief assets. "Entirely self-centred," at this moment of supreme crisis he listened "to nobody's views: I just went straight ahead."[26] His mighty strategic decisions at this juncture included sending the only armored division in Britain to Egypt and refusing to commit more RAF squadrons to France.

The hide and the constitution of a rhinoceros were vital characteristics for the man at the epicenter of an imperial war effort and a global political and military alliance. So, too, was the ability to conceptualize events taking place all over the world and the implications they had upon one another. "Those working closely with him," wrote Sir Ian Jacob, "were impressed by the fury of his concentration . . .

[as he] relentlessly focused on the problem in hand."[27] The unsurpassed burden of eighteen hundred days of war leadership would have destroyed anyone with less than monumental strength and ability. Surviving the bleak, desolate moments when personal strategies failed, disasters unfolded, and losses mounted—the fall of Tobruk and Singapore, the sinking of the *Hood* and the *Prince of Wales*, knowledge of the imminent V-2 campaign—presented a test unparalleled in British history. The decisions Churchill was obliged to take were often unspeakably unpleasant—whether to press on and authorize the bombardment of the French fleet at Oran, to reinforce or not to reinforce doomed garrisons, or to watch (and indeed condone) the tightening of Russia's bloody grip on Poland, the ally for which Britain had gone to war. One wonders if anyone else in the world could have performed so well under such pressures. From June 1940 until December 1941, "Churchill carried the world on his shoulders. The burdens he bore, and the anxieties he endured, would have crushed many lesser mortals."[28]

Everything that had gone into the making of Winston Churchill—his parents' genes and his childhood, his experiences on the frontiers of empire and his father's fall from grace, as well as his own tempestuous experience of the vicissitudes of democratic politics—had steeled him for the unparalleled demands of a global war of national survival. Churchill's achievements during the Second World War, and the epic nature of Britain's struggle, have been allowed to overshadow the significance of his achievements before the war and after. Aneurin Bevan wrote on Churchill's death that he would have admired him more if he had not appeared to enjoy the war so much and suggested that it was easy to understand why this was so: "the war rescued him from political oblivion and gave him wings."[29] It can only be said that most modern politicians, including Bevan, would have envied the career leading up to that "oblivion," and that such claims are quite ridiculous if one moves away from the central narrative of Churchill as war leader, in training before 1939, and from 1945 in an elegant decline that personified the decline of his nation. As we have seen, though out of office during the 1930s,

Churchill's life blossomed, and his political contribution to Britain was greater than that of anyone beyond the charmed circle of the Cabinet. Even during the so-called wilderness years, Churchill was still a member of Parliament, a political commentator of international significance, and the most powerful backbench opponent of government policy in the land. He was now, with the world at war, about to become as close to a savior as a nation is ever likely to get.

On May 10, 1940, Churchill went to Buckingham Palace and was formally asked by the king to form a government, then returned to the Admiralty and set about forming a War Cabinet of five, contacting the leaders of the opposition parties as he sought to build what would be a remarkably successful wartime coalition government. "I felt as if I were walking with destiny, and that all my past life had been but a preparation for this hour and for this trial." Yet despite this roseate view of the "man of destiny" assuming his appointed place, a view entrenched in history and national mythology, his appointment was not universally welcomed and, following Attlee's refusal to join a Chamberlain-led coalition, owed more to the Labour Party than to the Conservative. Halifax had been a more popular choice as prime minister among many senior figures; Eden despaired of Churchill's political judgment; the Canadian prime minister, William Mackenzie King, recorded a conversation with King George VI in June 1939 in which "the King said he would never wish to appoint Churchill to any office unless it was absolutely necessary in time of war. I confess I was glad to hear him say that because I think Churchill is one of the most dangerous men I have ever known."[30] For the staff at 10 Downing Street, according to Jock Colville, the thought of Churchill as boss "sent a cold chill down the spines" (and he feared the arrival of Churchill and his "mermidons," Brendan Bracken, Professor Lindemann and Desmond Morton). Colville himself, however, was later to write of the utter transformation in opinion across Whitehall within two weeks of Churchill's taking up his post.

But on the other hand, there were plenty who recognized that Churchill was the man for the hour. His old friend David Lloyd

George, Father of the House, responded to his "blood, toil, tears, and sweat" speech by saying that "we know the Right Honourable gentleman's glittering intellectual gifts, his dauntless courage, his profound study of war, and his experience in its operation and direction . . . it is fortunate that he should have been put in a position of supreme authority."[31] Now Churchill had the bridge to himself. A life in preparation had led to this moment.

THE MACHINERY OF GOVERNMENT
AND WAR DIRECTION

Churchill's tasks as prime minister were legion and fell into a number of broad categories: acting as a signal box and processor for the manifold activities of a global empire during a time of total war; shaping the machinery of government and strategic direction and providing the political stability without which commanders cannot effectively wage war; providing a focal point of leadership and inspiration for the people of Britain, the empire, and the world in opposition to the dictators; and acting as the nation's public face in all dealings with foreign powers, concentrating in his own hands control of British foreign and defense policy.

Churchill's first notable achievement was the formation of a truly representative national government that included the other main parties and did not ostracize leading Chamberlainites, many of whom had until very recently been thoroughly opposed to him serving as a Cabinet member, let alone prime minister. Chamberlain stayed on as leader of the Conservative Party, and his supporters remained powerful in both party and parliamentary affairs. Chamberlain and Halifax were wisely included in Churchill's government. So, too, was Clement Attlee, leader of the Labour Party, and Churchill's old friend Sir Archibald Sinclair, leader of the Liberals. The Labour ministers were the staunchest supporters of Churchill as prime minister for quite some time, reflecting the legacy of hostility and suspicion within Conservative ranks and Churchill's lack of a parliamentary power base. Ernest Bevin, a leading trade unionist but not a member of Parliament, was made minister of labor, and Sir John Anderson was brought in to chair the Cabinet Home Affairs Committee.

Churchill immediately established an iron grip on British grand strategy and took possession of the bridge connecting strategic direction and military action by making himself minister of defense, effectively relegating the three service ministers, who were not to be members of the War Cabinet. They were no longer responsible for strategic planning and the day-to-day conduct of operations; that responsibility now rested with the Chiefs of Staff Committee, which was harnessed to the prime minister. As his appointment of Bevin and several ministerial uses of Lord Beaverbrook showed, like Lloyd George in the First World War, Churchill was prepared to make unorthodox appointments in order to get the job done. Churchill's arrival instilled a hitherto unknown sense of urgency throughout Whitehall: a new dynamo had been installed at the core of Britain's political system and war machine, and it lit up like a Christmas tree. Military assistant secretary to the War Cabinet Sir Ian Jacob gave an excellent description of this phenomenon:

> The total war effort was an interconnected battery of powerful engines—the Departments of State, the Forces, the civilian bodies within the country, the Dominions and Colonies within the Commonwealth, and beyond that our allies. What was needed—and it is easier to see it now than it was then—was some single unifying human force to drive the whole contraption: a power at the center strong enough to move even the wheels at the periphery. And Churchill was by nature such a prime mover. . . . Previously we had seen this human dynamo threshing around unharnessed and uncentred, dislocating and disrupting, even destroying from time to time. Now, with the dynamo in the right place, it was a different story. . . . Once the prime minister had been more or less harnessed to the machinery, the effects were terrific. Things began to hum, and they hummed till the end of the war. It is impossible to put into words the change that we felt. His power seemed to be turned on all the time.[32]

Churchill's presence, spirit, and voice braced the nation at a moment when the threats of invasion and mass bombing raids were very, very real. Untainted by the mark of the "guilty men" that had blighted his predecessor, he was a figure of defiance, resolve, purpose, and hope. The fact that he had so often been branded an enthusiast for war now became a positive asset, not a stick with which to beat him. Here was someone who knew about war, indeed welcomed it. Clement Attlee believed that he was the only man who could have performed the required role—"I saw nobody around who could qualify except Winston. . . . [He] knew what war meant in terms of suffering of the soldier, high strategy, and how generals got on with their political bosses."[33] Churchill offered hope in eventual victory, despite the odds. "The tunnel may be long and dark, but at the end there is light."[34] The confidence and even overconfidence, the energy and exuberance that led some to question his reliability, seemed uniquely appropriate when harnessed to a national struggle for survival.

> By a paradoxical accident of history it was this very unwillingness to com-promise with the forces of the modern world that enabled him to avoid the error of being reasonable with Hitler. What had once earned him the ugly reputation of being a reactionary and a warmonger was the same quality that enabled him to save civilization from one of the greatest dangers it has ever faced. . . . His great hold on his countrymen in the years of the Hitler war lay in the extraordinary fact that he seemed to reach back across the security of the Victorian era and to revive in us all the qualities of an older Britain.[35]

Nevertheless, there remained people who opposed the lioniza-tion of Churchill, choosing instead to focus upon his failings. For months, many Conservative members of Parliament refused to be convinced, harping on about old crimes and Churchill's "notorious" methods and character.

Churchill sought to fashion a highly centralized "war machine" in which politicians were not bossed around by military leaders and in which the prime minister exercised effective ultimate control. There was to be no repeat of the situation that pertained under the Asquith administration during the First World War: "It took Armageddon to make me prime minister, but now I am there I am determined that power shall be in no other hands but mine. There will be no more Kitcheners, Fishers or Haigs."[36] As minister of defense, he had the right not only to summon the chiefs of staff, but also to instruct them. This meant that he was literally able to run the war and its military aspects, in conjunction with the three most senior officers in the army, the navy, and the RAF. All of this enhanced his ability to direct across the field and meant that the British war machine was far less fractious than the American equivalent. Clement Attlee, writing on Churchill's death, expressed the magnitude of Churchill's achievement in this field: "I rate him supreme as Britain's leader in war because he was able to solve the problem that democratic countries in total war find crucial and many find fatal: relations between the civil and military leaders. . . . Winston's concrete contribution to the war effort, namely the setting up of the intra-governmental machine that dealt with the war, was most important."[37]

Though Churchill exercised overwhelming power at the center of Britain's war machine, and despite his forcefulness and impetuosity, he was a democratic warlord and the servant of king and the Cabinet. He sought support from the War Cabinet and appeared often before Parliament. What is more, despite his position, he appointed service chiefs—Dill (followed by General Sir Alan Brooke), Portal, and Cunningham—who were able to pay him back in kind and hold their ground. In bossing them around, Churchill never pushed them to the point of resignation. No matter how much he harried the chiefs of staff, he never overruled them. "He knew the limits of his proper constitutional role," Attlee wrote, "and of theirs." Alan Brooke ventured the opinion that "if Hitler had acted in the same way the outcome of the war might have been different."[38] Though Churchill hounded the chiefs of staff and senior commanders in the field, he did so with purpose and could eventually be made to listen. He acted constitutionally and maintained his respect for the role of Parliament even in a time of extraordinary national crisis. Clementine also acted as a restraint on her husband, as when on June 27, 1940, she censured him for his "rough, sarcastic, and overbearing manner."

While the normal procedures of government, such as Cabinet meetings and committees, continued during the war, they were bound to be modified, and much was achieved by the prime minister outside of office hours and often in less conventional settings— over lunch, in the dead of night, and by summoning generals and proconsuls to his side during his regular overseas peregrinations. Churchill and his government showed initiative in their willingness to create ad hoc ministries and agencies when necessary, institutions such as the Ministries of Economic Warfare, Food, Fuel and Power, Supply, and Reconstruction. Another innovation was the system of Cabinet-ranking resident ministers sent out to coordinate civil-military affairs in the Far East, the Middle East, Northwest Africa, and West Africa. Churchill's experiences of government in the First World War, especially his stewardship of the Ministry of Munitions, suited him well for the task of streamlining government to manage national war mobilization, and he presided over an enormous expansion of the state apparatus. He was always ready to sponsor and support new or peripheral military initiatives. He nurtured Bletchley Park and prized the unexpurgated daily intelligence reports it provided him, telling the head of the Secret Intelligence Service in September 1940 to send all original transcripts to him every day ("Where are my eggs?" he would ask, referring to the latest box of intercepts); he was enthused by the prospect of Special Operations Executive activity around the world; he supported the establishment of the commandos and heard, without derision, the schemes proposed by the Combined Operations Command he had created; and he fostered the careers of men such as Percy Hobart (the armored warfare specialist), Mountbatten, and Wingate.

In gearing up the British government to total war, Churchill was aided by his willingness to delegate and allow colleagues to get on with the job, and to be influenced, even if after much debate, by colleagues and advisers. His maverick approach to politics aided both his and the nation's cause. As the linchpin of the British war effort, it was better to have someone who conceived of himself as a statesman and strategist rather than as a party politician. As the war progressed, he grew increasingly detached from party politics and immune from criticism in the minds of the majority of the public (though ultimately this damaged his party's electoral prospects). He managed to foster as well as personify national unity and purpose, and to identify himself with the fears and hopes of the nation.

Churchill's impact on the conduct of the war was immense, though not uniformly successful. But it should always be remembered that there was no chance whatsoever of conducting war on such a massive scale and over so many years without mistakes being made. Those who search gleefully for Churchill's errors in order to attack him do little more than confirm the unremarkable fact that in war, mistakes are unavoidable and losses inevitable. Churchill's command over generals and admirals was incredible, and it is difficult to see any other contemporary politician achieving such a degree of civilian control and strategic direction or having the confidence, knowledge, and ability to even try. He was prepared to chastise, harry, and sack senior commanders, at times revealing his ignorance of logistics in the process as well as his sometimes unhelpful passion for ceaseless action. Churchill was the generals' bane, and Attlee recorded that "some of the generals out in the field thought that Winston was like Big Brother in Orwell's book, looking down on them from the wall the whole time,"[39] an impression strengthened by his access to secret intelligence. ULTRA intelligence was invaluable in his dealings with the chiefs of staff and field commanders, as it enabled him to keep abreast of the war in different theatres and to think across its many fronts, though it also encouraged his tendency to act as if he were a general himself. Even Hitler is said to have been impressed by the abandon with which Churchill sacked his generals. His judgment on these matters was sometimes excellent, sometimes lucky, and often influenced by the opinion of people he liked. It was sometimes wrong. Thus the taciturn Wavell was less to his taste than the urbane Alexander or the zealous and unorthodox Wingate (though Churchill's interest in him was transient; Lord Moran, on board the *Queen Mary* on August 8, 1943. as Churchill sailed for Quebec, wrote that "Wingate is only a gifted eccentric. He is not another Lawrence. When this became plain to the PM he lost interest in him, and presently forgot all about his presence on the ship").[40] That having been said, when he wasn't frustrating commanders on the ground with unreasonable suggestions or demanding information that was the business of a quartermaster sergeant rather than a prime minister, Churchill created the space in which commanders could operate and backed them up with all the support he could give. As General Ismay wrote to Auchinleck, he "is head and shoulders above anyone the British or any other nation could produce" as a war leader, "indispensable and irreplaceable."[41] Jan Smuts told Lord Moran that Churchill was "indispensable. He has ideas. If he goes, there is no one to take his place."[42] "Churchill's return to power," reflected Sir Ian Jacob, "in a war where knowledge and technique were as important as the gift of command was, I think, perhaps the most original aspect of his many-sided career."[43]

THE FALL OF FRANCE

Notwithstanding Churchill's ascent, the situation facing Britain in the summer of 1940 was dire. Many of the best-informed people in the land believed it was hopeless. Even if an invasion could be prevented, defeating Germany seemed impossible. Churchill became prime minister just as Germany's westward onslaught was about to restart: having absorbed Austria, Czechoslovakia, and Poland between March 1938 and September 1939, through political bullying and invasion, Germany had stood like a greedy pig digesting what had thus far been devoured. Now Germany's quest for "living space" continued, in a series of brilliant, lightning-quick campaigns, and between April and June 1940, Belgium, Denmark,

Holland, France, and Norway were secured for the Reich. From the point of view of British survival, the loss of the French army—a vital pillar in British defense planning in any conflict with Germany or Italy—was an utter disaster. It totally altered the nature of the war that Britain had to fight. Britain's grand strategy and military planning had been firmly founded upon the belief that any war would be fought with France as a fully functioning military ally, and its massive army was considered vital given the smallness of Britain's own land forces. All around the world, the alliance with France had been pivotal. Now the fall of France was to fundamentally weaken Britain's strategic position, not only in Europe, but also in the Mediterranean and the Far East.

Churchill, who realized that the war had begun for Britain the moment Hitler had set his heart on continental domination, contended with the pressing problems from abroad that Allied impotence and German power were creating. As the Low Countries fell and Paris was threatened, so began a spurt of frenzied shuttle diplomacy aimed at keeping France in the fight once the Maginot Line had been breached. Churchill never wavered in his determination to go on, persuading the Cabinet that this was the only course. A war that had seemed distant had become an eyeball-to-eyeball encounter and a war of national survival.

Given the central importance of the alliance with France, Churchill faced harrowing decisions regarding British military support for its foundering partner across the Channel as the German invasion gathered pace. Despite French appeals, he decided not to overcommit British air power lest it be lost, leaving Britain bereft of fighter cover should the Luftwaffe venture in strength across the Channel. A crucial, and as it was to transpire, correct decision (though the RAF actually sustained greater losses during the Battle of France than during the Battle of Britain). Meanwhile he sought to steel the resolve of the French government and show Britain's shoulder-to-shoulder commitment. During the agonizing weeks of French collapse, Churchill demonstrated his imperial instincts, using language that contributed to a sense of involvement throughout the British world. His thought and speech were instinctively suffused with an awareness of the British Empire, and he was the most empire-minded politician of his age. Regarding the question of sending more aircraft to France, he said that "we should hesitate before we denude still further the heart of the Empire"; during the fighting before Dunkirk, he signaled the local commander, exhorting him to "hold Calais for the good of the British Empire" (this was on May 26, a black day on which, with Whitehall waiting anxiously for news of the first wave of Dunkirk evacuations, Churchill had intervened to issue a "fight to the death" instruction, which silenced him at dinner and made him feel physically sick).

In the fateful days of May, as French military power and political will wilted, Churchill strove to gauge the truth of the situation and rally French spirits. These days were "extraordinary, in some ways unreal, phases in the history of the nation . . . one beautiful summer's day succeeded another."[44] He flew to France on four occasions, rekindling memories of his frequent cross-Channel flights during the final year of the First World War and presaging the summitry that was to characterize his approach to the strategic planning of the war. But his efforts to bolster the French were to little avail. The Dutch army capitulated on May 14, and large parts of the French army (and almost the entire British Expeditionary Force) looked as if they would be cut off by a German dash for the Channel. With the British commander in France recommending an evacuation by sea on May 22, Churchill's hopes were momentarily raised as General Weygand, newly appointed to command the armies, spoke resolutely about military recovery. But the plan was not put into action, and four days later, the British government ordered the execution of Operation Dynamo, the attempt to evacuate the British army, then massing on the French coast and threatened with death or capture. To the surprise and relief of a watching world, over the next nine days, this epic maritime feat, involving a mass of vessels from the Royal and Merchant Navies, fishing fleets, yacht clubs, and pleasure boats, embarked over 338,000 British and French soldiers and brought them safely to England. The RAF, though largely unseen, performed heroically as it kept the full might of the Luftwaffe away from the chaotic evacuation beaches.

On May 31, Churchill flew to France for a third time and observed at first hand the fatal equivocation at the heart of the French government. Reynaud supported the continuation of the struggle but his vice premier, Marshal Pétain, appeared to favor an armistice while terms could still be negotiated from a position short of abject defeat. Feelings were running high, as everyone shared a sense of terrible history in the making. Reynaud's mistress, who supported an armistice, tried to physically attack Churchill in the courtyard at Tours, only to be fought off by the faithful bodyguard Walter Thompson. Back in Britain, on June 4, Churchill apprised the House of the magnificent achievements of Dunkirk and went on to intone his famous national manifesto:

> We shall defend our Island,
> Whatever the cost may be,
> We shall fight on the beaches
> We shall fight on the landing grounds
> We shall fight in the fields and in the streets,
> We shall fight in the hills;
> We shall never surrender.

Resolution, defiance, and an inspiring, romanticized vision of the "island story" that had reached, after a thousand years, its most dramatic page. "Where the people of this country might have been depressed by the brute facts of Dunkirk," wrote Aneurin Bevan, "Churchill was persuading them to think about Queen Elizabeth and the defeat of the Armada."[45] But he was also reminding them that "wars are not won by evacuations."

As France fell, problems mounted on other fronts; on June 10, Italy chose its moment to join the victor-elect in sharing the spoils, declaring war on the British Empire. Further east, in a theater that would remain inactive for the better part of another eighteen months, the British closed the Burma Road—a lifeline to Chinese forces resisting Japanese invasion. It was an ignoble act, though one based on the sound, stark strategic assessment that risking war with Japan at this stage was folly. On the day that Italy became an enemy, threatening Britain's manifold interests in the Middle East, North Africa, and the Mediterranean, Churchill made his fourth visit in a month to France to attend a meeting of the Supreme War Council at a château on the Loire. He returned to London on June 13 and then flew out again the following day, already established as the most peripatetic national leader of the war, entrusting to no one but himself the high-level diplomacy that, he believed, could only be conducted through personal meetings. This visit confirmed for Churchill that the French were ready to be defeated—and that the young and relatively junior Charles de Gaulle was the only person prepared to fight on. On June 14, General Sir Alan Brooke, commanding Britain's remaining 150,000 troops in France, was given permission to evacuate across the Channel, and two days later, the War Cabinet agreed to France seeking terms with Germany (though on condition that the French fleet sailed for British ports).

Even as the minute hand approached the midnight hour and French sovereignty was about to be extinguished, de Gaulle was in London drawing up, with Desmond Morton, a declaration of union between Britain and France. The War Cabinet approved the text, and it was telephoned through to Reynaud. Another Churchill trip to France was planned but abandoned when the British ambassador warned of a crisis in the French government and Reynaud's resignation. De Gaulle broadcast to the French people on the BBC. Seizing upon de Gaulle as leader of Free France was an astute move on Churchill's part, even if supporting him was often a thankless task. As Churchill wrote to Roosevelt, "I am no more enamoured of him than you are. But I would rather have him on the committee than strutting about as a combination of Joan of Arc and Clemenceau."[46] All the time, Churchill was trying to get Roosevelt to make a commitment to the Allied cause that might steel the French to carry on, even hoping for an American declaration of war. From the start of his premiership, Churchill viewed America as the key to ultimate and absolute victory. But it was all to no avail. With the fall of France, things looked grim for Britain and Churchill's government, and there were murmurings from within his Cabinet about the need for a change at the top. Churchill's speech on the fall of France shored up his position with its powerful appeal beyond the Cabinet circle to the House of Commons and the British nation it represented. It scotched all thoughts of Britain seeking terms with the enemy and ensured that Britain would fight on. The Battle of France was over. The Battle of Britain was about to begin. "Upon this battle depends the survival of Christian civilization. Upon it depends our own British life, and the long continuity of our institutions and our Empire." Churchill's position was strengthening to such an extent that senior ministers no longer dared air their criticisms and concerns in public.

Churchill achieved an extraordinary level of communication with the British people, holding out hope when despair seemed more fitting, offering the spectacle of military success as defeats mounted. Though Churchill's voice was heard on the radio less frequently than is sometimes thought, and many of the famous "wartime" broadcasts were actually recorded after the war had ended, his speeches were numerous and of great importance. Most of his renowned wartime speeches were delivered from the dispatch box in the House of Commons, some recorded thereafter for radio. On June 18, the 125th anniversary of Waterloo, Churchill told the House of Commons "the Battle of France is over. I expect that the Battle of Britain is about to begin. . . . Let us therefore brace ourselves to our duties, and so bear ourselves that, if the British Empire and its Commonwealth last for a thousand years, men will still say: 'This was their finest hour.'"[47] Reluctantly, Churchill repeated this speech later in the day for a radio broadcast, which meant that his brilliant words were heard by millions across the world.

At this moment of crisis, Churchill demonstrated his quality and became the embodiment of national defiance and resolve. French warships in British ports around the world were seized; the powerful squadron at Oran in French North Africa was given the option of sailing for neutral or British ports or of being destroyed. The French admiral refused, and there followed a short bombardment from Admiral Sir James Somerville's Force H based at Gibraltar, in which the warships of the French squadron were either destroyed or badly damaged and over 1,300 French sailors killed. To sanction this presented Churchill with a terrible decision, but one that he did not shirk. It was imperative that the French fleet did not fall into German hands. It was also imperative that the watching world, particularly America, was left in no doubt as to Britain's resolve to carry on the fight, whatever disasters might befall continental Europe, particularly given the fact that the American president had tired of the defeatism that pervaded Chamberlain's administration.

On July 4, Churchill received an ovation as he explained the action against the French navy to the House of Commons: "A large proportion of the French Fleet has, therefore, passed into our hands or has been put out of action or otherwise withheld from Germany by yesterday's events. . . . I leave the judgment of our action, with confidence, to Parliament. I leave it to the nation, and I leave it to the United States. I leave it to the world and history."[48] This speech also made optimistic comments about Britain's capacity to resist a German invasion, as the contours of what would become known as the Battle of Britain began to emerge. Churchill sat down at the end of his speech "with tears pouring down his cheeks," but it was a significant parliamentary triumph. Aneurin Bevan wrote that "he was tremendous. History itself seemed to come into the chamber and address us. Nobody could have listened and not been moved. This was his *forte*. There has never been anybody who could speak for history as Churchill could."[49]

It was crucial at this moment of European disaster that Churchill exerted himself to define Britain's war aims. Others in his Cabinet advocated, or considered, seeking an immediate end to the war. Beaverbrook favored a negotiated peace, an "honorable" settlement that would allow Britain to retire behind its imperial frontiers. What, they asked, could Britain hope to do without an ally on the European mainland? But Churchill remained immovable, and sent a telegram to Roosevelt assuring him that Britain would never parley, setting out a strident and defiant national policy that his Cabinet had not agreed to. In arguing his case in Cabinet and in his speeches to Parliament and the nation, Churchill held out the possibility of American aid and a hope for the future. What was at stake, in the glorious vision sketched by Churchill, was civilization itself. Connecting with a thousand years of history, Churchill saw a battle and a hope beyond the ken of men like Halifax. For his part, Halifax thought that Churchill talked "the most frightful rot" about the terms on which he would listen to a peace offer from Hitler—after he had relinquished all of his conquests. Even at this stage, Churchill's position was vulnerable, and he could not afford Halifax's resignation. But Churchill exuded rocklike resolution. There could simply be no peace with Hitler, and it was better to fight and lose than not fight at all. He passionately believed in decency, and that British influence in the world promoted it. To compromise with Nazi Germany, therefore, was impossible—"What justification was there for the Empire and British power, if not to fight against Hitler and all he stood for?"[50]

With France now defeated and German forces on the other side of the Channel, the prospect of invasion and national defeat, not experienced since Napoleon's planned invasion of 1803, dominated the high summer of 1940. Though the threat of Napoleonic invasion had been viewed with the utmost seriousness and elaborate measures taken for home defense, as long as Britain remained master of the Channel, there had been no chance whatsoever of Napoleon's transporting the large army he had amassed at Boulogne across the water to the Kent and Sussex coast. In 1940, however, there was the entirely novel threat of more than 2,500 German bombers and fighters, mostly operating from airfields in nearby Belgium and France. Against this force, Air Chief Marshal Sir Hugh Dowding mustered only 650 RAF Spitfires and Hurricanes. Adolf Hitler, master of continental Europe since the armistice with France, could now turn his attention to the one remaining problem—the offshore kingdom, its empire, and its navy. Air power would neutralize the

threat of the RAF; German transports would then brave the perilous Channel and the might of the Royal Navy and transport German troops to British shores. On July 16, Hitler issued his order for
Operation Sealion, the invasion of Britain.

In the face of mounting military disasters, the British desperately needed to rebuild their armed strength after the losses suffered at Dunkirk, when so much precious equipment had been lost
(2,000 heavy guns, 60,000 vehicles, 70,000 tons of ammunition,
and 600,000 tons of fuel). To make matters worse, the army had
been the poor relation in interwar defense spending, greater priority having been given to the RAF. So there was much work to be
done, and this included the formation of the Local Defence Volunteers (renamed the Home Guard on Churchill's initiative). Defence
Regulation 18b gave the government a range of emergency powers, and enemy aliens were rounded up on Churchill's orders. On
August 20, during his Commons speech praising the gallant efforts
of "the Few," Churchill also summarized the work of the army and
the Home Guard, stating that "nearly 2,000,000 determined men
have rifles and bayonets in their hands tonight. . . . We have never
had armies like this in our Island in time of war. The whole Island
bristles against invaders, from the sea or from the air."[51] Meanwhile,
Lord Beaverbrook, as minister for aircraft production, was working
frantically to increase the frontline strength of Fighter Command,
the navy was prepared to defend the coast, likely landing sites were
fortified, and the army drew up its plans of defense should the
invader come. Barrage balloons, antitank trenches, dragon's teeth,
and pillboxes sprouted across Britain. Churchill traveled to inspect
as much as he could, and the country braced itself, literally, to fight
on the beaches and landing grounds.

The Battle of Britain developed into a dramatic war of attrition
as the vapor trails of skirmishing fighters crisscrossed the summer
skies and Göring's bombers targeted RAF airfields. But despite German advantages, the RAF was fighting at home, and the Luftwaffe
felt its losses (of aircraft, but particularly of aircrew) even more
keenly than its opponent. Of even greater consequence was Hitler's

strategic blunder in switching the attention of his bombers to London and other major cities from September 7 and ceasing to target the RAF and its airfields in an attempt to sweep Fighter Command from the sky. This change in strategy came about when Churchill ordered an attack on Berlin following a mistaken Luftwaffe raid on central London on August 24, which incensed Hitler. Despite Göring's claims, RAF Fighter Command never reduced in strength, largely because of the prodigious efforts of Beaverbrook's Ministry of Aircraft Production, nearly 352 new fighters being rolled out each month during this crucial period.

The new German strategy was intended to wear Britain down by blitz bombing ("cruel, wanton, indiscriminate bombings" of cities, as Churchill put it),[52] and this meant that by late September, the Battle of Britain had been won. During this period, Churchill tended to work from 10 Downing Street, sleeping in the Downing Street Annex and regularly watching the action from rooftops. He and Clementine had moved out of Downing Street and into the annex flat, which had been specially constructed from former government offices on the first floor at Storey's Gate overlooking St. James's Park. The flat, built at the height of the Blitz, was directly above the underground War Rooms, which themselves had been built in 1938 as the likelihood of enemy bombers appearing over London escalated. Churchill made special efforts to inspect bomb damage and in the War Cabinet advocated a more generous compensation scheme for the victims. This, as Clement Attlee noted, showed his "gift of immediate compassion for people who were suffering."[53]

While all of this was going on, Churchill had to attend to affairs of state relating to the global war effort and the cultivation of key allies. In September, he quietly and wisely assumed the leadership of the Conservative Party upon Chamberlain's retirement (he died the following month), securing his power base. Given the visceral hatred with which many in the party had viewed Churchill, this was a remarkable personal triumph.

THE AMERICAN CONNECTION

Churchill believed that America was crucial to victory. He thus set about wooing the reluctant superpower-in-waiting in any way he could. Despite some jaundiced remarks in the 1920s when he had been chancellor, his well-documented enthusiasm for his mother's native country stood him in good stead and was in marked contrast to Chamberlain's views on America. It showed an intellectual suppleness and pragmatism, as in his heart of hearts and despite his bombastic assertion of British might and the continuing relevance of the British Empire, Churchill knew that America was outstripping Britain in terms of raw power. It was, furthermore, not a new or circumstantial move. As early as June 1903, he had told the Commons that "I have always thought that it ought to be the main end of English state-craft over a long period of years to cultivate good relations with the United States."[54]

From June 1940, Churchill was making efforts to get America into the war, usually eliciting depressing responses. But Churchill persisted, remaining gracious and patient. Right from the outbreak of war, he recognized the need to court American opinion and to do everything possible to involve America on Britain's side, as a noncombatant at first. Hence the deal to exchange fifty old American destroyers for ninety-nine-year leases on sites on British Caribbean islands that was concluded in August 1940. The British received some much-needed additions for convoy escort, and the Americans were able to extend their eastern seaboard and Atlantic defenses by building military facilities on British islands. But there was much more to the deal than this, as Churchill knew. It tautened the psychological, military, and political bonds across the Atlantic. Churchill, with his American ancestry and interest in America as a world power (he had begun writing his *History of the English-Speaking Peoples* before the outbreak of war, delivered to Cassell in autumn 1939 as a 500,000-word typescript, though not, as it turned out, the final one) was better qualified than any other British politician to appeal to American opinion and to convince America that he was the man to trust in resisting Hitler. In pursuing this line, Churchill understood that the American public needed to see the British war effort close up—to view its military encounters as well as the war's impact on the home front. Thus he warmly welcomed American guests into his circle and sought to show them around his battered but unbowed country.

The message to the American people was sent in other ways, too, and Churchill's image was burnished through pro-British propaganda disseminated by British information services and pro-British Americans. Americans were generally unaware of his colorful and controversial political past, which was a good thing. They were enthralled by his extrovert style and bulldog appearance. Americans came to love Churchill. As the *New York Times* put it, "This is the kind of leadership a free people deserve. . . . He has refused to treat his people like children, and they are responding gloriously with all they have and all they are." Roosevelt was greatly impressed by Churchill though was obliged by American political realities to avoid being seen to commit too much or too little to the British cause.

Churchill forged relations with America as a matter of priority. In November 1940, while staying at Ditchley Park in Oxfordshire, he was visited by Lord Lothian, ambassador to Washington, at a moment when economic disaster loomed. He sent a telegram to Roosevelt on November 16, telling him of a long letter that would be delivered to him upon Lothian's return to the American capital. Churchill viewed this letter "as one of the most important I ever wrote," for it contained the seeds of the Lend-Lease scheme that was to provide Britain's financial base for the rest of the war. In the month following Roosevelt's receipt of the letter, January 1941, Churchill (again at Ditchley) received the president's personal envoy, Harry Hopkins. The prime minister lost no time in establishing a warm relationship with him and doing all he could to ensure that he was well placed to report to his master on the British war effort and the man at its center. The Americans still needed to be convinced that it was worth backing Britain. Much as the British might look askance at the American attitude, asking why they were not rolling up their sleeves and joining the war against a tyrant who would sooner or later threaten them, this was the way things stood in a land far removed from the din of European battle. Hopkins was welcomed into the Churchill circle, and the prime minister took to his humor, his gambling, his dress, and his colorful past. He took him to Scapa Flow to see Lord Halifax depart aboard the battleship HMS *King George V* to take up his position as ambassador to America following the death of Lothian. Churchill entertained Hopkins at Chequers, where, snug in his siren suit (an all-in-one garment, designed to be put on over nightclothes when the air raid sirens sounded), the PM fared better than his guest, who experienced the house's renowned chilliness. Hopkins accompanied Churchill on a tour of Swansea and Bristol, both men receiving honorary degrees at Bristol University, a city bearing the scars of heavy German bombing.

Lend-Lease resulted from Churchill's personal appeal to Roosevelt and his dire warning that unless Britain was supported with material aid, it could be defeated and America left exposed. He had said on February 9, 1941, that his response would be to assure President Roosevelt that "we shall not fail or falter; we shall not weaken or tire. Neither the sudden shock of battle nor the long drawn-out trials of vigilance and exertion will wear us down. Give us the tools, and we will finish the job."[55] Churchill's logic, in addressing the American government, was to argue that America must help Britain in any way possible, even when Britain ran out of cash to pay for goods. America could not afford to allow Britain to fight alone; Hitler's onward march, and possible British defeat, was a problem for America just as much as it was for Europe. Lend-Lease, dubbed by Churchill the "most unsordid act in any nation's history," duly received congressional approval in March 1941, and over thirty billion dollars' worth of American-produced material would galvanize the British Empire's war effort over the next four years. (Nearly ten billion dollars flowed in the other direction, known as Reverse Lend-Lease.)

Churchill and Roosevelt had their first wartime meeting at Placentia Bay, Newfoundland, in August 1941. This trip presaged what was to become a familiar aspect of wartime communication and decision making: the globetrotting summit meeting among the major Allied leaders, with Churchill emerging tens of thousands of miles in the lead, signified his enormous appetite for travel, no matter what the dangers and discomforts, and his Herculean efforts to forge the Grand Alliance and conduct policy making in person.

HMS *Prince of Wales*, Britain's newest battleship, transported a delighted Churchill across dangerous Atlantic waters. He took to the venture like a schoolboy let loose for the holidays, spurred on by the whiff of danger and sense of a historic moment in the making. The journey was made in great secrecy, the prime minister and his entourage of officials, chiefs of staff, and newsmen traveling by rail from Marylebone Station to Scapa Flow. On both the outward and homeward journeys, Churchill entertained the ship's wardroom each evening with a picture show, having brought with him a variety of films, from American comedies and westerns like *High Sierra* to stirring British historical dramas like *Lady Hamilton* (which made Churchill weep), to cartoons and slapstick like Donald Duck's *Foxhunting* and Laurel and Hardy's *Saps at Sea*. Each day, Churchill would wander about the ship and spend hours closeted with his chiefs of staff or in bed with his papers, conducting the empire's war effort from the high seas. He also found time to read a novel, C. S. Forester's *Captain Hornblower RN*.

The meeting at Placentia Bay set the tone for the wartime summits that were to see Churchill and his chiefs of staff, together with the attendant flock of advisers and journalists, venture to such places as Bermuda, Cairo, Casablanca, Quebec, Tehran, Washington, and Yalta. There was a great deal of ceremony aboard the battleship and the president's cruiser, culminating in a joint church service that filled the *Prince of Wales's* deck with sailors and the strains of "Onward, Christian Soldiers." The result of the meeting was the Atlantic Charter, a document that with its promise to "respect the right of all peoples to choose the form of government under which they will live" was to reverberate throughout the British Empire and would be cited ad infinitum by nationalists seeking a greater share in the direction of their countries' destinies. This was a cat that Churchill was to rue letting out of the bag, for he had had only the territories overrun by Germany in mind when framing it—not Britain's extensive collection of colonies. The charter was greeted with some disappointment in Britain, and indeed among the company of the *Prince of Wales*, who had hoped that the historic meeting would be the drumroll for an American declaration of war on the side of the British Empire. For a while, Churchill actually thought he had succeeded in obtaining from Roosevelt a commitment to join the war, though he soon understood that the president's encouraging words stopped short of this. But, as Churchill said in an explanatory broadcast to the nation on August 24, 1941:

> The meeting was . . . symbolic. That is its prime importance. . . . Would it be presumptuous of me to say that it symbolizes . . . the marshaling of the good forces of the world against the evil forces which are now so formidable and triumphant? . . . This was a meeting which marks for ever in the pages of history the taking up of the English-speaking nations amid all this peril, tumult, and confusion, of the guidance of the fortunes of the broad toiling masses in all the continents.[56]

For Churchill, the meeting and the charter bound America more closely to Britain's cause and moved America a step closer to joining the war as a full belligerent—including the agreement to extend America's responsibility in securing the Atlantic sea lanes—a process that was completed four months later as American battleships burned at their moorings in Hawaii and Germany joined its eastern ally and declared war on America. Returning from this first meeting with Roosevelt, the *Prince of Wales* caught up with a convoy of seventy-two vessels plowing the Atlantic swells on its way to Britain. Churchill stopped off briefly to visit Iceland, where British and Canadian troops were deployed in aid of Atlantic defense.

WORKING WITH THE MAN

Churchill's energy and drive were legendary, along with the manner in which he kept all around him on their toes. His work rate and ability to tirelessly deal with innumerable people and issues across a vast spectrum of war was phenomenal and without equal in history. He was a dynamic information processor and decision maker at the center of a well-oiled machine. Brigadier Jacob captured a typically frenetic opening to the day: "Sawyers brings the breakfast; then Kinna is sent for to take something down; meanwhile the bell is rung for the Private Secretary on duty who is asked for news, and told to summon someone, say CIGS [Chief of the Imperial General Staff] or Pug. Then it is the candle for lighting cigars that is wanted. Then someone must get Hopkins on the phone. All this while the Prime Minister is half sitting, half lying, in his bed, breathing rather stentoriously, and surrounded by papers."[57] His attitude to his work is perfectly summed up by his reaction in Quebec in August 1943 when, at midnight, Cordell Hull rose from the table to go to bed. "W. was scandalized," Eden wrote, "and explained in reply to Hull's protest that it was late, 'Why man, we are at war!'"[58]

His capacity to work without respite inspired people but presented challenges for those not used to the peculiar rhythm and pace of Churchill's life, made more unusual and taxing by the demands of war. Senior figures in the autumn of their years (like Churchill himself) found it difficult to keep up with him and didn't necessarily appreciate the demand to do so or his verbal blitzes. They would despair when, after a late-night conference on the heels of a tiring day, they were obliged to sit up with their leader and watch a film. Throughout the war, Churchill drove himself with scant regard for his health. Even his journeys overseas, accomplished in de Havilland Flamingos, battleships, Liberator bombers, destroyers, troopships, and the like, never seemed to ruffle him, and his gift of a smiling, pugnacious, calm, and confident front was a boon to colleagues and commanders both at home and overseas. Even when abroad, his staff attempted to stick as closely as possible to what amounted to Churchill's routine—the morning hours spent working in bed, regular baths, formal dinners, and after-dinner games.

Those who worked alongside him have left a rich record of the man observed at close quarters. May Shearburn, a typist, recalled the need to endure petulant insults and his "genius for not recognizing other people's problems." But she also experienced his kindness and was aware of the incalculable strains under which he worked. "Are you ready?" he might begin a session of dictation, the secretary poised over a specially silenced typewriter. "I'm feeling very fertile tonight." Sometimes, with a twinkle in his eye, he would say that he would need two young ladies tonight. As he dictated and tried sentences aloud, he would walk up and down the room, muttering phrases to himself, sometimes dictating, sometimes rehearsing the delivery of the speech that was forming. Of course, he loved powerful prose and evoking men of action from British history, such as Henry V, Drake, Marlborough, and Wellington. He often employed suitably archaic language: "Yes. The time is right for another feat of arms," Sir Ian Jacob recalls him saying.

His moods ranged from "charming, amusing, light-hearted and talkative to moody, bad-tempered, irascible and silent."[59] Fortunately, most people who saw the bad side also got to see the good. As his friend Brendan Bracken put it, it was like being in love with a beautiful woman who infuriates you but can smile and be forgiven in a moment. On the whole, Churchill's secretaries wrote of their time with him in tones of affection and admiration: they knew how great was their master's load, how great the moment of history in which they had the chance to share. Elizabeth Layton wrote: "He was simply *sweet* all the time."[60] On Christmas Day 1942, he worked in bed "in a grand temper," Layton recalled, then "sat up in bed and read a book . . . looking like a benevolent old cherub."[61] "The more one is with him, the more one gets to understand his funny little ways," she wrote, "and why he gets cross at this or that. One can anticipate his wants sometimes, and he always appreciates that. He likes one to know what kind of a smoke he wants, or when he wants a different type of pen passed to him. . . . There is nothing in the world he hates more than to waste one minute of his time!"[62] On Marian Holmes's first encounter with him as a secretary, Churchill said, "You know you must never be frightened of me when I snap. I'm not snapping at you but thinking of the work."[63]

Churchill's secretaries, while often overworked and harangued, were at least given the courtesy of being acknowledged and treated as part of the entourage. They had an important and difficult job to do. Elizabeth Layton, a personal secretary, found that his speech impediment made dictation difficult, as did the presence of a fat cigar between his lips. She would work for three consecutive days from two in the afternoon until two or even four thirty in the morning, with duties at Chequers every other weekend and regular dictation in the car between Downing Street and Chequers. He could be demanding and could tease or bark at her. But she endured these trials, aware that her master was "the spearhead of our stand against Nazism" and aware of his occasional smile, his gratitude, and his concern about her eating properly and keeping warm in the winter. Churchill rode his personal secretaries hard, expecting dictation straight onto the silent typewriter and the production of an almost instant, accurate typescript of what he had said, and always ready to go off "like a rocket" if an error was made or the unfortunate secretary fidgeted. But they understood the situation: "I didn't mind—we were all so impressed by the stature of our master, so engaged in the tremendous task to which he was unsparingly devoting himself, that we would take anything from him."[64] Often, he was playful: "Gimme more work," he might proclaim, or "Stop muckin' me about," when told there were no more papers in his Box.[65]

His robust style of interaction with colleagues and subordinates, so much in contrast to the skills of diplomacy he displayed in his dealings with Roosevelt and the American leadership, was well known. As Sir Ian Jacob wrote, "Having decided at the start exactly what he wanted to do, Churchill would first try to beat down opposition by a deluge of argument." None of his ministers found him easy to deal with; he was combative and made no attempt to curb his pugnacity. "He was always ready to contend that opposition to his particular friends must be the result of inertia, orthodoxy, or jealousy of Government departments." He had a soft spot for the eccentric or the man who incurred the hostility of officials. General Sir Alan Brooke's war diaries give a fascinating insight into the challenges and frustrations of working with such a dynamic, assertive superior and of the ways in which he could be handled. Eden once suggested he should not go and interfere with commanders in the Middle East. "You mean like a great bluebottle buzzing over a huge cowpat?" Churchill enquired. (He went anyway and sacked Auchinleck.) The previous November (1941), he had even removed the most senior soldier from his post, the chief of the Imperial General Staff, Sir John Dill. His dispatch to Washington as Churchill's personal representative and chief of the British Joint Staff Mission, and replacement as CIGS by Alan Brooke, were inspired moves.

Churchill's fascination with war, travel and danger had many outlets during his first prime ministership. His desire to watch dogfights was almost childlike, and he frequently strained at the leash in his urgency to get to the front line to witness military action, or as close as the restraining stratagems of his peers and advisers would allow him. A trip to France that involved a voyage by submarine was "a tremendous lure for this man of adventure," as was his penchant for taking over the controls of aircraft in which he was being conveyed, even of the superliner *Queen Mary* on a transatlantic crossing (insisting during lifeboat drill that a machine gun be mounted in his boat). When driving around London, Churchill's cars would move fast, jump traffic lights, and take roundabouts on the right-hand side. He had a special train for his not infrequent movements around the country and early in the war visited most places on the British coast where an enemy landing might take place. The Churchills would descend upon Chequers or Ditchley Park in a wave of secretaries, policemen, valets, and often soldiers.

Churchill shared the danger of the people of London, insisting on working from the prime minister's official residence, 10 Downing Street. The house was hit by a bomb, and he was persuaded to make use of the abandoned Down Street tube station off Piccadilly ("the Burrow"). Then there was the Downing Street Annex. While running the war effort from the imperial capital, he would take regular strolls in St. James's Park, often in the dark. After his bodyguard Walter Thompson had walked into a tree, it was decided to procure a walking stick fitted with a torch.

Close-up accounts of Churchill's private habits and character abound as he became one of the most observed men on earth. His foibles included a loathing of whistling and of paper clips, which he insisted be removed from incoming mail and documents before they came to him. He wore silk vests and slept with a black satin band over his eyes. After his second bath of the day, he might emerge in his famous siren suit, then after dinner change again, sometimes into a dressing gown, before settling down to bagatelle. His bodyguard Thompson described him as looking like a teddy bear. He would occasionally listen to music, his taste embracing popular tunes such as Noël Coward's "Mad Dogs and Englishmen," "Run Rabbit Run," and "Home Sweet Home." As the gramophone played, he might hum the tune and mark time with his hand, and he had been known, if sufficient floor space presented itself, as in the Great Hall at Chequers, to march in time to military music or waltz with his daughter Sarah to the "Blue Danube." He sang "There Is a Happy Land Far Far Away," "The Glory Song," "A Wandering Minstrel I," and "Keep Right On to the End of the Road."

AN INDECISIVE YEAR

After the Battle of France and the Battle of Britain, with their contrasting outcomes, the British war effort fell into a series of distinct patterns. Churchill presided over and inspired an unprecedented mobilization of the British home front; the RAF and Luftwaffe traded blows across Europe; the navy and the merchant marine fought a deadly battle with German submarines; and the army, licking its wounds and manning the defenses of Britain, began extensive operations in Africa following Italy's entry into the conflict. In the air, Britain continued to endure German bomber raids against cities and towns. The RAF, meanwhile, built up its strategic bomber offensive against German cities and industrial sites. The prevailing wisdom still decreed that heavy bombing could shorten the war by knocking out important elements of the enemy's war machine, from U-boat pens to munitions factories, and that its impact upon civilian morale would weaken the enemy's resolve. Both contentions have been hotly debated ever since, as symbolized by the intense controversy surrounding Air Chief Marshal Arthur "Bomber" Harris. From the British point of view, the air campaign against Germany had another, more political value once Hitler had invaded Russia. From June 1941, unable to launch the "second front" offensive (the reinvasion of Nazi-occupied Western Europe) that Stalin so vociferously demanded, Bomber Command's activities were presented by Churchill to the Russians as a significant military threat to the enemy's homeland and contribution to winning the war. A strategy involving the destruction of German industrial cities and the "de-housing" of the population was hardly a grotesque response to the way the war was turning out; it had been at the heart of British air power doctrine and national strategy since the interwar years (while the valiant Coastal Command remained a Cinderella service compared with the richly endowed Bomber Command). The advice Churchill received from experts of various shades, including Professor Lindemann, was that bombers were better employed raining destruction upon Germany, not operating against shipping and coastal targets.

On land, with the Allies booted out of Europe, the Middle East became the focus of Britain's war effort. The fall of France meant that the war in the west was now over, Britain momentarily safe following the Battle of Britain, though a renewal of the German offensive was entirely possible and there was no time for complacency. The question was, how could Britain act against Germany now? Where, on land, could it meet the enemy given Germany's complete success in conquering Europe? Where could Britain strike a blow? The old British strategy died with the fall of France. Churchill now cast about for new means to take the fight to the enemy, seizing upon initiatives such as the Special Operations Executive and the creation of commando, paratroop, and combined-operations capabilities. While not decided upon by choice, it transpired that Africa became the one place where Britain was facing the German enemy on land, after Hitler's frustrated decision to reinforce the Italians in the Western Desert with the dispatch of General Erwin Rommel and the Afrika Korps. This was after a period of dramatic British and imperial victories over Italian forces in East and North Africa in 1940–41 under General Sir Archibald Wavell, commander in chief Middle East. By February 1941, General Wavell's troops, never exceeding 30,000 in the front line, had advanced five hundred miles in ten weeks, completely destroyed an Italian army, and captured 130,000 prisoners, for a cost of fewer than 2,000 killed and wounded. It said much about the contrasting fortunes of war that while for the British, the war in the Western Desert became the main thing, for Germany it was always a sideshow, an entanglement born of Italy's ineptitude.

While unable to make any dramatic inroads into Nazi-dominated Europe, Churchill continued to exude confidence. Dealing robustly with those who criticized his government's record, he painted an optimistic picture, telling the Commons in May 1941: "When I look back on the perils which have been overcome, upon the great mountain waves through which the gallant ship has driven, when I remember all that has gone wrong, and remember also all that has gone right, I feel sure we have no need to fear the tempest. Let it roar, and let it rage. We shall come through."[66] In the following month, he told a conference of Dominion high commissioners and Allied ministers that "our solid, stubborn strength has stood the awful test. We are masters of our own air, and now reach out in ever-growing retribution upon the enemy. The Royal Navy holds the sea."[67]

Throughout 1941 and the first half of 1942, campaigns in the Mediterranean and North Africa went badly. Elsewhere in these theatres, Churchill took the guarantee of Greek independence seriously and hailed a coup in Yugoslavia that installed a government favorable to resisting the Nazis. It led him to conceive the idea of a large-scale Balkan front, though the Yugoslavian government hesitated about joining a military alliance. Events in both these countries moved quickly. General Wavell was obliged to weaken his North African front by moving troops for the defense of Greece (the alternative was to shamefacedly abandon an ally). Though often portrayed as an example of poor Churchillian decision making, Britain's ill-fated Greek campaign was in fact an initiative proposed by commanders on the spot and sanctioned collectively by the War Cabinet. German invasion of both countries soon followed, Yugoslavia being defeated within two weeks. The invasion of Greece came in March 1941, and Churchill accepted the advice of Eden and Wavell and sent imperial troops, overrun in the following month and hastily evacuated, 43,000 of 55,000 deployed getting away. In May and June 1941, Crete, to which 26,000 of these men had been transferred, fell to German paratroops, and the army was again taken off by the hard-pressed vessels of the Royal Navy, 16,000 escaping to Alexandria. Churchill thought that Wavell could have done more to save the island.

In June 1941, Operation Battleaxe, a counteroffensive in the Western Desert promising a long-overdue British victory, got under way. Churchill had pressured Wavell into this offensive earlier than the general would have liked. As reports of the battle filtered back to Britain, Churchill was at a deserted Chartwell, shut up for the war, roaming the valley deep in thought. But the operation fared badly, and Wavell's time was up. He had had the misfortune to command the world's most active theatre of war with woefully inadequate resources once the Italian pretenders had been resoundingly defeated under his command. These several setbacks greatly deflated Churchill, but he continued to believe, and to convince those around him, that Britain could not be beaten. In Cairo, Auchinleck replaced Wavell, and Wavell replaced Auchinleck in Delhi as commander in chief India. Churchill hated inactivity. The Eastern Fleet, performing a valuable role in the face of Japanese naval superiority, was often labeled "idle." And he never allowed Middle East Command to rest. "The Army is like a peacock—nearly all tail," he said. "I intended North Africa to be a springboard, not a sofa."[68]

The spring and summer of 1941 were trying times as the British war effort continued to founder. But British action in "peripheral" theatres (which are never "peripheral" to those who fight and die in them and usually have a strategic purpose) was impressive, largely stimulated by Churchill's intuition, enthusiasm for action, and understanding of the global nature of Britain's war effort. Likely as it was that Iraq might be next on Germany's list following their series of victories in the Mediterranean, the British acted against the pro-German Iraqi regime in order to ensure that this region, containing vital oil resources, did not fall to the enemy. Vichy Syria was also conquered, and in August 1941, Anglo-Russian forces invaded Iran so as to forestall Nazi penetration, guard oil supplies, and open a new Anglo-American supply route to Russia via the Gulf and the Caspian Sea.

Meanwhile, in May 1941, a major naval triumph occurred when the world's most powerful warship, the *Bismarck*, was destroyed after she had accounted for the Royal Navy's iconic HMS *Hood*. Churchill had issued the order "Sink the *Bismarck*," which spurred a period of frenetic naval action. Elsewhere at sea, the campaign to keep open the world's sea lanes and protect British, Allied and neutral vessels from the predations of Axis raiders and U-boats continued. In particular, the Battle of the Atlantic raged around Britain's key lifeline with North America, but the entire empire needed to be defended and held together, and this meant a constant, often bloody, vigil for the Royal Navy all over the world. From its overseas bases in places such as Sierra Leone, Cape Town, Durban, Mombasa, Aden, Colombo, and Bombay, British and imperial warships engaged the enemy and sought to protect the thousands of merchantmen flying the Red Duster, as well as the ensigns of other friendly powers, while seeking to interdict enemy shipping and blockade enemy coasts.

The Royal Navy enjoyed success against the impressive Italian fleet and U-boats sent by Hitler into the Mediterranean, but not without severe losses, epitomized by Italian frogman raids on Alexandria and the epic Malta convoy battles. Meanwhile, the Japanese menace to British possessions in Asia and the Far East loomed, though it was to an extent underplayed—because there was little chance to reinforce, given the state of affairs closer to home, and because of the hope that, in alliance with America, Japan could be deterred. This was a reasonable, if unpalatable, assessment; it was believed that Japan would not be rash enough to go to war against the combined might of the world's two largest navies. Unfortunately, when it did, defending British possessions in Southeast Asia and the Far East had slipped further down the list of strategic priorities, and Churchill made the unpleasant, though strategically correct, decision to send military aid (including the most modern fighter aircraft) to Russia rather than to Malaya. Keeping Russia in the war as a fighting ally was more important than saving Singapore.

In the autumn of 1941, Churchill hatched numerous schemes for coastal landings in Northern Europe and the Mediterranean theatre. Churchill's bamboozling tried the chiefs of staff severely. As General Sir Alan Brooke put it, "He cannot grasp the relationship of various theatres of war to each other." Deciding on grand strategy and its military execution from a position of extraordinary power at the center of an emergency wartime British government, Churchill was comfortable playing the strategist. Some argued, however, that he was too hotheaded to be a great strategist because of his demand for action all the time. As Sir Ian Jacob put it, his "predilection for continuous feats of arms had to be curbed. It was a weakness in his strategic thinking. He always wanted to be doing something himself, and the forces to be doing something; hammering away, engaging the enemy at all points on all fronts."[69] Churchill's attitude to global strategy was that resources should be centrally directed toward clearly understood priorities. Thus supplying Russia with arms was deemed more important than sending aid to Singapore, and Churchill vehemently opposed the Australian government's desire to have its divisions returned from the Middle East as Japan threatened, arguing that American divisions would make up the shortfall—strategically logical, though trampling on Australian sensibilities. Churchill's belief that Japan would not invade Australia was correct, and the fact that Churchill was insensitive to Australian feelings is not much of a criticism; "feelings" count for little in war, and Churchill was famously uninterested when it came to the feelings of others.

Throughout his life, Churchill "lived the imperial theatre" and was one of the few politicians who understood the implications of Britain's unique imperial status and the Anglo-Saxon heritage. He was acutely aware of the imperial nature of Britain's fight, and the empire was rarely far from his mind, as shown repeatedly in his speeches and broadcasts. He understood that British world power depended upon the empire, and that Britain—unique among the Great Powers of the world—was an imperial state. He was not, however, keen on consulting the Dominions, firmly believing that the center of the empire's war effort was London and that London should therefore have the power to decide upon the movement of all imperial resources. This was evidenced by his relations with the Australian government and with the Canadian prime minister, who said that when hosting Churchill and Roosevelt for conferences in Quebec, he was treated rather like the general manager of the Hotel Frontenac. Churchill's thinking, on Dominions or smaller allies alike, was revealed in a speech to the Commons in January 1942, in which he said: "To hear some people talk, however, one would think that the way to win the war is to make sure that every Power contributing armed forces and branches of these armed forces is represented on all the councils and organizations which have to be set up, and that everybody is fully consulted before anything is done. That is, in fact, the most sure way to lose a war."[70] While always mindful of Britain's imperial status and responsibilities, Churchill's concentration on Europe and the Middle East was a sound, war-winning strategy. As Richard Toye puts it: "[We] need not conclude from his repeated invocations of Empire that his vision for the war was an imperial one. Of course, imperial resources were highly welcome to him. . . . [But] Churchill's method—and it was undoubtedly sound strategy—was not to rush all possible help to under-defended out-posts, but rather to exploit the imperial periphery in order to defend the metropole."[71]

NEW ALLIES: RUSSIA AND AMERICA

Evidence mounted in 1941 of an imminent German attack on Russia, though Stalin did little to heed Churchill's intelligence-led warnings. When Operation Barbarossa was launched, Churchill was keen for Britain to do all it could to help its newfound ally, showing political acumen in jettisoning long-held prejudices against Russia and embracing a new ally as the tectonic plates of global power shifted imperceptibly. He broadcast his encouragement over the airwaves, setting the tone for British support of what would become a mighty but awkward ally—but most important, one capable of smashing the German army. In July 1941, an Anglo-Soviet agreement committed both powers to not making separate peace deals with Germany. In the following month, the first Arctic convoy departed from Scapa Flow, bearing two squadrons of Hurricanes to bolster Russia's attempt to repel the German onslaught. Churchill shared intelligence from his treasured ULTRA source. An Anglo-American supply conference in London in September decided to allocate munitions to Russia that had been destined for Britain under the Lend-Lease agreement.

This policy of supporting Russia in any way possible demonstrated Churchill's ability to make immensely difficult decisions at the highest strategic level and to change his tune when circumstances demanded. As General Sir Alan Brooke lamented, the policy of supporting Russia removed precious military resources from British battlefronts. (As Churchill signaled to Attlee from Ottawa in December 1941, "If Malay Peninsula has been starved for sake of Libya and Russia, no one is more responsible than I and I would do exactly the same again.")[72] What was more, the Russian ally was invariably ungrateful and ungracious. The policy also meant that from this moment, Britain was allied to a power whose political system was anathema and whose vision of the postwar world differed fundamentally from those of the Western allies. But the war against Germany had to be won, so any German enemy was automatically Britain's friend. Churchill overcame his potent hostility to the Soviet regime, proclaiming that "if Hitler invaded hell I would at least make a favorable reference to the Devil in the House of Commons." "No one has been a more consistent opponent of Communism than I have for the last twenty-five years. I will unsay no word that I have spoken about it. But all this fades away before the spectacle of what is now unfolding. The past with its crimes, its follies, its tragedies flashes away."[73]

While Churchill had deeply held concerns about Russian intentions and saw the descent of the Iron Curtain and the battle lines of the Cold War long before anyone else who mattered, he realized the need to build a relationship with Stalin in order to attempt to influence him. Becoming an ally of Russia brought foul dilemmas later in the war—standing as an onlooker, for example, while Russia clamped its authority upon Poland, the very country for whose freedom Britain had gone to war. But in terms of realpolitik, it is difficult to see what else Churchill could have done. Russia was an emerging superpower and a key ally; Poland a weak and relatively unimportant one that bordered Russia, not Britain. Russia, furthermore, had gained notable (if undeserved) prestige in the eyes of many British people, and Churchill's support of Russia played well with the public. So at this moment of Soviet need, as German troops and tanks poured eastward, Churchill bravely committed resources for which British commanders around the world were crying out. This was in support of a country that, according to the best available intelligence, would collapse under the weight of German invasion within a couple of months (though, shrewdly, Churchill himself did not share this gloomy assessment).

The British Empire in Asia and the Far East was gravely threatened by the Japanese. Nevertheless, Churchill's uncompromising focus on the Western theatres was absolutely correct. Simply stated, the security of the eastern empire was less important than that of the British Isles themselves, the Atlantic bridge, and the Mediterranean and Middle East. But this verdict would have brought little cheer to those marooned in Burma, stunned by the failure to hold Singapore, or those watching anxiously from Australia as Japan spread its martial wings. Though the chiefs of staff believed the defense of Singapore was more important than the defense of the Suez Canal, Churchill disagreed. Being forced to choose between them was an awful position to be in but represented the reality of fighting worldwide war and defending a worldwide empire from a position of unpreparedness. It was, in Churchill's words, like having to decide whether your son or your daughter should be killed. Churchill's position, however, was one that many others would have supported. Though the chief of the Imperial General Staff wanted to send reinforcements to the Far East in spring 1941, Churchill did not share the sense of alarm. On the one hand, Singapore was thought to be an impregnable fortress, which could hold out indefinitely until relieved; Churchill was absolutely shocked when it fell and it became apparent how fragile it was. On the other hand, he had a very low opinion of the fighting prowess of the Japanese. Along with the Foreign Office and many other informed observers on both sides of the Atlantic, he believed the Japanese were unlikely to enter the war until Russia had been knocked out by the Germans.

Things were about to change dramatically, as the "Day of Infamy" altered the course of the war. On Sunday, December 7, 1941, Churchill was at Chequers, in the company of the American ambassador to Britain, John Winant, and Averell Harriman, the American Lend-Lease administrator. Just before nine at night, the butler announced that there had been something in the news about a Japanese attack upon the American fleet. He was asked to bring a wireless into the room. Thus they listened, on a portable radio that Harry Hopkins had given Churchill, to news of Japan's attack on Pearl Harbor, America's naval stronghold in the Pacific. Afterward, Churchill left the room to telephone Roosevelt. That evening, digesting the news of this momentous event, the prime minister radiated confidence at the prospect of the full mobilization of America's martial power. He was instantly aware of what Pearl Harbor meant, whatever tribulations might lie ahead. "We should not be wiped out. Our history would not come to an end . . . we had won the war. England would live."

Simultaneous Japanese attacks had also been launched elsewhere across the Far East–Pacific region, including against Britain's possessions on the Malay Peninsula, and three days after Pearl Harbor, British naval power east of Suez suffered a severe blow when HMS *Prince of Wales* (aboard which Churchill had so recently visited Roosevelt at Placentia Bay) and HMS *Repulse* were sunk in the Gulf of Siam, the first capital ships to fall victim to aircraft. Churchill was appalled; he had expected the two vessels to disappear into the vastness of the Pacific "like rogue elephants," representing a thorn in Japan's side thereafter. The war having now become genuinely global, and with Japanese aggression in the Far East, dating from the early 1930s and now conjoined with the European struggle, Churchill saw a unique role for himself as the linchpin of a nascent "Grand Alliance." It would be his task to forge a global coalition in order to oversee the strategic prosecution of the war in disparate locations with disparate forces drawn from nations with divergent interests, histories, and postwar visions. In particular, channeling American energy into the European war, rather than simply focusing America's rage against the Japanese, was a priority. For this reason, Churchill was prepared to travel vast distances, extending his shuttle diplomacy in order to do everything possible to please, coax, and influence America. Roosevelt, understandably wanting to remain at the center of the momentous events unfolding in America, felt unable to travel to meet Churchill, who had proposed a meeting in either the British colony of Bermuda or Washington.

Days after Pearl Harbor, therefore, Churchill was at sea aboard the battleship HMS *Duke of York*, bound for the American capital. During the war, the two leaders were to meet nine times and to spend a total of four months in each other's company. The seas were rough as Churchill crossed to America. On December 21, no one was allowed on deck, and Churchill was confined to a "lovely cabin" in the bridge structure. "Being in a ship in such weather is like being in a prison," he wrote to Clementine, "with the extra chance of being drowned." He traveled with his staff, including twenty-seven cipherers for official telegrams and secret traffic. Arriving on December 22, he was accompanied on the War Cabinet's insistence by the physician Sir Charles Wilson (about to be created Lord Moran in the 1942 New Year's honors list).

Roosevelt paid Churchill the signal honor of waiting on the tarmac for his arrival by air in Washington. Close and cordial relations were established during an intimate stay at the White House. Over an extended period, the Arcadia Conference enabled the two nations' military staffs to work closely together. But bad news piled up during Churchill's visit. Hong Kong fell on Christmas Day; Churchill had hoped it would hold out for much longer. Despite the bitter pain of such blows, he was able to remain focused on the bigger strategic picture. "We must expect to suffer heavily in this war against Japan, and it is no use the critics saying, 'why were we not prepared?' when everything we had was already fully engaged. The entry of the United States into the war is worth all the losses sustained in the East many times over. Still these losses are painful to endure and will be very hard to repair."[74] This assessment, sent to Clementine, was spot-on. All of the Western imperial powers in the East—America, Britain, France, and Holland—were caught hideously unprepared by the Japanese onslaught; all sustained losses that dealt irreparable damage to their standing and sped the end of empire. But Churchill was aware of the fundamental fact that American power meant that the Allies could not lose the war. Lord Moran noted his mastery of detail, writing on January 14 that Churchill was "drunk with the figures of US production estimates. I think Winston, more than anyone here, visualizes in detail what this program means to the actual conduct of the war."[75] Churchill also understood, ahead of everyone else, that the emerging Anglo-American alliance was the only way to preserve British power in the world.

On Boxing Day, Churchill addressed a joint session of Congress, sharing his vision of the two great English-speaking powers standing shoulder to shoulder and observing that "if my father had been American, and my mother British, instead of the other way round, I might have got here on my own." He reviewed the world war to date, dwelling on the combined might of America, the British Empire, Russia, and China when compared with that of Japan, in the light of which "it becomes still more difficult to reconcile Japanese action with prudence or even sanity. What kind of people do they think we are? Is it possible they do not realize that we shall never cease to persevere against them until they have been taught a lesson which they and the world will never forget?"[76]

Roosevelt was impressed with the war plans the British had brought with them, including the scheme for an invasion of Northwest Africa, eventually to come to life as Operation Torch (which was to see an Anglo-American force of over 100,000 men land in Vichy-controlled Algeria and Morocco). Churchill accepted Roosevelt's proposal for a united command in the South West Pacific, and the Americans admired the thoroughness of British preparation and planning, many feeling that it had a decisive influence at the conference. The Americans agreed to a general statement confirming that, despite the Japanese war, "Europe first" was to be the policy. The aim was to take the offensive against Germany in 1943 and begin the liberation of the continent. While in America, Churchill suffered a minor heart attack after reporting severe chest pains. Still, on December 30, he moved to Ottawa, where he addressed the Canadian Parliament and made his famous "Some chicken! Some neck!" gag after recounting that a French general had said that Britain would "have her neck wrung like a chicken" within three weeks of the fall of France. Returning to America, a tired-looking prime minister was persuaded to take a brief rest in Florida.

Churchill went home via Bermuda in a flying boat, which he was allowed to pilot for much of the way. In the House of Commons, he spoke at length about the tragic loss of the *Prince of Wales* and *Repulse*, the decision to supply Russia, and the formation of a combined Anglo-American Chiefs of Staff Committee. This was a singularly important achievement of his visit to Washington (and an impressive example of wartime alliance integration). He also spoke of the first fruition of this Anglo-American arrangement, the new unified command for the South West Pacific that the Americans had been keen on, the ill-fated American-British–Dutch-Australian Command. Losses in the Far East had depressed Britain, as had mounting losses in the Atlantic following an intelligence shutout of U-boat signals. Harold Nicolson, referring to growing discontent about the course of the war, feared "a slump in public opinion which will deprive Winston of his legend."[77] But a vote of confidence on January 29 was won by a thumping 464 votes to 1. In his speech during this debate, Churchill said, "Could you have any higher expression of democracy than that? Very few other countries have institutions strong enough to sustain such a thing while they are fighting for their lives."[78] He continued:

> There never has been a moment, there never could have been a moment, when Great Britain or the British Empire, single-handed, could fight Germany and Italy, could wage the Battle of Britain, the Battle of the Atlantic and the Battle of the Middle East—and at the same time stand thoroughly prepared in Burma, the Malay Peninsula, and generally in the Far East against the impact of a vast military Empire like Japan.[79]

Nicolson noted that during this two-hour speech, "One can actually feel the wind of opposition dropping sentence by sentence."[80] Following the censure debate, while preparing for bed on the evening of January29, Churchill turned to his physician Lord Moran and said, "-—is a silly bastard. There are about half a dozen of them; they make a noise out of all proportion to their importance."[81]

Churchill was able to quell parliamentary frustration about the disastrous events in the east, though the national mood was not improved by the apparent failure of British sea power when the German ships *Gneisenau, Prinz Eugen,* and *Scharnhorst* sped through the English Channel and escaped the clutches of the Royal Navy and the RAF (though Enigma decrypts revealed that all had been badly damaged). Even worse was the stunning blow landed on February 15, when the "impregnable" fortress of Singapore surrendered to the Japanese, ending a campaign in which 130,000 British and imperial servicemen died or went into Japanese captivity. Yet even with this latest evidence, this latest measure, of the unpreparedness of the Allies to face the might of the dictators, Churchill remained confident of ultimate victory. He told the Commons on the day Singapore fell: "Tonight the Japanese are triumphant. They shout their exultation round the world. We suffer. We are taken aback. We are hard pressed. But I am sure even in this dark hour that 'criminal madness' will be the verdict which history will pronounce upon the authors of Japanese aggression."[82]

Despite his brave words, and the accurateness of his prophecy, Moran noted how the fall of Singapore "stupefied" the prime minister. He fretted about the quality of British arms and the shame of defeat, though in part Singapore's ultimate strategic goal had been to ensure American involvement in a war against Japan. There was a suggestion that Sir Stafford Cripps might replace him; there was criticism in the press, from the likes of Frank Owen and H. G. Wells, who wrote that "a boy scout is better equipped. He has served his purpose and it is high time he retired upon his laurels before we forget the debt we owe him." Churchill brooded on Singapore for a long time. Months later, Moran wrote, Churchill stopped drying himself after a bath and gloomily surveyed the floor—"I cannot get over Singapore," he said sadly. But Churchill refused to yield. As he told the Commons ten days after the calamity, "However tempting it might be to some, when much trouble lies ahead, to step aside adroitly and put someone else up to take the blows, I do not intend to take that cowardly course but, on the contrary, to stand to my post and persevere in accordance with my duty as I see it."[83] But though, as Churchill said, it seemed as if the fall of Singapore was "everyone's fault," the problem, and the great challenge facing the Allies, was that, as he told Roosevelt, "Democracy has to prove that it can provide a granite foundation for war against tyranny."[84]

In a measure designed to bolster confidence, Churchill again reorganized his government. Beaverbrook became minister of war production (despite Clementine's advice to remove him from office altogether), replaced soon by Lyttelton when ill health supervened. Sir Stafford Cripps became Lord Privy Seal and Leader of the House of Commons and entered the War Cabinet, where he ranked behind only Churchill and Clement Attlee (who became deputy prime minister), effectively bringing into the inner circle a potential rival for the premiership. Churchill was desperate for a victory and harried his commanders. Lord Moran, who had frequent contact with Churchill, recorded a day in February 1942 when Churchill was "in an explosive mood." He had learned that Auchinleck would not be ready to take the offensive until June. "That bloody man does not seem to care about the fate of Malta," the prime minister raged.[85] (When, in August, the island was finally relieved, Moran wrote that "the PM's relief is a joyful sight.")[86]

Close colleagues and family noticed that Churchill's understandable fatigue was affecting his performance, and that the business of government lacked firm direction. The Allied war effort seemed becalmed, if not actually going backwards. "When I reflect how I have longed and prayed for the entry of the United States into the war," Churchill telegraphed Roosevelt on March 5, "I find it difficult to realize how gravely our British affairs have deteriorated since December 7."[87] Military reverses continued. Rangoon fell to the Japanese (March 1942), and the mass retreat of British imperial arms and hundreds of thousands of civilians from Burma into India began. Pressure from within Labour ranks and, even more unwelcome, from America led to the Cripps mission to India, an attempt to persuade the Indian National Congress to get behind the war and desist from using it as an opportunity to push for Britain to "quit India" immediately. The offer was simple—constitutional reform leading to full independence after the war in return for support now. Churchill was not too distraught when this offer was rejected. Importantly, it was a gesture to the nationalists that was noted in Washington, as Churchill had intended. Churchill deeply resented

American interference in Indian affairs, though while he could make his views known in no uncertain terms, he had of course to take account of American opinion and the fact that American military resources in the China-Burma-India theatre were of growing importance. Roosevelt's telegram on India infuriated Churchill and led to a string of cusswords lasting for two hours. India was one of the very few issues on which Churchill was prepared to risk his alliance and friendship with Roosevelt. The failure of the Cripps mission meant that the British could take a firm stand against civil disobedience and lock up the opponents while attempting to get on with the war and defending India from a Japanese invasion that in the spring of 1942 looked an entirely plausible prospect. In Washington the following year, Roosevelt mischievously invited a vocal campaigner for Indian independence, Mrs. Ogden-Reed, to lunch.

Mrs. Ogden-Reed: "What are you going to do about those wretched Indians?"

Churchill: "Before we proceed further, let us get one thing clear. Are we talking about the brown Indians in India, who have multiplied alarmingly under the benevolent British rule? Or are we speaking of the Red Indians in America who, I understand, are almost extinct?"[88] Mrs. Ogden-Reed was rendered speechless, Roosevelt convulsed with laughter.

All of the advances toward consultation and shared government in India since the First World War were threatened by this reversion to old-style imperialism. The cost of this imperial intransigence, and the suppression needed to quell the civil disobedience that was to come, would be great. It might not have been this way, and India might have enjoyed an easier wartime career, with less reliance placed upon it as a military stronghold, if it had not been for the imperial defeats in Malaya and Burma. In February 1942, Chiang Kai-shek also stuck his oar into British-Indian affairs while visiting the subcontinent. Churchill's reaction to this intervention, from a leader whose importance he considered to be grossly inflated beyond his own or his country's significance by virtue of American foreign policy alone, can only be imagined.

On April 2, 1942, Churchill signaled Cripps to spell out the fact that this was the final offer. A late American flourish saw Roosevelt's personal representative, Colonel Louis Johnson, arrive in Delhi. His meetings with Cripps and Nehru, however, led to exasperation in London, and Roosevelt was obliged to limit Johnson to his initial role as assessor of India's need for American war materials. Harry Hopkins in London had to extricate Johnson and the president's name from a potentially embarrassing situation, and Churchill was able to signal Cripps (one imagines with some relish) to say that Johnson had in fact no presidential backing beyond the munitions issue.

The Cripps mission failed in part because of INC immobility and, it is claimed by some, because of Churchill's conservatism regarding India (and his fear of splitting the Conservative Party). Fundamentally, neither he nor Viceroy Lord Linlithgow would accept the fact that the end of the war would bring the end of the Raj. As Wavell, Linlithgow's replacement as viceroy in 1943, recorded in his diary, "The Cabinet is not honest in its expressed desire to make progress in India." Casting Churchill and his viceroy as the villains, however, may well attribute more influence to them than is their due. The Indian nationalists refused to cooperate; as a result, stern action was required so that their activities did not derail India's war effort during the critical phase of the Japanese assault on Britain's Asian empire. It was not long in coming, and in August 1942, Churchill told Lord Moran that "we have clapped Gandhi into prison."[89] The point to grasp is that this moment in 1942—before the Allies had won any significant offensive victories—was the most dangerous the British Empire faced during the war, and Churchill was determined to ensure that nothing jeopardized the chances of resisting the Japanese onslaught.

ALAMEIN AND ALLIANCE PLANNING

As these dramatic events were unfolding in South Asia, General Marshall and Harry Hopkins arrived in Britain to attempt to persuade Churchill that the invasion of mainland Europe should take place as soon as possible. The British chiefs of staff, however, were adamant that 1942 was too soon, and that a premature attempt would court disaster. Furthermore, General Sir Alan Brooke was successful in convincing Churchill of the potential for the Mediterranean theatre to deliver victory. The two Allies agreed, in principle, on joint war strategy, the Americans agreeing that the time was not yet right for a cross-Channel invasion of Europe and agreeing to a joint invasion of North Africa. Churchill felt the need to ensure that Roosevelt was thoroughly happy with all of this, recognizing that the American president was the most important man in the world in terms of delivering Allied victory. In June 1942, therefore, Churchill was again on the other side of the Atlantic enjoying the president's hospitality. The two leaders were together when Churchill received one of the greatest shocks of the war—news of the fall of Tobruk on June 21 and the surrender of a large imperial garrison. Churchill felt embarrassed, disoriented, and in despair ("defeat is one thing; disgrace is another"). It was then that Roosevelt made his famous offer of help and immediately undertook to provide what Churchill asked for—three hundred tanks and one hundred guns sent to Egypt without delay. At moments like these, Churchill's extraordinary strength and mental and physical resilience came into their own. Lord Moran, who was with him in Washington, described his "buoyant temperament" as a "tremendous asset." After the news about Tobruk hit him, in Moran's words, he "refused to take the count; he got up a little dazed, but full of fight. . . . There is never any danger of him folding up in dirty weather. My heart goes out to him. I do like a full-sized man. With our military prestige at zero, he dominated the discussions."[90]

Back at home, the fall of Tobruk generated the most intense criticism that Churchill's government had to withstand during the war. Everywhere, it seemed, apart from in "sideshow" campaigns, British land forces seemed unable to hold the enemy, let alone beat him. Aneurin Bevan's cruel jibe—that the prime minister "wins debate after debate and loses battle after battle"—hurt Churchill.[91] Given this catalogue of reverses, it was no surprise that, when General

Auchinleck won a defensive victory in the desert ("first" Alamein), Churchill wanted to head off to Cairo, only prevented from doing so by pressure from his Cabinet colleagues. A vote of "no confidence" in the House was defeated by 475 to 25. "Good for you," telegraphed Roosevelt.

In terms of grand strategy, divergent British and American imperatives were emerging. The British chiefs of staff insisted that there could be no D-Day-style assault on Hitler's Europe in 1942, and it was Churchill's hope that there could be some joint concentration in the Mediterranean region. Out of all of this came Roosevelt's approval for Operation Torch, the Anglo-American landings in North Africa. The fact was that, despite British hopes for a cross-Channel invasion in 1943, the American buildup of troops and landing craft was too slow to permit this. In July, Churchill was allowed to go to Cairo, where, after a flight in a Liberator, he met his great friend and supporter General Smuts and inspected the 8th Army. Out of this visit came his decision to replace General Auchinleck with General Sir Harold Alexander as commander in chief Middle East, and to replace Major General Neil Ritchie as commander of the 8th Army. The choice to replace him was Lieutenant General William "Strafer" Gott, but his aircraft was destroyed as he flew into Cairo on the same route that Churchill had flown the day before, and the choice devolved upon Lieutenant General Bernard Montgomery. On August 9, Churchill told Clementine that he had been "so busy at anxious work since I arrived nearly a week ago. . . . It was absolutely necessary that I should come here. This splendid army, about double as strong as the enemy, is baffled and bewildered by its defeats." On August 19, Churchill was in high spirits. Lord Moran wrote that "I heard the PM singing in his bath this morning," delighted because he was "about to be driven, jolted, across the desert from the British Embassy in Cairo, in blinding heat, to visit Montgomery in the field."[92] After a day with the men of the 8th Army, "the PM was full of all he had seen. He talked late into the night, while his little audience, reveling in this new experience, marvelled at the man—his boyish enthusiasm, his consuming vitality, his terrific vocaulary."[93] During his stay, Churchill also decided to split the enormous Middle East Command, in telegram consultation with the Cabinet, and this astute decision gave birth to the Persia and Iraq Command.

From Cairo, Churchill flew to Tehran, before flying on to Moscow to meet Stalin. "I am not looking forward to this part of my mission," he told Clementine, "because I bear so little in my hand, and sympathize so much with those to whom I go." The purpose of his visit was to break the bad news to the Russian leader concerning the Anglo-American decision not to launch a second front in Western Europe that year, showing once again his stamina, appetite for travel, moral courage, and faith in his own brand of face-to-face diplomacy. It was, Churchill said, "like carrying a large lump of ice to the North Pole."[94]

The Russian leader found it impossible to understand that landing the British Army in France and opening the "second front" was not a realistic prospect. Stalin, as expected, was furious and submitted a complaint on paper. This angered Churchill, who also replied on paper, leading to a strained atmosphere when the two attended an official dinner at the Kremlin on August 14. Stalin also accused the Royal Navy of running away during the battle for Convoy PQ 17. As Churchill reported to Lord Moran, "Stalin says we've broken our word about a Second Front" and was "most uncomplimentary about our army. . . . Stalin didn't want to talk to me. I closed the proceedings down. I had had enough. The food was filthy. I ought not to have come."[95] All of this was reported to Moran at a quarter to four in the morning, the physician noting how despondent Churchill was after this meeting, though that he still felt he could work with Stalin if only he could break down the language barrier.

But a second meeting went far better, and Stalin was impressed with the news of Operation Torch (to illustrate which, Churchill drew a picture of a crocodile and used it to show how he intended to attack its soft underbelly as well as its hard snout). Churchill later used a globe to demonstrate the advantages of clearing the Mediterranean. Averell Harriman "listened mesmerized" as Churchill answered Stalin in "the most brilliant of utterances."[96] Churchill earned Stalin's respect and withstood his sometimes insulting harangues, and there were some late-night toast-drinking sessions, one of which saw Stalin tuck into a suckling pig at one thirty in the morning, after having offered Churchill the head. The British party were all asleep in armchairs when at half past three the delighted prime minister burst in. During the visit, Churchill also met General Anders, commander of the Polish forces forming under British command in Iran. Returning from Moscow via Egypt, Churchill stayed in General Montgomery's caravan and, sporting a vast sombrero, bathed in the ocean. Singing in his bath at the prospect of visiting the troops, Churchill was in high spirits. By the time he reached London, he had traveled ten thousand miles in the space of a month, a tremendous feat that demonstrated his mental and physical robustness. General MacArthur, America's Pacific supremo, said, "My first act would be to award the Victoria Cross to Winston Churchill. No one of those who wear it deserves it more than he. A flight of 10,000 miles through hostile and foreign skies may be the duty of young pilots, but for a Statesman burdened with the world's cares, it is an act of inspiring gallantry and valour."[97]

In October 1942, Montgomery's 8th Army recorded a major victory in the Western Desert at the Battle of Alamein, which secured the region for the Allies. With the Russians successfully stemming the German thrust toward the Caucasus, British interests in the Middle East were now safe. The church bells rang out across the empire to mark this turning point. Churchill had believed that only a victory in the field could extend his time in office, and now it had come. There soon followed, in November, the joint Anglo-American landings in Northwest Africa intended to extinguish all enemy activity in North Africa and secure the entire Mediterranean for the Allies (completed in May 1943). Churchill and Roosevelt had agreed to the invasion in early September. "Hurrah," telegraphed Roosevelt. "Okay full blast," replied Churchill.[98] Churchill's next major overseas venture was a meeting with Roosevelt in January 1943, which it was hoped in vain Stalin might attend. The conference took place in Casablanca, where both British and American forces met in arms. Lord Moran recalls how elated the prime minister was at the prospect of the trip, "full of zest."[99] "When he gets away from his red boxes and leaves London, he puts his cares behind him."[100] The journey out, however, gave Moran occasion to worry about Churchill's well-being. There were two mattresses in the stern of the bomber, one for Churchill, the other for his physician. Concerned that the improvised heating might ignite the mattresses, they endured the cold.

> I awoke to discover the PM on his knees, trying to keep out the draught by putting a blanket against the side of the plane. He was shivering: we were flying at 7,000 feet in an unheated bomber in mid-winter. . . . The PM is at a disadvantage in this kind of travel, since he never wears anything at night but a silk vest. On his hands and knees, he cut a quaint figure with his big, bare, white bottom.[101]

Harold Macmillan, the Cabinet's resident minister appointed to Eisenhower's headquarters, described Churchill, during this visit, drinking, with the atmosphere "a mixture between a cruise, a summer school and a conference." "He ate and drank enormously all the time, settled huge problems, played bagatelle and bezique by the hour, and generally enjoyed himself."[102] At the conference, Churchill and his staff advocated their preference for the Mediterranean strategy aimed at knocking Italy out of the war early and wooing Turkey to the Allied side, and Roosevelt agreed that once the Axis forces had been cleared out of Tunis and completely ejected from the African continent, an invasion of Sicily would come next. Despite justifiable pride in their achievements in Africa, it can't have escaped the attention of many people that although (as Churchill put it to Congress) "one continent at least has been cleansed and purged forever from Fascist or Nazi tyranny,"[103] the fact was that it was not the continent in which Axis strength lay still in undefeated abundance.

The question now on everyone's minds was how to go about getting onto the core continent, Europe, and once there how to set about defeating an enemy of unparalleled strength and ruthlessness. With victory assured in what Churchill called the "Third Front—the great flanking movement into North Africa," all thoughts came to focus upon the long-awaited second front.[104] Though until recently Churchill had supported the idea of a cross-Channel assault on Fortress Europe in 1943, the chiefs of staff had gone a long way to convincing him that this was not at all ideal, and Roosevelt in turn was persuaded to delay D-Day until 1944. Churchill was not prepared precipitately to sacrifice an estimated 100,000 men on an assault on Europe just to relieve pressure on Russia. Persuading the American president required another Churchill journey to confer with Roosevelt, heralding a new year—1943—that was to be dominated by international conferences for the peripatetic British prime minister. What General Ismay dubbed "conference year" brought trips to Casablanca, Washington, Quebec, Moscow, Cairo, and Tehran.

Churchill's first summit of the year entailed another joint meeting between the American and British chiefs of staff. As he wrote on January 24, 1943:

> We have now covered the whole vast war scene and have reached a complete agreement both between the two countries and between the military and political authorities. This entailed not only the plans but the distribution of material between 5 and 6 different theatres of war all over the world and the timing and emphasis of all that should be done. It is in every respect as I wished & proposed.[105]

Churchill was also very much aware of events on the Russian front, where, in his words, "The astounding victories . . . are changing the whole aspect of the war."[106]

During the course of this North African sojourn, Churchill took Roosevelt for a day trip to Marrakech; "You cannot come all this way to North Africa without seeing Marrakech . . . I must be with you when you see the sun set on the Atlas Mountains." It was "the most lovely spot in the whole world."[107] Here something like a family party, complete with songfests, ensued. After Roosevelt

departed for America, Churchill remained for a time, correspond-
ing with the War Cabinet, and painted his only known canvas of the
war, a view of the city and its twelfth-century Katoubia Mosque set
against the backdrop of the snow-capped Atlas Mountains. This he
subsequently gave to Roosevelt as a memento. From Casablanca,
bursting with plans for the Mediterranean theatre, Churchill flew
to Cairo, where he decided that a mission would be sent to Tito
in Yugoslavia, and also visited Turkey, a yearned-for ally. He spent
a night in the British colony of Cyprus, where he visited the regiment of his distant junior officer days, the 4th Hussars (of which he
was colonel in chief). It was then back to Cairo and a trek all along
the Maghreb coastline visiting troops and headquarters. Arriving
back in London after nearly a month away, he was greeted on the
platform at Paddington Station by thirteen of his ministers. He was
shortly afterward diagnosed with pneumonia and required a full
month's convalescence.

By spring 1943, Churchill felt the need, yet again, for talks with
Roosevelt, convinced as he was that the invasion of Sicily (Operation Husky) should be the next big operation, given the growing
signs of an end to the fighting in North Africa. Again he set off
for America and the Trident Conference, a voyage accomplished
aboard the *Queen Mary*, serving as a troop transport and on this
occasion loaded with thousands of German prisoners. Roosevelt
met him off the train in Washington and took him to Camp David.
During his visit, Churchill was invited to address Congress for a
second time, and the Combined Chiefs of Staff were able once again
to engage in person. There was broad agreement at this conference,
though the signs of future Anglo-American strategic (and technological) divergence were present. While the American chiefs of staff
wanted the earliest possible attack across the Channel, a telegram
was sent to Stalin informing him of the news that there would, in
1943 as in 1942, still be no second front. Churchill and the British
chiefs of staff had got their way in the face of significant American
reluctance. It was agreed that D-Day would come by May 1, 1944.
Secretly, Churchill and Roosevelt also agreed to work jointly on the

atom bomb. Addressing Congress on May 19, Churchill said that "by singleness of purpose, by steadfastness of conduct, by tenacity and endurance such as we have so far displayed—by these and only these—can we discharge our duty to the future of the world and to the destiny of man."[108] His return journey involved flights to Newfoundland, Gibraltar, and Algiers aboard a flying boat (which was at one point struck by lightning), Churchill quartered in what he termed "the bridal suite." In North Africa, he touted his Mediterranean plans to the local Anglo-American commanders, attempted to smooth relations between the Free French and Vichy French leaders, and bathed in the sea off the Algerian coast. On June 5, he arrived back in London after a month away. The campaign in Africa had finally been brought to a successful conclusion, and his admired general, Alexander, had signaled on May 13 that "the Tunisian campaign is over. All enemy resistance has ceased. We are masters of the North African shores."[109]

Churchill has been variously praised and blamed for preferring a Mediterranean or Balkan strategy to an early cross-Channel attack, though Sir Michael Howard captures Churchill's motivation when he writes that "it was the spirit of the chase, and not any dedication to 'peripheral strategy'—much less any calculation of postwar political advantage—which led the British now to urge impatiently that their recent victories in North Africa should be exploited to the full." Barrie Pitt agrees, arguing that Churchill was not advocating "pinprick war" or an "indirect" approach and that his impatience for operations in the Mediterranean and Italy was "more an indication of keenness to grapple with the enemy where they were to hand" and to give immediate help to Russia. Churchill was determined that the armies assembled in the Mediterranean and North Africa should not become redundant—and Fascist Italy provided an obvious target against which they might be thrown, forcing the Germans to transfer resources from the Eastern Front and from the defense of the Atlantic Wall in the west. Operations in the Mediterranean also offered the chance for Allied sea power to be brought to bear against an enemy possessing a formidable and entrenched army. Churchill was also influenced by a British strategic mindset that valued the Middle East and eastern Mediterranean above most other regions in the world (whereas the Americans knew little of it). It was the "swing door" of the British Empire, its essential fuel dump, and the meeting place of so many rival interests. Viewing the war as a whole, it was little surprise that this region tended to dwarf the affairs of Asia and the Far East in Churchill's mind, reflecting his realization that it was the one overseas region without which Britain could not survive. Clement Attlee captured this well, writing that the "policy of exploiting our success in Africa and of stroking what he [Churchill] called the soft under-belly of the Axis power was sound. It was entirely in line with the strategic lessons of our past. We had succeeded by exploiting British sea-power."[110] As for Russia, again disappointed by the postponement of a cross-Channel invasion, Churchill told Stalin, "It would be no help to Russia if we threw away a hundred thousand men in a disastrous cross-Channel attack. . . . I cannot see how a great British defeat and slaughter would aid the Soviet Armies."[111] As he then told Britain's ambassador in Moscow, "You should adopt a robust attitude to any further complaints. They themselves destroyed the second front in 1939 and 1940 and stood by watching with complete indifference what looked like our total obliteration as a nation. We have made no reproaches, and did our best to help them when they were attacked."[112] On June 26, he said as much directly to Stalin.

The invasion of Sicily by Anglo-American forces began on July 9, 1943, and the island was conquered within five weeks. Mussolini was dismissed by the Italian king on July 25, and an armistice was signed on September 7. Admiral Cunningham was soon able to echo General Alexander and report to Churchill and the War Cabinet that the "Italian battlefleet now lies beneath the guns of Malta." Despite Italy's defeat, however, German reinforcements and defensive skill significantly lengthened the Italian campaign. On the collapse of Italy (itself a momentous event), Churchill and Roosevelt met at Quebec in August 1943 for the Quadrant Conference, the prime minister accompanied by his daughter Mary as aide-de-camp, an example of the discreet but important support Churchill received from family members. Excited as usual by the prospect of travel, as the Churchills waited for the train to take them to Scotland and Scapa Flow, Churchill strode up and down the platform singing a W. S. Gilbert ballad.[113] At Quebec, the differences of opinion between the British and American chiefs of staff came to a head, some Americans believing that the British were shy of fighting in the Western European theater and fixated with Italy and the Mediterranean. Churchill was reluctant to remove British and American divisions from the Mediterranean to contribute to the buildup in Britain for the invasion of France (Operation Overlord) and still harbored schemes for an invasion of Rhodes and for bringing Turkey into the war. The Americans, however, led by General Marshall, insisted that the major strategic objective for 1944 must be the cross-Channel invasion of Europe. It was decided at this conference that the supreme commander for D-Day would be an American, a decision that wounded General Sir Alan Brooke deeply, particularly given the offhand manner in which Churchill, who had promised him the command, carelessly conveyed the news. At this time Churchill was greatly worried by what, in a telegram to Attlee, he called "The increasing bearishness of Soviet Russia." Worrying about the return flight to Britain of his main lieutenants, he said, "I don't know what I should do without you all. I'd have to cut my throat. It isn't just love, though there is much of that in it, but that you are my war machine. Brookie, Portal, you [Eden], and Dickie. I simply couldn't replace you."[114]

Soon another summit beckoned Churchill away from British shores, and he boarded HMS *Renown* at Plymouth on November 12, 1943, bound for Algiers and then Malta. Churchill had been enraged by the Russians the previous month, to the point that a message about the Arctic convoys had been returned to the Russian ambassador. Another visit to Uncle Joe was required, with an Anglo-Chinese-American conference en route. Churchill met Roosevelt at Heliopolis Airfield in Cairo, and there the Anglo-American planning circus reconvened for the Sextant Conference, which gave primacy to Allied strategy in the war against Japan. The two Western leaders consulted in Cairo with Chiang Kai-shek about the war in the Far East, as well as with Admiral Lord Louis Mountbatten, supreme allied commander, South East Asia. Churchill considered China and its leader a distraction from the main business of the conference, though was beguiled by Madame Chiang—"I withdraw all unfavourable remarks which I may have made about her," he wrote to Clementine. Though impressed by Chiang and his wife, he could not bring himself to consider that their influence in his conversations with the Americans was useful and complained of important conversations distracted "by the Chinese story, which was lengthy, complicated, and minor."[115] But for the Americans, China was one of the major keys to the postwar future, and therefore it had to be endured.

The conference agreed that the main thrust in the war against Japan would come in the Pacific, but Churchill harbored dreams of a British-led field action in Southeast Asia gaining a decisive victory over Japanese forces in that region and winning back the lost colonial estates of Britain, France, and Holland. This conference highlighted the divergence of opinion between Churchill and the chiefs regarding British strategy against Japan. Churchill was determined that Britain's main effort east of Suez should be to liberate colonies conquered by the Japanese and to achieve this by British imperial arms, crucial to rebuilding prestige and ensuring the empire's survival. The chiefs, however, while understanding Churchill's point of view, realized that the key to defeating Japan as quickly as possible lay in the Pacific, specifically in the Japanese home islands, and that therefore contributing to American efforts to win in this theatre should be Britain's main aim, thus foreshortening the war and strengthening Britain's alliance with the increasingly dominant United States. While the chiefs focused on trying to overcome Admiral Ernest King's often xenophobic objections to British imperial forces being involved in the Pacific theatre, Churchill expatiated on the benefits of operations such as Culverin, an attack upon Sumatra. Churchill was also driven by his restless desire to make use of the bases and forces that Britain had so laboriously and at such cost amassed in such places as the Middle East, Ceylon, and India.

The battle between Churchill and the chiefs of staff over strategy east of Suez was a drawn-out one. While Churchill was happy to commit forces to the assault on Japan—at one time contemplating building up a bomber force of fifteen hundred aircraft for the purpose—he was adamant that this must not interfere with British-led operations in Southeast Asia and the reconquest of the lost colonies. Churchill would invoke Admiral King's objections, or support received from Anthony Eden and the Foreign Office, or a positive assessment of what could be achieved in Burma and Malaya by Admiral Mountbatten, or personal correspondence with President Roosevelt in order to try to outmaneuver the chiefs. They, for their part, worked tirelessly to ensure that Churchill's "Indian Ocean" strategy ("as is known, I consider that all United Kingdom forces should operate across the Indian Ocean and not in the South-West Pacific") did not blunt Britain's contribution to the war in the Pacific, to such an extent that Churchill accused them of ganging up on him and withholding crucial information from him—an example of how Churchill was checked, counterbalanced, and sometimes thwarted by Britain's military hierarchy.

This ongoing debate certainly hampered Britain's activities in the east of Suez region. As General "Pug" Ismay commented, the "waffling that there has been for nearly nine months over the basic question of our strategy in the Far East will be one of the blackest spots in the record of the British Higher Direction of the War which has, on the whole, been pretty good."[116] When it came to getting Churchill to support them or to abandon a policy of which the chiefs disapproved, Admiral Pound wrote that standing up directly to Churchill brought out the worst in him. It was better to agree in principle and then let evidence accumulate about the impossibility of the scheme. General Sir Alan Brooke acted as a brake on his "passion for premature offensives,"[117] and as Ismay noted, "not once during the whole war did he override his military advisers on a purely military question." Arthur Marder wrote that he rarely failed to accept expert advice even if he thought the admirals "too plodding and lacking sufficient fire."

In the eastern theatres, while Churchill was intimately involved in plans and discussions, with the chiefs and with the Allies, his imprint was less visible than in Europe, the Mediterranean, and North Africa. This reflects four facts: the first, that specifically British-led operations in Asia and Southeast Asia were often determined by what could be accomplished by the resources that were available; the second, that the war effort of India was in many ways autonomous and not subject to London's direct control, reflecting the manner in which the Government of India and Indian Army had developed over the centuries; the third, that the chiefs of staff and subordinate commanders often had their way when it came to the direction and execution of operations (one of the reasons for Churchill's strong support for the new South East Asia Command was because it was his invention and would help wrest control of the war effort in the region from GHQ India); and the fourth, that America dominated in the war against Japan and so ultimately decided strategy—even by its control of resources, which could either make an operation in the east (such as the use of American transport aircraft at crucial moments during key battles in the Burma campaign) or break it (scuppering numerous planned amphibious operations because of the lack of landing craft).

This is an important perspective, because it diminishes Churchill's role as Britain's sole strategist of the war, helping us better understand Churchill as a man working with, and having to take account of, others around him, rather than working entirely alone. Churchill was of course the dominant force in developing Britain's war strategy. But he was not the *only* force and did not dominate *every* aspect of British foreign policy and military operations. Admiral Cunningham, talking to Lord Moran about Churchill's contribution to British strategy after the war, said, "Well, anyway, it did not amount to much."[118] This goes too far, though it gives a sense of the manner in which senior military commanders felt they had been able to shape, channel, or bypass Churchill's strategic directives, a sign of the healthy balance that was achieved as Churchill, the chiefs of staff, and senior commanders and ministers argued with each other and countered each other as British strategy was hammered out. Unlike in the First World War, military leaders were unable to dominate their civilian masters, but neither were the civilian masters—and the brooding, fertile, and ingenious mind who led them—able to walk over the admirals and generals. Always present was the threat of the chiefs resigning, and this put a brake on Churchill. Meanwhile, his energy and mind for detail and interference provided, in the words of Jock Colville, "guidance and purpose for the chiefs of staff and the Foreign Office on matters which, without him, would often have been lost in the maze of inter-departmentalism or frittered away by caution and compromise."

Heated discussions and much frustration were generated as British strategy was thrashed out. Churchill drove the chiefs of staff hard, believed that his chivying and ceaseless demands for action helped the chiefs overcome their caution. As he said to Harold Macmillan, referring to the chiefs: "You may take the most gallant sailor, the most intrepid airman, and the most audacious soldier, put them at a table together—what do you get? The sum of their fears." The man most frequently exposed to Churchill's strategic initiatives and arguments—as well as his goading, shouting, and fist shaking—was General Sir Alan Brooke. He poured his woes into his diary. "The wonderful thing is that three-quarters of the population of the world imagine that Winston Churchill is one of the Strategists of History, a second Marlborough, and the other quarter have no conception of what a public menace he is and has been throughout this war!"[119] In the cold light of day, Brooke significantly modified this view, while Churchill would wholeheartedly have agreed with the three-quarters of the world's population to which he referred.

It was in 1943 that Britain's lessening grip on Allied strategy became manifest, auguring a postwar world in which Britain was to be a distant third behind America and Russia in international affairs. In Cairo, Churchill took Roosevelt to see the pyramids and the Sphinx, having first checked it was possible to get a car close enough so that the president did not have to alight. Churchill was still trying to get the Americans to sign up more fully, through the commitment of resources, to the Mediterranean theatre. One thing that particularly upset Churchill at this time, and exposed both the limits and the wishful thinking of his loftier visions for an English-speaking alliance, was Roosevelt's refusal to permit them to present a united front to Stalin. Before heading off to Tehran to meet the Russian leader, Churchill had hoped that he and Roosevelt could agree on a common front. But Roosevelt wanted to talk to the Russians on his own, having distinct American policies—regarding the Pacific war and the future of the postwar world—that did not necessarily align with, and in some cases were directly opposed to, British interests and policies. Churchill concealed his disappointment and remained true to his conception of his role in the Grand Alliance, as well as his resolve to let no difference with America jeopardize it. That was the priority; all else was subordinate to it. Roosevelt's tactics failed to impress Stalin, who disliked his apparent disloyalty to his foremost ally. Lord Moran recorded Churchill's vexation during this visit. He wrote that the prime minister had a "glimpse of impending catastrophe." Of Stalin, Churchill said, "I believe man might destroy man and wipe out civilization. Europe would be desolate and I may be held responsible. . . . Why do I plague my mind with these things, I never used to worry about anything." According to Moran, Churchill asked himself whether Stalin would "become a menace to the free world, another Hitler. . . . The PM is appalled by his own impotence."[120]

On December 2, 1943, Churchill and Roosevelt flew back to Cairo, where the Sextant Conference resumed. While Churchill was pleased when Roosevelt agreed that an assault on the Japanese-held Andaman Islands in the Indian Ocean was not worthwhile, he could not persuade him to divert precious landing craft for the operation against Rhodes that he cherished. On December 11–12, 1943, Churchill flew to Tunis to stay with General Eisenhower. Here, exhausted, he slept for a full day, though he complained of a splitting headache. He felt so ill that he decided to stay for a rest. Lord Moran telegraphed for assistance and an X-ray machine arrived. Military doctors with appropriate specialties converged from across the Mediterranean theatre. Pneumonia was discovered on the lung, and Churchill suffered a fibrillation of the heart. His physician expected him to die over the weekend, so serious was the attack. "In what better place could I die than here—in the ruins of Carthage?" was Churchill's brave sally from his sickbed. But he rallied and made a remarkable and speedy recovery. An eighteen-day convalescence period at Marrakech began, and Clementine arrived on December 15. In an illuminating entry, Moran recorded that "the PM received the news of her arrival with considerable emotion, but when I told her later how pleased he had been, she smiled whimsically: 'Oh yes,' she said, 'he's very glad I've come, but in five minutes he'll forget I'm here.'"[121] During the course of this visit, Churchill was pleased to learn of the sinking of the *Scharnhorst* and of a delay in removing landing craft from the Mediterranean to Europe for D-Day, which allowed a new amphibious assault upon the Italian coast to be undertaken, two Allied divisions landing at Anzio in January, a surprise invasion within forty miles of Rome. Inspecting French troops with de Gaulle in Marrakech on January 13, Churchill was deeply moved by the cries of "Vive Churchill," which trumped those of "Vive de Gaulle."

The strain of wartime travel cannot be overestimated. Captain Richard Pim, who managed Churchill's mobile map room, calculated that since the outbreak of the war the prime minister had traveled 110,000 miles by ship and plane. The map room was a daily feature of Churchill's war, enabling him to keep up with progress on all fronts. All the maps were kept up to date, and those surviving bear the marks of a thousand pinpricks, as individual units were marked with colored flags, Churchill seated in a swivel chair in their midst and able to survey the world at war. A commemorative map celebrating his many journeys was published under the title *Dunkirk to Berlin: Journeys Undertaken by the Right Honourable Winston S. Churchill OM, CH, FRS, MP in Defence of the British Empire.* It showed the wartime journeys on a map, and the methods of travel, which included a BOAC flying boat; RAF Skymaster, Liberator, and York aircraft; the converted liner *Queen Mary*; the sister battleships HMS *Duke of York, King George V,* and *Prince of Wales*; the battle cruiser HMS *Renown;* and the destroyer HMS *Kelvin.* Churchill visited Newfoundland for the Atlantic Charter meeting with Roosevelt; went to Washington three times, Quebec twice, and Moscow three times (involving major conferences en route in Cairo and Tehran); Bermuda, Casablanca, Normandy, Italy, and France during the invasion of southern Europe, Greece, and Malta; and, after D-Day, made separate visits to Belgium and Holland, Normandy, Paris, and the Rhine, with a final appearance at Potsdam.

1944 AND THE ROAD TO VICTORY

After two months away from Britain, in mid-January 1944, Churchill left Marrakech by aircraft for Gibraltar, feeling well enough to take the controls of the aircraft, thence to England aboard HMS *King George V.* The full Cabinet met him at Paddington after he had traveled overnight from Plymouth. Two hours after arriving in London, he made a triumphant surprise appearance in the Commons, where a "gasp of astonishment" passed over first the Labour benches when he was seen, then all the MPs were jumping up, shouting, and waving their papers in the air. "Winston very pink, rather shy, beaming with mischief, crept along the front bench and flung himself into his accustomed seat." "Flushed with emotion," two large tears rolled down his cheeks.[122] At one thirty, he then dined with the king. The year 1944 was to see the epic battle of Monte Casino as the campaign in Italy dragged on, the continuation of the war at sea, the beginnings of imperial recovery in Burma, and telling American victories against the Japanese in the Pacific. It also brought an increase in the Anglo-American strategic bombing offensive after its discussion at Casablanca and Churchill's explanation to Stalin about its extent. Now the American 8th Air Force was to join Bomber Command in flattening Germany, though the year saw a diversion of resources to target the launch sites of the dreaded V-bombs (buzz bombs) that had begun to menace London and other parts of Britain. The main event of the year, however, was to be the Anglo-American-Canadian invasion of Nazi-occupied Europe (Operation Overlord).

Churchill committed himself fully to supporting preparations for this offensive despite personal anxiety. He presided over a regular meeting of Cabinet ministers and chiefs of staff and reviewed progress on things such as the Mulberry harbors. Fortunately for Churchill's health, 1944 brought far less foreign travel, the prime minister spending less than two months of the year away from Britain. Those close to him recognized how much had been taken out of him by illness and the monumental demands of his position. While victory moved perceptibly closer during the course of the year, Britain's purchase in Allied councils waned, as the "Big Three" became more like the "Big Two-and-a-Half." Churchill worried increasingly about the postwar world and the looming power of Russia but was unable to get Roosevelt to view things in the same way. He also invested considerable energy in Greek affairs, attempting to resist Russian ambitions and end the nascent civil war at the expense of the Communists.

Churchill was able to draw some comfort from the 1944 Dominion heads of government conference in London, which emphasized Commonwealth togetherness despite the many international and regional strains of war all had been subjected to. He was praised for delaying the opening of a second front until the time was right, Dominion governments being as anxious to avoid more Gallipolis or Dieppes as the British government was to avoid more Sommes. Churchill, along with senior British commanders, had been deeply marked by the losses sustained on the Western Front during the First World War and was desperate to avoid a full-scale invasion of a fortified coastline manned by the world's best soldiers. Commando raids were one thing; putting entire divisions ashore from the sea was quite another. This understandable aversion to casualties also meant that Churchill, along with many others, was naturally drawn to flanking theatres through which a shattering blow might potentially be delivered against the enemy. But events in Italy never moved as swiftly and shatteringly as he earnestly hoped; as he described the Anzio landings, "I had hoped that we were hurling a wild cat onto the shore, but all we got was a stranded whale."[123] The Americans, with their own good reasons, were never convinced of the significance of the kind of operations in the Mediterranean and the Balkans that the British believed had so much potential, seeing the beaches and countryside of northern France as the starting point for the defeat of Hitler's Germany. For them, the Mediterranean was peripheral, and they were always wary, here as elsewhere, of the specter of British imperialism. Nevertheless, it is important to remember that even America's vaunted enthusiasm for Overlord was initially based on the understanding of a sufficient buildup of Allied forces in Britain and upon a German collapse. In short: cross-Channel if the Germans happened to crumble in 1942 or 1943; an all-out invasion in 1944 if that did not occur. American impatience to put troops across the Channel is rendered more intelligible when one considers the president's and General Marshall's need to "get active" in the European theatre as quickly as possible or risk Admiral King and the navy winning the debate and having the lion's share of resources committed to the war against Japan.

During the course of 1943, Churchill had been away from Britain for four months and missed nearly half the meetings of Cabinet. Now reestablished in Whitehall and Westminster, he made the planning for D-Day his top priority. When the vast armada of over 7,000 vessels supported by over 11,000 aircraft and carrying a first wave of over 150,000 men and their equipment went in, Churchill was roughly dissuaded from watching the landings, the War Cabinet having to enlist the aid of King George VI in order to restrain him. The fear of massive casualties was not realized, and casualty rates for this, the greatest seaborne invasion of all time, were relatively light. Churchill did set foot in liberated France on June 21, and was on board the destroyer HMS *Kelvin* as she fired at enemy targets on land after he had pressed her captain to have, as he told Roosevelt, "a plug at the Hun."[124] He returned at Montgomery's invitation in

July, established offshore aboard the cruiser HMS *Enterprise* and allowed to survey the forward positions from the air.

At this stage of the war, Churchill had less involvement with the British Commonwealth armies than during any of the war's other major operations. This signaled the fact that not only was America on board, but the need for Churchill had diminished. As he wrote to Smuts, "Our armies are only about one-half the size of the American. . . . it is not so easy as it used to be for me to get things done." The downsizing of Churchill's prominence was also due to the fact that the war was going well and its command structures working efficiently. A winning team had been put in place. Eisenhower, for example, was a superlative supreme commander and political general, adept at managing Anglo-American commanders on the ground.

In the Mediterranean theatre, Churchill had one of his pet schemes, a proposed attack on the Ljubljana Gap to reach Vienna before the Russians, flatly rejected by the Americans, though his great interest in the region remained despite the Allied advance toward Germany from the north. On August 10, he flew to Algiers and then onward to Naples, believing that his personal intervention was needed in the affairs of Italy and Yugoslavia. He met Tito and the Ban (the governor of Croatia), "trying to unite all against the Germans." It was a thankless task, and as he wrote to Clementine, "unhappily Tito is now using the bulk of the ammunition we gave him to fight the Serbs." In the midst of all this war business he found time to visit the Blue Grotto at Capri and to enjoy a "lovely expedition to the Island of Ischia." "I thought the Blue Grotto wonderful," he wrote, and he had "four bathes which have done me all the good in the world." He even managed to get away and see some more live military action; despite his opposition to Operation Dragoon, Churchill wangled a trip on the destroyer HMS *Kimberley* to watch the invasion in progress, sailing within a few miles of Saint-Tropez. Churchill found himself "in an immense concourse of ships all sprawled along 20 miles of coast with poor San Tropez in the center." Churchill was there to "show public support" for what he considered a "well conducted but unrelated [to the wider war] operation." In fact, he bitterly regretted the loss of resources in Italy caused by this American-inspired campaign. His relish for action was undimmed. On August 26, 1944, while visiting General Alexander's armies, he was allowed to witness at close quarters the beginning of a new Allied offensive. The party pursued the action by car. From a hilltop village near Florence that had recently been shelled there was "a magnificent view from the ramparts of bygone centuries," Churchill wrote.[125] "The whole front of the Eighth Army offensive was visible." But with only puffs of smoke visible, he wanted to get closer. They crossed the River Metauro, where "Hasdrubal's defeat had sealed the fate of Carthage," he noted. Stopping at a minefield, they found a building held by British troops. "Here one certainly could see all that was possible. The Germans were firing with rifles and machine-guns . . . about five hundred yards away. Our front line was beneath us . . . this . . . was the nearest I got to the enemy and the time I heard most bullets in the Second World War."[126] A photograph captures Churchill observing the fighting from this advanced position, as does the unique painting on the cover of this book. "He absolutely loved it," Alexander wrote. "It fascinated him—the real warrior at heart."[127]

Following this latest trip, Churchill returned to Britain, again in a bad state of repair, suffering from a high fever and a patch on the lung. He was nursed in the Downing Street Annex, though a mere six days later he hauled his seventy-year-old frame off to Canada. On September 5, 1944, he set sail for Quebec on the *Queen Mary* for the all-important Octagon Conference. It had become Churchill's primary role in the war to manage the Anglo-American alliance and attempt not only to win the war but to shape the peace that would follow. At the Octagon Conference, Churchill sought to both gain American support for his military plans and secure a massive extension of Lend-Lease. He also sought to strengthen Britain's role in an alliance increasingly controlled from Washington. In a revealing letter to Clementine, he explained what he hoped to achieve at this conference:

This visit of mine to the President is the most necessary one that I have ever made since the very beginning as it is there that various differences that exist between the Staffs, and also between me and the American COS, must be brought to a decision. We have three armies in the field. The first is fighting under American Command in France, the second under General Alexander is relegated to a secondary and frustrated situation by the United States' insistence on this landing on the Riviera. The third on the Burma frontier is fighting in the most unhealthy country in the world under the worst possible conditions to guard the American air line over the Himalayas into their very over-rated China. Thus two-thirds of our forces are being mis-employed for American convenience, and the other third is under American Command. The casualties in Burma amounted in the first six months of this year to 288,000 sick and 40,000 killed and wounded. These are delicate and serious matters to be handled between friends with careful and patient personal discussion.[128]

During the sea voyage, Churchill and the chiefs of staff considered the prospect of transferring resources from the Mediterranean to the Far East, where plans for the reinvasion of Malaya were gaining ground under Mountbatten's South East Asia Command. Beyond this, the British were thinking about the substantial contribution they wanted to make in the Pacific theatre when events elsewhere permitted, lest the Americans believe that the British contribution to the defeat of Japan had been negligible.

Churchill told the chiefs that Britain's policy "should be to engage Japanese forces with the maximum intensity, and at the same time to regain British territory."[129] He bemoaned American control over landing ship tanks [sic], the lack of which thwarted his plan to put an army into Istria to bid for Vienna and a stake in Central and Eastern Europe. The landing craft formed part of a "common pool," he complained, Britain having agreed to concentrate on the construction of other forms of hardware. It was at this conference that Churchill saw the plan for the postwar pastoralization of Germany, a scheme that he and Roosevelt initially approved only to be forced to back down by the Foreign Office and the State Department. As regards the Far East theatre, the Americans were anxious to clear the Burma Road in order to sustain China and build up air bases there for the assault on Japan. Churchill knew how strongly American public opinion felt about China, commenting that "it is almost true to say that the American public would be more concerned if China fell out of the war than if Russia did so." He did not relish the prospect of a campaign in the Burmese jungle and preferred to strike at the Japanese home islands from Russian Asia, though was persuaded that a forward move in Burma was necessary. The Americans were focused very much on Overlord; Churchill was still keen on the Mediterranean and the increasing need, as he discerned it, to keep Russian influence as far to the east as possible, hence his desire to prevent Tito from seizing Trieste, to be the first to Austria, and to beat the Russians to Berlin. After the Octagon Conference, Churchill was again a guest at the White House, indulging in some fishing at Snow Lodge (though as Lord Moran noted, when relaxing—fishing here, for example, or in Canada the previous August—"he feels he is playing truant").[130] On September 6, he visited Harvard to receive an honorary degree. In his speech, he told the American people that they could "not escape world responsibility" and that the "responsibilities of this great Republic [are] growing."[131]

"Churchill, in excellent form," according to Admiral Cunningham,[132] arrived back from the Octagon Conference aboard HMS *Renown* in late September. Friends and colleagues noted a rejuvenation, and eleven days later he was off again, believing it was essential that he talk to Stalin. Thus on October 7, 1944, he left for another marathon trip to Moscow via the Middle East, accompanied by Anthony Eden. His intention was to get some resolution about how postwar Europe might look. He wanted to reach agreement about Poland, the Balkans, and Greece. His belief in one-to-one diplomacy was unwavering ("What an ineffectual method of conveying human thought correspondence is . . . they are simply dead, blank walls compared to personal-personal contacts"[133]), as was his burning desire to come to an arrangement with Stalin, especially about the postwar division of spheres of influence in Europe. On these issues of postwar Europe he faced the agony of abandoning the Baltic republics and letting down the Poles. As a result, Stalin withdrew Russian support for the communist guerrillas in Greece, Churchill playing a leading role in saving Greece from communism. When the German army withdrew from Greece in that month, a British occupation force arrived and intervened decisively in the civil war that was brewing between monarchists and communists. At this meeting, Churchill and Stalin drew up their "Naughty Document" on a half sheet of paper, divvying up by percentage British, American, and Russian "influence" in Rumania, Greece, Hungary, Yugoslavia, and Bulgaria. "After this," Churchill wrote, "there was a long silence. The penciled paper lay in the center of the table. At length I said, 'Might it not be thought rather cynical if it seemed we had disposed of these issues, so fateful to millions of people, in such a manner? Let us burn the paper.' 'No, you keep it,' said Stalin."[134]

On October 13, Churchill wrote to Clementine telling her that the conference was going well. "We have settled a lot of things about the Balkans & prevented hosts of squabbles that were maturing." Churchill was growing to like "the Old Bear" and believed he was making headway—"<u>Now</u> they respect us here & I am sure they wish to work with us—I have to keep the President in constant touch & this is the delicate side." Churchill's party left Moscow on October 19. In Cairo, Lord Moran was again forced to summon specialists because Churchill was ill. The physician recorded changes in the prime minister's mood throughout the war. On this latest trip to Russia, he wrote that he "is less certain of things now than he was in 1940, when the world was tumbling around his ears." Churchill fretted about Russia in the postwar world—"Good God, can't you see that the Russians are spreading across Europe like a tide?"[135] Caught between the devil and the deep blue sea, on the other side he had to face growing American indifference to his warnings. On his trip to America that September, Moran had found him "waiting for the chance to put in a word with the President. One has to seize the occasion," he had said.[136]

In November 1944, Churchill visited newly liberated Paris, where he joined General de Gaulle in a procession down the Champs Elysées. In the following month, he was in Greece to try to broker a settlement after he had authorized General Scobie in Athens to open fire on communist guerrillas. His sudden departure for Athens ruined a rare family Christmas at Chequers, Churchill arriving a day late and then announcing he was off the following day, Christmas Eve. This left Clementine in tears. The episode underlined the extent to which Churchill had become public property, as his family well understood, and the extent of his desire to be at the center of affairs, build peace in Europe, and make history. Instead of a well-earned break in the bosom of his family, Churchill found himself at a Boxing Day conference with the various political parties set against the backdrop of incessant gunfire in the streets and a view of the fighting north of Piraeus. He earned little thanks for this Greek intervention and was criticized in the American press. In Parliament in January, however, Churchill vigorously defended his policy and actions. He spoke of the principles for which Britain was striving on behalf of the liberated countries and the "repentant satellite countries." This principle was "government of the people, by the people, for the people, set up on the basis of free and fair universal elections."[137]

Constant overseas travel meant less time for the business of government at home, and this occasioned a stinging rebuke from Attlee. In his letter of January 19, 1945, the deputy prime minister wrote of "the method or rather the lack of method of dealing with matters requiring Cabinet decisions." It was felt that Churchill should trust colleagues' views on civil affairs, which, owing to his concentration on war strategy, he had ignored. Attlee also complained that he relied too much on Beaverbrook and Bracken. This was a common criticism, though no one, not even his close advisers and confidants, ever had him in their pocket. Attlee's warning reflected growing concern among senior colleagues about the way government was being conducted. Churchill's lengthy absences and preoccupations elsewhere meant that he was often unable to read Cabinet papers. With things going relatively well in Western Europe and reflecting the greater role of America in Allied affairs, Churchill was far less active on the fighting front than he had been in the first four years of conflict. With the development of a sophisticated inter-Allied command structure, Churchill's power to sack people diminished. So, too, did his purchase on Roosevelt; from 1943 onward, American advisers thought it was safe to let the president be alone with the prime minister without fear of the former's head being turned by Churchillian bright ideas or deviations from agreed American strategy. At a staff conference in December 1944, Churchill spoke of how, since Quebec, "events had been the cause of much disappointment. The Germans were holding fast on the Western Front and in Italy, and in Burma the advance was slow."[138] Reinvigoration was necessary.

By this time, inter-Allied conferences tended to be about the postwar world as much as war strategy. In early 1945, Churchill traveled to the Yalta Conference along the familiar Mediterranean route, meeting Roosevelt at Malta on February 1. At Yalta, Churchill pressed for an occupation zone in Germany for the French, for fear America might leave Europe after the war and leave Britain to face the growing menace of Russia alone (Churchill said that he regarded "the restoration of France as one of the great powers of Europe . . . a sacred duty from which Great Britain will never recede").[139] The conference's two main issues were the establishment of the United Nations and the future of Poland. Churchill did what he could to argue for the Poles, but from a position of weakness. The conference was noted for its cordiality, and Stalin described Churchill flatteringly as a man born once in a hundred years. But beneath the surface, this was a conference about American and Russian ambitions rather than British. The Russians gained more concessions from the Allies, and the Americans were anxious to please them in order to win Russian participation in the war against Japan and in the foundation of the United Nations. The world was changing, and Churchill's frustration was a barometer of declining British power, in terms of the Allied war effort, and more generally in terms of Britain's ability to shape world affairs. Churchill was not blind to the auguries. On the journey to Malta, he had been reading Beverley Nichols's book *Verdict on India*. Ruminating on its message, he wrote to Clementine:

> I have had for some time a feeling of despair about the British connection with India, and still more about what will happen if it is suddenly broken. Meanwhile we are holding on to this vast Empire, from which we get nothing, amid the increasing criticism and abuse of the world, and our own people, and increasing hatred of the Indian population, who receive constant and deadly propaganda to which we can make no reply. However out of my shadows has come a renewed resolve to go on fighting as long as possible and to make sure the Flag is not let down while I am at the wheel.[140]

Increasingly, Churchill viewed the world with a jaundiced eye, though remained determined to meet challenges in a robust and enthusiastic manner. Contemplating the horrendous plight of German refugees, he wrote that "the misery of the whole world appals me and I fear increasingly that new struggles may arise out of those we are successfully ending." But he found the strength to carry on and to remain ebullient and determined to fight Britain's corner while attempting to sculpt the postwar world. In particular, he was a champion of the new United Nations organization and was determined that something stronger than the League of Nations would be created this time around. As he told the Commons in May 1944:

> Scarred and armed with experience, we intend to take better measures this time than could ever previously have been conceived in order to prevent a renewal ... of the horrible destruction of human values which has marked the last and the present world wars. We intend to set up a world order and organization, equipped with all the necessary attributes of power, in order to prevent the breaking out of future wars.[141]

He was an ardent believer in such an organization shaping the future, underpinned by the power of the Anglo-American alliance.

In September 1944, he was angered when Admiral Cunningham commented that the proposed United Nations would "never be any use to anyone." Churchill turned on him, saying: "I don't know why you say that; it is the only hope of the world."[142]

The Yalta Conference was taxing as well as dispiriting. It was, as Churchill wrote in March 1946, "extremely favorable to Soviet Russia," though the agreement was concluded at a time "when no one could say that the German war might not extend all through the summer and autumn of 1945, and when the Japanese war was expected to last for a further eighteen months from the end of the German war."[143] Churchill's performance was regarded as superb, and the War Cabinet took the unusual step of telegraphing their congratulations. Roosevelt, in contrast, was nearing death and apathetic. Upon the conclusion of the conference, Churchill drove with his daughter Sarah to Sevastopol on February 11, where the *Franconia* awaited them. They spent two days on board resting and touring the Balaclava battlefield. But, as ever, the respite was brief. On February 14, Churchill flew to Athens. Since Christmas, when his visit had been accompanied by the sound of gunfire, things had changed, and he was now able to drive with the regent in an open-topped car. A crowd of around forty thousand people greeted him in Constitution Square, where he delivered an emotional speech. That night, the Acropolis was lit up in his honor, the first time this had happened since the German occupation. But such moments of triumph and optimism were increasingly rare. Though Churchill remained "on form," he was increasingly worried about Russia, America's apparent nonchalance in the face of communism's spread, and Europe's security in between. At dinner with Sir Edward Bridges and Air Chief Marshal Sir Arthur Harris at Chequers on February 23, 1943, he said, "After this war . . . we should be weak, we should have no money and no strength and we should lie between the two great powers of the USA and the USSR."[144] The difficulties of persuading the Americans to join with Britain in protest at Russia's treatment of Poland highlighted the fact that after Yalta, as Churchill wrote, "Britain, though still powerful, could not act decisively alone."[145]

In late March 1945, Churchill visited General Montgomery in the field. Then, on the last day of April, came news of Hitler's suicide in his bunker in Berlin, and a week later of Germany's surrender. For Churchill, the moment of victory was tempered with regret. The looming power of Russia worried him profoundly, and the world that Britain had gone to war to save in 1939 looked very different from the perspective of 1945. Churchill was also aware that through no fault of his own he had presided over a contraction of British power in international affairs, as the war had exhausted the empire's resources and thrust America and Russia to superpower status. As if to mark the speed with which events had moved, and how the old contours of world power had shifted, on May 12, Churchill made his first use of the term "iron curtain" in a message to president Truman outlining his fears for the future of Europe. The battle to rid the world of one menace had ended, but another was about to begin. President Roosevelt had died on April 12. Not going to meet his successor, Churchill was later to claim, was his greatest mistake of the war. "During the next three months tremendous decisions were made, and I had the feeling they were being made by a man I did not know."[146]

THE END OF CHURCHILL'S WAR

So a sense of difficulties to come, rather than euphoria, occupied Churchill's mind as the Second World War came to an end. "Both our great enemies are dead," he wrote to Clementine on May 2 (Mussolini having been summarily executed by communist partisans on April 28). Despite this, he was busier than ever, looking after the work of the Foreign Office in Anthony Eden's stead in addition to his own duties. "My hours are shocking but I am very well," he wrote. He was preoccupied with building the postwar world, striving for "a complete understanding between the English-speaking world and Russia . . . as this is the only hope for the world." Three days later, he wrote again to Clementine, saying that "it is astonishing one is not in a more buoyant frame of mind in public matters."[147] Really, it was no surprise at all. He was exhausted, and winning the peace was, from a British point of view at least, going to be remarkably difficult. During the last three days he had learned "of the deaths of both Hitler and Mussolini; Alexander has taken a million prisoners; Monty took over 500,000 yesterday and far more than a million today." While the country geared itself for Victory in Europe Day, Churchill told his wife that "I need scarcely tell you that beneath these triumphs lie poisonous politics and deathly international rivalries." On May 7, 1945 Lord Moran recorded that "the PM does not seem at all excited about the end of the war."[148] "I feel alone without a war," he said. "Do you feel like that?"[149] Shortly after, capturing the sense of loss and the extent to which politics ruled his life, Churchill told Moran: "It would have been better to have been killed in an aeroplane, or to have died like Roosevelt."[150]

Despite his despondency, Churchill lavished praise on the British people in their great moment of victory. Speaking from the balcony of the Ministry of Health, he said:

> God bless you all. This is your victory! [the crowd shouting back, "No—it is yours."] It is the victory of the cause of freedom in every land. In all our long history we have never seen a greater day than this. Everyone, man or woman, has done their best. Everyone has tried. . . . My dear friends, this is your hour. This is not victory of a party or of any class. It's a victory of the great British nation as a whole. We were the first, in this ancient island, to draw the sword against tyranny.[151]

An avalanche of congratulatory telegrams descended. Eden's read: "All my thoughts are with you on this day which is so essentially your day. It is you who have led, uplifted and inspired us through the worst days. Without you—this day could not have been."[152] Churchill had expected a new coalition government to be formed in order to see the war to its conclusion so was surprised by Attlee's refusal of his offer on May 21, 1945. This meant a return to party politics, which Churchill found difficult to cope with. What had escaped the notice of most people, including Churchill, was that while the war had elevated him to a unique position above the din of party wrangling, it had caused the most profound leftward swing in British political history. Churchill found it difficult to descend from the plateau of international statesmanship and return to bread-and-butter national politics. The world was emerging from its darkest hour and a new international system taking shape, one in which the Cold War was to be the defining feature. Churchill believed that no other British politician could influence this process as much as he could so had little appetite for domestic arguments over coal or town planning. The system of government forged by Churchill had allowed the successful delegation of responsibilities in this sphere to Tory and Labour ministers. Nevertheless, Churchill had to enter the electioneering bear pit and put his back into attacking the "socialism" of the Labour Party and sparring with Attlee in the press.

As had been the case at the end of the First World War, the electorate was uninterested in Churchillian warnings about the emerging threat of Russia or his attempts to puncture unrealistic hopes about what the postwar world held for the British people. With Anthony Eden laid low with an ulcer, the main burden of the Conservatives' election campaign fell upon Churchill's shoulders, and he took to it with gusto. The Conservatives hoped to cash in on his war-leader status, and he raged against Labour, conflating his attacks upon it with those on the Soviet Union. His warnings about Labour "totalitarianism"—especially his notorious "Gestapo" accusation—did little to help the Tory campaign.

On May 23, 1945, two weeks after the end of the war in Europe, Churchill formally resigned and was invited by the king to form a new caretaker government ahead of a general election on July 5. Ministers were drawn from all parties. Churchill did not realize that few people had been as thrilled by the war as he had been, and such was his focus on winning the war and shaping the postwar landscape that he was not in tune with the domestic aspirations of the people. In his defense, however, it should be remembered that the war was not yet over. While a state of euphoria might have gripped the British people on VE Day, it was widely believed that the defeat of

Japan would take up to a year and a half, and there were plans to dramatically increase the British role in the Pacific campaign.

The Labour Party's pledge of national insurance, new homes, and family allowances caught Churchill and the Conservatives on the hop. To some, Churchill looked like a fox in a hen coop and decidedly old-fashioned. His opponent and soon-to-be-successor, Clement Attlee, summed up the problem: "If Winston couldn't talk about the war he'd rather not talk at all. The only part of home affairs he was interested in were those which bore upon the war effort."[153] He could also be reactionary; "whenever the Cabinet committee put up a paper to him on anything not military or naval, he was inclined to suspect a Socialist plot."[154] During the election campaign, Churchill traveled the country in a train that acted as his mobile communications headquarters. He was greeted warmly by cheering crowds and developed an unrealistic sense of his party's electoral prospects, for cheering crowds do not necessarily translate into votes. "I shall be glad when this election business is over," he told Lord Moran. "It hovers over me like a vulture of uncertainty in the sky."[155] On July 22, he was complaining to those around him about "this bloody election."

Churchill's lack of appetite for the return of party politics and electioneering was perfectly understandable. There was a war still to win and grave concerns about Britain's ability to influence world affairs in the face of more powerful allies and rivals. In these very weeks, he was preoccupied by the prospect of using the atomic bomb in order to foreshorten the war against Japan. From the outset, Churchill had been ready to share scientific and technological advances with America, an indication of the way in which he saw the two nations walking hand in hand to victory in war and the stewardship of the postwar world thereafter. Britain's nuclear bomb project had officially begun in August 1941, when Churchill sanctioned research on "tube alloys," though as the Anglo-American dimension developed, Britain found America unwilling to reciprocate and was brusquely shut out. This was in spite of Churchill and Roosevelt's spoken agreement in June 1941 to freely exchange knowledge and results. In August 1943, Churchill and Roosevelt had signed the Quebec Agreement, and the Hyde Park Agreement followed in September 1944. Churchill was mindful of how the bomb could shape the postwar balance of power in Europe as well as how it could be used to terminate the war. On July 4, 1945 he was asked for, and gave, his consent to the use of the bomb against Japan.

Before the Potsdam Conference, Churchill elected to go on holiday at the Château de Bordaberry in Bordeaux, flying on to Potsdam on July 15. The following day, he toured Berlin and viewed Hitler's bunker and on July 18 conferred with President Truman. By this time, the Americans had detonated an atomic bomb. Churchill, in company with Attlee and Bevin, flew back to Britain on July 25 and prepared for the election results. On the following day, before the counting was complete, Churchill tendered his resignation to the king in what he described as "a very sad meeting." After thanking the British people for their support, Churchill left Downing Street and headed for Chartwell.

Despite Churchill's popularity and unique reputation as a war leader, the general election was a party political vote, not a presidential contest. Labour had simply campaigned better and offered the British people more of what they wanted, in particular a vision of a world that would be better for the average person than that which had followed the last war. The temperature of British politics had altered significantly, as wartime special elections had indicated. When the results were known and the full extent of Labour's victory clear, Lord Moran remarked on the "ingratitude" of the voters. "Oh no," said Churchill. "I wouldn't call it that. They have had a very bad time."

Winston Churchill's war was over. The chief of the Imperial General Staff wrote:

> I wonder if any historian of the future will ever be able to paint W in his
> true colors. It is a wonderful character, the most marvellous qualities
> and superhuman genius mixed with an astonishing lack of vision at
> times, and an impetuosity which, if not guided, must inevitably bring

him into trouble again and again. . . . He is quite the most difficult man to work with that I have ever struck, but I would not have missed the chance of working with him for anything on earth.[156]

In assessing Churchill's war leadership, Stephen Roskill wrote:

His ability to see issues in the cold hard light of reality was sometimes clouded by his eagerness to take the initiative. His zeal and confidence in improvisation had contributed to the Norwegian failure. Toward the Far East, he had shown an imperfect grasp of Japanese strength. Yet, on the most important strategic questions, his sense of realism prevailed over other considerations.

Admiral Pound summed Churchill up by saying that "at times you could kiss his feet—at others you feel you could kill him."[157] Admiral Tovey wrote to Admiral Cunningham that Churchill "as prime minister is magnificent and unique, but as a strategist and tactician he is liable to be most dangerous. He loves the dramatic and public admiration." The war against Germany had been managed much better than the First World War, and this was "due in part, if not entirely, to his leadership." Even as a strategist, Churchill deserves more credit than his senior generals and admirals were wont to give him. The general thrust of his grand strategy—above the level at which even chiefs of staff and commanders-in-chief operate—was right. "As a manager of war he was nonpareil," Ronald Lewin wrote.[158] "He never espoused any truly unwise strategic course."[159] Perhaps most important of all, he had offered his country and the world a lead in 1940 that no one else on the planet had been able to give. As Clement Attlee wrote, at that moment of profound crisis, only "one man qualified martially—I saw nobody around who could qualify except Winston. He knew what war meant in terms of suffering of the soldier, high strategy, and how generals got on with their political bosses."[160] His accession to the premiership invigorated Whitehall and "presented an extraordinary optimism against the odds." He was, in John Charmley's words, "the essential man."[161]

Furthermore, he was then the chief architect of a potent and victorious alliance, "unique," as Charmley put it, "in all the history of alliances." Churchill's own assessment of his wartime significance was accurate and spoken privately and not immodestly: "My death would have been a loss to our war-making power no one could measure."[162]

8

A Higher Vision:
Postwar Government
and a Changing World

Sometimes accounts of Churchill's life portray everything that happened after July 1945 as an anticlimax, whether intentionally or not. Churchill appears as a personification of Britain and of British decline. His lifeline tails off as the colossal politician who achieved greatness as leader of the free world in wartime fades against the sinking sun of the "finest hour." Churchill's life, so this teleological reading goes, had until 1940 been all about achieving the moment of destiny. What followed was the ineluctable descent from the summit after the attainment of political greatness. This familiar periodization is, of course, as much a reading of *British* national decline as it is of Winston Churchill's, a rendition of the accelerating loss of British world power as the "great" moment of war and "standing alone" receded into the background. A new postwar world emerged in which Britain was, by some margin, no longer top dog, and for the first time in centuries, British statesmen had to get used to an international chessboard dominated by others. According to the iconoclast John Charmley, Churchill had presided over a fatal weakening of

British imperial power, the arrival of socialism, the appeasement of a European dictatorship, and the dawning of British dependence upon the United States of America—the exact reverse of what he had strived for.

This reading of the Churchill story between 1945 and his death in 1965—what one might call the "decline" narrative—intermingles with another trend in Churchill biography: the "splendid anachronism" narrative. This latter narrative suggests that Churchill was unfit to govern in the 1950s and was increasingly out of touch— "gloriously unfit for office," as Roy Jenkins puts it—and reflects, among other things, a common condescension toward age. While Bevan's quip that Churchill looked "like a dinosaur at a light engineering exhibition" fits readily with popular perceptions of Churchill's personality and physical appearance, it also strikes a chord because it implies he was unfit for postwar government because he was old and unmodern. This is a shallow portrayal; older people are often more intellectually supple and balanced than their younger peers, and being over sixty-five is not a bar to service or utility. Churchill, in fact, was no different from the vast majority of aging people. What is more, the image of Churchill the dinosaur sits ill alongside clear evidence throughout his life of adaptability to changing circumstances and resilience in the face of both personal and public change and tragedy. He kept abreast of a rapidly changing international landscape and the ramifications of a nuclear age, focusing firmly on the future, revering aspects of the past, yet always able to act effectively in the present. "If we open a quarrel between the past and the present," he said, "we shall find that we have lost the future."[1] "I have no fear of the future. Let us go forward into its mysteries, let us tear aside the veils which hide it from our eyes, and let us move onwards with confidence and courage."[2] Churchill positively embraced change, even if he did not necessarily like it: "Without measureless and perpetual uncertainty," he acknowledged, "the drama of human life would be destroyed."[3] What is more, in addition to this mental suppleness in his sunset years, Churchill lived the life of Riley into his eighties, smoking, drinking, buying racehorses, expanding the

Chartwell estate, establishing a college for science and technology, gambling on the Riviera, and yachting with exotic friends such as Aristotle Onassis. Some dinosaur!

Churchill had been accused of being backward-looking throughout most of his career. Leopold Amery said in 1929 that the key to Winston was to see him as a mid-Victorian, "steeped in the politics of his father's period, and unable ever to get the modern point of view."[4] This was as unfair then as it is now, implying that the vast concourse of British politicians of the mid-twentieth century were habitual modernists moving swiftly with the changing times, bending to every new wind and seeking to preserve little of the past. It was simply not true that Churchill's world view remained stuck in the 1890s (or that there was a set Victorian view). To see Churchill as being "in decline" and "out of touch" in the postwar period is unhelpful and tells us little more than that he was aging and that, as ever, Britain and the wider world were changing. If one looks at his achievements, and the portentousness of some of his pronouncements about the world, a quite different image emerges. This is particularly the case during the decade following the end of the war, the period between his seventy-first and eighty-first birthdays. To have won a Nobel Prize and produced the most influential work on the Second World War in six dense volumes, to have completed scores of paintings of distinction and commercial value, and to have become prime minister for a second term while dominating a major political party is achievement beyond the wildest dreams of even the most overachieving men in history. At the time, his achievements received due acclamation; *Time* magazine named him "Man of the Year" in 1950 (not "old man" of the year), and as the aging process really began to erode Churchill's mental and physical abilities after a stroke in 1953, the press, his friends, and colleagues drew a discreet veil around him so that the wider public was unaware of the extent of his decline.

Harsh assessments of Churchill's capacities (or incapacities) are also sometimes founded on the tendency to view him in isolation and to judge him by more exacting standards than those normally applied to politicians and noted public figures. Too often, Churchill is portrayed as a giant in a historical landscape that he could (or should) have dominated, one largely devoid of other people and the swirling movement of real life and the manifold forces that shape it. Of course, life isn't like this, and even the most powerful men cannot command the tides of history, even if, on rare occasions, they have the opportunity to influence them. Should Churchill have known and understood everything? No one else would have. Other prime ministers, both in war and peace, have shown gaps in their political skill, knowledge, and interest; previous and subsequent prime ministers have variously been bored by domestic issues or impassioned by them, have bestrode the international stage either with ease or with the gaucheness of youth. Moreover, Winston Churchill cannot be blamed for having achieved greatness, or for the fact that those around him (particularly from within his own party) were not ambitious enough, ruthless enough, or clever enough to supplant him. One cannot blame the sun for shining if the night will not come, and Churchill's longevity as a leader after 1945 owed much to the paucity of first-class challengers, as well as to his burnished reputation and his phenomenal array of talent.

The 1945 general election demonstrated Churchill's well-known limits as a party politician, as well as the gulf that had opened between his position as national leader and talisman during the crisis of war, and the position of the Conservative Party in the country. The landslide Labour victory should not have been a surprise. As Ross McKibbin notes, the war had overthrown the Tory hegemony that had emerged after the Wall Street Crash. The collapse of the Tory government in May 1940 led to the creation of a Conservative-Labour coalition in which Labour was overrepresented, leading to the government's radicalization and pointing to a novel postwar political climate. While Churchill awoke on July 26, 1945, in almost physical pain, his wife considered defeat a blessing in disguise for her and her husband, though Winston's great depression over the ensuing months gave substance to his retort that if it was a blessing in disguise, it was very well disguised. "What I shall miss is this,"

Churchill told Lord Moran on July 27, pointing to red dispatch boxes full of papers. "It is a strange feeling, all power gone," he mused. "I had made all my plans; I feel I could have dealt with things better than anyone else."[5] He had no illusions about the "problems of the aftermath" of war, telling the Commons in June 1946 that "the moral and physical exhaustion of the victorious nations, the miserable fate of the conquered, the vast confusion of Europe and Asia" together combine "to make a sum total of difficulty, which, even if the Allies had preserved their wartime comradeship, would have taxed their resources to the full. Even if we in this island had remained united, as we were in the years of peril, we should have found much to baffle our judgment, and many tasks that were beyond our strength."[6] Britain had been particularly hard hit. As he told the Commons in January 1945, "We have sacrificed everything in this war. We shall emerge from it, for the time being, more stricken and impoverished than any other victorious country."[7]

Electoral defeat did, however, save Churchill from the potential ignominy of a term in office in which his gilded wartime reputation as national savior and his place in the pantheon of great statesmen was eroded by the humdrum of peacetime politics and the severe economic plight of austerity Britain. Of course, this point is a retrospective one and tells us little about Churchill; for him, living life forward, it was a massive loss of the power he craved and the lifestyle to which he had become so accustomed. Already he found himself upon the precipice of old age and gentle but inevitable decline. Now, with the elixir of power gone, the risk was that there might be no pause in the descent. He was fully cognizant of the grim facts of life for postwar Britain: the war had weakened the country and strengthened Russia and America to an extent that no one had thought possible, and Lord Moran noted before the election that Churchill dreaded the "financial consequences of the war, and even the housing problem depresses him."

Defeat at the polls meant good-bye and thank you, Mr. Churchill. There was no ceremony to stand on; he was beaten and out, and that meant leaving his home of the past five years and finding somewhere new to live in London, the city of politics and power that held him like a moth to a flame. The incoming prime minister, Clement Attlee, offered the Churchills time to leave Downing Street. But they would not hear of it. On July 30, 1945, Winston and Clementine left Downing Street and began a period as vagrants, putting up at Claridge's Hotel, then lodging at their son-in-law Duncan Sandys' flat at Westminster Gardens and spending weekends at Chartwell, which had lain largely unoccupied for six years (on wartime visits, the family had used Orchard Cottage, where Churchill had had an Anderson air-raid shelter erected. Canadian troops billeted there had camouflaged the house and concealed the ponds).

Soon there was a new house in Hyde Park Gate, Kensington, to decorate, then a long-overdue holiday, taken on Lake Como as a guest of General Alexander. Alexander knew how to please his erstwhile supremo. He painted alongside him and gave him a brace of young officers from his old regiment, the 4th Hussars, as aides-de-camp. Arriving at the Italian lakes just before the sixth anniversary of the start of the war, Churchill found space in which to contemplate his wartime memoirs. In the usual absence of his wife on such trips, he passed the time with his daughter Sarah. Churchill needed time to adjust from the unique atmosphere of war and ultimate political power. But he continued to brood on the future, especially given the Soviet threat and America's apparent unwillingness to face it square on. Yet again, people who craved peace did not want to hear Churchill discoursing on war, though he "took no pleasure in hoisting storm signals" in these postwar years.[8] Being overseas worked its magic; he found pleasure and absorption once more in painting, losing some of his interest in news from home. He was pleased as punch with his paintings, writing to Clementine to say that he hoped she could resist the temptation to open them when they arrived back at Chartwell, as he wanted to unveil them in person. After three weeks in Italy he spent two weeks on the French Riviera before going home, but this was to be a transient interlude, for Churchill had international obligations, including honors to accept in numerous European countries and an important appointment in

America. He had been awarded the Order of Merit in the 1945 New Year's Honours List (membership of this exclusive order is limited to twenty-four and is in the gift of the sovereign).

In early 1946, Churchill traveled to Missouri to lecture at Westminster College in Fulton. President Truman and Churchill arrived in Missouri, the president's home state, by train. Here, in a seminal speech on March 5, the British statesman erected a historic landmark by speaking openly of the undeclared Cold War already being waged. Churchill's internationally reported speech called for the new United Nations to be granted genuine military capabilities, for Britain and America to keep the secret of atomic weaponry to themselves, and to continue a special relationship based on the ties established over the past five years. That Western powers needed to forge an effective alliance was the main burden of his message. In facing up to Russia, he argued for strength, unity, and military alliance and famously identified an "iron curtain" that had descended across the European continent. He had earlier used the term in a letter on September 24, 1945, in which he described the future as "full of darkness and menace." Churchill's warning about the intentions of the erstwhile Grand Alliance partner attracted criticism. The "warmonger" cap was dusted down once more, and he was accused of advocating a return to an old-fashioned, discredited form of alliance-based international politics in which one bloc sought to counterbalance the destructive power of another. Churchill the dinosaur, so they claimed, was lumbering across the plains once more.

But Churchill was simply developing themes that had become clear to him during the war, and his fear of the dangers posed by Stalin's westward march and the Soviet system of rule were sound, and no less correct because of the unpopularity of his message. His Fulton speech was "a message about the fragility of peace,"[9] from a statesman not seeking renewed war but instead calling for a lasting peace built upon a realistic assessment of the lie of the international landscape as it existed rather than as it might exist in an ideal world. Furthermore, though his views attracted criticism, many in government in Britain and America knew the truth of them and welcomed his advocacy, as Baldwin had welcomed it in the face of the German menace in the 1930s. The speech exhorted America to accept the responsibility thrust upon it: "The United States stands alone at this time at the pinnacle of world power. It is a solemn moment for the American Democracy. For with the primacy of power is also joined an awe-inspiring accountability to the future."[10] Preventing war and forging a global political organization "will not be gained without what I have called the fraternal association of the English-speaking peoples. This means a special relationship between the British Commonwealth and Empire and the United States."[11]

Churchill outlined other key postwar themes. Further developing his ideas on international politics and the balance of power in the new postwar world, he expounded the cause of a united states of Europe that would prevent another such devastating conflict ever occurring, while enabling the West to better stand up to the growing Russian threat. As his support for the emergence of a strong France from the Second World War demonstrated, Churchill believed in the continuing need for strong European states (Britain and France foremost among them) to maintain the balance of power in Europe. The rise of America and Russia might have transformed the old European order, but this did not mean that the European states they had eclipsed could abnegate responsibility for their own security and the fate of the continent. A speech in Zurich on September 19, 1946, opened his campaign for a united Europe, blazing a trail that others would follow. Like many other leading politicians and commentators of the time, Churchill was easily able to reconcile this Europeanism with a fundamental attachment to the transatlantic alliance and commitment to the empire-Commonwealth. He desired Britain to be as involved in Europe as possible, without detriment to Britain's unique global role and its "special relationship" with America. At the time, when it was still by no means apparent that Britain's ambitions to remain a major international power were unrealistic, this attitude was natural.

The Russian threat to European security and liberty was underlined by the communist takeover of Czechoslovakia in 1948 and the developing crisis in Berlin in the same year, which required the famous Berlin Airlift to keep Allied zones supplied once the Russians had severed the ground links. When Russia became an atomic power in 1949, the problems of peace (even of the survival of the human race) became central to Churchill's conception of his role. He was preoccupied in these years with the Cold War and the need to perform, both personally and nationally, an international role in the name of peace. Released from party politics and occupying a position of international renown shared by no one else, he became a symbol of resistance to communism and the search for peace through strength. Churchill's willingness to contemplate nuclear weapons was born of a conviction that there was a line in the sand that the Russians must not be permitted to cross, and that ultimately they would respond appropriately to this threat and the evolving politics of deterrence, of which Churchill was an early and prominent advocate. This meant nuclear weapons, with all of the associated risks. But there was no choice, even if, as he told the Commons in March 1952, "moralists may find it a melancholy thought that peace can find no nobler foundations than mutual terror."[12]

Despite its electoral defeat in 1945, there was overwhelming backing within the Conservative Party for Churchill's continuation as leader. He had long since become a talisman who transcended national and party politics. In June 1948, he told Moran: "A short time ago I was ready to retire and die gracefully. Now I'm going to stay and have them [the Labour Party] out."[13] For Churchill, 1946 had been a "Year of Recovery" as he farmed, painted, and wrote at Chartwell. During these years of opposition, Churchill appeared infrequently in the House of Commons, leaving the lion's share of the business to his understudy, Anthony Eden. As his parliamentary enemy, the "squalid nuisance" Aneurin Bevan, put it, "Though he loved a big fight, the ceaseless skirmish of party conflict bored him."[14] Churchill's position was understandable, as he had become something much more than a domestic politician and had, in fact, always seen himself as a great statesman. He now occupied the stage he'd always dreamed of. His lack of interest in domestic affairs had been apparent since leaving the Treasury and finding his mark in the realms of defense and foreign affairs in the 1930s. Now, in the second half of the 1940s, he was the unchallenged leader of his party. There was no chance of the Labour government calling a general election until it had to, and that was a good five years away. Yet reverence for Churchill was never universal, and some Labour MPs even dared to mock him. His elevated position and continued leadership of the Conservative Party also came at a cost, because it encouraged party inactivity, and while Churchill retained ultimate authority and responsibility for the party, those left to run its day-to-day affairs were unable to shape it according to their will. Churchill retained the power but shirked much of the responsibility and work.

During Labour's period in office between 1945 and 1951, Churchill criticized Indian independence and lamented Mountbatten's influence, watching—"with deep grief," as he put it—"the clattering down of the British Empire." He criticized Labour for not being more robust in the face of the Iranian government's nationalization of the Anglo-Iranian Oil Company's installation at Ibadan. He bemoaned the fact that it now seemed as if anyone could take a pop at Britain without expecting retaliation and worried about Britain's declining power in the world. "Her great Indian Empire has gone down one drain," he said in 1948, and the "Home Fleet down another. Can you wonder, with these weapons, that you are checked by Chile, abused by the Argentine and girded at by Guatemala?"[15] There was a desperate need, he said in July 1951, to renew "the glory of our island home."[16] As he told the Lord Mayor's Banquet in November, "I hope to see a revival of her former influence and initiative among the Allied powers, and indeed with all powers." He was determined to overcome what he perceived to be a growing sense that Britain was on the slide. "There is hardly any country in the world where it is not believed that you have only to kick an Englishman hard enough to make him evacuate, bolt or clear out." Naturally, much of the blame for this sorry state of affairs, Churchill claimed, could be laid squarely at the Labour

Party's door: "Six years of Socialists have hit us harder in our finance and economics than Hitler was able to do."

He was deeply perturbed by the military vacuum emerging in Western Europe. On the home front he accused Labour of perpetuating shortages and failing to address the chronic lack of housing. Rab Butler was tasked with developing new policy lines for the Conservatives to try on the electorate, though Churchill was not keen on presenting too many hostages to fortune; *not* having fixed policies was, to his mind, one of the benefits of being in opposition. On 11 January 1950 Attlee announced the dissolution of Parliament and the prospect of a general election brought Churchill home from a holiday in Madeira. His campaign speeches and broadcasts were more listened to than those of Prime Minister Attlee, demonstrating his political and personal celebrity despite age and opposition. But although the Conservatives performed much better than in the election of 1945, their recovery was not sufficient to achieve power, though enough to ensure that Attlee's second Labour government could be nowhere near as radical as the first. Churchill's attacks on Labour often lacked resonance with the wider electorate, even if they titillated the converted. Addressing the Scottish Unionist Conference in Perth, he said "we are oppressed by a deadly fallacy. Socialism is the philosophy of failure, the creed of ignorance and the gospel of envy."[17] Another election soon followed, and this time the Labour government was ousted.

PRIME MINISTER AGAIN

Having won the 1951 general election, Churchill was back in 10 Downing Street, his London abode at Hyde Park Gate rented out to the Cuban ambassador. The change of government did not lead to a great deal of political flux, Churchill's administration basking in the light of a recovering economic position that permitted Britain to become independent of Marshall Aid in 1951. Churchill relished the job, the bustle associated with purposeful activity, and the exercise of power. Advisers, secretaries, and red boxes came and went, though his desire to avoid complicated domestic issues or lengthy papers, tendencies that had become noticeable during his previous stint as prime minister, remained. Churchill enunciated his reasons for staying in office and for not, as he put it, taking the easy course of "retiring in an odour of civic freedoms," a course of action that "had crossed my mind frequently some months ago":[18]

> If I remain in public life at this juncture it is because, rightly or wrongly, but sincerely, I believe that I may be able to make an important contri-bution to the prevention of a third world war and to bringing nearer that lasting peace settlement which the masses of the people in every race and in every land fervently desire. I pray indeed that I may have this opportunity. It is the last prize I seek to win.[19]

Despite his having frequently inveighed against "socialism" and its alleged erosion of the incentive to work and to excel, there was no chance of the Conservatives turning the clock back on the legis-lative achievements of the Attlee government. This was an era of broad agreement between the two major parties on most domestic and international issues. Denationalization was not a central policy plank of the new Conservative government, and the architecture of the National Health Service was left alone. Collectivism and nation-alization were in vogue, and even the Conservatives did not entirely abstain. The new era of the managerial and welfare state was to be a bipartisan endeavor. It was also one that Churchill had already been involved with, as it was under his wartime leadership that state intervention in people's lives, and state ownership, had advanced to an unprecedented degree. The Labour government had created a broad network of social services to protect people and brought about 20 percent of the country's productive capacity under public own-ership. Unemployment remained a problem throughout the period of Attlee's government, and food rationing lingered depressingly. The Conservatives were pledged to major social reforms, including the construction of 300,000 new homes a year. Furthermore, the love affair between sections of British society and the Soviet Union was beginning to cool as the chill of the Cold War set in. The "Uncle Joe" image of Russia was being replaced by a more sinister picture of a brutal state. Freedom, once again, was juxtaposed with totalitarianism, the state versus the individual.

In appointing his new government, Churchill ignored the claims of the Tory party and appointed wartime colleagues and men from outside of politics. General Ismay became secretary of state for Commonwealth Affairs, General Alexander (from March 1952) served as Minister of Defense. Eden returned to the Foreign Office, and Harold Macmillan was tasked with delivering the manifesto's housing pledge. At seventy-seven, Churchill relished the task but was less capable than he had been. He was going deaf, domestic affairs often bored him, and he did not have the appetite for working nights that he once had had and never regained the discipline required to keep on top of voluminous paperwork. But he still had fight; as he said in May 1952 in the Commons, "The spectacle of a number of middle-aged gentlemen who are my political opponents in a state of uproar and fury is really quite exhilarating to me."[20] He dominated his Cabinet and clearly viewed many of his colleagues as rather unimportant necessities. Chancellor Adenauer opined that if he were recreating the world, he would "put a limit on man's intelligence without putting a limit on man's stupidity." "That would not do," Churchill replied, "because it would deprive me of many of my Cabinet members."[21] In 1953, he agreed that a minister be relieved of office but not be granted a peerage. "No, but perhaps a *disappearage*" was his comment.[22]

As had been the case during the war, Churchill was happy to allow others to look after domestic matters. As long as they kept things steady, he preferred to concentrate on foreign policy. His overwhelming focus in this period was on restoring Britain's world position, the menace of the Cold War, and the proper restoration (as he saw it) of the "special relationship" with America. It was against a backdrop of Britain's declining place in the world that Churchill had to act. "We are resolved to make this Island solvent, able to earn its living and pay its way . . . we have no assurance that anyone else is going to keep the British Lion as a pet."[23] As he wrote on July 11, 1952, "It is a very bleak outlook—with all our might, majesty, dominion & power imperiled by having to pay the crashing Bill each week. I have never seen things so tangled & tiresome. But we must persevere."[24] Ten days later, he described his government's labors: "Inside our circle we toil continuously at plans to pay our way. The problems are baffling & bewildering because of their number & relationship. What to cut, & all the hideous consequences of the choice. . . . Indeed we were left a dismal inheritance! Beneath all the party malice there is a realization of the facts. But the nation is divided into 2 party-machines grinding away at one another with tireless vigor," he said, giving voice to his lifelong dislike of the party system. The decisions he was required to take, he said, were worse than those of the war years. Yet humor and fun remained part of Churchill's makeup. In 1952, considering the merits of British or American rifles, Field Marshal Slim had said: "I suppose we shall end up with some mongrel weapon, half British and half American." "Pray, moderate your language, Field Marshal," Churchill said. "That's an exact description of me."[25] Opposing a proposal to fly forty MPs to Italy in a single plane, Alan Lennox-Boyd said, "You don't want to have all your eggs in one basket." The reply: "On the contrary, I don't want all those baskets in one egg."[26]

Churchill's overriding concern about the Cold War and his undiminished faith in face-to-face diplomacy meant more summits (including four transatlantic visits during his second tenure as prime minister). In January 1952, he went to see President Truman and visited Canada. A year later, he was in Washington to see President Eisenhower, his wartime friend, followed by a holiday in Jamaica. In December 1953, there was a conference in Bermuda, and in June 1954, Churchill was a guest in the White House and again visited Ottawa. Churchill believed that peace in the face of the Soviet threat could only be preserved through rock-solid Anglo-American unity and resolve. He was, however, often disappointed by the response of the Americans, which in part reflected the extent to which Washington had supplanted London as the capital of the

Western alliance and the extent to which America preferred a uni-
lateral approach to Moscow as opposed to the united approach
advocated by Churchill. President Truman did not see an alliance
with the British empire-Commonwealth as desirable. For many
Americans, alliance with an "empire" about which they had historical reservations was problematic. For his part, Churchill was disturbed by Eisenhower's apparent inability to see just how dangerous
the atomic bomb was.

The early months of Churchill's second administration brought
echoes of both the old and the new. When in 1952, for the third time
in his life, he addressed both houses of Congress, a congressman's wife
remarked: "I felt that the British Empire was walking into the room."[27]
Churchill remained committed to the empire, despite the loss of
Burma, Ceylon, India, Palestine, and Pakistan under the Labour government, though he left general policy matters to his subordinates
and presided over negotiations to end Britain's base rights in Egypt,
even though he regretted having to do so, largely at the insistence
of Eden and the Foreign Office. Though Labour derided his apparent "scuttle" and Churchill hated bearing "the odium" of "Anthony's
policy," the strategic sense of quitting Egypt was as undeniable as its
reflection of changing power balances in the world. His Commons
speech elegantly disarmed the critics by casting the withdrawal
against the nightmare background of "the incredible calamities of
a war of annihilation."[28] As he put it to the Commons in July 1954,
"the strategic value of Egypt and the Canal has been enormously
reduced by modern developments of warfare."[29] As regards the British empire beyond the Middle East and South Asia, there was not
much going on in terms of the next wave of decolonization, which
occurred *after* Churchill had left office (the Sudan gained independence in 1956, Ghana and Malaysia in 1957). "The Empire I believed
in has gone," he said, though he did all he could to preserve Britain's
position in the world.

Another key area Churchill focused upon was Europe, where,
despite his advocacy of closer unity, he disliked French proposals
for a European Defence Community, seeing in it the potential for

military inefficiency and weakened national control. This signaled the parting of the ways between Britain and the early advocates of European integration, as the six major players (Belgium, France, Luxembourg, Italy, the Netherlands, and West Germany) decided they would have to go forward alone. Thus the Coal and Steel Community came into being in August 1952, and then the six founders, through the Treaty of Rome in 1957, went on to found the European Economic Community. Signifying at this time Britain's belief in a continued independent world role despite commitments and constraints emanating from America and Europe, in October 1952, the first British nuclear tests took place in the Montebello Islands off North West Australia, making Britain the third power to possess the bomb. This was central to a defense policy, advocated by both Churchill and many others in the main political parties, based upon deterrence. It meant a declining focus on conventional forces and an increase in capabilities able to support the deterrence policy, such as V bombers to carry the atomic bombs to the Soviet Union in the event of war. But the economy remained a worrying threat to Britain's ability to perform the functions of a Great Power. As Churchill wrote in October 1952, "It seems hard indeed that we shd get no credit for saving the country from Bankruptcy."

Churchill earnestly desired an equal partnership with America on atomic weapons, though America reneged on wartime agreements and the postwar Labour government had been unable to protect them. Churchill's belief in Anglo-American partnership had always tended toward the wishful, especially as the special relationship became an unequal one. On this front, Churchill displayed a naive ignorance of American politics. The McMahon Act of 1946 prevented America from sharing atomic information with any other power, and writing to Truman was not going to change this. When Churchill returned to power, he found Eisenhower impressively stubborn on relations with Russia and resistant to his campaign of personal diplomacy.

In April 1953, the Order of the Garter was conferred on Churchill. Founded by Edward III, the order represented Britain's highest honor, in the personal gift of the sovereign and consisting of only twenty-five knights. On his investiture, Churchill wore the insignia that his forebear the 1st Duke of Marlborough had worn when admitted to the order in 1702. The summer of 1953 brought the coronation of Queen Elizabeth. Churchill was resolved to play his part, and the determination to assist the new monarch strengthened his appetite for staying in office, further delaying Anthony Eden's anticipated accession. Churchill presided over five plenary sessions of the Commonwealth conference and entertained the Dominions' leaders, now including the leaders of independent South Asia, at 10 Downing Street. He attended the Coronation Fleet Review at Spithead, but his health let him down on June 23, 1953, when, while entertaining the Italian prime minister at Downing Street, he suffered a severe stroke. The stroke came when Churchill felt he was "at the peak of my opportunities" regarding world affairs and his quest to establish better relations with Russia and its allies.[30] Though his recovery over the rest of the summer was remarkable, and secrecy surrounded the extent of his illness, this was a hammer blow from which Churchill never fully recovered. Many have suggested that it was the God-appointed time for him to have left office. But he soldiered on, because he believed he could "save the world," and because he feared that only death awaited him once he retired. Medically, his recovery was astounding; amphetamines ("majors," "minors," "dwarfs," "babies," and "Morans") regulated his sleep, and meticulous preparation, including a reversion to rehearsing set-piece speeches (such as to the Tory conference in Margate in October 1953) in the "Looking-Glass," helped the performance. Winston "seems to a doctor's eye," Moran wrote, "to be designed on lines quite different from the rest of mankind."[31]

The Tory party and the government carried on without him, and without Eden, too, who was also ill. Rab Butler deputized as acting prime minister, and Churchill did not appear in the House of Commons again until October. He went to the Riviera in September to aid his recovery though still did not believe it was time for him to leave office, focused as he was upon the need for a summit with the Russians. A meeting with Eisenhower, scheduled to take place in Bermuda in July but delayed because of his illness, finally took place in December 1953. In this period, Churchill was in conversation with himself about whether he should stay or go. Sometimes, feeling like "a specimen, a kind of survival" or a physical "hulk, eating and excreting," he thought he should give the job up to Eden. The next moment, however, he would defiantly claim that Eden wasn't up to the job and that only he could secure a brightening of relations between West and East. This was "the one consuming purpose," shaded, too, by the fear of retirement and the loss of power. Lord Moran kept a regular eye on his health, and his son-in-law Christopher Soames and his long-standing secretaries kept an eye on his work and the opinions of colleagues and the Tory party. Those around him noted a new serenity, as well as a loss of tenacity and a tendency to be a lazy prime minister. He was hurt by press suggestions that his time was up and particularly by Harold Macmillan's efforts to get him to go in January 1955.

Clementine thought her husband should not have returned to office, partly because he had so much to lose in terms of reputation and partly because of the strain upon his health and home life. Surely now card games, writing, and painting were the appropriate pursuits of a man of international renown, a time to reap the rewards of unparalleled status. But Churchill loved being before the public and loved power. More important, he felt that he could do a job as an international statesman that no other British politician could. He pursued the holy grail of a top-level meeting with the Russian leader that would reduce the likelihood of nuclear Armageddon that threatened the planet. As it was, he was able to some extent to combine a semiretirement from politics with his manifold other pursuits: bezique became a passion, and he read more novels than he'd done since his youth, C. S. Forester's *Death to the French* being observed in his hand as he flew from Gander in Newfoundland to Bermuda in late 1953. He read *Wuthering Heights*, *Quentin Durward*, and Trollope. He was a laissez-faire leader of the Conservative Party and now only an occasional parliamentary performer.

Churchill sought unity with America while that country sought, among other things, to supplant Britain's international position. Perhaps America was only responding to the logical impulse of power—to subordinate weaker peers and potential competitors until they became at best junior allies and, at worst, proxies. The British, during their days of pomp, had done the same to the Portuguese and the Dutch. Churchill has been accused of neglecting Europe in favor of the white rabbit of the "special relationship," even though it was clear in the spheres of trade, foreign policy, and nuclear technology that the Americans were not prepared to welcome Britain and were in some cases hostile toward it. Truman did not share Churchill's vision of a postwar world in which a still *imperial* Britain walked hand in hand with America as a leader of the "free world." His successor, Eisenhower, thought Churchill's conception of international realpolitik too sentimental by half and had stubborn opinions on the evils of communism that had little time for summitry as a major tool.

But Churchill's pursuit of America is emblematic of a central fact of Britain's history after the First World War. America was the foundation of British security, and the security of a world Britain had forged during its period as "top nation." As Churchill wrote in May 1954, the Americans "are the only people who can defend the free world even though they bring Dulles to do it." ("Dull, Duller, Dulles" was Churchill's flippant summary of the American secretary of state.) American power had become a fact of life, and everyone was ultimately dependent upon it and, should America choose, subject to it. America could not help but expand its power, often into spheres where the British could no longer hold the line, even though the Americans might be content for them, in their junior role, to do so. The Truman Doctrine, for example, signaled America's willingness to step into a region where Britain was simply unable to sustain the burden of responsibility, for its own purposes as well as those of the emerging Western alliance. While Churchill was the first to openly declare the Cold War, he was also the first to achieve some détente in the 1950s, convinced as he was that the fate of humanity rested upon attempting to do so. The opportunity for this increased after Stalin's death in 1953, and Churchill played a unique role in preserving world peace.

BEYOND POLITICS

In the postwar years, as in the 1930s, much of Churchill's activity had little to do with Westminster politics or international affairs. He remained a hugely successful professional writer and a prolific and successful amateur painter. The construction of his massive memoir-history of the Second World War occupied a great deal of time, though work on it was interrupted in August 1949 when, staying on the Riviera, he had a stroke, from which he made a full recovery. The large advance payments for this work were invested in a trust fund for his family and helped sustain the cottage industry that attended his literary productions. In 1948, *Life* magazine and the *Daily Telegraph* began to serialize the book. The *Telegraph* paid £555,000, and the American book and serial rights sold for $1.4 million. The work was compiled by "the Syndicate," a team of researchers and experts who conducted research and prepared essays that Churchill then incorporated into his narrative. Among them were Lieutenant General Sir Henry Pownall, Commodore Gordon Allen, Air Chief Marshal Guy Garrod, Captain William Deakin, and General "Pug" Ismay. Along with his ensemble, Churchill produced what Roy Jenkins described as "the ultimate literary achievement of the outstanding author-politician of the twentieth century."[32] "This is not history, this is my case" was how Churchill described the resulting multivolume work. No one else was going to make Churchill's case, certainly not as forcefully as he could, and he had occupied a unique position throughout the conflict.

As with any memoir or description of a sequence of related events, there was plenty of room for alternative focus and interpretation. But if Churchill wrote in order to vindicate his role, it was only because he thought what he had done had been, on the whole, right. He never claimed to be definitive or beyond question. As he put it, "The tale is told from the standpoint of the British prime minister, with special responsibility, as Minister of Defence, for military affairs. . . . It would be easier to produce a series of after-thoughts, when the answers to all the riddles were known, but I must leave this to the historians, who will in due course be able to pronounce their considered judgements."[33] In *The Second World War*, Churchill demonstrated his understanding of the nature of war and its relationship to international affairs. Britain, as in the days of Marlborough, was responsible for resisting continental tyranny and forming an effective alliance to overcome it. Critics said that too often in the book, wartime decisions and actions appear to be solely down to Churchill, rather than having been taken as part of a dialogue with other politicians and military leaders. Critics also took issue with the extent to which the errors of the Chamberlain government made it an "unnecessary war," and Churchill's failure to emphasize the strategic backdrop against which appeasement was set—the prospect of three militarized industrial states attacking the British Empire simultaneously.

The work did not exist in a vacuum, because many other leading figures were beginning to write their own accounts. Published diaries and memoirs sometimes took Churchill to task over specific issues—not giving enough prominence to the role played by the chiefs of staff; emphasizing Montgomery's victory at "second" Alamein while downplaying Auchinleck's earlier defensive battle; underplaying the role of the Red Army; or slighting a particular commander-in-chief or divisional commander. Churchill's six-volume history of the war, like any other, has to be treated with critical caution. He wrote history in order to generate tomorrow's account of today, as well as to make the money that fueled his career as a politician. As he once said to Stanley Baldwin in the Commons, "History will say that the Right Honourable gentleman was wrong in this matter. I know it will, because I shall write that history." Churchill's account of the global drama in which he was a central actor reveals his personal sense of how the war unfolded, and how it was to be *remembered* to have unfolded. As a measure of his success in doing this, subsequent works of history and the received public version of the war in Britain reflect in large measure Churchill's periodization of the conflict: the view of the 1930s as a decade marred by the West's lack of resolve in the face of the dictators; the concept of the phony war (ending, unsurprisingly, soon after Churchill became prime minister); the glorious months of the "finest hour" when Britain stood defiant; the post-Alamein turning of the tide— all are familiar chapter breaks in the memory of the war, just as Churchill intended them to be.

Churchill was extremely quick off the mark in producing his history of the war, aware of the fact that the public history of the conflict would take time to set firm. He intended to be the principal architect when that historical edifice emerged, and he was determined to build on a global scale. Churchill's history was heavily marked by his desire to "set the record straight," and to account for policies that turned out to be less than successful (or to justify his position on issues like the "second front" in Europe). Churchill pursued into the postwar world and onto the written page his differences with certain politicians and servicemen while continuing to burnish the reputation of his favorites. Lauding Montgomery, for example, Churchill pursued his beef with Auchinleck to the point that Eric Dorman O'Gowan (Dorman-Smith during the war), Auchinleck's deputy chief of staff in the summer of 1942, launched proceedings for libel.

Elsewhere, Churchill's account of the war was colored by the shadow cast by subsequent political events. In the 1950s, for example, as he acted on a global political stage dominated by the Cold War while simultaneously penning his Nobel-prize-winning book, Churchill was not averse to casting himself in the role of lone wartime prophet of the perils of Soviet Russia (just as he had cast himself as the interwar seer pointing to the menace of Nazi Germany). His treatment of certain issues in his war history was affected by the political milieu of the postwar decade. He would, for example, write sensitively on an issue that might cast Stalin in a bad light for the sake of current, postwar relations or approach subjects like the wartime politics of atomic weapons in a way calculated to buttress his postwar attempts to revive the transatlantic alliance. The "I told you so" perspective on the causes of the war, and also the causes of the Cold War, mingled with Churchill's basic human instinct to seek to augment or restore his own reputation and to present an account of how things had appeared to him.

Churchill's extraordinary historical feat was achieved on the back of privileged access to highly confidential government documents, the bedrock of the entire project. Access to these documents required some planning on Churchill's part, and his intention to write a book influenced his production of minutes and telegrams during the war, as well as his recorded comments upon those produced by other people. It became a standing joke in Whitehall that Churchill penned minutes and telegrams with one eye on using them in his future memoir. Shortly before leaving office after the Labour landslide in 1945, he arranged it so that Cabinet ministers could take with them copies of War Cabinet memorandums and other documents they had written, could have access to Cabinet documents issued to them, and could quote from such documents, a gift to the historian. In August 1945, Churchill had sixty-eight monthly volumes of minutes and directives and understandably had some confidence in his ability to write a history of the war. In August 1945, the Cabinet secretary, no less, wrote "our general doctrine is that Mr. Churchill, and those who are helping him with his book, should be given all possible facilities and assistance."[34]

As well as his writing, in the postwar years, Churchill was able to resume his love affair with brush and easel that war had interrupted. His talent was considerable in this field; a brace of paintings, one showing the River Loup in the Maritime Alps, were submitted under the pseudonym David Winter and accepted by the Royal Academy in 1947, three more under his own name in 1948. He was appointed honorary academician extraordinary. A number of his paintings appeared in color in *Life* magazine (though he turned down $75,000 to write three articles for it).

"Genius has many outlets" was Churchill's saucy reply to someone who marveled that he had time to paint and to do it so well. He did not lack for suitable subject matter, by virtue of his access to the best country houses in England and the choicest European locations. After the war, Churchill was often to be found, along with other members of the elite, at rest or play in eye-catching continental locations, usually in southern Europe. His hosts included the Duke of Westminster, Lord Beaverbrook, Consuelo Balsan, and Maxine Elliot. The venues for his postwar peregrinations, and the subjects for his canvases, included Aix-en-Provence, Antibes, Cannes, Madeira, Marrakech, and Lakes Carezza, Como, Garda, and Lugano. The Atlas Mountains, the Dolomites, and the pyramids were all subject to the Churchillian brush, as were vistas discovered in Bruges, Genoa, Jamaica, Miami, Monte Carlo, Sicily, Strasbourg, Switzerland, and Venice. He wrote to Clementine from Marrakech in December 1947, saying that he was painting better than ever and making immense progress on his war memoirs. But he was still a politician and leader of a political party, and Clementine, as well as some of his colleagues, felt that he wasn't putting enough into it. It was the subject of one of Clementine's periodic stinkers: in a letter on March 5, 1949, she outlined the work that she did on her husband's behalf in his constituency. "But now & then I have felt chilled & discouraged by the creeping knowledge that you do only just as much as will keep you in Power. But that much is not enough in these hard anxious times."

Churchill also took up horse racing in this period, largely under the influence of his son-in-law Christopher Soames. One of his horses, a French gray colt called Colonist II, won him thirteen races and nearly £12,000, its jockeys wearing Lord Randolph's racing colors. (When it was suggested he be put to stud, Churchill said, "And have it said that the prime minister of Great Britain is living off the immoral earnings of a horse?")[35] Churchill invested in thirty-seven horses. Despite his vintage years and a life of achievement, money remained an issue for the Churchills, and writing continued to be the main solution. In the postwar years, the "abyss of debt" had opened up once more, but matters were considerably eased when Lord Camrose established the Chartwell Trust to manage the property and other Churchill assets.[36] A group of Churchill's friends bought the house in 1946, charging Churchill a nominal rent, and with the intention of giving the house to the nation via the National Trust when its famous occupants died. This guaranteed Chartwell as the Churchills' home for the rest of their lives and also created a literary trust for the profits from the lucrative publication of Churchill's war memoirs, intended to benefit Clementine and their descendants.

Clementine remained Churchill's lodestar in these postwar decades, as she had been for half a century. But her general physical and mental health continued to be fragile, a condition not helped by worry about her husband and his exertions. In the summer of 1955, for example, Clementine "was in a thoroughly exhausted and depressed state."[38] Their daughter Mary wrote candidly of Clementine's "neuritis" and recorded that in Churchill's final spell as prime minister, Clementine was "touchy and difficult" and fundamentally opposed to his remaining in office. "Winston himself could be maddening," Mary wrote, "and on occasions behaved like a spoilt child." But Clementine and Winston's love and partnership was rock solid, even if, as had been the case throughout their life, it was often at a distance, Churchill perhaps on the Riviera or Clementine on one of her occasional trips to such places as Ceylon. They still fussed over each other; in the mid-1950s, Clementine was battling with Churchill's weight, a battle in which Churchill proved an ineffectual ally. In May 1954, he wrote to say that he weighed "15 stone [210 pounds] exactly on your machine." A week later, however, he detected a loophole that potentially offered a relief from dietary tyranny: he reported that a new set of scales were saying

I'm 14 stone and a half compared to the previous version of 15 stone on your machine and 15 stone and a half on the broken down one at

Chartwell. The two in London are to be tested on Tuesday next and if your machine is proved to be wrong you will have to review your conclusions, and I hope abandon your regime. I have no grievance against a tomato, but I think one should eat other things as well.

In July 1953, he told his doctor that he was trying to cut down on alcohol. "I have knocked off Brandy and take Cointreau instead," he reported mischievously.[38] Churchill remained keen on drink as well as food. Bob Boothby described a scorching-hot day with the Churchills in Provence in 1948:

"I find alcohol a great support in life," he said. . . . "If I become prime minister again, I shall give up cigars. For there will be no more smoking. We cannot afford it." "What," I said, "None at all?" "Well, only a small ration for everyone" . . . [In a bistro, the trio were served beer.] "It is cool, but not cold," Winston said with truth. Two pails of ice immediately appeared. Clemmie ordered a lemonade, and peace was gradually restored. "I hate the taste of beer," Clemmie said. "So do most people, to begin with," he answered. "It is, however, a prejudice that many people have been able to overcome."[39]

It was with immense reluctance that Churchill stood down as prime minister and leader of the Conservative Party. He made his last major speech in March 1955, devoted to the threat of nuclear holocaust hanging over the world. It was a great finale. Churchill was determined to produce an exceptional speech, and to prove that, although he was finally standing down as leader, he remained fully capable. He said that disarmament all around the world would be the best way to guarantee world peace, but that that wasn't going to happen. Therefore, nuclear deterrence was the only option, and it was incumbent upon Britain to pull its weight and "make a contribution of our own to the West's nuclear security"; it couldn't all be left to the Americans. "Our moral and military support of the United States," he said, "and our possession of nuclear weapons of the highest quality and on an appreciable scale, together with their means of delivery, will greatly reinforce the deterrent power of the free world, and will strengthen our influence within the free world."[41] Deterrence was the key; even though atomic and hydrogen bombs were appalling, Britain had to possess them in order to wield influence in order to prevent conflict. For Churchill, this was part of a long, ongoing narrative of Britain trying to save itself and Europe from tyranny and act as a force for good in the world. In striving to retain Britain's Great Power status and exert influence in Washington and Moscow, Churchill earnestly believed that he was serving the cause of world peace and the avoidance of nuclear conflict.

Above all others, it was no surprise that Clementine best understood her husband's awful dilemma as age finally forced him to give up the premiership. As she said a couple of weeks after his triumphant valedictory Commons speech, "It's the first death—and for him, a death in life."

9

Symbol of the Nation

Churchill having finally relinquished power and left government for the last time, his family, his estate, bezique, and painting at long last were to have a fair chance of absorbing his energies. Holidays abroad could be arranged without reference to parliamentary timetables: a week after presiding over his final Cabinet meeting on April 5, 1955, Winston and Clementine set off for a holiday in Syracuse, and from January to April 1956 he was on the Riviera. He continued to be feted by those grateful for his role in defending the world from extremism: in May 1956, he received a prize in West Germany for his contribution to European peace and unity, and in 1963, Congress conferred honorary American citizenship upon him.

It was, of course, completely in character for Churchill to eschew sedentary retirement. While his mind and body held out, he refused to be inactive. Even at eighty, he remained surprisingly busy and peripatetic. Though supposedly retired, Churchill continued to act as an orator, writer, and painter at a tempo few manage at the height of their careers. The first volume of *A History of the English-Speaking Peoples* was published in 1956. This grand work was designed to demonstrate the common heritage and destiny of Britain and America and was well received on both sides of the Atlantic. Churchill's unique conception of history suffused this work, and F. W. Deakin, one of his long-term literary assistants, said that he had gained more of a sense of history while at Chartwell than while at university. This is not difficult to understand, for Churchill was a historical figure even before the Second World War elevated him to unparalleled celebrity status. It wasn't just his age; it was also the fact that he had been involved in so many famous historical events—the Battle of Omdurman, the People's Budget, the First World War, the General Strike—had known so many famous people, stretching back to the likes of Rosebery and Kitchener, and had occupied high office for half a century. Listening to him expatiate at dinner one night, talking about the Boer War, Lord Moran remarked upon the power of the man and how, even to a group of men themselves at an advanced age, it was "like listening to living history" because of his status as "a figure out of history."[1]

Financial arrangements encouraged Churchill to indulge his love of the continent, because money earned in America could be spent in France without the tax man getting involved. Thus Monte Carlo's Hôtel de Paris and the Hôtel Roi René in Aix became regular haunts. So too did the private villas of friends, including Beaverbrook's La Capponcina at Cap d'Ail and Emery Reves's villa La Pausa near Roquebrune, where Churchill began an important friendship with Aristotle Onassis. Between 1958 and 1963, he stayed eight times on Onassis's yacht *Christina*, playing games and reading in luxury away from strangers and overbearing guests.

Painting now occupied more of his time than ever before. He exhibited annually at the Royal Academy, showing the bold, colorful canvases depicting seas, skies, and fine buildings. The postwar years brought requests from all around the world for Churchill to loan or exhibit paintings, which were generally refused. In 1958, he allowed an exhibition tour of America at Eisenhower's suggestion, which continued on to Canada and Australia and then to London. At the Royal Academy, the collection of sixty-two Churchill works was viewed by 141,000 people in five months. On March 13, 1959, Clementine wrote to Winston to tell him that the "One Man Show" had opened and that 3,210 people had seen his exhibition on the first day, compared with a mere 1,172 who had attended the first day of a Leonardo da Vinci exhibition the year before.

His work was widely acclaimed. On a visit to the studio at Chartwell, the president of the Royal Academy, Sir Charles Wheeler, remarked, "I can't think how you have found time in your life to do anything else but paint." Churchill replied that "if it weren't for painting, I couldn't live; I couldn't bear the strain of things."[2] Reviewing Churchill's output after his death, Sir John Rothenstein, sometime director of the Tate Gallery, wrote that "the astonishing fact about Churchill the painter is that in spite of obstacles that would have prevented other men from painting at all, he painted a number of pictures of rare beauty."

But, having emphasized Churchill's continuing, post-"retirement" activity, there is no doubt that part of his being died as soon as he left politics. The depression that he had managed extremely well throughout his life became more prominent, and, according to Anthony Storr, "The last five years of his life were so melancholic that even Lord Moran draws a veil over them."[3]

Churchill remained politically engaged during the final decade of his life, serving as a member of Parliament until 1964, though his parliamentary appearances were rare and often accomplished in a wheelchair. Churchill was distressed by the Anglo-American breach caused by the Suez Crisis and was consulted by the queen on the choice of Anthony Eden's successor as prime minister. He devoted energy to supporting causes calculated to maintain and improve Britain's standing in the world. In 1958, for example, he launched a trust to help produce technological and scientific experts, leading to the foundation of Churchill College, Cambridge. This was partly motivated by Churchill's desire to create a British equivalent to the Massachusetts Institute of Technology, and the college became a national memorial to him. In May 1959, he made his final visit to America, staying at the White House as of old, and over the radio,

Clementine, back in London, heard his voice "strong, clear and res-
onant" as he greeted the president.

In the final decade of his life, Churchill suffered numerous strokes
and endured the indignities of the aging process, as well as sadness
brought about by the loss of friends. There were also family tribulations and tragedies, including the broken marriages of two of his
children and the suicide of his daughter Diana in 1963. He found it
increasingly difficult to write "in my own paw" and complained that
"original composition is a greater burden than it used to be." "An
anti-slobber device," as he called it, could be put around his cigars,
and he struggled with a hearing aid. It was, Clementine admonished
him, "just a question of taking a little trouble, my dear. Quite stupid
people learn to use it in a short time." This sally led him to twinkle
and pat her hand affectionately.[4] His mobility declined markedly. At
such an advanced age, even the most rudimentary ailments could lay
him low. In February 1958, for example, he developed a chest cold
that turned into pneumonia while staying in the south of France and
was not well enough to return home from the Villa La Pausa until
April. In March 1959, he wrote that he was finding it difficult not to
drop food while eating, and in the following month, he had another
small stroke. In November 1960, he fell down at Chartwell and broke
a vertebra on the top of his spine. A fall in Monte Carlo's Hôtel de
Paris in the summer of 1962 led to a broken hip and an operation at
Monaco Hospital, and it was widely held that he was never the same
again after this accident. On January 15, 1965, Winston Churchill
suffered a serious stroke. Just after eight o'clock on the morning of
Sunday, January 24, seventy years to the day after his father's death,
he passed away in the presence of his family.

THE FINAL JOURNEY

The journey to Oxfordshire was deliberately slow. Across the south
of England, people scrambled to catch sight of the train, just as
their London compatriots had crowded to see the funeral procession and the launch on the River Thames. Football matches around

the country observed a two-minute silence. The platforms of all the stations through which the train passed were lined with people. "A Thames lock keeper, all alone, came to attention and saluted. The winter fields had little groups of people—families with their children and dogs; a farmer, taking his cap off; children on shaggy ponies—all waiting in the chill of a winter's afternoon, to watch Winston Churchill's last journey home."[5] As the train steamed through Oxford, the Great Tom bell in Christ Church was muffled. In Yarnton, people crowded the bridge and the railway platform. The locomotive's cross-country trek ended at the tiny railway halt of Long Hanborough, where the coffin was met by a hearse for the short journey to the neighboring village of Bladon, half a mile down a road lined with people. Throughout the entire journey from London, the bells of the Church of St. Martin, where the Churchills rested amid three hundred moss-stained graves, rang Plain Bob Minor 5,040 times, the ring half-muffled at the precise moment of the interment.

For three days previously, Churchill had lain in state in the Great Hall of Westminster, cavernous, dark, and empty except for the catafalque and Union Flag–draped coffin flanked by six tall amber candles in gilt candlesticks and four guardsmen, "heads bowed, hands clasped on the hilts of their naked swords."[6] On the coffin, on a black silk cushion, rested the collar, garter, and star of the Knights of the Garter. At the catafalque's head stood a gold and jeweled cross. Over 320,000 people streamed by noiselessly along a carpeted path, "the mesmeric effect of a river flowing past."[7] The funeral was held in St. Paul's Cathedral, yet, fittingly, the interment took place in Bladon, a stone's throw from the room in which Churchill had been born. Winston had for a long time wished to be buried at Chartwell ("under the croquet lawn," he once told Harold Macmillan), but, on a visit to Blenheim a few years before he died, he had walked in the graveyard of the Church of St. Martin, where his parents and brother, Jack, already lay. Here he changed his mind and told Clementine that he would like to be buried there with them, and his last will contained this amendment.

But before the burial, there was the funeral to be considered, and Churchill's achievements since becoming prime minister in 1940 had guaranteed him a state funeral. A funeral on this scale— the "last burial in the British tradition of imperial ceremony"— took years of preparation. Queen Elizabeth II told the government in 1953 that he should have "a public funeral on a scale befitting his position in history—commensurate, perhaps, with that of the funeral of the Duke of Wellington."[8] In 1957 Prime Minister Harold Macmillan commissioned research into the funerals of Nelson, Pitt the Younger, Wellington, and Gladstone. In March 1958, the Cabinet Office drew up its first detailed master plan for the funeral, known privately as Operation Hope Not. Many revisions were to come, because, as Mountbatten noted, "Churchill kept living and the pall-bearers kept dying." The BBC prepared to make it a fittingly grand event, and when the day came, over forty cameras lined the route of the funeral procession, with Richard Dimbleby providing a dignified commentary.

"On the morning of 30 January 1965, the wind was full of daggers of ice. The day kept the quality of a persistent dawn: numbing, grey, empty, flattened, drained of color by the dull shroud of nimbus pressed down upon it."[9] By 9:45 a.m. the pallbearers had arrived at the West Door of St. Paul's. They were twelve in number, the youngest, Lord Mountbatten, sixty-four years old, the eldest, Lord Attlee, eighty-three. From the lying in state at Westminster Hall, a bearer party from the Grenadier Guards carried the coffin to a waiting gun carriage, drawn by naval ratings. Churchill's son, Randolph; son-in-law Christopher Soames; other male family members; and his secretary, Anthony Montague Browne, followed behind. Clementine and the ladies rode in five of the queen's carriages, given rugs for their knees and small hot-water bottles for their hands in order to combat the chill. As Big Ben struck ten, the Duke of Norfolk, charged with the task of organizing the funeral at the queen's command, led the procession out. The funeral music of the bands and drums accompanied the procession, along with the sound of horses' hooves, and as it passed St. James's Park, a ninety-gun salute crashed out, one for each year of Winston's life, and the only time that a commoner had received more than seventeen.

Crowds estimated at over one million lined the route from the City of Westminster to St. Paul's in the City of London. They stood in silence as the massed ranks of uniformed men passed slowly by, many having arrived hours before, greeted by the aroma of bacon and eggs cooked on camping stoves. The Queen's Own Oxfordshire Hussars had a place of honor, Churchill having been colonel in chief of the regiment until the moment he drew his last breath. The Queen's Own contingent were the fifth detachment of soldiers in the order of march, ahead of all the guards regiments. The cortege progressed up the Strand, along Fleet Street, "past a City church where the priest and his white-robed choir crowded out onto the church steps, golden cross held aloft in hope and blessing, and—at last—into the forecourt of St. Paul's."[10]

Here the ladies alighted. Randolph gave his mother his arm as they followed the bearer party up the steps and into the cathedral's shining vastness, where three thousand people waited and the choir sang "I Am the Resurrection and the Life" as the coffin swayed gently along the aisle. "There for the first time up close were the eight Grenadier Guardsmen with their heads bare, their bearskins laid aside, and beads of sweat on their faces from the exertion that their duty cost them. The coffin is of solid oak. They laid their cheeks against the sides and took the weight on their shoulders and reached across each of them, under the coffin, to grasp a handful of greatcoat on the other side as an insurance against a slip."

Breaking all precedent, the queen and her family awaited the arrival of this most renowned of commoners, as did representatives of 112 foreign nations. "Ever since his death we, his family, had realized that he belonged as much to others as he belonged to us— perhaps more—and that we were only a small part of the laying-to-rest of Winston Churchill," wrote his daughter.[11] For the service, Clementine and the family had chosen his favorite hymns. There was "Fight the Good Fight," "He Who Would Valiant Be," "O God Our Help in Ages Past," and "Mine Eyes Have Seen the Glory of the

Coming of the Lord," "the words of which Winston knew from start to finish."

Following the service, Churchill's casket was embarked at Tower Pier and piped aboard the Port of London Authority launch *Havengore* for the journey down the Thames to Waterloo, still guarded by the Grenadiers. As it moved upstream toward Festival Pier, the cranes along the route slowly dipped their "giant giraffe-necks." The band played "Rule Britannia" as the launch moved into the center of the river, and a seventeen-gun salute rang out. Overhead, sixteen Lightnings of Fighter Command flashed by. At Waterloo Station, a Battle of Britain train named "Winston Churchill," pulling a freight car for the coffin and five cream-and-black Pullman cars for the family, waited to begin his final journey, and the guard was taken over by men from Churchill's old regiment, the 4th Hussars.

Stress had been laid on the strictly private nature of the burial service at Bladon, including a personal request from Clementine that there be no press or television coverage for the last and private part of what had so far been a national event. This wish was scrupulously respected. The police sealed off the village; the international press stayed away. Reverend J. E. James, Rector of St. Martin's, met the coffin and the Hussars Bearer Party at the lych-gate and led the way to the graveside. The only people present, apart from the priest and members of the family, were the Duke of Norfolk, Anthony Montague Browne, Jock Colville, Leslie Rowan, Lord Moran, and Grace Hamblin (the longest-serving member of Churchill's secretarial staff). "After the committal and the lowering of the coffin into the grave, Clementine first of all, and then all of us one by one, filed past and bade our last farewell. . . . Before we left, two wreaths were placed on the grave: Clementine's red roses, carnations, and tulips, bearing a card, 'To My Darling Winston. Clemmie'; and a wreath of exquisite spring flowers from the Queen, with a card in her own hand, 'From the Nation and the Commonwealth. In grateful remembrance. Elizabeth R.'"

As twilight fell, the family took their leave of Winston Churchill for the last time. Back at 28 Hyde Park Gate that night, as she prepared to go off to bed, Clementine turned to her daughter and said, "You know, Mary, it wasn't a funeral—it was a triumph."[12] By ten o'clock on Sunday evening, 125,000 people had filed past the flower-strewn grave, and thousands more waited their turn, forming a line three abreast and a mile long that stretched far beyond the village. A ten-year-old local boy said: "I never realized what history was until we became part of history through the greatness of Sir Winston Churchill."[13]

Epilogue

The memoirs and diaries of those who knew Winston Churchill intimately or had the chance to observe him at close quarters over extended periods of time provide the best measures of the man. Lord Moran's books, for example, provide many colorful sketches: of breakfasts of omelette, grouse, melon, toast, and marmalade, and of Churchill's focus, ambition, and egotism: "If I were ten years younger I might be the President of the United States of Europe," he mused toward the end of the war.[1] "He's an egoist, I suppose, like Napoleon," Clementine said to Moran. "You see, he has always had the ability and force to live life exactly as he wanted."[2] Perhaps this affected his judgment, which was often commented upon during his life, and Moran endorsed the view that he had "no nose for charac-ter; he is not very good at spotting a wrong 'un."[3] Moran noted that he "resented every moment taken from his work" and was often too "engrossed in his own thoughts to notice the mood of those around him." This made him a poor companion to those who did not know him or matter to him: he was "the poorest hand imaginable at small talk, or even at being polite to people who do not interest him,"[4] and presented "formidable ramparts of indifference," especially to women.[5] In interacting with his fellows, Churchill preferred to hold the floor—"they bat, and the other fellows field,"[6] as Moran put it, or as Hastings remarked, furthering the cricketing analogy, "The

PM can be relied upon to score a hundred in a Test Match, but is no good at village cricket." Moran wrote that Churchill did not submit to inhibitions of any kind: "After all, they imply a desire to placate, and Winston is singularly free from that urge."[7]

These eyewitness accounts also offer instances of Churchill's humor: queried about the new A22 tank, he replied that it had "had many defects and teething troubles and when these became apparent it was appropriately rechristened the Churchill." He had the following exchange with his valet:

> Getting ready for his afternoon sleep, he cried out irritably: "Sawyers, where is my hot-water bottle?"
>
> "You are sitting on it, sir," replied the faithful Sawyers. "Not a very good idea," he added.
>
> "It's not an idea, it's a coincidence," said the PM, enjoying his own choice of words, and without a trace of resentment.[8]

The portraits of Churchill painted by contemporaries and intimates can help isolate the qualities that made him so unique. One was the fertility of his mind: as his doctor wrote, "The PM has views on everything, and his views on medicine are not wanting in assurance."[9] Moran regarded his strength of will as his foremost quality, and wrote that "what his critics are apt to forget is that you cannot measure inspiration."[10] "I have seen him take a lot of punishment and not once did he look like a loser. Not once did he give me the feeling that he was in any way worried or anxious about the outcome of the fight. Gradually I have come to think of him as invincible."[11]

Clement Attlee also provided illuminating insights. He believed that "if Winston's greatest virtue was his compassion, his greatest weakness was his impatience."[12] His compassion was a virtue that "has never properly been appreciated. It was his compassion, coupled to his energy, that made him so 'dynamic.' Cruelty and injustice revolted him."[13] Attlee also saw fit to comment that Churchill's "range of interests and curiosities was so vast that they seemed more those of a child than a grown man. Indeed, the idea of a child sometimes comes to mind when one considers many things about him. His naughtiness, for example, and his short-term sulkiness, which were soon followed by complete oblivion of who or what it was that had upset him." Attlee also wrote that Churchill was "a generous enemy, perhaps the most magnanimous of his generation."[14]

Winston Churchill was wonderfully alive in so many ways and beguiles us still because of his communicable humanity as well as his achievements and extraordinary character. While many figures from the past remain black and white to all but their most intimate admirers, Churchill is cast in 3D Technicolor in the minds of millions, few of them experts. Phyllis Moir, Churchill's secretary during his American tour of 1931, noticed his "exceptionally keen visual sense. . . . When he sees a beautiful woman, his face lights up with pleasure and admiration." Scores of commentators have remarked upon the sheer fascination he attracted.

Churchill had a remarkably long life. In the year he was born, General Sir Garnet Wolseley defeated the Ashanti, and the Sultanate of Perak was added to the British Empire. In the year he died, the Beatles were introduced to LSD and given MBEs. His public life was also incredibly lengthy. By the time he retired from the premiership, it was fifty years since his first appointment to the Cabinet, and he had served under six sovereigns. As a young man, he met much older men in high positions whom he was later to work with on an equal footing or as their superior, such as French, Curzon, Milner, Kitchener, and Roberts. He overtook his seniors and outlasted juniors, such as Anthony Eden.

Because of his longevity, his social class, and the fact that— like the majority of people—he was something of a conservative, Churchill is far too often presented as a stick-in-the-mud, unable or unwilling to come to terms with the onward march of time. David Cannadine describes him as

a nineteenth-century personality living most of his life out of his own time. . . . [He] became disillusioned about a parliament elected on a mass franchise, he worried that the national will to rule was weakening . . . he looked back nostalgically to the settled social order and firmly grounded monarchies of his youth, and his elaborate, Victorian style of oratory seemed increasingly out of touch and out of date. In short, he did not adapt well to the changed circumstances of the twenties and thirties, and it pained him to see that there were others who did so much more easily. . . . [He] died a sad and disappointed man. . . . [D]espite his heroic efforts to prevent it, Britain ceased to be a great power or a great empire, crowns vanished and thrones tottered . . . and Chartwell was destined to go to the National Trust.[15]

This interpretation reflects a desperately ageist and teleological way of looking at things and focuses entirely on the negative. It appears to blame Churchill for getting old and conflates postwar British decline with Churchill's. It also suggests that Churchill's life was about nothing other than politics and national leadership, and fails to register his achievements in disparate other spheres, such as family, literature, and painting. Contrary to this image of Churchill as the disappointed, backward-looking conservative unable to adapt to the twentieth century, one could equally portray him as a modern man who embraced change and spurned the conventions of his time and his class. In contrast to the disappointed dinosaur tramping awkwardly through the mid-twentieth century, one might prefer to remember the irascible Churchill whooping it up on the Riviera in his sunset years, mixing with unconventional and racy people and the kind of "gangsters and crooks" that had led George VI and the establishment to so oppose his elevation to the premiership. One might further emphasize his fascination with new technology, with pioneering aviation, weapons systems, and nuclear energy. As opposed to disappointment, we might remember him as a pensioner painting in exotic locations and sucking pleasure out of life while still working as a mass-circulation pulp journalist and trendsetting historian.

What this common interpretation of Churchill's "declining years" also fails to acknowledge is the fact that everyone who avoids an untimely death gets old and suffers physical and mental decline.

It ignores the fact that most people become more conservative as they age and that the vast majority of people approaching ninety will inevitably spend time reflecting on the past and will probably not like contemporary pop music or the policies of the government of the day. In short, virtually everyone who survives beyond their three-score years and ten could be portrayed as backward looking and "unmodern"; to single Churchill out is unfair and unprofitable and ignores the surprising range of interests and activities he enjoyed in his sunset years. This view also insinuates that looking to the past or regretting some elements of change is inherently wrong. It is not. The bold fact is that even when approaching his eightieth birthday, Winston Churchill was Britain's foremost politician, its leader by popular election. He was the most important international statesman seeking to prevent nuclear conflict and the most influential chronicler of twentieth-century history.

Some historians have found it necessary to attempt to moderate Churchill's reputation and the high regard in which he is commonly held. This stems partly from the fact that too much praise has been heaped upon him because of his extraordinary role as a war leader and that he was the only British politician of the twentieth century to become an enduring national hero. But while Churchill did what he could to cement his reputation, it was not his fault that others made him into something superhuman. Acclaim for Churchill as a war leader "concealed the views of critics for whom he was at best a hero with feet of clay, and agnostics for whom he had never been a hero at all."[16] He had from childhood a powerful and unwavering belief in himself as a man of destiny. Throughout his career, his heroic self-image was "communicated to the world through a stupendous barrage of publicity in which oratory, journalism and history were all pressed into service."[17] But he was not a saint and cannot be judged as anything other than a man. It is also the case that *anyone* whose actions and words over many decades are subjected to forensic scrutiny will inevitably be found "guilty" on some accounts and that evidence will be found to support one disparaging case or another. But such endeavors have remarkably limited value, because they distort and decontextualize human affairs and often fail to spot the difference between things said in earnest and things said with a mischievous twinkle in the eye.

Balanced accounts, aided by the work of revisionists, have helped to remove some of the hagiography that surrounds Churchill's life. Like an antique table stripped of its varnish, the natural material that this reveals is far more interesting. Balanced accounts remind us that Churchill's reputation was more equivocal among contemporaries than the historical record has allowed, especially before the Second World War. "Churchill the racist, Churchill the social Darwinist, Churchill the glutton"—some biographers have been desperate to demythologize him, and this has led to "the revival, in fact, in different guise, of the unflattering portrait that was dominant before 1940."[18]

Churchill possessed great abilities, including indestructible energy, remarkable eloquence, and a streak of genius, as well as some of the more amiable qualities of the mischievous schoolboy. But some people always preferred to dwell upon other aspects of his personality, portraying him as a shameless egotist, an opportunist without principles or convictions, an unreliable colleague, an erratic policy maker, and a reckless amateur strategist with a dangerous passion for war. But Churchill's self-regarding, ruthless, and inconsiderate streaks were integral parts of his character, inseparable from any assessment of his performance as a national leader. His character also contained strong streaks of decency, patriotism, humanity, and courage, and these characteristics were better able to do their work *because* of the drive provided by his egotism. Andrew Roberts writes that Churchill "was a young man in a hurry who always broke the rules. It was the secret behind his greatness." Geoffrey Best writes that "great men come in all kinds and colors, and are not the same thing as saints; a Gandhi or a Hammarskjöld would not have saved Britain (and more than Britain) in 1940."[19] In 1949, Isaiah Berlin described Churchill as "the savior of his country, a mythical hero who belongs to legend as much as to reality, the largest human being of our time. . . . Wherever he appeared, he cast fantastic shadows, a distorting effect that laid him open to myth-making of both a negative and a positive kind."[20] Paul Addison wrote that "Churchill himself changed little, but perceptions of him were transformed when late in life he overthrew a long-established critique of his strengths and weaknesses in favor of his own vision of himself as a man of destiny."[21] Capturing the manner in which Winston Churchill the sentient human being with blood coursing through his veins has differed from the historical image of Churchill "the greatest Briton," Lord Moran wrote:

> As one reads of these now-distant days, they seemed to be smoothed out, and as it were edited; the terrifically alive, pugnacious, impatient and impulsive Winston Churchill has been dressed up as a sagacious, tolerant elder statesman, pondering good-humouredly on the frailty of men and the part chance plays in their fluctuating fortunes. He himself once said that he was not designed by nature for that particular role.[22]

More than this, any final attempt to summarize Winston Churchill must capture how very different he was from other men. "This astonishing creature," as Moran wrote, who "obeys no laws, recognizes no rules."

Robert Rhodes James offers a brilliant summary of Churchill. He was

> a genius, and such people are complicated, much larger than life, self-enfolded, hungry for power and fame, passionately ambitious, and often inconsiderate of others. In Churchill's case these aspects were softened by his humanity, kindness and capacity as a conversationalist. . . . To dehumanize Churchill, to make him an all-wise automaton that poured out speeches, books, articles, and military decrees, does him no service at all. Indeed, it was his very humanity, his failures as well as his triumphs, his weaknesses as well as his strengths, that make him so fascinating.[23]

We can glimpse the great man in our mind's eye, clambering over the rubble of a bombsite, brandishing a defiant "V" sign, or sitting up in bed with the contents of a dispatch box spilled around him, a parliamentary flourish forming in his mind and a lunchtime brandy in the offing. The memory of Winston Churchill has been attended by hundreds of accomplished servants, and his greatness has been resoundingly endorsed. Some commentators remain frustrated by the fact that Britons refuse to relinquish their memory of the Second World War, and with it their reverence for Churchill. But those interested in history need great men and momentous events to collide, and their stories need to be told. Churchill dominated British politics in an age shaped by industrial war and totalitarianism. Britain—now shorn of the power present when Churchill helmed the ship of state—is unlikely ever again to produce a statesman of such talent, controversy, longevity, and endless fascination.

FURTHER READING

When contemplating the preparation of a bibliography, it is often hard to resist the temptation to list all of the works that the author has consulted. But when the subject is the life of one of the world's most famous people, a life that has inspired an enormous and ever-growing literature, there is little point in doing this. So here instead is a summary of the type of work available and some suggestions about extensive source lists.

First, there are of course the writings of Winston Churchill himself. They include books, some in multiple volumes, as well as collected essays and articles and collections of speeches. Authors such as Ronald Cohen, Charles Eade, Buckley Barrett, and Richard Langworth have produced extensive bibliographical guides, and it is to these that the reader should turn if he or she wants to make a systematic study of Churchill's writings. Churchill's own words are the natural place to start when studying the man. Many of his speeches were recorded and are readily available as audiobooks. Starting with the words of Churchill himself enables one to focus on what he said, as opposed to what others say he *meant*. Quotation books form a distinct category of published Churchill work, from tiny souvenir "wit and wisdom" volumes to exhaustive themed studies. In this vein, the Churchill Estate has launched a "famous quotes" application for mobile phones, and Richard Langworth has edited some definitive collections.

Moving on from Churchill's own writings, there is the indispensable official biography, an unrivaled monument running to eight huge volumes and sixteen companion volumes. It is still not complete. Randolph Churchill was appointed his father's official biographer but died after the first two volumes had been completed. Sir Martin Gilbert took over the job and produced the remaining volumes and the extensive companion volumes that accompany them. Another distinct area of Churchill material has been produced *by* members of his family, such as Mary Churchill, Minnie Churchill, Sarah Churchill, and Celia Sandys, or written *about* members of his family and shedding light upon his life, such as the biographies of Clementine Churchill, of his mother and father, Lord and Lady Randolph Churchill, and of Winston's son, Randolph. There is also a study of the Churchill family *en masse*. Many books focus on Churchill's relations with other people—Clementine, his brother (Jack), Lloyd George, Roosevelt, Hitler, Gandhi, Adenauer, de Gaulle, Beaverbrook, "the Prof" (Professor Frederick Lindemann), Stalin, Robert Menzies. Another distinct area of literature are the compilations written by Churchill's contemporaries, produced during his life (such as the volume edited by Charles Eade) or upon his death (the *Observer*'s appreciation written by "his contemporaries"), or A. J. P. Taylor, Robert Rhodes James, J. H. Plumb, Basil Liddell Hart, and Anthony Storr's appreciation of Churchill as statesman, politician, historian, military strategist, and as a psychiatric study.

There are then the general biographies that appear annually, written by the likes of Roy Jenkins, Richard Holmes, Michael Rose, William Manchester, John Charmley, Paul Addison, Henry Pelling, Geoffrey Best, Paul Johnson, and Piers Brendon. Added to these should be what one might call themed biographies, covering things such as Churchill's life as a soldier, the "young Winston," his time at the Colonial Office, his opposition to Bolshevism, and his attitudes toward and experiences of the British Empire. A particularly rewarding biographical approach is that which assembles in a single volume a host of Churchill experts writing about different aspects of his life (Lord Blake and William Roger Louis's volume stands out).

Another distinct area of literature for those interested in the life of Winston Churchill is the books written about a particular topic upon which Churchill's career impacted. Some of these books, while adopting the obvious marketing ploy of having "Churchill" in the title, actually have little to do with him, and the appearance of "Churchill and . . ." books is so common, one wouldn't be surprised to come across *Winston and the Argonauts* or *Winston Churchill and the Goblet of Fire*. "Churchill and . . ." titles often relate to particular places—Blenheim, Chartwell, Harrow, Malta, Palestine, India, Finland, Spain, the Dardanelles, Ireland, America, Singapore. Or they relate to specific themes: Churchill and the Jews, and intelligence, and secret service, and the British constitution, and the admirals, and the generals, and appeasement, and the Royal Navy, and the bomb, and war. There are also books that relate to Churchill as a painter (such as those written by his daughter Mary) and Churchill as a historian (for example, those by Robin Prior, David Reynolds, and Maurice Ashley).

Naturally, Churchill's role as a wartime leader is the area of his life that has attracted most attention. Books on this multifaceted topic are legion, featuring overall biographical studies of Churchill "at war" (Max Hastings, Carlo D'Este, Walter Reid) and books on particular features of Churchill's war, such as his numerous journeys overseas, or aspects of the war with which he was associated, such as the construction and use of the Cabinet War Rooms (*Churchill's Bunker*); military intelligence (*Churchill's Toyshop*); deception (*Churchill's Wizards*); British resistance (*Churchill's Underground Army*); evacuee children (*Churchill's Children*); his personal aircraft (*Churchill's Navigator*); specially designed weapons (*Churchill's*

Secret Weapons); the Royal Navy patron service (*Churchill's Pirates*); relations with Turkey (*Churchill's Secret War*); or his impact on the Bengal famine (also *Churchill's Secret War*). Diaries or memoirs written by people close to Churchill during the war are particularly illuminating (such as those by Oliver Harvey, General Sir Alan Brooke, Lord Moran, his bodyguard Walter Thompson, Churchill's valet Norman McGowan, and wartime secretaries such as Elizabeth Nel). So, too, are those of renowned parliamentary diarists (such as Harold Nicolson). Other diaries and memoirs relate to Churchill's life over a longer time span (such as those by Violet Bonham Carter and his longtime private secretary, Eddie Marsh).

Finest Hour: The Journal of Winston Churchill is published by the Churchill Centre, a treasure trove of information for the student of Churchill's life. There are, then, of course, archival sources, such as the Churchill Papers at the Churchill Archives Centre at Churchill College, Cambridge. The most obvious places to visit for those interested in Churchill's life are the Cabinet War Rooms in London (part of the Imperial War Museum); Chartwell, his home in Kent now run by the National Trust; and Blenheim Palace, near Woodstock in Oxfordshire, the home of the dukes of Marlborough and a World Heritage Site open to the public. Bletchley Park, home to Britain's wartime code breakers, houses a "Churchill Collection."

NOTES

Introduction

1. From Norman McGowan, *My Years with Churchill* (London: Pan Books, 1959), quoted in "The Hero and His Valet," in *Churchill by His Contemporaries: An* Observer *Appreciation* (London: Hodder and Stoughton, 1965), p. 127.
2. Geoffrey Best, *Churchill: A Study in Greatness* (London: Hambledon and London, 2001), p. ix.
3. Randolph Churchill, *Winston S. Churchill: Young Statesman, 1901–1913*, volume II (London: Heinemann, 1967), henceforth Official II, p. 451.
4. Martin Gilbert, *Winston S. Churchill: The Challenge of War, 1914–1916*, volume III (London: Minerva, 1990), henceforth Official III, p. 329.
5. Waugh writing to Ann Fleming three days after Churchill's death. Quoted in Charles Moore, "Why the World Is Still in the Shadow of Churchill," *Daily Telegraph*, January 29, 2005, from *The Letters of Evelyn Waugh*.
6. Randolph Churchill, *Winston S. Churchill: Youth, 1874–1900*, volume I (London: Heinemann, 1966), henceforth Official I, p. 246.
7. Richard Langworth, *Churchill's Wit: The Definitive Collection* (London: Ebury Press, 2009), p. 185.
8. Richard Holmes, *Churchill's Bunker: The Secret Headquarters at the Heart of Britain's Victory* (London: Profile Books, 2009), p. 152.
9. G. Best, *Churchill*, p. 4.

Chapter 1

1. J. H. Plumb, "The Historian," in A. J. P. Taylor et al., *Churchill: Four Faces and the Man* (London: Allen Lane, 1969), p. 119.
2. D. W. Riley, "Expansion of Small Towns—Planned and Unplanned," *Journal of the Town Planning Institute*, 43 (1957), p. 106.
3. Official I, p. 13.
4. Quoted from *The Reminiscences of Lady Randolph Churchill*, in David Green, *Sir Winston Churchill at Blenheim Palace* (Oxford: Alden and Company, 1959), p. 13.
5. Henry Pelling, *Winston Churchill* (London: Macmillan, 1974), p. 20.
6. Official I, p. 2.
7. Ibid., p. 2.
8. J. H. Plumb, "The Historian," p. 119.
9. D. Green, *Sir Winston Churchill*, p. 20.
10. John Forster and Jeri Bapasola, *Winston and Blenheim: Churchill's Destiny* (Woodstock, Oxfordshire: Blenheim Palace, 2005), inside front cover.
11. Anita Leslie, *Jennie: The Mother of Winston Churchill* (Maidstone, Kent: George Mann, 1992), p. 33.
12. Ibid., p. 51.
13. *The Reminiscences of Lady Randolph Churchill* in D. Green, *Sir Winston Churchill*, p. 18.
14. Postmarked from Blenheim in January 1882 and reproduced in Official I, p. 43.
15. J. Forster and J. Bapasola, *Winston and Blenheim*, p. 1.
16. Official II, 268.
17. Mary Soames (ed.), *Speaking for Themselves: The Personal Letters of Winston and Clementine Churchill* (London: Black Swan, 1999), p. 44.
18. Ibid., p. 23.
19. Ibid., p. 46.
20. D. Green, *Sir Winston Churchill*, p. 8.
21. John Graham, *Ditchley Park: The Story of a House and an Institution* (Derby: English Life Publications, n.d.).
22. David Niven, *The Moon's a Balloon* (London: Penguin, 1994), p. 230.
23. J. Graham, *Ditchley Park*.
24. Mary Soames, *Clementine Churchill: The Revised and Updated Biography* (London: Doubleday, 2002) p. 369.
25. D. Green, *Sir Winston Churchill*, p. 12.

Chapter 2

1. Winston Churchill, *My Early Life: A Roving Commission* (London: Odhams Press, 1949), p. ix.

2. Ibid., p. 1.
3. Ibid., p. 19.
4. Ibid., p. 6.
5. Ibid., p. 8.
6. See Anthony Storr, "The Man," in A. J. P. Taylor et al., *Churchill: Four Faces and the Man.*
7. Official I, p. 52.
8. Ibid., p. 55.
9. W. Churchill, *My Early Life*, p. 13.
10. G. Best, *Churchill*, p. 7.
11. Official I, p. 45.
12. H. Pelling, *Winston Churchill*, p. 34.
13. Official I, p. 102.
14. Ibid., p. 114.
15. Ibid., p. 131.
16. W. Churchill, *My Early Life*, p. 41.
17. The last verse of his poem "The Influenza," written in 1890. See "The Complete Poems of Sir Winston Churchill," compiled by Douglas Hall.
18. Official I, p. 143.
19. Ibid., pp. 154, 157.
20. Ibid., p. 164.
21. Ibid., pp. 196–97.
22. W. Churchill, *My Early Life*, p. 34.
23. Ibid., p. 35.
24. Ibid., pp. 45–46.
25. Ibid., p. 44.
26. H. Pelling, *Winston Churchill*, p. 40.
27. Philip Guedalla, *Mr. Churchill: A Portrait* (London: Hodder and Stoughton, 1941), p. 47.
28. Official I, p. 259.
29. Ibid., p. 397.
30. W. Churchill, *My Early Life*, p. 67.
31. Paul Addison, *Churchill: The Unexpected Hero* (Oxford: Oxford University Press, 2005), p. 3.
32. W. Churchill, *My Early Life*, p. 44.
33. Ibid., p. 76.
34. Ibid.
35. Ibid., p. 77.
36. Ibid., p. 83.
37. Ibid.
38. Winston Churchill (ed.), *Never Give In! Winston Churchill's Speeches* (London: Pimlico, 2006), p. 30.
39. W. Churchill, *My Early Life*, p. 88.
40. Ibid., p. 92.

41. Official I, p. 281.
42. Ibid., p. 288.
43. W. Churchill, *My Early Life*, pp. 101–2.
44. Official I, p. 296.
45. W. Churchill, *My Early Life*, p. 103.
46. Official I, p. 299.
47. W. Churchill, *My Early Life*, p. 110.
48. A. J. P. Taylor, "The Statesman," in A. J. P. Taylor et al., *Churchill: Four Faces and the Man*, p. 11.
49. Richard Toye, *Churchill's Empire: The World That Made Him and the World He Made* (London: Macmillan, 2010), p. 121.
50. A. J. P. Taylor, "The Statesman," p. 12.
51. H. Pelling, *Winston Churchill*, p. 48.
52. Clement Attlee, "The Churchill I Knew," in *Churchill by His Contemporaries*, p. 22.
53. Official I, p. 371.
54. David Notley, *Winston Churchill Quotations* (Andover, Hampshire: Pitkin, 2008).
55. W. Churchill, *My Early Life*, p. 121.
56. Official I, p. 256.
57. Richard Holmes, *In the Footsteps of Churchill* (London: Basic Books, 2005), p. 50.
58. W. Churchill, *My Early Life*, p. 136.
59. John Charmley, *Churchill: The End of Glory—A Political Biography* (London: Sceptre, 1993), p. 22. Churchill's four books on the colonial campaigns he took part in between 1896 and 1900 can be read in an abridged form in Winston Churchill, *Frontiers and Wars* (London: Eyre and Spottiswoode, 1962).
60. Official I, p. 365.
61. Sean Lamb (ed.), *The Wisdom of Winston Churchill: Words of War and Peace* (London: Arcturus, 2010), p. 45.
62. Official I, p. 381.
63. Tom Hartman, "Foreword" to Winston Churchill, *Savrola: A Tale of Revolution in Laurania* (London: Leo Cooper, 1990 edition).
64. Official I, p. 384.
65. Ibid., p. 396.
66. Ibid., p. 397.
67. Ibid., p. 426.
68. W. Churchill, *My Early Life*, p. 172.
69. Ibid., p. 174.
70. Ibid., pp. 177–79.
71. Ibid., p. 188.
72. Ibid., p. 192.
73. Ibid., pp. 192–93.

74. Ibid., p. 194.
75. Ibid., p. 195.
76. Official I, p. 421.
77. W. Churchill, *My Early Life*, p. 200.
78. W. Churchill (ed.), *Never Give In!*, p. 4.
79. Official I, p. 422.
80. Ibid., p. 429.
81. W. Churchill, *My Early Life*, p. 222.
82. Ibid., p. 226.
83. Ibid., p. 273.
84. Ibid., p. 294.
85. Official I, p. 507.
86. W. Churchill, *My Early Life*, p. 295.
87. Ibid., p. 302.
88. Ibid.
89. Ibid., p. 315.
90. Official I, p. 524.

Chapter 3

1. Official I, p. 510.
2. W. Churchill, *My Early Life*, p. 355.
3. Official II, p. 69.
4. Ibid., p. 4.
5. W. Churchill (ed.), *Never Give In!*, p. 9.
6. "Power of Speech," *Saga Magazine* (February 2003).
7. Official II, p. 29.
8. W. Churchill (ed.), *Never Give In!*, p. 11.
9. Ibid.
10. Official II, p. 39.
11. *The Star*, 7 March 1903.
12. W. Churchill (ed.), *Never Give In!*, p. 13.
13. H. Pelling, *Winston Churchill*, p. 87.
14. Earl Winterton, "Memories of a Friend," in *Churchill by His Contemporaries*, p. 47.
15. Official II, p. 47.
16. Ibid., p. 57.
17. Ibid., p. 53.
18. Roy Jenkins, *Churchill* (London: Pan Books, 2002), p. 109.
19. Official II, p. 93.
20. R. Jenkins, *Churchill*, p. 90.
21. A. Leslie, *Jennie*, p. 276.
22. Official II, p. 207.

23. Ibid., p. 321.
24. R. Jenkins, *Churchill*, p. 120.
25. R. Toye, *Churchill's Empire*, p. 112.
26. Ronald Hyam, "Churchill's First Years in Ministerial Office," in Hyam, *Understanding the British Empire* (Cambridge: Cambridge University Press, 2010), p. 301.
27. Winston Churchill, *My African Journey* (London: New English Library, 1972), p. 105.
28. Ibid., p. 7.
29. Official II, p. 228.
30. W. Churchill, *My African Journey*, p. 11.
31. H. Pelling, *Winston Churchill*, p. 102.
32. W. Churchill, *My African Journey*, p. 60.
33. R. Jenkins, *Churchill*, p. 105.
34. Official II, p. 249.
35. M. Soames, *Clementine Churchill*, p. 73.
36. Ibid., p. 50.
37. A. Leslie, *Jennie*, p. 281.
38. M. Soames, *Speaking for Themselves*, p. 13.
39. M. Soames, *Clementine Churchill*, p. 81.
40. M. Soames, *Speaking for Themselves*, p. xvi.
41. Ibid., p. xx.
42. Ibid., p. xvi.
43. Official II, p. 242.
44. W. Churchill (ed.), *Never Give In!*, p. 33.
45. R. Jenkins, *Churchill*, p. 149.
46. M. Soames, *Speaking for Themselves*, p. 38.
47. G. Best, *Churchill*, p. 29.
48. Official II, p. 322.
49. W. Churchill (ed.), *Never Give In!*, p. 35.
50. Ibid., p. 38.
51. S. Lamb (ed.), *The Wisdom of Winston Churchill*, p. 306.
52. R. Holmes, *In the Footsteps of Churchill*, p. 81.
53. Robert Lloyd George, *David and Winston: How a Friendship Changed History* (London: John Murray, 2005), p. 48.
54. Official II, p. 315.
55. Ibid., p. 308.
56. W. Churchill (ed.), *Never Give In!*, p. 41.
57. Official II, p. 518.
58. Ibid., p. 364.
59. G. Best, *Churchill*, p. 41.
60. Lord Attlee, "The Churchill I Knew," in *Churchill by His Contemporaries*, p. 27.
61. Official II, p. 400.

62. Ibid., p. 363.
63. Ibid., p. 341.
64. Official III, p. 121.

Chapter 4

1. S. Lamb (ed.), *The Wisdom of Winston Churchill*, p. 316.
2. W. Churchill (ed.), *Never Give In!*, p. 46.
3. Basil Liddell Hart, "The Military Strategist," in A. J. P. Taylor et al., *Churchill: Four Faces and the Man*, p. 160.
4. M. Soames, *Speaking for Themselves*, p. 30.
5. Ibid., p. 65.
6. Peter Padfield, *Maritime Dominion and the Triumph of the Free World: Naval Campaigns That Shaped the Modern World, 1852–2001* (London: John Murray, 2009), p. 121.
7. M. Soames, *Speaking for Themselves*, p. 84.
8. Official III, p. 121.
9. Stephen Roskill, *Churchill and the Admirals* (Barnsley: Pen and Sword, 2004), p. 21.
10. W. Churchill (ed.), *Never Give In!*, p. 53.
11. S. Roskill, *Churchill and the Admirals*, p. 24.
12. W. Churchill (ed.), *Never Give In!*, p. 55.
13. Alfred Gollin, *The Impact of Air Power on the British People and Their Government, 1909–1914* (Stanford, California: Stanford University Press, 1989), p. 181.
14. Official II, p. 526.
15. S. Lamb (ed.), *The Wisdom of Winston Churchill*, p. 276.
16. Official II, p. 581.
17. M. Soames, *Speaking for Themselves*, p. 26.
18. Official II, p. 455.
19. W. Churchill (ed.), *Never Give In!*, p. 49.
20. Official II, p. 500.
21. Ibid., p. 669.
22. Ibid., p. 682.
23. Official III, p. 30.
24. M. Soames, *Speaking for Themselves*, p. 96.
25. Ibid., p. 95.
26. Winston Churchill, *The World Crisis, 1911–1918* (Harmondsworth: Penguin, 2007), p. 109.
27. H. Pelling, *Winston Churchill*, p. 178.
28. R. Jenkins, *Churchill*, p. 213.
29. W. Churchill (ed.), *Never Give In!*, p. 59.
30. D. Notley, *Winston Churchill Quotations*.

31. Official III, p. 37.
32. G. Best, *Churchill*, p. 51.
33. Ibid., p. 52.
34. Ibid.
35. S. Roskill, *Churchill and the Admirals*, p. 29.
36. Official III, 125.
37. Ibid., p. 129.
38. Ibid., p. 113.
39. S. Roskill, *Churchill and the Admirals*, p. 55.
40. Michael Howard, "Churchill and the First World War," in Robert Blake and William Roger Louis (eds.), *Churchill: A Major New Assessment of His Life in Peace and War* (Oxford: Oxford University Press, 1993), p. 136.
41. W. Churchill (ed.), *Never Give In!*, p. 63.
42. S. Roskill, *Churchill and the Admirals*, p. 42.
43. Official III, p. 273.
44. S. Roskill, *Churchill and the Admirals*, p. 51.
45. Official III, p. 313.
46. P. Addison, *Churchill*, p. 79.
47. Official III, p. 453.
48. Ibid., p. 457.
49. Ibid., p. 571.
50. Ibid., p. 473.
51. David Coombs with Minnie Churchill, *Sir Winston Churchill's Life Through His Paintings* (London: Chaucer Press, 2003), p. 30.
52. Ibid., p. 107.
53. W. Churchill (ed.), *Never Give In!*, p. 69.
54. Official III, p. 579.
55. Official III, p. 607.
56. M. Soames, *Speaking for Themselves*, p. 157.
57. Ibid., p. 149.
58. Official III, p. 632.
59. Ibid., p. 658.
60. *Lord Kitchener and Winston Churchill: The Dardanelles Commission, Part 1: 1914–1915* (London: The Stationery Office, 2000), p. 34.
61. Ibid., p. 105.
62. Martin Gilbert, *Winston S. Churchill, 1916–22*, volume IV (London: Heinemann, 1975), henceforth Official IV, p. 17.
63. Official IV, p. 5.
64. Ibid., p. 22.
65. H. Pelling, *Winston Churchill*, p. 229.
66. Official IV, p. 32.
67. Ibid., p. 38.
68. Ibid., p. 47.
69. Ibid.

70. W. Churchill (ed.), *Never Give In!*, p. 75.
71. Official IV, p. 133.
72. M. Soames, *Speaking for Themselves*, p. 209.
73. Ibid., p. 215.
74. Official IV, p. 151.
75. M. Soames, *Speaking for Themselves*, p. 217.
76. W. Churchill, *The World Crisis*, p. 839.
77. Gordon Craig, "Churchill and Germany," in R. Blake and W. Louis (eds.), *Churchill*, p. 28.

Chapter 5

1. Official IV, p. 180.
2. G. Best, *Churchill*, p. 93.
3. R. Langworth, *Churchill's Wit*, p. 137.
4. W. Churchill (ed.), *Never Give In!*, p. 77.
5. S. Lamb (ed.), *Wit and Wisdom*, p. 57.
6. Official IV, p. 915.
7. R. Lloyd George, *David and Winston*, p. 166.
8. Gordon Pirie, *Imperial Airways* (Manchester: Manchester University Press, 2009), p. 31.
9. M. Soames, *Speaking for Themselves*, p. 249.
10. Official IV, p. 528.
11. R. Langworth, *Churchill's Wit*, p. 79.
12. W. Churchill (ed.), *Never Give In!*, p. 83.
13. Ibid., p. 85.
14. M. Soames, *Speaking for Themselves*, p. 268.
15. W. Churchill, *The World Crisis*, p. xvii.
16. Lord Moran, *Churchill at War, 1940–1945* (London: Constable and Robinson, 2002), p. 229.
17. R. Jenkins, *Churchill*, p. 416.
18. M. Soames, *Speaking for Themselves*, p. 300.
19. S. Roskill, *Churchill and the Admirals*, p. 73.
20. Ibid., p. 79.
21. R. Jenkins, *Churchill*, p. 396.
22. M. Soames, *Speaking for Themselves*, p. 274.
23. Ibid., p. 330.
24. Ibid., p. 331.
25. Ibid.
26. J. Charmley, *Churchill*, p. 219.
27. Ibid., p. 219.
28. Graham Stewart, *Burying Caesar: Churchill, Chamberlain and the Battle for the Tory Party* (London: Weidenfeld and Nicolson, 1999), p. 45.

29. M. Soames, *Speaking for Themselves*, p. 340.

30. Robert Rhodes James, "The Parliamentarian, Orator, Statesman," in R. Blake and W. Louis (eds.), *Churchill*, p. 508.

31. Charles Murphy and John Davenport, "The Lives of Winston Churchill," *Life*, May 21, 1945, p. 100.

32. H. Pelling, *Winston Churchill*, p. 327.

33. M. Soames, *Speaking for Themselves*, p. 328.

34. Ibid., p. 313.

35. Ibid., p. 280.

36. Ibid., p. 281.

37. D. Coombs, *Sir Winston Churchill's Life Through His Paintings*, p. 126.

Chapter 6

1. G. Best, *Churchill*, p. 152.

2. G. Stewart, *Burying Caesar*, p. 48.

3. R. Langworth, *Churchill's Wit*, p. 21.

4. M. Soames, *Speaking for Themselves*, p. 354.

5. W. Churchill (ed.), *Never Give In!*, p. 97.

6. Ibid., p. 98.

7. R. Langworth, *Churchill's Wit*, p. 133.

8. M. Soames, *Speaking for Themselves*, p. 370.

9. G. Stewart, *Burying Caesar*, pp. 52–53.

10. W. Churchill (ed.), *Never Give In!*, p. 48.

11. R. Langworth, *Churchill's Wit*, p. 102.

12. G. Stewart, *Burying Caesar*, p. 62.

13. Ibid., p. 199.

14. G. Craig, "Churchill and Germany," p. 36.

15. W. Churchill (ed.), *Never Give In!*, p. 101.

16. Ibid., p. 107.

17. Ibid., p. 108.

18. G. Best, *Churchill*, p. 150.

19. S. Lamb (ed.), *Wit and Wisdom*, p. 58.

20. M. Soames, *Speaking for Themselves*, p. 408.

21. W. Churchill (ed.), *Never Give In!*, p. 122.

22. M. Soames, *Speaking for Themselves*, p. 402.

23. W. Churchill (ed.), *Never Give In!*, pp. 153–54.

24. Ibid., p. 155.

25. *Harold Nicolson Diaries and Letters, 1930–1964* (London: Collins, 1980), p. 106.

26. S. Lamb (ed.), *Wit and Wisdom*, p. 279.

27. Ibid., p. 21.

28. M. Soames, *Speaking for Themselves*, p. 402.

29. Ibid., p. 427.
30. Ibid., p. 433.
31. W. Churchill (ed.), *Never Give In!*, p. 163.
32. R. Jenkins, *Churchill*, p. 472.
33. W. Churchill (ed.), *Never Give In!*, p. 166.
34. Ibid., p. 178.
35. Ibid., p. 183.
36. G. Stewart, *Burying Caesar*, p. 341.
37. R. Jenkins, *Churchill*, p. 541.
38. Ibid., p. 540.
39. G. Stewart, *Burying Caesar*, p. 372.
40. Winston Churchill, *The Second World War*, volume I, *The Gathering Storm* (London: Cassell, 1948), p. 320.

Chapter 7

1. W. Churchill (ed.), *Never Give In!*, p. 197.
2. S. Lamb (ed.), *Wit and Wisdom*, p. 261.
3. W. Churchill (ed.), *Never Give In!*, p. 198.
4. R. Jenkins, *Churchill*, p. 559.
5. S. Roskill, *Churchill and the Admirals*, p. 93.
6. Sir Ian Jacob, "Churchill as a War Leader," in *Churchill by His Contemporaries*, p. 77.
7. Lord Attlee, "The Churchill I Knew," in *Churchill by His Contemporaries*, p. 19.
8. Lord Moran, *Churchill: The Struggle for Survival, 1945–1960* (London: Constable and Robinson, 2006), p. 408.
9. Ibid., p. 419.
10. *Harold Nicolson Diaries*, p. 167.
11. Martin Gilbert, *Winston S. Churchill: Finest Hour, 1939–1941*, volume VI (London: Minerva, 1983), henceforth Official VI, p. 49.
12. J. Charmley, *Churchill*, p. 373.
13. S. Lamb (ed.), *Wit and Wisdom*, p. 354.
14. Official VI, p. 298.
15. R. Jenkins, *Churchill*, p. 577.
16. Official VI, p. 333.
17. W. Churchill (ed.), *Never Give In!*, p. 206.
18. Enoch Powell interview, "North Africa 1939–1945," Department of Sound Records, Imperial War Museum, accession number 0044/08. Thanks to Dr. Andrew Stewart for this reference.
19. Martin Gilbert, "My Life with Churchill."
20. A. J. P. Taylor, "The Statesman," in A. J. P. Taylor et al., *Four Faces and the Man*, p. 38.
21. R. Langworth, *Churchill's Wit*, p. 92.

22. Martin Gilbert, *Winston S. Churchill: Road to Victory, 1941–1945* (London: Minerva, 1990), henceforth Official VII, p. 511.
23. Commentator, "Churchill: Spokesman of Empire," *Empire Review* (June 1943), p. 17.
24. G. Stewart, *Burying Caesar*, p. 387.
25. *Harold Nicolson Diaries*, p. 167.
26. Lord Moran, *The Struggle for Survival*, p. 409.
27. Sir Ian Jacob, "Churchill as a War Leader," in *Churchill by His Contemporaries*, p. 75.
28. P. Addison, *Churchill*, p. 182.
29. Aneurin Bevan, "History's Impresario," in *Churchill by His Contemporaries*, p. 62.
30. P. Addison, *Churchill*, p. 154.
31. R. Lloyd George, *David and Winston*, p. 228.
32. Sir Ian Jacob, "Churchill as a War Leader," in *Churchill by His Contemporaries*, pp. 68–69.
33. Lord Attlee, "The Churchill I Knew," in *Churchill by His Contemporaries*, p. 33.
34. Edmund Warde, *The Silver Lining* (Lyminge, Kent: Edmund Warde, 1941), p. 5.
35. "Friend of a Nation," in *Churchill by His Contemporaries*, pp. 11–12.
36. *Finest Hour; The Journal of Winston Churchill*, p. 134 (2007).
37. Lord Attlee, "The Churchill I Knew," in *Churchill by His Contemporaries*, p. 14.
38. Dean Acheson, "The Supreme Artist," in *Churchill by His Contemporaries*, p. 39.
39. Lord Attlee, "The Churchill I Knew," in *Churchill by His Contemporaries*, p. 17.
40. Lord Moran, *Churchill at War*, p. 127.
41. P. Addison, *Churchill*, p. 182.
42. Lord Moran, *Churchill at War*, p. 61.
43. Sir Ian Jacob, "Churchill as a War Leader," in *Churchill by His Contemporaries*, p. 66.
44. R. Jenkins, *Churchill*, p. 589.
45. A. Bevan, "History's Impresario," in *Churchill by His Contemporaries*, p. 61.
46. R. Langworth, *Churchill's Wit*, p. 109.
47. Official VI, pp. 570–71.
48. W. Churchill (ed.), *Never Give In!*, p. 233.
49. A. Bevan, "History's Impresario," in *Churchill by His Contemporaries*, p. 59.
50. Richard Holmes, *In the Footsteps of Churchill*, p. 19.
51. W. Churchill (ed.), *Never Give In!*, p. 242.
52. Ibid., p. 252.
53. Lord Attlee, "The Churchill I Knew," in *Churchill by His Contemporaries*, p. 17.
54. S. Lamb (ed.), *Wit and Wisdom*, p. 26.

55. Official VI, p. 1010.
56. H. V. Morton, *Atlantic Meeting: An Account of Mr. Churchill's Voyage in* HMS Prince of Wales, *in August 1941, and the Conference with President Roosevelt That Resulted in the Atlantic Charter* (London, 1943).
57. Official VII, pp. 308–9.
58. Ibid., p. 480.
59. Sir Ian Jacob, "Churchill as a War Leader," in *Churchill by His Contemporaries.*
60. Official VII, p. 238.
61. Ibid., p. 282.
62. Ibid., p. 358.
63. Ibid., p. 372.
64. Sir Ian Jacob, "Churchill as a War Leader," in *Churchill by His Contemporaries*, p. 86.
65. Official VII, pp. 964, 1296.
66. W. Churchill (ed.), *Never Give In!*, p. 281.
67. Ibid., p. 285.
68. R. Langworth, *Churchill's Wit*, p. 22.
69. Sir Ian Jacob, "Churchill as a War Leader," in *Churchill by His Contemporaries*, p. 66.
70. S. Lamb (ed.), *Wit and Wisdom*, p. 361.
71. R. Toye, *Churchill's Empire*, p. 182.
72. S. Lamb (ed.), *Wit and Wisdom*, p. 310.
73. Official VII, p. 34.
74. M. Soames, *Speaking for Themselves*, p. 460.
75. Lord Moran, *Churchill at War*, p. 26.
76. W. Churchill (ed.), *Never Give In!*, p. 322.
77. *Harold Nicolson Diaries*, p. 225.
78. W. Churchill (ed.), *Never Give In!*, p. 325.
79. Ibid., p. 327.
80. *Harold Nicolson Diaries*, p. 223.
81. Lord Moran, *Churchill at War*, p. 29.
82. S. Lamb (ed.), *Wit and Wisdom*, p. 318.
83. Ibid., p. 91.
84. Official VII, p. 65.
85. Lord Moran, *Churchill at War*, p. 54.
86. Ibid., p. 83.
87. Official VII, p. 71.
88. R. Langworth, *Churchill's Wit*, p. 13.
89. Lord Moran, *Churchill at War*, p. 84.
90. Ibid., p. 45.
91. R. Jenkins, *Churchill*, p. 697.
92. Lord Moran, *Churchill at War*, p. 79.
93. Ibid., p. 80.

94. Official VII, p. 172.
95. Lord Moran, *Churchill at War*, p. 72.
96. Official VII, p. 186.
97. Ibid., p. 217.
98. Ibid., p. 226.
99. Ibid., p. 94.
100. Ibid., p. 96.
101. Ibid., p. 95.
102. Ibid, p. 306.
103. W. Churchill (ed.), *Never Give In!*, p. 352.
104. S. Lamb (ed.), *Wit and Wisdom*, p. 334.
105. M. Soames, *Speaking for Themselves*, p. 474.
106. Official VII, p. 339.
107. Lord Moran, *Churchill at War*, p. 99.
108. Official VII, p. 409.
109. Ibid., p. 404.
110. Lord Attlee, "The Churchill I Knew," in *Churchill by His Contemporaries*, p. 26.
111. Official VII, p. 431.
112. Ibid., p. 432.
113. Ibid., p. 484.
114. M. Soames, *Speaking for Themselves*, p. 487.
115. Nicholas Sarantakes, "Churchill Versus the Chiefs," in Sarantakes, *Allies Against the Rising Sun: The United States, the British Nations and the Defeat of Imperial Japan* (Lawrence, Kansas: Kansas University Press, 2009), p. 84.
116. Colin Baxter, "Winston Churchill: Military Strategist?," *Military Affairs* (February 1983), p. 8.
117. N. Sarantakes, "Churchill Versus the Chiefs," p. 37.
118. Ibid., p. 42.
119. Ibid., p. 113.
120. Lord Moran, *Churchill at War*, p. 171.
121. Ibid., p. 187.
122. Official VII, p. 655.
123. R. Langworth, *Churchill's Wit*, p. 158.
124. Official VII, p. 807.
125. Ibid., p. 914.
126. Ibid., p. 915.
127. Ibid., caption to photograph 31.
128. M. Soames, *Speaking for Themselves*, p. 500.
129. Official VII, p. 951.
130. Lord Moran, *Churchill at War*, p. 138.
131. S. Lamb (ed.), *Wit and Wisdom*, p. 347.
132. Official VII, p. 971.
133. Ibid., p. 968.
134. Ibid., p. 993.

135. Lord Moran, *Churchill at War*, p. 198.
136. Ibid., p. 224.
137. Official VII, p. 1151.
138. Ibid., p. 1107.
139. S. Lamb (ed.), *Wit and Wisdom*, p. 154.
140. M. Soames, *Speaking for Themselves*, p. 512.
141. S. Lamb (ed.), *Wit and Wisdom*, p. 369.
142. Lord Moran, *Churchill at War*, p. 227.
143. S. Lamb (ed.), *Wit and Wisdom*, p. 372.
144. Official VII, p. 1233.
145. Ibid., p. 1298.
146. Lord Moran, *Churchill: The Struggle for Survival*, p. 56.
147. Official VII, p. 1332.
148. Lord Moran, *Churchill at War*, p. 305.
149. Ibid., p. 310.
150. Lord Moran, *Churchill: The Struggle for Survival*, p. 6.
151. W. Churchill (ed.), *Never Give In!*, p. 391.
152. Official VII, p. 1351.
153. Lord Attlee, "The Churchill I Knew," in *Churchill by His Contemporaries*, p. 16.
154. Ibid., p. 19.
155. Lord Moran, *Churchill at War*, p. 341.
156. Barrie Pitt, *Churchill and the Generals* (Barnsley, Pen and Sword, 2004), p. 123.
157. S. Roskill, *Churchill and the Admirals*, p. 125.
158. Ibid., p. 282.
159. John Keegan, "Churchill's Strategy," in R. Blake and W. Louis (eds.), *Churchill*, p. 328.
160. Lord Attlee, "The Churchill I Knew," in *Churchill by His Contemporaries*, p. 33.
161. John Charmley, "Once a Whig . . . ," *Guardian*, October 13, 2001, review of Roy Jenkins, *Churchill*.
162. M. Gilbert, "My Life with Churchill." *Sunday Express Magazine*, January 2, 1994

Chapter 8

1. D. Notley, *Winston Churchill Quotations*.
2. S. Lamb (ed.), *Wit and Wisdom*, p. 256.
3. Ibid.
4. J. Charmley, *Churchill*, p. 17.
5. Lord Moran, *Churchill at War*, p. 353.
6. S. Lamb (ed.), *Wit and Wisdom*, p. 17.
7. Ibid., p. 136.

8. G. Best, *Churchill*, p. 256.
9. Geoffrey Best, *Churchill and War* (London: Hambledon and London, 2005), p. 216.
10. W. Churchill (ed.), *Never Give In!*, p. 414.
11. Ibid., p. 418.
12. W. Churchill (ed.), *Never Give In!*, p. 333.
13. Lord Moran, *Churchill: The Struggle for Survival*, p. 22.
14. A. Bevan, "History's Impresario," in *Churchill by His Contemporaries*, p. 58.
15. R. Langworth, *Churchill's Wit*, p. 66.
16. W. Churchill (ed.), *Never Give In!*, p. 465.
17. Ibid., p. 446.
18. S. Lamb (ed.), *Wit and Wisdom*, p. 305.
19. Ibid., p. 290.
20. Ibid., p. 271.
21. R. Langworth, *Churchill's Wit*, p. 19.
22. Ibid., p. 68.
23. Ibid., p. 125.
24. M. Soames, *Speaking for Themselves*, p. 566.
25. R. Langworth, *Churchill's Wit*, p. 3.
26. Ibid., p. 4.
27. Alistair Cooke in *Manchester Guardian*.
28. Lord Moran, *Churchill: The Struggle for Survival*, pp. 299, 304.
29. S. Lamb (ed.), *Wit and Wisdom*, p. 330.
30. Lord Moran, *The Struggle for Survival*, p. 119.
31. R. Langworth, *Churchill's Wit*, p. 110.
32. R. Jenkins, *Churchill*, p. 824.
33. Winston Churchill, *The Second World War*, volume IV, *The Hinge of Fate* (London: Cassel, 1951), p. ix.
34. David Reynolds, *In Command of History: Churchill Fighting and Writing the Second World War* (London: Allen Lane, 2004), p. 405.
35. R. Langworth, *Churchill's Wit*, p. 188.
36. G. Best, *Churchill*, p. 316.
37. M. Soames, *Speaking for Themselves*, p. 593.
38. Lord Moran, *Churchill: The Struggle for Survival*, p. 158.
39. R. Rhodes James, "The Parliamentarian, Orator, Statesman," in R. Blake and W. Louis (eds.), *Churchill*, p. 505.
40. W. Churchill (ed.), *Never Give In!*, p. 495.

Chapter 9

1. Lord Moran, *Churchill at War*, p. 293.
2. M. Soames, *Winston Churchill, His Life as a Painter, A Memoir by His Daughter* (London: Collins, 1990), p. 180.

3. A. Storr, "The Man," in A. J. P. Taylor et al., *Churchill: Four Faces and the Man*, p. 207.

4. Lord Moran, *Churchill: The Struggle for Survival*, p. 412.

5. M. Soames, *Clementine Churchill*, p. 544.

6. Ibid., p. 541.

7. Edward Bacon, "Thousands Queue Up to Offer Homage," in *Illustrated London News*, February 6, 1965, p. 6, and M. Soames, *Clementine Churchill*, p. 541.

8. R. Jenkins, *Churchill*, p. 911.

9. Iain Hamilton, "The Captains and the Kings Honour the Great Commoner," in *Illustrated London News*, February 6, 1965, p. 18.

10. M. Soames, *Clementine Churchill*, p. 543.

11. Ibid., p. 543.

12. Ibid., p. 545.

13. David Moller, "Sir Winston Lies at Rest in an Oxfordshire Country Churchyard," in *Illustrated London News*, February 6, 1965, p. 40. See also *Sir Winston Churchill and the Bladon Connection* (The Parish Church of St. Martin, Bladon, n. d.).

Epilogue

1. Lord Moran, *Churchill at War*, p. 301.

2. Ibid.

3. Ibid., p. 156.

4. Ibid., p. 239.

5. Ibid., p. 324.

6. Ibid., p. 8.

7. Ibid., p. 81.

8. Ibid., p. 274.

9. Ibid., p. 264.

10. Ibid., p. 132.

11. Ibid., p. 133.

12. Lord Attlee, "The Churchill I Knew," in *Churchill by His Contemporaries*, p. 20.

13. Ibid., p. 23.

14. Ibid., p. 24.

15. David Cannadine, *In Churchill's Shadow: Confronting the Past in Modern Britain* (London: Penguin, 2003), p. x.

16. P. Addison, *Churchill*, p. 1.

17. Ibid., p. 3.

18. Richard Gott, "The Man, the Myth, the Muck," in *Guardian*, May 4, 1994.

19. G. Best, *Churchill*, p. 31.

20. P. Addison, *Churchill*, p. 238.

21. Ibid., p. 6.

22. Lord Moran, *Churchill at War*, p. 77.

23. R. Rhodes James, "The Parliamentarian, Orator, Statesman," in R. Blake and W. Louis (eds.), *Churchill*, pp. 504, 503.

ACKNOWLEDGMENTS

Thanks are due to John Foster, Head of Education at Blenheim Palace, Dr. Tony Lemon of Mansfield College, Oxford, Dr. Andrew Stewart of King's College London, His Grace the Duke of Marlborough, Caroline Anderson of the Oxfordshire Museum, Chris Galloway, Bursar of Ditchley Park, Joshua Ireland, Tony Morris, Richard Milbank, and Richard Milner. For allowing the use of his painting on the cover of this book, special thanks are due to Hugh Bourn. Thanks also to my wife Andrea for her enthusiasm and support for my work.

PHOTOGRAPHY CREDITS

INDEX